INFINITE SKY
Infinite Sky Learning, LLC
2024 West 15th St. Ste F-106
Plano, TX 75075-7363

First published in the United States in 2022
Copyright © Sandy Wall, 2022

All rights reserved. No part of this publication may be reproduced or transmitted in any form or by any means, electronic or mechanical, including photocopying, recording, or any information storage or retrieval system, without prior permission in writing from the publishers.

ISBN: 979-8-8264545-3-4

Infinite Sky Publishing books may be purchased for business or promotional use. For information on bulk purchases, please contact support@islpublishing.com.

www.islpublishing.com

For:

The unsung men and women who wear the badge in the Houston Police Department and the community they protect and serve. Especially those that gave the ultimate sacrifice.

My Academy classmates #75 and all the brave crime fighters I served with over the years, your names and faces may not be known by many, but I will never forget you.

My support system of friends and family who helped me in my career, especially my loving wife for her patience, coaching, and proofing of this piece of work so that my story could be told.

A special thanks to Johnny Bonds, Kelley Siegler, and Kristi McCown Betts for their time and efforts in test reading and encouragement throughout this process. I must also mention Ronnie Parker who provided so much material for me to write about through the years.
I love you, Captain Dynamite!

I hope you enjoy Andy Wallace's journey as much as I did reminiscing the good times, bad times, and challenges on the long road home.

"People sleep peaceably in their beds at night only because rough men stand ready to do violence on their behalf."

George Orwell

ONE

It was a beautiful summer day in southeast Texas, the landscape surrounded by incredibly lush green grass from recent rains. The fat cows feeding in pastures on both sides of the two-lane road reminded Andy of home. He slowed to a stop at the guard shack and the first layer of security at the state prison. Nervously, he rolled his window down, handed the guard his identification, and hoped for the best. The guard handed back the ID and waved him on towards a meeting that Andy hoped would set things right.

Driving through the checkpoint, Andy thought back on what led him to this visit and how lucky he was to be here. With wounds still healing, Andy needed crutches to get around but was gaining strength every day.

Parking near the front gate, he struggled to get out of his truck. He winced in pain until he was able to accurately adjust his crutches in place to steady himself. Andy started toward the tall wire fence entrance to the prison visitation center and glanced up at the picket tower where an armed guard stood watch over the parking lot. As he walked closer to the prison, he couldn't imagine what it must be like to live here as an inmate.

The time had come to bury the hatchet and settle an old feud. Thankfully, it wasn't too late to start over, and his near-death experience made him appreciate how precious life is and how quickly it could be taken away. A fresh start required putting this behind him for both his and his family's futures.

Once he signed the register, the registrar instructed him to take a seat in a waiting area and listen for his name to be called. Sitting there looking at the plain white brick walls, he wondered how it all came to this—recalling each moment that had gone tragically wrong and the fate that led him to this day. His thoughts began to drift back to a simpler time, 22 years ago, when he embarked on a new life in Houston. Then, he was a young man beginning a new journey. Much like today, he was leaving a part of his life behind and looking forward to an uncertain future. He leaned back, closed his eyes, and remembered that day like it was yesterday.

The year was 1976, and Andy was moving away from his small hometown, same as many others he drove past on his 2-hour drive to Houston. That part of the Texas coastal plains was plain and unremarkable, like the loving home he was leaving.

His Dad had worked most of his career as a pipeline engineer, and his Mom was a full-time homemaker, although she dabbled with side jobs to make ends meet. Both of Andy's parents were children of the depression and had come from sparse beginnings. They had a strong work ethic, appreciated hard work, and knew how to stretch a penny. Downhome people who did everything they could to make a home for their kids.

Andy grew up with three older brothers; each of them had been a stand-out in one way or another. The eldest and most intelligent of the bunch, Melvin, graduated from the University of Texas with a degree in Aerospace Engineering. He was now working with NASA to build satellites and married a local gal he met in college. They started a family with two small boys and subsequently moved to Houston to be near NASA. The entire family was proud of what he had accomplished.

Next in line, was Mike, who had been a football and track star in high school. He had made it to the state finals in track three years in a row and appeared to have something special. Mike's talent earned him a full scholarship to run for the University of Wyoming, but he grew tired of the cold weather and returned home after a couple of years. When Mike returned home, he married his high school sweetheart and was hired as a lab technician for a local chemical plant. On the side, he dabbled in bodybuilding, and he was actually a good amateur bodybuilder. Regularly won state-level competitions and he even did well in some national meets. Even with all of these strengths, Mike also had a devilish side that got him in trouble from time to time. Nothing too serious growing up but surely enough for people to notice. Dad always admired the fact that nothing seemed to stick to Mike. Dad joked, "Mike could fall in a toilet and come out smelling like a rose."

That knack would serve him well for years. Maybe a little too well now that he was an adult and dealing with laws that had actual lifelong consequences, but Mike still thought he was invincible.

Lastly, just two years older than Andy was Tommy, another gifted athlete in High School. He lettered in football and track three years in a row and won All-District honors. Mr. Everything of his High School class and won a scholarship to play football for Texas Lutheran University until he suffered a career-ending back injury. Following the back injury, he returned home to work construction and married his High School sweetheart... just like Mike. Although Tommy and Andy were close, Andy always felt in his shadow. But he did not mind; in fact, he was just as proud of his big brother as his parents.

Lastly, there was Andy, who didn't thrive in much of anything. Pegged as the class clown growing up, Andy was known for telling a good joke or merely wasting time. Without taking anything all that seriously, he worked just hard enough academically to get by in High School. He barely crossed the threshold to make the team in sports but did show up for the games. Mainly, his interests consisted of hunting, fishing, and having a good time!

He still had several good high school friends, and they would remain close for life. Andy attended a local University for a couple of years but lost interest. To be blunt, he hadn't taken anything in his life very seriously until now. Determined to make something of himself, he drove north on US-59 to the big city and the new life that awaited him.

Becoming a police officer was not the career choice his parents would have chosen for him. As all mothers do, she feared for his safety in Houston, and his Dad wanted him to stay in college and get a degree like his oldest brother. However, Andy felt that he needed to make a clean break from his existing path and start over. Deep within himself was a strong urge that this was the right course of action for his life, and he had to follow it. Andy had acquired an ability to lock things away in his mind and not focus on them. This talent would serve him well in the years to come as he embarked on this new adventure.

The Houston Police Department had recruited him, and the idea of becoming a big city cop seemed like an exciting career. If he was going to become a police officer, he was going to be all in. Unfortunately, Houston had more than its share of crime and could be a dangerous city. Andy had no idea how dangerous, but that didn't matter right now.

Occasionally when watching the evening news, Andy noticed when a Houston officer was killed in the line of duty. Andy didn't have a death wish, but he was willing to take that chance. This new career was his entire focus now, and nothing else mattered. He was determined to finally accomplish something for himself and make his parents proud. Come hell or high water!

In far northwest Houston, Andy turned into the driveway of his Aunt Peggy and Uncle Chris's place. Reminiscent of the summers he used to spend with them here as a child. His Aunt and Uncle welcomed him to stay for a few days while he looked for an apartment. With only a week before his first day at the Police Academy, he aimed to find a place closer to downtown. All he had in his possession were his clothes and some personal items, the meager beginnings of a young adult venturing out onto their own. Furniture would have to wait while he focused on the necessities.

Gene Wallace, another Uncle, lived near downtown Houston. Gene was the wheeler-dealer type and knew where Andy could get a deal on a bed, a TV, and a chair. Unfortunately, that would be all he could afford for now until he started getting some paychecks from the city.

Within a few days, Andy leased an apartment near a major highway that led directly into downtown. A strategic location for his commute to the Police Academy, and he could still easily visit his parents.

He spent the first night in his new apartment with nothing more than a small TV propped up on a cardboard box and a beanbag to sit on. Unable to afford a box spring, he laid his mattress directly on the floor. His meager assortment of clothing hung in the closet until he picked an outfit to lay on the bed for the following day. Because he had no means to cook anything, his meals for the first few weeks consisted of predominately fast food.

It was an unimpressive start. Andy didn't want anyone coming over to see his new place so sparse but knew things would improve soon enough. Once he got a few weeks under his belt at the Academy, he could afford what he needed to make his apartment more livable. Unfortunately, that process would prove to be more difficult than he thought.

The First Day

Andy's alarm clock sounded bright, and early at 5 am that Monday morning. Despite a lack of sleep, he sprang to his feet with anticipation of what this day would bring. This small-town kid woke up in a vast city, and he was about to embark on the first day of the rest of his life. Unsure how to prepare himself or what to expect, he wore the only sports coat and tie he owned. Better to be overdressed rather than underdressed. As he grabbed his briefcase walking out the door, he couldn't shake the feeling that he wasn't ready. A nagging sensation in the back of his mind that maybe he wasn't good enough or he wouldn't compare to the rest of the recruits.

After pulling out into the crowded street during Houston's morning traffic, Andy quickly realized he had grossly underestimated his commute time. While driving the route yesterday from his west side apartment to the Police Academy, the drive was far less time-consuming, but morning traffic was quite different. Stuck at a snail's pace in bumper-to-bumper traffic for as far as the eye could see. He was anxious and impatient, knowing he wouldn't make it to the classroom by the 7 am start time. With his heart pounding, he nervously glanced back and forth between the road and the clock on his dashboard, watching the minutes quickly tick by. Thoughts of just turning around and forgetting the whole thing swirled in his mind, but he couldn't. Failure was not an option because of everything he had put into this opportunity.

As he pulled into the Central Police Departments' employee parking lot at 7:05 am, he thought to himself; this is NOT good. He still had to navigate through the lot to find an available space and walk to the Academy. The Police Academy was located inside an old building on the police complex, right across from the jail sally port. The building contained a complete fitness gym and a locker room with showers for the cadets. The officers often used the space to grab a quick workout before their shift.

Flushed with nervous energy, Andy hurried through the main door of the Academy. On his immediate left, Andy noticed the office of Captain A.W. Milan. The entrance to the office was open, and an attractive young woman was sitting at the reception desk. Momentarily, she glanced up at Andy and then looked back down at her desk, smiling, knowing that this cadet had already screwed up. This only further added to Andy's uneasiness as he approached what appeared to be the cadet classroom door. Peering through a window in the door, he noticed several young men and women sitting at desks facing away from him. Andy hesitated as he realized the cadets were listening to someone speaking at the front of the room. His worst fears were now actualized; there was no way to covertly slip into the back of the room without being noticed.

Again, he thought about just turning around and walking out. Maybe this wasn't meant to be. Perhaps this was a sign, but he had already come too far to turn back. Andy couldn't return to his small hometown and face his friends and family as a total failure. No matter what was going to come his way, he had to walk in and face the consequences.

Inhaling a deep breath, Andy tried to open the door quietly to avoid being noticed. A tall, uniformed officer stood at the front of the room, speaking to the cadets. He was standing on a slightly elevated platform as he casually leaned against the podium. The stately man was dressed in a complete Class-A uniform. Abruptly, he stopped talking and looked at Andy for what felt like an eternity. The glare from his piercing eyes felt like it cut right through him.

The officer stiffened his posture as if he was coming to attention. "Well, well, well. There's always one," the officer said condescendingly. "Now we know who it is."

Seventy-two cadets quickly turned around in their seats to look at who the officer was referring to. All Andy could do at this point was stand tall and try not to show how scared he was.

Unbeknownst to Andy at the time, the officer at the podium was James Hurley. As a former Marine drill sergeant, Hurley was a stickler for promptness, rules, and uniforms. He loved to make examples of anyone that drew his attention, and Andy was directly in his sightline. Standing behind Hurley on the stage stood the rest of the Academy's training staff. All assigned as full-time employees, their main job was to ensure the cadets followed the rules, passed the courses, and graduated in six months. Six long months of grueling college-level curriculum, physical training, and practical exercises. The Academy training was designed in a military-style format to prepare young cadets for their police careers.

Andy could feel every eye in the room on him as he tried to say something. The thought of begging for forgiveness immediately came to mind, but his instincts told him to be strong and stand up for himself. "Sorry, sir, the traffic was more than I had anticipated," he yelled out firmly.

Several cadets turned back to see Hurley's response as the tense confrontation played out. Hurley was not impressed but decided to move forward with the program and deal with Andy later. "What's your name, son?" Hurley blurted out.

"Andy Wallace, sir."

"Well, Wallace, find your name and take a seat. We'll talk later," snapped Hurley.

Andy glanced across the room and spotted an empty chair. Sure enough, his last name was taped to the back of it. The staff had arranged everyone in alphabetical order. Quickly sitting down, Andy hoped that the worst was over.

The orientation went on for about an hour, with the Academy staff taking turns to describe the program and outline the expectations of the cadets for the next six months. Andy tried to pay attention, but his mounting embarrassment was challenging to ignore. As he tried to concentrate and listen to each presentation, he wondered what everyone thought of him. Already assuming he would be labeled a screw-up and pegged as a perpetual problem, Andy was determined to change their minds and do whatever it took to get back in good standing.

Their first break arrived at 8:15 am, and the cadets were instructed to be back in their seats by 8:30. For 15 minutes, they were free to do whatever they chose. Andy stood up to locate a restroom, but Hurley was already waiting for him as he walked out into the hallway.

"WALLACE, come with me!" Hurley barked out as he turned and started walking away. Hurley made sure that he spoke loud enough for everyone to hear. The entire class couldn't help but notice what had just occurred. Andy's tardiness was not going to be overlooked, and he was about to pay the price.

Andy nervously followed Hurley across the gym floor and up a flight of stairs to the staff offices. Hurley was walking quickly without saying a word or even looking back to see if he was following. He entered his office door with Andy close behind. Andy stepped just inside the door and stood there as Hurley sat down behind his desk across the room.

Andy thought it would be presumptuous to take a seat until told to do so, but he soon found out that he was wrong no matter what he did.

"Sit your ASS down, Wallace!" Hurley screamed. "What do you think this is, a fucking inspection?"

"Yes, sir," replied Andy softly as he sat down in the chair directly across from Hurley.

"What did you say?" barked Hurley.

"I said yes, sir, officer Hurley!"

"Stand up when you talk to me!" Hurley yelled, loud enough to be heard by everyone downstairs.

Andy jumped to his feet without saying a word.

"When I say something to you cadet, you answer, do you hear me?" Hurley continued yelling.

"Yes, sir," Andy replied as he stood there, unsure what to do next.

"Shut the damn door, cadet!" Hurley screamed.

Andy turned to shut the door, and Hurley jumped to his feet, up close to Andy's face.

"Did I not just tell you to answer me when I speak to you?" Hurley yelled.

"Yes, sir," Andy replied with Hurley standing eye to eye with him.

Andy's heart was pounding as he absorbed Hurley's wrath. Hurley towered over Andy at 6'3", with a slim but well-built frame. Staring down into Andy's eyes, it was as if Hurley could see right through him. He knew he was paying the price for being late but still wasn't sure what the consequences would entail.

Pacing back and forth across his office floor, Hurley proceeded to lecture Andy for 10 consecutive minutes on how being late was unacceptable, only occasionally stopping to stare into Andy's eyes for dramatic effect. Hurley droned on and on about how Andy should have more respect for himself. Hurley's responsibility was to determine who did not meet the Academy's rigorous standards. And Andy was already well on his way to being the first one expelled. Nothing would give Hurley greater satisfaction. Finally, Hurley told Andy that he would be on the Coffee Squad for two weeks.

"If you make it that long!" Hurley quipped.

Any cadet assigned to the Coffee Squad was required to arrive an hour early each morning and make coffee for the Academy staff. Additional responsibilities included cleaning the break room and setting up the cups, napkins, and utensils needed throughout the day.

"Get out of my sight and close the door behind you," demanded Hurley.

"Yes, sir," Andy replied as he walked out of the office, careful to close the door quietly.

There wouldn't be time for a restroom break. The next class was already underway as he walked back into the classroom. Once again, everyone looked back at Andy, but this time not with a look of surprise. They looked almost forgiving of the delay this time. Everyone had heard the yelling and already knew what Andy had just endured. Andy walked quietly to his desk and sheepishly settled in for what he hoped would be his last class disturbance.

During the next break, Andy walked outside for some much-needed fresh air. There was a small landing area where cadets gathered during breaks to watch what was going on at the jail. Officers would drive up in their patrol cars and escort prisoners out of the back seat for a final search before walking them into the jail for booking. Although a very mundane task for a veteran police officer, it was quite fascinating for a young cadet. The cadets stood there pondering what the prisoners could have done and waited anxiously to see if something exciting would happen.

A fellow cadet named Herman Munich walked shyly over to Andy to introduce himself, "Hi, I'm Herman."

"Hi," Andy replied and shook Herman's hand.

"What a way to start your first day, huh?" Herman commented.

"Yeah, it could have gone better," Andy replied nodding his head in agreement. They both chuckled.

Herman was small in both size and stature. When shaking Herman's hand, the first thing that Andy noticed was how soft and small his hands were in comparison to his. Almost like a girl, he marveled. His skin was pale with small freckles spotted across his nose and a face adorned with thick-lensed glasses. Obviously shy by nature, Herman had difficulty making eye contact as he tried to awkwardly carry on a conversation. Sizing up Herman, Andy was thoroughly unimpressed and couldn't help but wonder how he had made it through the selection process. Someone else had noticed Herman as well...James Hurley.

Herman leaned over and told Andy in a low voice, "I don't think Hurley likes me either."

"Why, what happened?" asked Andy.

Herman recounted how he arrived early that morning, but that was a mistake. Hurley arrived early as well, waiting to size up the cadets as they first walked into the Academy. Herman was the first to walk into the room and Hurley was ready to strike. Embarrassingly, Herman explained that when he walked into the classroom Hurley was sitting near the podium just glaring at him. Hurley continued staring at him without saying a word, much like he did when Andy walked in.

"I asked him if this was where cadet class 75 was meeting but he just kept staring. It was weird! I didn't know what to do. He got up and walked toward me like he wanted to beat the hell out of me or something. Then he asked me if I wanted to be a Houston Police Officer. I told him 'Yes, sir,' and he said that I had a tough row to hoe." Herman added, "It was like I could feel his eyes piercing through my brain!"

Andy suspected Herman was holding some details back about the encounter and that he wanted to say more.

"That Hurley is a real asshole," Andy said.

"No doubt," Herman replied.

They walked back into the classroom and prepared for the next speaker. Andy had made a friend, but he wasn't sure if that was a good thing. At this point, he was thankful to know anyone and wasn't going to be choosy. Looking around the room, he wondered who else he could break the ice with. Maybe he should be more assertive in making friends but right now he was still licking his wounds from this morning's blunder.

During the next few breaks and lunch, Andy spent time trying to size up his fellow classmates. Most of them were young and new to law enforcement but there were a few older cadets that had been officers in other cities. For one reason or another, they decided to start over in Houston.

One such cadet was Charlie Oats. Charlie had come from the New Orleans Police Department and as luck would have it, he was late that morning as well, just not as late as Andy.

Charlie approached Andy after lunch and asked, "Did you get on the Coffee Squad?"

"You know it," replied Andy.

"Me too! I guess I'll see you at 6 am tomorrow. Just don't be late again," Charlie commented.

"No way," Andy replied and appreciated the fact that he wasn't the only one.

The class was dismissed at 5 pm and Andy couldn't wait to get out of there. Although he was not off to a good start, he was thankful he made it through the first day! All he wanted to do was grab a bite to eat on the way home and go to bed for an early wakeup. He was exhausted, but he was NOT going to be late for the Coffee Squad. Whatever it took, he would be there on time and ready to go.

Dealing With Hurley

When the alarm went off the following morning at 4 am, Andy sprang to his feet. After the exhaustion from his first day, Andy had slept soundly and felt rejuvenated when his alarm sounded. Fearful of being late again, he quickly dressed and ran out the door. The drive downtown was a breeze because of the earlier commute time. When Andy pulled into the Academy parking lot, he was 45 minutes early, and it was still pitch-black outside. The Academy was left open all night for nightshift officers to use it, but the break room and offices were locked. Andy began to pace back and forth in front of the building while waiting for one of the Academy staff to show up. With the extra time, he watched the officers off-load prisoners.

"You're early," Charlie Oats yelled out as he walked out of the darkness.

"Yep, a team of wild horses couldn't hold me back this morning!" replied Andy.

About that time, a voice from beyond the lights of the building said, "OK ladies, let's not gaggle." Hurley appeared from the shadows, "You two losers can swap spit later," Hurley said as he walked up the steps of the Academy and past them without even a glance.

A rather disturbing comment to make about two subordinates thought Andy. Another interaction that only solidified how he felt about Hurley. Andy and Charlie followed him inside as he unlocked the break room door. "There you go, girls, get to making coffee!"

Andy and Charlie quickly got to work figuring out where the supplies were and how the coffee makers functioned. Hurley stood staring at them in the doorway, not offering any assistance or guidance. The smirk on his face showed how much he enjoyed watching the two cadets nervously fumble through the process. Andy had never developed a taste for coffee and didn't know how to make it; thankfully, Charlie was a well-versed barista from his days as a New Orleans police officer. Hurley became bored when it appeared that the two of them had figured out the coffee routine and walked off when he realized he didn't have anything to bitch about.

The remainder of the day went about the same as the first. Andy thought it was best to try and stay in the middle of the pack. Hopefully, this way, he could avoid being noticed because Hurley was always on the perimeter. Watching like a wolf watches a herd of elk, he was biding his time, waiting for the weakest to fall behind.

Academy courses were fascinating, consisting of different expert speakers lecturing on police code for criminal procedures, arrest laws, search and seizure, and so much more. Assistant District Attorneys predominately taught the law courses; they prosecuted cases in Harris County. They would elaborate using stories from their more exciting cases. Some classes were not as captivating, although equally important, like Departmental Procedures or how to become a member of the credit union.

The cadets were issued their uniforms, and Hurley went into great detail on where creases should be in their pants, how to wear them, and how to properly stand at attention. A stickler for every detail, Hurley even discussed something he called the gig line, where the seam of the front of the shirt lined up with the seam of the pants zipper. Heaven forbid if those two did not line up! Detail, discipline, and uniformity meant everything to Hurley. Mess up on any of those, and you would catch his wrath.

Strangely, Andy was fascinated by how Hurley seemed like two people in one body. The strict disciplinarian who prided himself on following the rules and the image of professionalism, then the other side of Hurley, the side that enjoyed making other people's lives miserable for his amusement. Primarily preying on the weak and vulnerable, Hurley loved to abuse cadets physically and mentally, and being in a position of power, he could. Andy witnessed Hurley slap cadets on the back of the head as he walked by if they were in his path or said something he disagreed with. Frequently, he sneaked up behind cadets and would goose them to get a reaction, laughing hysterically as he walked off. He relished his dominance over subordinates; Andy despised that side of Hurley.

While observing the other cadets, Andy noticed a fellow cadet, John Frost, who he was interested in getting to know better. John was a big guy with an athletic build and a kind way about him. He appeared unassuming and unsure of himself, even though he was one of the biggest guys in the class. Andy found John's personality endearing, so he started a conversation on break. "Hey John, I'm Andy."

"Hi," John replied and nothing more. John was a man of few words, especially if he didn't know you. While chatting awkwardly for a few moments, Andy learned that John was from Houston. He had been a High School football star and played college football in Louisiana. Unfortunately, college academics weren't a good fit, so he decided to drop out and give police work a try. As their break ended, Andy felt that John was someone he could relate to. He reminded Andy of his big brother, Tommy, so he made a point to hang out with him every chance he got.

Nearly every time Andy and John were kidding around, Herman would attempt to intrude. Due to Herman's nerd status and lack of popularity, Andy avoided the relationship. Instead, Andy would politely reply to Herman but find any excuse to disengage and walk away. Because Herman was kind and meant well, Andy didn't want to be rude, but unfortunately, he wasn't getting the hint.

With day two behind him, Andy was relieved the second day went more smoothly. Starving after a long day of training, he stopped at the McDonald's drive-thru and grabbed a hamburger and a Coke on his way home. As soon as he arrived at his apartment, he immediately phoned his Mom and Dad to recap the past two days' events. Never wanting to worry or disappoint his parents, Andy attempted to sugarcoat everything as best he could. He devoured his soggy hamburger while they chatted and ended the call with a promise to come home for the weekend.

Once Andy had the morning commute down and learned the better ways to avoid Hurley, the remainder of the week flew by without issue. The cadets were learning to march and sound cadence. As Andy became more comfortable in his new routine, he started to feel a sense of belonging. During daily inspections, Hurley continued to jump Andy for minor details about his uniform. Typically, this meant his shoes were not shined enough and didn't meet Hurley's unrealistic standards, but Andy was starting to become callused to the attacks. Andy endured the abuse in silence, and over time, it became less bothersome and anticipated. However, as Hurley started to sense Andy's indifference to his attacks, he became more and more agitated.

After a few days, Hurley had locked in on the weakest of the herd, Herman. Sensing that his abuse was getting to Herman only fueled the flame. Every time Herman trembled in his presence, the abuse came more frequently. Similar to the first morning when Andy was called into Hurley's office, Herman could do nothing right, leaving the other cadets grappling with how much more he could endure. It seemed unlikely that someone as fragile as Herman could handle much more. Many of the cadets pitied him, but it was every man for himself at this point. Andy was focused on surviving each day and staying out of Hurley's way.

Next week would begin the physical aspect of their training, starting with the physical training (PT) program. Added to their daily curriculum would be an hour of PT every morning. Andy and John were eager for the physical portion because it would allow them to excel and stand out. For others, like Herman, it was another opportunity for Hurley.

On Friday afternoon, Andy planned to head home as soon as his day at the Academy concluded. Before leaving that morning, he packed his car for the trip, so he didn't have to stop at the apartment on the way out of town. Fighting traffic out of Houston gave him time to reflect on the past week.

When he pulled into the driveway, his Mom came running out of the house. She wrapped her arms around him in a big hug like they hadn't seen each other in years. Even though she was being melodramatic, he didn't mind. Andy looked sharp in his cadet uniform, which made his Mom and Dad proud for a change.

Andy spent the next couple of hours rehashing his first week at the Academy with them. To save his parents from worry, he left out anything regarding Hurley. Instead, he focused on the exciting parts and the aspects he was looking forward to.

Upon asking about his brothers, Andy learned Mike had opened a new gym in town that included a full spa and café. Mom and Dad were gushing with pride at Mike's success, and Andy was glad to hear that his brother was doing well. He was looking forward to seeing the gym sometime this weekend, but right now, he was exhausted from this past week and needed a good night's sleep.

The following day Andy tried to call some of his old friends to hang out, but they had already made plans. Attempting to get caught up on regular chores, he worked on his car and mowed the lawn, but that was the extent of the day. Before he knew it, the weekend was over, and he was driving back to Houston with freshly washed laundry, thanks to Mom.

TWO

It All Blows Up

Right after inspection on Monday morning, they began PT. Everyone was required to be standing in formation until their dismissal, and then a mad dash for the locker rooms followed. In unison, sixty male cadets rushed to undress and put on their workout clothes in less than 10 minutes. Pure chaos ensued as all of the cadets struggled to finish in such a short period. Amid the commotion was a lot of unintentional pushing and shoving. Tensions were high, with everyone trying to avoid the Tardy Squad. No one relished the thought of staying in at lunch and more PT. The female cadets had a separate, smaller locker room, but it seemed adequate because they always beat the guys back to formation.

Academy staff officer John Shockley conducted PT. He had a tall and slim build like Hurley, but their similarities ended there. Shockley was the spitting image of professionalism and sort of funny with an arid sense of humor. An excellent PT coach who knew his stuff. He never really pushed anyone to do more than they could but always encouraged everyone's best effort.

The physical training sessions lasted for an hour and consisted primarily of stretching, calisthenics, and a 2-mile run or sprints inside the basketball court. Later in the program, they would learn to box, but the current objective was to get everyone in good physical condition. Andy expected PT to be more like military boot camp and quickly realized he had overtrained. His daily fitness routine included two runs and circuit training. Circuit training included a variety of exercises, including push-ups, pull-ups, sit-ups, and weight training. In Andy's opinion, Academy PT felt like a challenging athletics course in college... not easy, but nothing that he couldn't handle even on his worst day. For some cadets, the physical training sessions were more challenging, especially for Herman. Hurley was ready to insult and demonize Herman every time he made a mistake or lagged behind. After only the first PT session, Herman and ten other cadets were assigned to the Olympic Squad and required to arrive an hour early each day for additional PT training.

After each PT session, there was a mad dash back to the locker room to shower and change into uniform. Everyone had 20 minutes to finish and be back in formation, or they would be assigned to the Tardy Squad. Once everyone was assembled, they would be dismissed for a 10 minute break. Enough time to grab a snack at the vending machine or snack on something brought from home before the next class began. Andy tried to blend into the pack by never being first or last to arrive in the classroom, knowing that Hurley was watching and ready to pounce on an outlier from the group.

Each cadet was required to keep their notes in a 3-ring binder, which could be inspected without warning. If a cadet's notes were deemed unsatisfactory, they would be placed on the Notebook Squad and required to stay after class until the skillset improved. Anyone who failed uniform inspection was placed on the Uniform Squad, and the Latrine Squad was a catch-all for non-specific disciplinary action. Hurley was itching to put someone on the Latrine Squad, knowing it was the most revolting squad to be assigned.

Andy and several other cadets walked across the street to Avenue Grill Cafe at lunch. The cafe earned its name because of its location on Houston Avenue, and it was your quintessential greasy spoon restaurant. The food was hot, and reasonably priced, and Andy loved it. Unfortunately, Herman would tag along with Andy any chance he got during lunchtime. Whenever possible, Andy would choose to sit at a table of cadets with only one remaining seat open. Herman's quirky mannerisms were beginning to get on his nerves, and even if he could only avoid him for a short lunch break, it was a nice reprieve.

Shockley was out sick on Thursday, so Hurley filled in and instructed PT. No one was looking forward to additional instruction from Hurley, and everyone knew he would attempt to exert his newfound authority. Hurley announced that they would go for a longer than usual run outside the gym. The cadets were instructed to run in unison and keep pace with the assigned peer leader. Fred Pierce was selected to set the pace and he could run like a deer with his frame as thin as a rail. Most cadets couldn't keep up with Pierce, and Hurley was looking to ostracize some cadets from the pack. When Pierce was picked to lead the run, Herman immediately dropped his head in defeat. With minimal effort, Fred was able to run a 7 minute mile pace endlessly, without breaking a sweat.

Andy intentionally lined up next to Herman outside to start the run. Herman glanced at Andy.

"Here goes nothing!" Herman said with a sheepish grin.

"Look, Herman, just run easy, take deep breaths, and relax your muscles. You'll do fine," Andy said encouragingly.

Hurley blew the whistle, and off they went under the Memorial Drive bridge to Buffalo Bayou, where the running track followed along the water's edge. Initially, Pierce set a leisurely pace, but this only agitated Hurley. In the distance, he began yelling that if Pierce didn't pick up the pace, he would be assigned the Latrine Squad. No matter how much Fred didn't want to hurt the other cadets, he wasn't going to let that happen. So Fred increased his pace to just under an 8 minute mile with three miles to go. Although that wasn't a problem for Andy, he knew Herman would fall behind. Recalling how dejected Herman looked before the run began, Andy kept glancing over his shoulder to see if Herman was still with the group, but he was slowly losing ground.

Most cadets remained in tight formation as they made the final turn towards the Academy. However, approximately eight cadets had fallen behind, and the stragglers were staggered out about fifty yards. Hurley eagerly waited at the finish line with a clipboard and pen to write down the names of any cadet who had lagged behind.

As Andy reached the finish line, he decided to circle back to Herman and motivate him to pick up the pace. Hopefully, with a bit of encouragement, Herman could pick up his speed, so Andy sprinted back, yelling at him to pick up the pace. "Come on, Herman, KICK!" Andy yelled, running alongside Herman.

Herman increased his pace but still fell short. As the two of them crossed the finish line, Andy was impressed by Herman's perseverance, knowing he had given it his all. Then, suddenly, Herman projectile vomited all over the street, directly in front of Hurley.

Hurley smirked and wrote Herman and Andy's names down on his list for Olympic Squad duty.

"Officer Hurley, am I on the Olympic Squad?" Andy asked, standing there gasping for air.

Hurley didn't answer, just continued writing. Andy had just finished on the Coffee Squad, but now it looked like he was going to be stuck on another, unnecessary detail.

"Sir, you saw me turn back. I was trying to help Herman," Andy said, pleading his case.

"Your problem, not mine," Hurley said with a smirk as he glanced back at Andy.

Unable to help himself, Andy mumbled "whatever..." under his breath as he turned to walk away, breathing still labored from the run.

"Latrine Squad too, smart mouth!" Hurley blurted out as he lowered his clipboard and glared.

"Yes, sir," Andy responded; knowing it would be a losing battle to say anything, he held his tongue and accepted his punishment.

"Munich! You're on Latrine Squad as well!" yelled Hurley.

"Why?" Herman asked, still bent over, gasping for air.

"For asking why and making a mess on my street!" Hurley replied.

The class walked back into the gym and assembled into formation, waiting for Hurley to dismiss them. Once he did, the mad dash for the showers was on. With his complexion as white as a ghost, Andy thought Herman would vomit again, but he held back. As Herman struggled to shower and get dressed, he slowly regained some color back in his cheeks. But, still lagging from the fiasco, he barely made it into formation on time.

Andy was fuming at Hurley, and honestly, he wasn't thrilled with Herman either. But, mostly, he blamed himself for turning around to help Herman in the first place. His own goals should always be the priority, and if he had watched out for himself, he wouldn't have been assigned to the Latrine Squad or Olympic Squad. Too late now, he would be cleaning toilets first thing in the morning alongside Herman.

The following day Herman and Andy were standing in the hallway waiting for Hurley to unlock the janitor's closet. With a swagger and smirk on his face, Hurley finally waltzes in and glances at them without saying a word. Then, after pulling the key out of his pocket, he leans in and unlocks the closet door. "There you are, ladies," Hurley said as he walked away.

With hands full of cleaning supplies, they headed for the men's restroom. Along the interior wall of the bathroom lined four urinals, followed by two toilets situated within privacy stalls. In addition, six sinks lined the opposite wall, positioned side by side with mirrors installed above each sink. Before their daily uniform inspections, the cadets would run into the restroom and check their reflections to ensure their uniforms met the prescribed standards.

"If you clean the urinals, I'll do the commodes," Andy said as they walked into the restroom. Herman nodded as Andy added, "I'll mop the floors if you want to wipe down the sinks."

Herman agreed, and they got to work. Andy poured some cleaner into the first toilet and circled the brush around the bowl. He hated being bent over the toilet in a small enclosed space, but there was no way around it. Further down, Herman was busy doing the same thing to the urinals.

Once Andy finished cleaning the first toilet, he moved over to the second stall and started on that one. While bent over, brushing the toilet, he was suddenly grabbed from behind by both hips and pulled backward with a quick thrust. Without any forewarning, Andy had been pulled into someone's crotch and was being aggressively humped from the rear while his assailant was squealing like a pig. Instinctually, Andy elbowed his attacker directly in the face. Andy realized it was Hurley about midway through pulling his arm back, but it was too late to stop; the swing was already in motion. The elbow landed on Hurley's nose, and the hit's force pushed him back against the other wall. With blood pouring down his shirt, Hurley tried to stop the bleeding by covering his nose with both hands. Then, leaning against the wall, he slowly slid down to the bathroom floor until his butt hit the tile, attempting to regain his faculties.

Herman heard the commotion and turned around just in time to see Andy elbow Hurley in the face. Andy and Herman stood still, in silence, both stunned by what had just happened. Unsure of what to do next, they stood staring at Hurley for a few seconds because he couldn't immediately get up.

Andy had reacted in the heat of the moment, and now that it was over, he was shocked he had hit Hurley and terrified of the potential repercussions. As his entire future flashed in front of his eyes, he feared he was going to hyperventilate.

While holding his nose, Hurley struggled to his feet and grabbed some paper towels from the container next to the sink. Blood covered the front of his shirt, but it appeared the bleeding had significantly slowed and possibly stopped. Hurley washed the blood from his face and grabbed a clean batch of paper towels from the dispenser to assess the injury. Andy and Herman continued to stand there in shock, expressionless, watching Hurley clean up. Finally, Hurley turned to walk out the bathroom door, ending the awkward silence. "I got your ass now! What goes around, comes around!" Hurley said without glancing back in their direction.

Andy and Herman looked at each other briefly, unsure what to do next. "Let's finish this," Andy said, and they got back to work. Anticipating Hurley would barge back in the men's room at any second, they hurried to finish without saying another word.

As two cadets walked into the Academy for the day, Hurley exited the men's room and walked down the hallway toward his office. Both cadets immediately noticed the blood on Hurley's shirt and how he was holding the wad of paper towels to his nose. Unable to stop staring at Hurley, they instinctually shuffled to the opposite side of the walkway to give him plenty of space to pass. Both cadets stood there with their mouths ajar as Hurley stomped down the hallway. He didn't utter a word as the two cadets looked on and then glanced back toward the restroom.

Just as Andy and Herman were finishing up their chores, the two cadets came running into the men's room to find out what had happened. "What the fuck happened to Hurley?" one of the cadets asked.

Neither one said a word; they kept their heads down and continued cleaning. Andy mopped the floor while Herman cleaned the remaining traces of blood left behind in the sink.

The two cadets looked at one another and then at the sink Herman was washing. They knew something had occurred, but it was apparent that Andy and Herman were keeping their lips sealed. The cadets rushed back into the hallway and quickly started gossiping about what they had just witnessed.

Lastly, Andy emptied the trash can, and they were finally finished. Quietly, Andy and Herman walked into the locker room to get dressed in their uniforms before inspection started. Internally, they were both waiting for the other shoe to drop.

As Hurley entered his office, he walked right past Shockley, standing near the door with a cup of coffee in hand.

"What the hell happened to you?" asked Shockley.

"I need you to run inspection for me. I'm going to the doctor!" replied Hurley.

"OK, but what happened?" Shockley asked again.

Hurley pretended not to hear him while he changed his shirt. Then he proceeded to pick up his things and walked out of the room. Stunned, Shockley stood there trying to figure out what had happened. "Are you going to tell me?" Shockley yelled as Hurley walked away.

Hurley didn't respond as he hurried down the stairs. Embarrassed, he wanted to get out of sight before any other cadets arrived, so he quickly exited through the back door of the gymnasium.

As everyone showed up for inspection, rumors of the morning events ran rampant through the class. The two witnesses told everyone that there must have been a fight. Only a few cadets had the nerve to ask Andy and Herman directly, but they both stuck to the same story and insisted nothing had happened.

They were both shaken and nervous from the morning's confrontation, but neither one wanted to talk about it. Going through the motions, they lined up for formation and silently brooded about what awaited them.

When Shockley came down to conduct the inspection, Andy breathed a sigh of relief. He assumed Hurley would tell the Captain all about the encounter, and it was only a matter of time before they came into the gym and drug him out by his limbs.

Still clueless about what had happened, Shockley conducted inspection as usual. Afterward, the class was dismissed for PT, and the mad dash to the locker room was on again. Petrified and anxious, Andy and Herman couldn't help but glance around every corner as they hustled to the locker room with the rest of the class. Hurley could be waiting anywhere to enact his revenge.

As they dressed for PT, Paul Gaye approached Andy.

"Is there anything I can do?" Paul asked.

Paul was the class President and had heard the rumors through the grapevine. Earnestly, Paul wanted to help if he could, but Andy refused to look up from tying his shoes.

"Nothing," replied Andy. It was apparent that he didn't want to talk about it.

"Look, I can't help if I don't know what's going on," Paul said.

Andy just nodded his head in agreement as he finished tying his tennis shoes. Then, finally, he stood up and looked at Paul. "I appreciate it, Paul, but I got this." Andy closed his locker door and walked briskly out of the locker room toward formation for what he assumed would be his last time in PT.

Ironically, the class started boxing instruction that morning with the heavy punching bags. Shockley opened the storage room facility door and instructed several cadets to drag out the heavy bags. For every two cadets, they assembled one punching bag. After their regular PT exercises had concluded, they took turns with a partner punching the bags. One cadet held the bag while their partner would take a turn punching with all their might. Shockley blew his whistle at the one-minute mark, and the pair switched places. The whistle sounded after another one-minute interval, and the pair swapped places again.

Growing up, Andy had done his fair share of boxing and even trained a little with a former professional boxer during his college years. He always found it an entertaining sport and an excellent skill to have, should he ever need it.

All of Andy's frustrations poured out of him as he rhythmically punched the bag... one-two, one-two, Andy punched the bag. For a brief moment, he was able to forget about his fears of expulsion, forget about the stresses of the Academy, and just let go. Shockley's whistle sounded to signal PT was over and the mad dash to the showers was on again.

Around every corner, Andy and Herman could hear the other cadets whispering about them. They ignored the gossiping and said nothing because they knew it would all come out into the open soon enough.

Andy hoped the entire ordeal would blow over if they ignored it. Yet, every time the classroom door opened, he feared it was the Captain and Hurley coming to remove them. Somehow that moment never came, and they managed to survive until the end of the day. Hurley didn't make it back to the Academy, and no one knew where he was or what he was up to. Shockley was at the front of the classroom, recapping the day and reviewing what they could anticipate in the upcoming week.

The class was dismissed, and as they walked out of the Academy doors, Andy had the feeling in the pit of his stomach that this was his last day as a Houston Police cadet. Of course, it was Friday, so the formality would have to wait until Monday, but Andy figured Hurley would be waiting, and he would have his revenge.

Dad's Wisdom

Andy decided he might as well make the 2-hour drive home for the weekend to spend some time with Mom and Dad. Slowly, he needed to prepare them for what was coming. After gathering some things from his apartment, including his dirty laundry, he made the drive home Friday night. By delaying leaving Houston, the traffic had an opportunity to die down, making the commute easier. While driving down 59, Andy had a lot of time to think about what had happened that morning and everything that had led him to this moment. He reflected on his regrets and the things he wished he could do all over again.

As he turned into his parents' driveway at 9 pm, he noticed the lights in the house were still on. Andy grabbed his laundry from the trunk and walked in the back door. His parents eagerly anticipated his arrival and were standing, waiting by the door for him. As Andy walked through the threshold, he could see both parents beaming, grinning from ear to ear.

"Are you tired, son?" asked his Dad.

"I'm fine," replied Andy. "You guys didn't have to wait up."

"We couldn't wait to hear about your week," Mom said.

They exchanged small talk, but Andy was vague about most of what had occurred at the Academy. Recalling just enough to satisfy their curiosity, they then had a nightcap together and caught Andy up on the news from home. About an hour into the conversation, everyone began to feel the exhaustion take over, and they decided to turn in and talk more in the morning.

As usual, Andy's Dad was up early the following morning. As a boy growing up during the Great Depression, his father would rise early to work in the fields. In Andy's lifetime, he had never witnessed his Dad sleep past 5 am, no matter what. Named Woodrow, but everyone called him by his nickname, Woody. Routinely every morning, Woody would wake up, brew his coffee, read the paper, and smoke a cigarette. He had picked up smoking as a teenager and never quit. He had tried to kick the habit on multiple occasions but was always unsuccessful. Unfortunately, smoking would eventually cost him his life.

Andy's Mom was named Emma, but most folks fondly called her Poodle. Woody had given her that nickname when they were dating in the early '30s, and it stuck. Even though they did not openly show affection, they were a down-to-earth, loving couple. They didn't publicly hug or kiss, but no one ever doubted they were wholly committed to one another.

Andy wasn't an early riser, but now that he had to get up for the Academy every day on his own, it was starting to catch on. He awoke to the smell of coffee and decided to have a cup with his Dad. He needed to begin the process of explaining what he knew was coming Monday.

"Morning, Dad," Andy said as he poured a cup of coffee.

"Morning, son," Woody replied. "How did you sleep?"

"Good! It's great to be out of the city and back home. I sort of think I made a mistake. I didn't think I would miss this place so much."

"Well, you can't live here forever," Woody replied. "Sooner or later, you were going to be out on your own anyway."

"Yeah, but maybe the big city was not the best choice," Andy replied.

"Something going on, son?" Woody asked.

Knowing Andy well, his Dad could sense that he was trying to say something. So Andy started in, "Well, as a matter of fact, I am having trouble with one of my Academy staff instructors. On Friday, he and I got into it, and I am not sure how this is all going to turn out once the Captain gets wind of it."

"Is it serious?"

"Serious enough to get me kicked out," Andy replied.

"Was it your fault?"

"I swear to God, Dad, I didn't do anything but defend myself," Andy replied passionately.

Woody could see the seriousness in Andy's eyes. "Well, let's keep this between us until we know for sure. No sense worrying your mother if it doesn't come to anything," replied Woody.

Andy nodded his head in agreement, and nothing else was mentioned. Andy could see how much his Dad cared and loved his mother and how he wanted to protect her for as long as possible.

The rest of the weekend, Andy relaxed, and it was just what he needed. He caught up with some of his old friends and blew off some steam, but he spent most of the time hanging out with Mom and Dad. Poodle's car was due for some much-needed maintenance, and since he loved to tinker on cars, this was an excellent opportunity to take his mind off his troubles and help his Mom out at the same time.

Hurley Gets His

Sunday evening came far too quickly as Andy started his drive back to Houston with a bag of freshly laundered clothes and his neatly ironed uniforms hanging in the back seat. While Andy was having a few beers with his friends, Woody had even given his shoes a good shine. Maybe my shoes will finally pass inspection now, he thought. Driving north on highway 59, Andy began contemplating how much his Mom and Dad had done for him, and he still hadn't had the opportunity to pay them back for his gratitude. Tears started to well in his eyes. He had hoped that becoming a police officer would make them proud. Now that it was his chance to shine, he was blowing it. How could he make his parents proud of him like his brothers? How could he ever come home and face them? No matter what, he knew he had to face the music tomorrow morning.

When the alarm went off at 5:30 am Monday, Andy was already awake. In anticipation of the day, he had barely slept. As he got dressed, he was nearly numb from all the emotions pouring through his mind. Over and over, he continued to dwell on what would happen when he opened the Academy doors.

As he pulled into the parking lot, he couldn't even recall the commute to the Academy. His mind was entirely focused on this moment; his heart was pounding. Walking up the Academy steps, he noticed the Captain's car was already there. This only confirmed his greatest fears because the Captain was never this early. He expected Hurley inside those doors, waiting for him. Several other cadets walked in, but no one said anything other than the usual morning greetings.

Another cadet held the door open for Andy as they walked into the building, appearing as though he was serving as a pallbearer to Andy's funeral. Andy immediately noticed the Captain's office door open. The Captain's secretary spotted him and motioned for him to come in.

'Ok, this is it,' Andy thought. The secretary informed Andy the Captain was waiting for him and that he should go straight in. Approaching the door, he overheard voices, but he could not decipher whom they belonged to or what was being said. He knocked on the office door.

"Come in," chimed Captain Milan.

Hurley was already seated in an office chair when Andy opened the door, eyes pointed directly at him. A slightly swollen nose, but other than that, he appeared to be his usual self. Andy withheld any reaction and directed his eyesight to Milan, outfitted in an entire Class A uniform. Typically, a Class A uniform was reserved for formal events, ceremonies, or meetings of particular importance.

'That figures,' Andy thought. "You wanted to see me, sir?" Andy asked.

"Sit down, cadet Wallace," Milan replied.

Andy sat down beside Hurley. Instantly, Hurley stiffened his posture.

"Is it true that you struck officer Hurley in the face last Friday?" asked Milan.

"Yes, sir," Andy replied in a matter-of-fact tone. Determined not to hang his head or fall on his sword, he would stick to the facts. Boastful and defensive behavior was ill-advised, and he would not reduce himself to that level. Instead, he would tell his story and let the chips fall where they may.

"Can you tell me why?"

"Because he grabbed me from behind and forced my butt onto his crotch when I was bent over cleaning the toilet," Andy responded.

Hurley suddenly stood up and exclaimed, "That's bullshit, Captain! That's a fucking lie!"

"SIT DOWN!" Milan yelled at Hurley.

With a disgusted look on his face, Hurley slowly sat back down.

Milan advised Andy to continue. "It was a reflex, sir. I didn't even know who it was, but I was not going to take that," Andy replied.

Milan turned his head to Hurley, "Is this true?"

"NO FUCKING WAY, CAPTAIN!"

Milan was a religious man, and no one had ever heard him utter a curse word. As such, he certainly didn't appreciate anyone else cursing either, especially in his office. "Watch your tongue, Hurley," Milan replied sternly.

Hurley glanced at Andy with an embarrassed expression, almost as if he didn't realize his reaction until after it had occurred. Andy sat still with a straight face, looking directly at the Captain, without regard for Hurley.

"Was anyone else present in the restroom?" Captain Milan asked Andy directly.

"Yes, sir," Andy replied. "Herman Munich was there, but I am not sure what he saw."

"Do you have anything else to say for yourself?" inquired the Captain.

"No, sir."

"You're dismissed, cadet Wallace."

"Yes, sir," Andy said, stood up, and walked out without delay.

Andy wasn't sure what would happen next, but he thought the meeting went as expected. Thankfully, he wasn't asked to turn in his uniforms, not yet anyway. As he entered the hallway on his way to formation, several other cadets were clustered together, chatting before inspection. Immediately all chatter stopped, and everyone looked in Andy's direction as if he were about to make an announcement, but he kept his gaze forward and walked to his spot. Several other cadets had already arrived, beginning to line up.

Paul Gaye walked over to Andy and asked, "How'd it go?"

"I don't want to talk about it right now, Paul. Let's just get this over with," replied Andy.

Paul nodded his head in understanding but was disappointed he could not help.

As the inspection approached, everyone was standing in line, attentively awaiting Hurley. Shock spread through the formation when Shockley walked down to conduct it. Curiously, they all wondered why Hurley wasn't present. Halfway through the process, the gym door opened, and the Captain's secretary shouted to Shockley. "Captain wants to see cadet Munich in his office."

Unsurprised, Shockley nodded his head in agreement. "Munich, fall out of formation!" Shockley advised.

"Yes, sir," Herman replied and started walking toward the door. Walking past Andy, their eyes locked in acknowledgment of what was about to happen. Herman attempted to walk confidently towards the Captain's office. The secretary pointed her head toward the closed door.

"Go on in," she told Herman.

Herman anticipated seeing Hurley upon opening the door, but it was just the Captain.

"Sit down, cadet Munich," Milan said.

Herman sat down and meekly glanced around the room. He had been curious about what the Captain's office was like, and now that he was getting the chance to see it, he was too nervous to take in any specific details.

"Cadet, I want you to tell me exactly what you saw happen in the restroom last Friday between officer Hurley and cadet Wallace."

"Yes, sir," replied Herman with a slight quiver in his voice. Herman vividly retold the Captain precisely what he had seen, which closely aligned with Andy's statement. For clarification, the Captain asked a few follow-up questions, but there wasn't any indication of pushback in his tone. Milan was thorough and wanted to ensure he had all the facts. He would repeatedly ask the same question but change the phrasing and how he asked it, a technique he heavily relied on during his detective career when checking for inconsistencies in a witness's statement. Herman had stayed the course.

"OK, dismissed cadet Munich," said Captain Milan.

Herman stood up and replied, "thank you, sir," and walked out. The class had already completed inspection and started PT, so Herman diverted to the locker room to change into his gym clothes. After taking off his uniform, Hurley suddenly appeared and violently slammed the locker door shut to demand attention.

"You little piece of shit!" Hurley snarled. "What the fuck did you just tell the Captain?"

Startled and scared to death, Herman instantly replied, "Uh, nothing, sir."

"Don't fucking lie to me, asshole. What the fuck did you say?"

Hurley leaned in toward Herman intimidatingly and stared at him.

"Nothing, sir. I promise," Herman said squeamishly. He couldn't bring himself to recount the conversation he had with the Captain. Herman had zero doubt that Hurley would kill him with his bare hands if he ever found out what was said.

"You sicken me, you little piece of shit. You don't want to fuck with me, Munich. I am NOT the guy you want to meet in a dark alley, and that is exactly what's going to happen if you fuck with me. Got that?"

"Yes, sir," Herman replied, trying not to piss his pants.

"What goes around, comes around," said Hurley as he turned and stormed out of the locker room.

Herman stood still for a minute, staring absently at his locker, petrified of Hurley ever discovering the truth. He was already terrified of conflict, particularly with Hurley. Finally, he finished dressing and joined the class in time for sprints. Just his luck; it was the part he hated most.

The rest of the day proceeded as usual. At every break or anytime someone opened the door to the training room, Andy was sick with anxiety. Hurley or the Captain could be there to deliver the bad news at any moment. He kept expecting to get the word to pack his stuff, but it never came.

At the end of the last lecture, Shockley reviewed their schedule and briefed everyone on what to expect the rest of the week. Finally, the Captain's secretary opened the door, and everyone turned. "The Captain wants to see cadet Wallace on his way out," she said.

Andy sank into his chair. 'This is it,' he thought. Although he had anticipated expulsion, it was still devastating to know he was on his way out of the program. His career as a cadet was now down to a few measly minutes.

Shockley nodded his head in acknowledgment and then looked at Andy. Andy returned a nod; nothing else needed to be said. He knew what to do.

"Class dismissed!" announced Shockley, and everyone got to their feet to shuffle out the door.

During his last encounter with his classmates on his way to the Captain's office, Andy was shocked by the number of fellow cadets that shook his hand in solidarity as they walked past him. Cadets that weren't within proximity waved or smiled, and many patted him on the back on the way out of the door. Quite the spectacle and the gesture warmed Andy's heart. Shockley stood at the front of the class and watched his cadet's display of camaraderie with pride and smiled. He didn't need to know the details of the incident to know that he didn't care for Hurley's moral character.

As Andy walked into the Captain's office, the feeling of fellowship was fleeting. The pit of his stomach instantaneously turned to butterflies when the secretary pointed at the Captain's door without uttering a word. She was gathering her stuff together to leave for the day and had no interest in staying. Andy slowly walked over and knocked on the closed door for the last time.

"Come in."

Andy stepped in, expecting Hurley to be present again, but he wasn't. Only the Captain was in the office.

"Take a seat, cadet."

There was a change to his tone from this morning. Earlier, he had the mindset of an investigator attempting to collect the facts; now, he appeared to be playing the role of the unhappy supervisor.

"Cadet Wallace, you have caused me a lot of grief in a very short period!" Milan said, staring directly at Andy. "My job is to run this Academy, and when something or someone causes my job to be more difficult than it has to be, I don't like it, and I don't like whatever or whoever is causing that problem. Officer Hurley wanted to file charges on you. Do you understand what I am saying?"

"Yes, sir," replied Andy making eye contact with the Captain.

"I'm not sure if he's going anywhere with that, but he could," Milan explained. "I told him that there was a witness that backed up your story."

Suddenly Andy realized Herman had stood up for him. When it counted, Herman had found the courage to do what was right. All at once, Andy was surprised, impressed, and thankful.

"Do you have anything to say for yourself?" Milan asked.

"No, sir," Andy replied.

Milan kept anticipating a reaction from Andy but found none. Andy remained calm and collected. Accepting the outcome as a foregone conclusion, he kept quiet and looked at his superior with respect. Milan was impressed by Andy's uncanny ability to remain unemotional during the high-stress situation, an admirable attribute that not many cops have. Indeed, not an easy skill to teach; the lucky ones were just born with it. Police officers who can remain unprovoked during challenging encounters increase the safety of both the officer and civilian; the Captain was witnessing the start of Andy's potential.

Thoughtful, Milan leaned back in his chair, removed his glasses, and slowly spun his chair to glance out the window. Andy could tell that he wasn't looking at anything in particular; instead, he was mulling the situation over in his mind attempting to determine how best to proceed. When Andy realized Milan was trying to make a final decision, he was surprised and struggled not to show it. Andy's mind raced through the possible implications as he sat anxiously waiting for Milan to decide his fate.

Milan briskly turned back around, placing both elbows on his desk, and leaned forward. He dropped his glasses on his desk in a deliberate fashion to emphasize his statement. "Look, I think you have potential," Milan said in a committed voice. "You could have the makings of a good cop, but you are also a screw-up. I don't know which one of you will win out, but the two are not compatible. You either get your act together, or I will have you out the door so fast your head will spin. Do you understand me?"

Andy wanted to stand and scream for joy, but he just sat there, momentarily stunned. Then, in all seriousness, he looked into the Captain's eyes with a sense of pure gratitude. "I will make you proud, sir."

"You see to it," Milan said, "but you're not getting out of this unscathed." Milan continued, "You're on the Coffee Squad and Knowledge Squad until I say otherwise. Officer Hurley will be given strict instructions to have nothing to do with you. Do you understand?"

"Yes, sir," replied Andy.

Milan finished by saying, "Look, you are never justified to hit an officer. There is always another way to handle these situations. However, I think everyone has the right to defend themselves. I disapprove of what Hurley did, and as a Christian man, I cannot condone any of these actions. Yours or his! This is a one-strike rule, and you will not get another one. Do I make myself clear!?"

"Yes, sir," Andy replied, and this time, he could not help but show a little emotion. He cracked a small smile, and tears started welling up in his eyes.

The Captain did not smile back, but just then, he knew for sure that he had made the right choice. "Now get out of here, and I better not see you in my office again, for ANY REASON! Dismissed!" Milan barked.

"Yes, sir," Andy replied as he got up and briskly walked out.

He went back to the classroom to grab his briefcase and then walked out of the Academy into the bright sun. It felt terrific on Andy's face like he had been given a new lease on life. He vowed to take full advantage of his second chance and do whatever he could not to disappoint. When he arrived at his apartment that evening, he couldn't wait to call his Dad and tell him the good news.

Woody was delighted, and they talked about how he should deal with Hurley in the future. "My suggestion is that you just ignore him and avoid him the best you can," said Woody. "You still have a long way to go, and this guy would like nothing more than to have your head on his mantel."

Andy agreed and told his Dad that he wouldn't be home this weekend, but next one for sure.

Woody said, "Ok, stay safe and watch your step."

Beaming with pride, Andy agreed and hung up. On his way to fulfilling his dream and finally giving his parents something to be proud of. Now to be ready for tomorrow and ready for Hurley.

THREE

Hurley Lays Off

Driving to work the following day, Andy was filled with anxiety, wondering if Hurley would be there. Would he follow the Captain's orders? Was he capable of being hands-off? Grateful for the bravery Herman showed by standing up for him and recounting the truth to the Captain, he couldn't wait to see him and thank him. Andy felt ashamed he had avoided Herman in the past, considering he truly understood what it was to be a friend.

As he walked into the Academy, Andy dropped off his stuff and headed straight to the breakroom to get the coffee started. While in the middle of making his first batch, Hurley walked in. Hurley's narrowed, anger-filled eyes honed in directly on Andy, but he said nothing. Not wanting to give him the satisfaction, Andy merely watched him out of his peripheral vision. After making himself a cup of coffee, he hiked his leg, cut a disgusting fart, and walked out of the room. Hurley found the stunt hilarious because he was uncontrollably laughing as he left the room and walked down the hallway. That only served to solidify Andy's disdain for the man.

The Captain arrived early that morning in preparation for his meeting first thing with Hurley. To ensure that Andy was fulfilling his additional obligations and grab a cup of coffee, he headed straight to the break room.

"Morning, sir," Andy said.

"Morning, Wallace," Milan responded, got his coffee, and walked out. The Captain wanted to return to business as usual, and Andy respected that. He just wanted to go back to blending in with the rest of the cadets and prove his worth.

After the Captain sat down in his office chair, he picked up his phone, dialed Hurley, and advised him he wanted to see him.

"I'll be right down, sir," replied Hurley.

On his way to the Captain's office, he came face to face with Herman in the hallway. Herman was walking in for the day, and Hurley gave him a go-to-hell look as they passed each other. Hurley intentionally took up the entire hallway so Herman was forced to slide to one side to let him pass.

Once Hurley got to the Captain's office, he knocked on the door, and the Captain invited him in. "Morning, sir," Hurley said.

"Morning. Take a seat," the Captain replied matter-of-factly. Then, the Captain rehashed the pertinent parts of his conversation with Andy and his subsequent punishment.

Hurley rolled his eyes, and as his anger continued to rise, he began squirming in his chair. Finally, when he could hold his tongue no longer, he interrupted the Captain, "You've got to be kidding me, sir! Why isn't he being discharged for striking a superior officer? I should have filed charges on the asshole when it happened."

"You should have done a lot of things!" Milan said, raising his voice. "For starters, you shouldn't have goosed him!"

Hurley interrupted again, "I didn't!" Now they were both yelling.

"I have an eyewitness!"

"You're gonna believe that piece of shit cadet over me?" Hurley asked.

Milan jumped up out of his seat, screaming in Hurley's face, "Watch your language in my office!"

Even though it was evident to Hurley that he had angered the Captain, he didn't care. With his emotions in hyperdrive, it was all he could do not to explode. First, seething over his confrontation with Andy, but now he was gunning straight for Herman. Without that eyewitness, this all would have ended differently.

As Hurley sat there looking at the wall in disgust, the Captain continued, "Look, Hurley, I'll be honest. I don't like you. I'm not too fond of your attitude, your language, and you don't have the temperament for this job. So, I want you to look for another place to work, and if you leave on your own without me having to transfer you, I will give you a good recommendation."

Hurley couldn't believe how the Captain was insulting him. Already the victim of an assault by a lowly cadet, and now he's the one to get transferred. What the fuck?! Keen to the fact the Captain was not in the mood to negotiate, he refused to make eye contact or acknowledge anything said.

Milan continued, "If I hear of you messing with Wallace in any way, you will be transferred immediately to the worst place I can find, and there will be disciplinary actions as well. It will be on your record indefinitely! Do I make myself clear?"

"You're clear, sir," Hurley replied curtly and then asked, "Are you finished?"

Milan was about to lose his patience, so he momentarily paused to regain composure. An awkward silence filled the room until finally, Milan said, "I'll give you a month to put your feelers out around the department. That should be plenty of time to find a new home."

Hurley remained silent, refusing to dignify the Captain's decision with a response.

"Dismissed," ordered Milan. Without a reply, Hurley got up and stormed out of the office.

The entire encounter further confirmed to Milan that he had made the right decision. Hurley was bad medicine, and Milan would be glad when he was no longer under his command.

Hurley kept mulling over what just happened on the walk back to his office, and the more he did, the angrier he got. 'That fucking little weasel snitched on me,' he thought. Technically, Hurley had been instructed to stay away from Andy; however, he was under no such orders regarding Herman. 'Packback is a real bitch!' Internally, Hurley waged a personal vendetta against Herman, but he was methodical about it. He couldn't afford any missteps. Herman had already proven himself to be a snitch and couldn't be trusted. Once a snitch, always a snitch. Deep in thought, Hurley slowly closed his office door and returned to his desk to plan his revenge.

The class schedule continued as planned the next day with only a few noticeable changes. Shockley was now running the program, with additional staff officers in support positions. In addition, special presenters were still being brought in from around the department to provide their expertise. Each day, the classes were gaining momentum and getting more interesting. The cadets learned to take fingerprints, plaster cast molds for tire tracks, and many other exciting techniques that they had only previously witnessed on TV.

The next day was their first field trip to the city morgue. It was a rather morbid and creepy experience to go there and see an autopsy firsthand, but also essential for their training. They needed to learn a basic overview of the Medical Examiner's responsibilities and what they required from first responders to execute their jobs properly.

The rest of the week included exciting trips to different areas of the police department. As the curriculum changed for the better, things improved for Andy too. While the cadets were on their feet and interacting with the various departments, they didn't have to report to Hurley. 'What a deal,' Andy thought.

Hurley Locks On

The next day after they conducted inspection and PT, the cadets were lined up for transport down to the city morgue. Fulfilling his Coffee Squad duties, Andy had already been at the Academy since 6 am. In addition, he stayed after class each day for the Knowledge Squad. But honestly, he didn't mind doing both. Several other cadets were on the Knowledge Squad, and occasionally he would have a partner to share responsibilities with.

Andy's jaw dropped when he saw Hurley get on the bus for the trip to the morgue. Although he constantly gave Andy the evil eye, he refrained from physical contact with him other than occasionally brushing against him as an intimidation tactic. Hurley's focus was now on Herman, and he did everything that was within his power to make his life a living hell. By nit-picking Herman's every action, Hurley managed to assign him to multiple squads, including the Olympic Squad. The Olympic Squad was Hurley's baby, and he took full advantage of it to physically punish Herman with extra sprints, push-ups, pull-ups, and anything else he could think of. Next, Hurley jacked with his uniform while Herman was showering in the locker room. Then when all the cadets lined up for formation, Hurley extensively ridiculed Herman for his uniform not meeting the proper specifications.

One day, Hurley thought it would be a good idea to drop Herman's towel on the wet tile floor. After his shower, Herman reached for his towel to discover it was damp and nasty. Out of fear, all the other cadets remained silent about the abuse they witnessed Herman endure. Plus, if Hurley was focused on Herman, they were less likely to be on the receiving end of his bullying. Unfortunately, the antics were getting to Herman, and Andy was afraid he would soon crack under the stress of it all.

Once they arrived at the morgue, the Deputy Medical Examiner gave the cadets a tour and explained their work process. The morgue was dark and quiet with a cold, sterile, uninviting feeling. Everything was constructed from stainless steel, similar to a hospital, and the stench of death constantly lingered in the air. Suddenly, a muffled scream filled the morgue, startling the cadets. The voice sounded familiar. Andy instinctively turned toward the direction of the scream, trying to determine what the hell had happened. It was Herman! Hurley was standing by the walk-in freezer with a shit-eating grin on his face, holding the door shut where the corpses were stored with Herman trapped inside. Shockley quickly shuffled through the group of cadets to investigate. As soon as Hurley saw Shockley coming, he quickly opened the door. Forcibly grabbing Herman by the front of his uniform, he pulled him out of the freezer and closed the door.

"What the hell are you doing?" demanded Hurley.

Hurley decided to pass it off as a joke, but the encounter had scared the hell out of Herman. He was visibly shaken from the experience, trapped in a completely dark freezer full of dead bodies and unable to open the door.

As Herman joined the rest of the cadets, Andy walked up behind him and put his hand on his shoulder.

"Are you OK?" Andy asked in a low voice.

Herman just nodded his head in response. His eyes were downcast with a mortified expression on his face. Believing Hurley just to be kidding around, some fellow cadets chuckled a little, but Andy knew it was much more beneath the surface. Unfortunately, Herman was taking the brunt of the abuse for standing up and telling the truth, and there was little Andy could do but console him.

Shockley yelled out for everyone to knock it off and pay attention. "Some of this will be on your test Friday!" Shockley said. Speaking as much for Hurley's benefit as anyone else's, he gave Hurley a disapproving glare. Hurley just shrugged his shoulders and grinned as if to say, 'What did I do?'

Once the tour ended, the cadets piled into the bus to return to the Academy. Andy hoped to sit beside Herman to cheer him up on the ride back, but Hurley had already taken the spot. Another way for him to zero in on his prey.

Certainly, not a good situation for Herman, and Andy knew it. Nevertheless, Hurley would not let up, and Andy hoped that Herman could weather the storm.

Once back at the Academy, Shockley stood up at the front of the bus facing the cadets and glanced at his watch. The time was 4:30 pm, the class was typically dismissed at 5 pm. "I don't see a point in returning to the classroom for less than a half-hour. Therefore, as a one-time exception, class is dismissed early for the day," announced Shockley.

A cheer rang out throughout the bus as everyone started to stand up and collect their belongings. Considering they had never been released early, this was a real treat.

Hurley then yelled out, "Except for you guys and gals on the Knowledge Squad!".

Andy, Herman, and a few other cadets were assigned to the Knowledge Squad. Herman dropped his head in defeat. Knowing Herman was fragile, Andy hoped he wasn't thinking about quitting. Andy thought about saying something to the Captain, but he remembered Milan telling him that he didn't want to hear anything from him again. Unable to handle any additional turmoil right now, Andy decided to keep his head down and his mouth closed. He couldn't afford for his efforts to backfire.

They exited the bus and walked to the classroom. Andy and Herman diligently worked on their notebooks and studied for their upcoming test on Friday. Several times, Hurley unnecessarily walked into the classroom and made sure to slowly walk past Andy and Herman. His obvious objective was to intimidate them and nothing more. Knowing how far he could push the boundaries, he said nothing, but it was nonetheless effective. Finally, at 6 pm, they were dismissed, and Hurley made sure he was in the hallway to stare them down as they walked out for the evening.

To ensure he was OK, Andy walked Herman to his car. He could sense Herman was reaching his breaking point, and Andy wanted him to stay strong and not give up. He chatted with Herman for a few minutes to lift his spirits and provide encouragement, and Herman appeared appreciative. After saying their goodbyes, Andy drove out of the parking lot, wondering if Herman could hang on.

The rest of the week went as planned. Hurley was spending more of his time making phone calls around the department, looking for a new place to work. Thankfully, this meant he had less time to mess with Herman, which seemed to boost his morale. Hurley would be transferred to wherever the Captain wanted if he didn't find a home soon. He had been calling around to anywhere in the department where he thought he could find a decent gig, but his reputation preceded him. No matter where he called, someone knew him or knew of him. All of his callbacks claimed there were no available openings. He was in a fix, and in his mind, it was all because of Herman.

Andy stayed at his apartment that weekend, catching up on his notebook and studying for the next week's test. They usually tested every Friday, and Andy didn't want to give Hurley anything to bitch about.

As usual, Andy made his weekly phone call home and caught up with Mom and Dad about the workweek. To an extent, they seemed interested, but they mainly wanted to talk about Mike's new gym and how successful it was. Of course, it made sense because Mike always had a knack for making things happen.

Everybody Loves a Fireman

On Monday morning, word came down from the Chief's office that the entire Academy class was invited to the Monster Jam at the Astrodome this upcoming Friday night. The extreme auto show features souped-up cars and trucks of various models, custom-built with massive tires and engine modifications. For everyone's viewing pleasure, a variety of obstacles were constructed for the vehicles to maneuver through to demonstrate their abilities in the middle of the Astrodome floor. The producers proposed that the Fire Department Academy and Police Department Academy cadets battle it out in a tug-o-war competition for thousands of screaming fans as halftime entertainment. A big PR event and both agencies could capitalize on the publicity as a method to recruit new cadets. Each Academy would pick fifteen of its most vital cadets to go head to head, with the winning team's Academy earning a $5,000 donation to their respective athletic program. The remaining cadets would receive free admission and sit in a special section to cheer on their classmates. The Chief wanted the money to expand the gym, but bragging rights were secretly just as important.

The curriculum was practically put on hold that week, with an extreme emphasis on winning the competition. Shockley was selected to pick the fifteen cadets for the team, which infuriated Hurley. Hurley saw this as his opportunity to shine and be noticed by the Chief, but it passed him by because of Herman's statement. Watching from the sidelines, he was seething with jealousy as Shockley instructed training.

Shockley scheduled team practice before classroom instruction every morning, during their intended lunch break, and even after class dismissal in preparation for the competition. If a cadet chosen for the team was scheduled to be on a squad that interfered with practice timing, the practice took precedence. The team's performance was the priority, and nothing else mattered.

Due to his strength and size, John Frost was the perfect candidate for team anchor. And John was just happy the team's practice got him off the Knowledge Squad for the week. When working for the police department in upstate New York, Paul Gaye had been part of their tug-of-war team. Every year, their department had tug-o-war competitions with the Canadian Mounties, located across the international bridge between Canada and the United States. Paul's tug-of-war system was exceptional, and as he began training the team using its techniques, they became more and more confident in their abilities.

Andy was chosen for the team; Herman wasn't. Herman was the designated waterboy and brought the team water and towels, but at least he would be at the Dome to cheer them on. A much-needed reprieve and break from what had been a rough couple of weeks for him. Herman needed this, and he needed an opportunity to build camaraderie with his peers and start to feel a sense of belonging. The constant ostracizing was lonely.

Friday arrived before they knew it, and Shockley decided to back off the physical training for the day to ensure they would be in peak physical condition for the competition that night. Instead, they focused on improving their technique, and the rest of the class showed up to encourage them and provide their support. After morning training, they finished the week's testing and went through with the day's scheduled classes, but the Monster Jam was all anyone could think about. As the anticipation mounted, they became caught up in the idea of doing something special for their class, the department, and to make the Chief proud.

Shockley had a personal contact at the local sporting goods store, and he arranged to have specially designed blue T-shirts donated to the team for the event. The T-shirts were decorated with 'HPD' letters printed in bold font across the back and adorned with a Houston police badge on the front left breast. The rest of the class would attend in their formal cadet uniform. Everyone agreed to stay late Friday afternoon to travel to the Monster Jam as a unified group.

Anxiously, the cadets lined up to walk out and board the bus for the trip to the Dome. All the cadets left their books and personal items at their desks to retrieve later. Herman was positioned towards the end of the line, and as he started walking to the exit, Hurley grabbed him by the arm. "Where do you think you're going?" snarled Hurley.

Herman, caught off guard by the peculiar question, replied, "The Monster Jam, sir."

"Not this time Munich," Hurley declared, "Someone has to pull security and watch our things while we're gone and that someone is you!"

Herman was visibly crushed. He searched Hurley's eyes, hoping that he had somehow misunderstood or that this was a cruel joke, but it wasn't. Hurley was dead serious, and there was nothing he could do to change his mind. At this point, everyone else was already out the door, even Shockley. Not that Herman would have had the nerve to stand up to Hurley or ask anyone for help anyway. It was done. Herman dropped his head in defeat as he realized he wouldn't get to go. The entire week had been a cruel exercise in futility. He was never going to be a part of anything.

Hurley laughed, put his uniform hat on, and walked out the door. "See you when we get back, sucker! I'll try to bring you back a souvenir," Hurley snarked over his shoulder.

Herman stood there watching out the door as the rest of his class boarded the bus without him. No one even seemed to notice he was left behind.

When the Houston Police Department bus pulled into the Astrodome complex, security officers directed them to a private loading dock. The Fire Department bus was already onsite and empty. They previously offloaded and entered the Dome. Shockley stood up and told the class to stay seated while he and Hurley found out where they needed to report. No one, not even Shockley, had noticed that Herman wasn't with them. And no one was aware Hurley had made him stay behind.

Shockley and Hurley returned to the bus and told everyone to fall out in single file. They quickly exited the bus and headed into the Dome down a long hallway. Andy could already hear the crowd, and he could feel the energy in the air as they walked toward the field. 'This must be what athletes feel like when they enter the Dome to play a big game,' he thought. They were all starry-eyed and filled with the thrill of the excitement.

When they arrived at their reserved seats, the cadets noticed they were seated directly across the aisle from the Fire Department cadet class. The Fire Department's uniforms were strikingly similar to the Police Department's uniform. Their fifteen cadets competing in the tug-o-war competition wore red T-shirts with 'HFD,' for Houston Fire Department, on their backs. As rivals, the two groups exchanged glances at one another, out of mere curiosity and in an attempt to size up their competition.

The Dome quickly filled to nearly capacity, and the crowd was rowdy. Every time a giant Monster Truck rolled out onto the Dome floor with flames shooting from the exhaust pipes, the crowd started screaming and yelling at the top of their lungs. The modified vehicles equipped with supercharged engines and after-market exhausts roared through the Dome at an ear-piercing decibel. The crowd's excitement, chanting, and shouting grew with every engine rev!

Andy was periodically scanning the stands and observing the spectators. Finally, he leaned in to whisper to John, "Most of the people here are rednecks, and the more beer they drink, the louder they get."

"Not a good combination," John replied.

Andy nodded his head in agreement.

The Dome staff came over to collect the tug-o-war teams just before the halftime show. The teams stood and walked in a single file line down the pathway leading onto the Dome floor behind the staff in unison. As their commander, Shockley followed the team to the floor while Hurley remained behind with the remainder of the class. The two groups listened carefully as the staff read the rules of the competition.

The rope was laid out in the middle of the Dome in a straight line. Once the competition was announced over the loudspeakers, both teams were instructed to run out onto the dirt floor and pick up their teams respective ends of the rope. A City Councilman was the special guest and ceremonial judge for the tug-o-war. Both teams nodded their heads to the other as a gesture of good sportsmanship.

The announcer began explaining the event over the PA and presented the Fire Department to the crowd first. Their team ran out onto the floor toward one end of the rope, and resounding applause and cheer emerged from the audience. Finally, the Police Academy team was announced to the center of the floor, and abruptly the audience's mood changed. The applause and cheers turned to a stark silence. As the police cadets ran out onto the floor and came into the viewing area, a series of loud "BOO's" erupted from the crowd. Andy was stunned at the adverse reaction! 'They don't like us?' he thought, 'Why are we the bad guys?' Andy felt dispirited; he had always thought the cops were the good guys. Not so much with this particular audience. The spectacle was catering to the roughneck, blue-collar types, and a lot of the audience had been drinking since at least the start of the event. The group was riled up and looking for their opportunity to give the police some grief; after all, it was perfectly legal.

The HPD team was undeterred and picked up the other end of the rope. The City Councilman stood in the middle, ready to call the winner. Andy was positioned towards the front of the team, and John Frost was last in line. Paul Gaye held a place in the middle and told the team to get into position just like they had practiced. The spectators were getting into it, and the arena's sound intensified. Andy struggled to hear Paul over the deafening noise, but apparently, they were about to start. The rope tightened, and the Councilman dropped his hand to signal the start. Andy leaned back and started pulling with all his might, in line with the cadence. At first, the rope didn't lean more one way or the other, but within about 10 seconds, it started inching toward HPD's Team. 'It's working!' Andy thought.

Paul continued his commands, and the rope was beginning to gain momentum in their territory now. They were going to win, and Andy was surprised at how quickly everything had happened. The Councilman waved his hands to signal the Houston Police Department won. The booing chants from the crowd grew louder. A little demoralizing, but Andy didn't care. He tuned it out as he and his teammates were jumping up and down and hugging each other in celebration. Finally, the HFD team came over and shook hands like good sports, and they all ran off the field together. The announcer attempted to put a good spin on the event by congratulating the HPD Team, but the crowd had none of it. As both teams ran towards the exit gate, the booing from the audience grew even louder. Closing in on the distance to the stands, projectiles were hurled at them from the bleachers. Wadded-up paper, hotdog plates, and empty beer cups closed in on the cadets from all directions.

The group covered their heads with their arms and continued running as fast as they could toward the exit. Obscenities were being shouted from the crowd. The rednecks saw this as their payback for previous traffic violations, and the cops couldn't do anything but run. Once the teams were under the protective cover of the bleachers, everyone took stock of their condition. Although everyone had all been hit with debris, thankfully, no one was injured. They reeked of beer, and everyone was hoping that's all it was. The cadets from the Fire Department commented on how much abuse the crowd gave the cops.

Shockley looked at them and said, "Everybody loves a Fireman!"

They smiled and started the walk back to the bus. No one had any inclination to go anywhere near those stands again. Shockley went within eyesight of the reserved section and signaled Hurley, along with the rest of the class to meet them at the bus for their trip home.

As the class boarded the bus, there were high-fives and yelling all around as they congratulated the team. Everyone was beaming with smiles as they pulled out of the Astrodome complex and got on the road heading back to the Academy. Shockley was radiating with pride, and even Hurley was in a good mood. The team made the department proud, and the idiots in the stands were just that. As they parked the bus back at the station, Shockley got up and addressed the class.

"You made us all proud tonight." Shockley said, "We'll have more time for celebration tomorrow, but for now, go in and grab your stuff and head home. I want you all to remember something about what you saw in that crowd tonight. That's not the typical behavior of the citizens of Houston, just a group of idiots! Don't let them get to you. And remember, if you can't handle the abuse from idiots, being a cop isn't the right job for you." Shockley ended with, "Dismissed!"

Tragedy in the Gym

Beaming with pride at their evening's success, the cadets exited the bus and walked back toward the Academy to collect their belongings. Paul Gaye reached the building first and immediately noticed the front doors were locked. Peering through the glass window in the door, Paul saw the lights were still on, except for the gymnasium. The situation appeared a bit unusual because the night shift cops occasionally use the gym to grab a quick workout. The doors typically remained unlocked and all lights on. The cadets started piling up at the front door when Hurley finally walked up and asked what the holdup was.

"The doors are locked, sir," Paul replied.

Hurley moved through the crowd and started reaching for his keys. "That little shithead Munich better not have locked the place up and left," Hurley said.

"Herman stayed behind?" asked Paul.

"Well, someone had to watch our stuff," he replied. Hurley unlocked the doors, and everyone started toward the classroom to grab their gear. Walking down the hallway towards his office, Hurley paused to turn on the gym lights to illuminate his pathway to the stairs. All of a sudden, he froze in his tracks. In shock, he stood there for a second, eyes wide, mouth ajar, unable to believe what he was seeing. Immediately, he couldn't help but wonder if he would be blamed for this.

Herman's body was hanging from the basketball rim, outfitted in his full cadet uniform. A leather belt was fastened to the carbon steel basketball hoop and wrapped around his neck. The step ladder from the maintenance closet was next to him; he must have used it to climb up to the height of the basketball rim to hang himself. Since Hurley hadn't uttered a sound and no one else could see inside the gymnasium from that angle of the hallway, at first no one noticed what he was glaring at. However, a few seconds later, when Shockley was walking past Hurley toward his office, he glanced over his shoulder to follow his gaze.

"Oh my God!" exclaimed Shockley as he started running toward Herman.

Hurley was still standing there in shock, then quickly snapped out of it and ran after Shockley as they both attempted to get Herman down from the goal.

"Oh my God! Call 911," Shockley yelled.

He immediately drew the attention of several cadets, who turned and ran towards the gym to see the commotion. One by one, everyone was shouting suggestions and attempting to help, but they were too late. Herman had taken his life some time ago; rigor mortis was already setting in. Shockley's first instinct was to perform CPR, but once he felt Herman's cold body, he knew he was gone. So he automatically changed gears, and his cop instincts kicked in. Because the situation changed from a potential medical emergency to a crime scene, he needed to get everyone back and preserve the evidence. Hurley made a feeble attempt to assist, but his mind was consumed with thoughts on how this might fall back on him.

Andy and John Frost were two of the last cadets to enter the Academy building, and they immediately noticed the commotion in the gym and heard Shockley yelling. "Get back! This is a crime scene, and we're contaminating it! There is nothing we can do for him now!" screamed Shockley.

As Andy and John picked up their pace and started hurrying towards the gymnasium, Andy wondered what could have happened to get Shockley so worked up, and then it hit him. On the gym floor, he could see someone approximately Herman's size and stature, and suddenly he realized he hadn't seen Herman the entire night. Where was Herman? Panic started to seize control of Andy as he tried to scan the crowd, searching for Herman. Shockley started herding the group back toward the gym doors and into the hallway to preserve the crime scene. Underneath the basketball goal, standing near the step ladder with his head down, Hurley just stared at the body. Herman was lying motionless on his back, blue in the face. Instantly, Andy knew he was dead.

With everyone back, Shockley walked over to the phone and called dispatch. An ambulance was required to arrive on the scene to pronounce the death, and an initial responding police unit would begin to conduct the investigation. In the end, Herman's death would be in the hands of the Homicide Detectives and the Medical Examiner's office, but those first steps needed to happen.

Unable to assist with the efforts, Andy stood as a bystander, watching the events unfold around him. Swirling through his mind was a litany of unanswered questions: Why did Herman stay behind in the first place? What brought him to take such drastic measures? Peering inside the gym, Andy noticed Hurley sitting in a chair near the gym wall with his head in his hands, slumped over, looking at the floor. 'Is it possible Hurley is grieving over Herman's death?!' thought Andy. Seems rather unlikely, but maybe he was wrong about Hurley. Maybe Hurley was merely trying to toughen Herman up in preparation for the job ahead.

What Andy didn't know was that Hurley wasn't grieving at all. He was only worried about how this would reflect on him. Hurley contemplated the evening events, forgetting about his inadvertent remark to Paul Gaye. He thought he could say that Herman wasn't feeling well and, on their way out, Herman asked if he could stay behind. Yes, that's the way he should spin this! He had to cover his tracks. If this blew up in his face, there was no telling where he would end up.

The rest of the evening passed by in a blur. No one was allowed to leave until Homicide decided who they wanted to speak with and who could be released. The ambulance EMTs and the initial responding patrol officers came and went. After the Homicide Detectives arrived on the scene, they directed the crime scene unit to take thorough pictures of every last detail. The Medical Examiner's office investigator arrived and started taking notes. Slowly, but surely, the press started collecting at the front steps of the Academy. A police cadet committing suicide in the Academy building was going to be a big, headliner news story.

With the exceptions of Shockley and Hurley, Homicide finally told everyone they could leave. They needed to go to the Homicide office and submit an official written statement. As he and his classmates walked outside, Andy was still in shock. Reporters from the news media were waiting for them. Even though they had been moved across the street, the cameras were still rolling, and the reporters were shouting out questions in an attempt to get a comment. The cadets were instructed not to speak to the press. Once all the facts were known, a Public Information Officer would provide a formal statement.

Andy assumed that at some point during his police career he would appear on television, but he never thought it would be as a cadet. Andy feared that his Mom, Dad, or another family member might see this incident on the news before he has a chance to speak with them. Probably best to call them first thing in the morning, it was already after midnight, and he was worn out. Feeling the toll of the physical and emotional exhaustion, he just wanted to get home and get some rest.

He desperately tried to forget this night that started on such a high note but ended in a nightmare.

Together, Shockley and Hurley walked up to the Homicide Division. Located on the 4th floor of the main police station and across the street from the Academy.

"Why did Herman stay behind? And why wasn't I made aware of it?" asked Shockley.

"As we were walking out the door to board the bus, Herman stopped me and said he felt sick. He thought he might throw up and he wanted to stay behind in case he got worse." Hurley continued, "I didn't want the boy to embarrass himself by making a mess on the bus."

"Why didn't you tell me?" asked Shockley.

"I don't know. We were all just so busy, I guess," Hurley replied.

Upon arrival at Homicide Division, they were ushered into separate witness rooms and handed a notepad and a pen to write their statements. Once they finished, they turned in their statements to a detective for review. The documents had to be signed and notarized, and then they were released for the night. Hurley stuck to the story he told Shockley. Although he was a little worried, he felt a lot better about the lie now that he had repeated the story several times.

Andy woke up Saturday morning, still exhausted. The image of Herman's lifeless body kept coming to the forefront of his thoughts, and he barely slept. He continually recalled how Herman had testified for him and how that action had drawn the ire of Hurley. Although he was emotionally devastated by the loss of his friend and fellow cadet, he knew he had to push through it. First, he needed to call his family and tell them what happened before they saw it on the news. Considering it had been a few days since he called them, it would be good to catch up anyway.

A police cadet hanging himself in the Academy gym made the headline news story. The reporters highlighted the trip to the Astrodome and how this one particular cadet reported to his superior that he was ill and stayed behind. Even though no one seemed the wiser about Hurley's story, to Andy, it just didn't make sense. Herman seemed fine just moments before they boarded the bus, and he was excited about the trip. Although Andy didn't trust Hurley or his story any further than he could throw him, it was in the detectives' hands now, and he trusted the system to find the truth.

Hurley Gets Transferred

The following week went by as planned, except for the mourning of Herman's death. Originally from New Jersey, Herman's parents decided to fly his body home. A ceremony wouldn't be held in Houston, and no one from the Academy was granted leave to go to the funeral services in New Jersey. Sadly, none of the cadets' could afford it right now anyway. So instead, the department would send a couple of Honor Guard members to escort the body and represent the department. It appeared as though Hurley was going to get out of this situation unscathed. The story of Herman's illness was sailing through the investigation unchallenged, and no one was the wiser. Herman had not mentioned Hurley's abuse to his parents or anyone else for that matter. Only Hurley, Herman, and Andy were aware of the extent of the bullying. Although Shockley and the rest of the class knew that Hurley didn't like Herman and that he was frequently badgered and teased by him, that was about it. Nothing that would have driven Herman to kill himself, and Herman didn't leave behind a note or any indication of the reasoning for his decision.

Captain Milan had the instincts of a good investigator, and he didn't like what he heard from Hurley. After reading Hurley's statement, he wasn't satisfied with his explanation of the events. He was disheartened and mortified that a cadet under his command had taken his life. Additionally, he didn't care for the way Hurley had acted since the incident, and deep down inside, he felt Hurley was somehow responsible. Repeatedly Milan reviewed all of the evidence collected, and he couldn't prove Hurley was involved, but just the same, he trusted his instincts and wanted him gone. So he picked up the phone and started arranging to have Hurley immediately transferred to the Northeast Patrol Substation. The worst possible place that Hurley would want to go and he was assigned to the night shift, where they would dole out his duties as they saw fit. Living on the far southwest side of town, he would have to commute to the opposite side of the city each day. Definitely, not an assignment that Hurley would have applied for himself.

Milan's secretary drew up the transfer papers, and once they were ready, he called Hurley into his office and broke the news. Hurley was to report to the Northeast Substation tomorrow at 11 pm for duty. Unsurprisingly, he didn't take the transfer well and stormed out of the Captain's office with transfer papers gripped tight in hand. Hurriedly, he went directly to his office and quickly threw everything in a box to leave. At this point, he had no desire to see a soul or say goodbye. He was utterly infuriated and boiling over with anger, and he knew exactly who was to blame. 'That little Wallace motherfucker,' Hurley thought. He certainly wouldn't give anyone the satisfaction of knowing this wasn't his decision and just how pissed off he was. Grabbing his boxed-up stuff, he walked out of the Academy, thankful that he would never have to see those damn cadets again.

Word spread quickly about Hurley's transfer, and no one was more relieved than Andy. 'Maybe Herman is getting his revenge in a way,' Andy thought. And some, small good that came out of this after all. Hopefully, with Hurley out of the picture, everyone could move on now, and Andy was sure things would be better without him at the Academy.

Graduation

Compared to everything he had already endured during his time at the Academy, the remaining months went by relatively easily. Finally, he was no longer assigned to any squads requiring additional duties, and Andy was committed to never being on one again. Each week, the curriculum became more engaging, adding in firearms training, tactical exercises, high-speed driving, and defensive tactics. All cadets were required to compete in three mandatory boxing matches, and Andy won all three; he was particularly proud of that. All of the pieces were coming together for him as the class grew closer to graduation. With their shared experiences, they were growing closer to each other too. He couldn't help but think about Herman from time to time, especially when they walked past the basketball goal.

As life in Houston and the Academy fell into a steady rhythm, Andy could afford to travel home more. He spent some of his weekend catching up with his old high school buddies. Andy shared stories from his Academy experiences, and they filled him in on the latest town gossip. Of course, they were still great friends, but everyone was moving in different directions in their lives. Times were changing.

Andy and John Frost quickly became good friends, and Andy even took John home to meet his parents. Poodle was an excellent cook, and John loved to put food away like nobody's business. The more he got to know John, the more he liked him. Their friendship would end up being one of the rare ones that last a lifetime.

Graduation day was fast approaching, and the entire class was starting to get a little nostalgic about their time together. The original seventy-two cadets that started together on day one were down to fifty-seven by graduation. Some cadets flunked; others were dismissed for one issue or another. A couple left for personal reasons, and a few others decided police work wasn't for them during the training process. Of course, Herman was the most tragic loss. The grief from Herman's death constantly lingered in the back of their minds.

Once they graduate and receive their work assignments, they may not see each other again. Houston was vast, and someone assigned to a remote substation may never run into another officer assigned to a substation on the other side of the city.

Following graduation, Andy and John Frost planned to get an apartment together. It would be an excellent way to share the cost of rent and household expenses and get to spend some of their off time with a friend. They included another cadet buddy, Doug Walling, in their new apartment plans.

Doug was quite different from Andy and John. Older, with a serious personality, Doug had been in the military and served in Vietnam. He was also a neat freak who required everything to be in its place and organized. Granted, Andy and John were more of the happy-go-lucky types and less likely to worry about clutter, but they were willing to give it a try as rookies and roommates.

Graduation day finally arrived, and the class had a rehearsal in preparation for the evening's ceremony. With the Chief of Police and most of the City Council attending, it would be a big deal. In addition, all the cadet's families were invited and encouraged to attend. The mayor was scheduled to give the graduation address. Andy was beaming with pride, knowing both his parents would be at the ceremony.

After a couple of practice runs, the class was given a break. Andy walked outside to get some air; Paul Gaye followed him. Paul turned to Andy, "You know, I am proud of you. When I first saw you, I didn't give you a snowball's chance in hell of making it to this day."

Andy smiled and replied, "Well, thank you... I think. To tell you the truth, Paul, I doubted it too." They both smiled. They enjoyed a moment of silence as they watched officers escort prisoners into the jail, then Andy said, "I wish Herman were here with us."

"Me too." Paul paused for a few seconds and then added, "If not for Hurley, I think he would be here."

Andy replied, "Yeah, Herman was fragile, and...well, you know."

There was a long pause, and then Paul turned to Andy and said, "You know I never mentioned this before, and maybe I should have, but Hurley's story was that Herman asked him if he could stay behind because he was sick."

"Yeah, so?"

Paul continued, "Well, when we got back from the Astrodome that night, we were locked out, and we had to wait for Hurley to show up with the keys. Hurley seemed surprised when he got to the door that they were locked. That's when he mentioned that Herman had stayed behind. I asked him why, and he said that someone had to stay behind and watch our stuff. Not once did he say anything about Herman being sick."

Andy was stunned. "You mean he lied?" Then, astonished and with a bewildered expression on his face, he asked, "You think Hurley told Herman to stay behind?"

Peering out toward the parking lot, Paul began to nod his head slowly and replied, "I think so."

For a few minutes, the two of them stood there gazing off into the distance, thinking back on that night and what happened. It felt like a moment of clarity for Andy; it all made sense now. Hurley forced Herman to stay behind by himself; maybe that was his breaking point. Andy's posture stiffened, and his fists began to clench in a fury, 'That son-of-a-bitch!' Andy thought. He was utterly infuriated, but there was nothing he could do. He swallowed hard, "Thank you for telling me. I kept going over the events of that day, over and over again. The story felt incomplete. Like something was missing, or there was something I was missing." Then, together, they turned and walked back inside.

After graduation, each cadet was handed their assignment in a sealed envelope. Everyone opened them up and proudly shared their jobs before leaving that evening. The following Monday they would report for their first day of duty. Andy was assigned to the Northwest Patrol, evening shift from 3 to 11 pm. Andy was initially hoping to be located in a rougher district than Northwest, but he was OK with it.

Northwest was referred to as the Ponderosa because it was in the city's outskirts where the development was sparse. Not much crime either. Far from what they called the ward or project areas of town. Andy was afraid that he wouldn't see much action, but it was close to where he lived, so that was convenient. As soon as he completed his 6-month probationary period, he would be eligible to transfer to anywhere in the city that he chose. Easing into police work was probably the best strategy anyway. 'No reason to rush this,' he thought. 'This will be a long career, and there will be plenty of time for crime-fighting.'

Andy drove back home for the weekend to celebrate with family and friends. After all of the stresses of training, he could use a couple of days of rest and relaxation before he buckled down to start his police career. Bright and early Saturday morning, Andy awoke to the smell of coffee brewing and the sound of hot bacon sizzling in the pan. Mom was up and cooking breakfast, and Andy's mouth was watering before his feet even hit the floor. He couldn't wait to dig in!

They talked about Andy's assignment to the northwest part of town during breakfast and what he expected. "After the rigorous training at the Academy, I'm ready for anything and cannot wait to get this show started!" Andy explained excitedly.

Mom and Dad were apprehensive, but all they could do was be supportive and smile encouragingly at their son.

After breakfast, Andy wanted to get in a workout, so he drove to town to check out Mike's new gym. Also, Andy wanted to spend some time with his brother and gain some much-needed brotherly advice before his first day.

The place was first class and, most definitely, the best gym in town. When Andy caught up with Mike, he was preoccupied with the business and his plans for company expansion. The conversation was dominated by his equipment purchasing plans and additions to their gym space before garnering much clientele. It seemed to Andy his actions demonstrated his impatience and inability to wait for success. But, he had to get it, and the cost was irrelevant. Andy wondered how Mike was managing to finance this whole endeavor, although it wasn't his concern, and he was proud of his big brother's success.

The weekend went by in a flash, and before Andy knew it, it was already Sunday afternoon and time to make the long drive back to Houston. Andy wasn't ready to leave. He knew once he got back on the open road, his thoughts would drift off to Herman and Paul's revelation.

Muscles stiff from the long car ride, he finally pulled into his apartment complex. Andy parked, unloaded his basket of clothes that Mom had washed and folded for him, and settled in for a quiet night before his big day.

FOUR

Northwest Patrol
First Day on the Streets

Andy cautiously pulled into the Northwest Patrol Substation parking lot, looking for an open space. He was simultaneously anxious and scared, imagining everything that could happen on his first day as a cop. Unable to stop pondering if he would become one of those harrowing statistics they studied at the Academy of becoming an officer killed in the line of duty. Or worse, would he screw up and accidentally shoot someone by mistake? Recalling all of the war stories from cops at the Academy, it sounded as though shootings are commonplace. However, the fact was that most Houston officers served their entire career without ever shooting anyone, so the odds were on his side.

Carefully observing his new surroundings, Andy walked into the Substation and introduced himself to the desk officer. The desk officer courteously directed him to Sergeant Mattis' office for assignment.

Mattis seemed in tune with younger officers, a young Sergeant with more energy than most. Mattis was focused on climbing the proverbial corporate ladder, so he was less determined to fight crime and more preoccupied with completing the checklist items necessary to reach his next promotion. Happy and currently content with being the station Sergeant, he aimed to get through each day with as little trouble as possible. Mattis was a fair and objective man who just expected his officers to do their job. The men liked him because he was predictable, honest, and fair. Certainly not the type to get excited, possibly because of what he had endured overseas.

A Vietnam veteran who had seen his share of action. Mattis earned several medals and even a purple heart throughout his time in combat. A rather humble man, Mattis rarely spoke about his accolades and time in the service. However, Andy and Mattis grew to become good friends over time, on and off duty. Later on, he recounted with Andy stories from his tour, including one particularly terrifying experience of his arrival in Vietnam. Mattis was forced to jump out of a Lockheed C-130 Hercules aircraft with the entire airfield under fire as it taxied down the runway. Just a young, inexperienced Army infantry grunt, Mattis had to scramble for cover in the nearest fox hole facing all of the pressure from incoming fire immediately once his feet hit the pavement. The C-130 Hercules continued to taxi down the runway as soldiers jumped from the plane and the flight crew pushed all of the large cases of supplies out of the plane. Never once coming to a stop, the plane turned around at the end of the runway and took off airborne again as quickly as possible.

Being thrown into a heavy fire combat situation during your first day in infantry was a complete shock to the system. Mattis was scared to death. The situation escalated throughout the night as the Viet Cong overran them. They were grappling with incoming fire from all directions, with the VC running past them, attempting to reach the military aircraft. Their objective was to cut off the infantry's access to their aircraft vehicles and decimate as much US military property as possible. After hours upon hours of turmoil and fire, the infantry was eventually able to fend off the attack, but the memory of that day was forever seared into the minds of those young soldiers. War is about survival.

Later on in his tour, while patrolling in the central highlands area, he was seriously wounded walking in formation along a dirt road. A soldier from his unit stepped on a landmine and was instantly killed directly in front of him. The explosion sent debris flying in all directions, and a large piece of shrapnel hit Mattis in the forehead. The impact of the blow skinned flesh from his head, knocked him unconscious, and then he plummeted to the ground with blood gushing from his wound.

Mattis regained consciousness to the deafening sound of a medivac helicopter landing nearby. The surface wind from the rotor wash was blowing grass and surrounding debris everywhere. As the foliage began pelting his body, he realized he was hurt but wasn't sure about the extent of his injuries. Fellow soldiers offered supportive words of encouragement while he was lying there. "Hang in there. If anyone can survive this, you can. Just hold on, transport is here to help you. Stay with us!"

One of Mattis' comrades kept the pressure on his forehead with a compress bandage. Then, as Mattis started to regain his faculties, he summoned the courage to reach up and feel the wound. Thankfully, his skull was still intact, so he assumed it was a deep flesh wound, and he could survive a nasty scar. Mattis laid there with his eyes closed, inhaled a deep breath to steady his nerves, and waited for a helicopter ride out.

After attending to too many injured soldiers, a medic finally made his way to Mattis to evaluate his injury. The medic prioritized care with mass injuries by determining if the injury was life-threatening, urgent but not life-threatening, not urgent, or an inevitable casualty. The medic carefully pulled the gauze back from his forehead. The medic triaged Mattis as a brain injury after glancing at the massive head wound. Considering the medic classified his injury as fatal, he assumed Mattis couldn't hear him. "Not this guy! He's not gonna make it," the medic hollered over his shoulder to his fellow evac-team. And Mattis fell unconscious again.

Several days later, Mattis abruptly awoke in a field hospital when the Doctor came around to check on him. With his mouth as dry as sandpaper, Mattis asked, "Am I going to make it?"

"You'll be fine. You're all patched up, but you need to heal for a day or two before we can release you to go home." The Doctor continued, "The good news is, you just got a one-way ticket back to the States."

"How long was I unconscious?"

"Three days. You were in a deep state of shock." Then, the Doctor explained, "I thought we were gonna lose you for a while. Not from the injury, but we couldn't get your vitals to stabilize. What happened out there?"

"The last thing I remember is the medic telling the evac team not to worry about me because I wasn't going to make it."

"That explains it," the Doctor chuckled, turned, and walked off.

Instinctually, Andy had a good feeling about Mattis; however, he was somewhat difficult to read. Just the same, he was comfortable in his presence as Mattis quickly ran down the list of rules of the station and his probationary period goals. Throughout his 6-month probationary period, Andy would be assigned to ride with a different senior officer every month. At the end of each month, the senior officer would write up an evaluation of Andy's progression. If Andy was on the receiving end of two inadequate assessments, he could be fired, reprocessed back through the probationary period, or even sent back to the Academy.

Throughout the probationary period, Rookies are not covered under the State's Civil Service protections from disciplinary action. Rookies are always wrong, and the senior officer is always right. They were instructed to do everything their senior officer advised them to do, short of an illegal act. Off the record, most Academy instructors informed the cadets that they should do everything asked of them by their senior officer, even if it violates policy or is a minor infraction of the law. The natural pecking order dictated that the senior officer was all-powerful in the patrol car, and rookies were loyal servants.

As Mattis finished his briefing, Andy's first assigned senior officer walked by. "Don come on over and meet your new rookie, Andy," Mattis called out to Don. Barber greeted Andy with a smile and a firm handshake. Don was a large man with dark, handsome features in excellent physical shape and he religiously weight trained to stay that way. Outside of policing, he also competed in powerlifting competitions and placed quite well. Courteous and polite to Andy from the start, Don was genuinely interested in getting to know him as they walked toward the roll-call room. After hearing all of the horror stories from others about their first senior officers, Andy was ecstatic to have an exemplary officer for his first time out. Sadly, some senior officers abused their power, similar to Hurley, while others were distrustful of everyone, especially rookies.

As they sat down for roll-call, Andy and Don got to know one another. About twenty officers were assigned for that shift. Andy was the only rookie present, so he was the lucky recipient of a few jabs from the others. Mainly directed towards Don with the intention that Andy would overhear. All lighthearted jokes and Andy took it in stride and enjoyed the camaraderie.

Mattis walked in and started roll-call by reading alert bulletins of wanted suspects who may be in the area. After covering a few Departmental updates, Mattis gave out the beat assignments for each patrol car. Most of the vehicles consisted of two-man units and the dispatcher usually sent them on the more dangerous calls, like family disturbances or robberies in progress.

After a quick uniform inspection, everyone headed out to the parking lot to locate their patrol car and load their equipment into their assigned shop. Shop was the police jargon used to describe their assigned patrol car.

Don drove first, and Andy was on the ground. While he was occupying the passenger seat, if they pulled a vehicle over for a traffic violation, Andy was responsible for writing the ticket with Don providing over-watch. Anytime they received a report call, the same was true. Throughout the probationary period, Andy would write most police reports, and Don would review their accuracy before submitting the files.

As they pulled out onto the street and drove toward their patrol beat, Andy's heart was racing, and sweat was starting to collect on his brow. Although he was attempting to do everything he could not to show how nervous he was, every time a car drove next to them, he kept envisioning an ambush. He knew his anxiety was getting the best of him, and he was overreacting, but he was still terrified that he would screw up or get his ass killed on the first day. It was both exhilarating and frightening to be in a patrol car and out on the streets of Houston. He was finally living his dream that he thought would never come true.

Andy and Don exchanged small talk as they drove down the major thoroughfares of northwest Houston. In the background, the police radio was squawking as the dispatcher directed outcalls and units called out during traffic stops. They would continue to patrol until a call close to them went out, or the dispatcher called their radio number.

Suddenly, Don spotted a vehicle with an expired inspection sticker and pointed, "There, expired sticker! This will be a good first stop for you to get your feet wet," Don encouraged. He turned on the overhead lights and pulled in behind the vehicle.

'Oh boy, here goes nothing,' thought Andy. With both vehicles off of the street and out of the way of traffic, Andy cautiously stepped out of the patrol car and walked to the driver's door. Don also stepped out of the vehicle to observe the area for anything that may be a danger to them and evaluate his rookie's first stop. Andy had his ticket book affixed to the clipboard in his off-hand (non-gun hand) so that if he needed to draw his pistol, there were no barriers. Andy was terrified as he walked to the car window. Peering inside the glass for any potential dangers, Andy was consumed by thoughts of possibly being shot. This could be his first and last stop.

When Andy reached the driver's side window and realized the driver was old enough to be his mother, he could hardly believe his eyes. She was visibly as terrified as he was, which gave him some solace. "We pulled you over today because your inspection sticker is expired. Driver's license, please?" Andy said with a slight crack in his voice, hoping that she didn't notice.

"What is an inspection sticker?" the woman asked. She claimed ignorance, and although Andy believed her, he knew Don was watching and expecting him to write a citation, so he told her to wait there as he walked back to the patrol car.

Sitting down in the passenger seat, Andy wrote the ticket as Don continued to stand and watch the area. Andy returned to the vehicle, asked the lady to sign the citation, and released her. As Andy walked back to the car, he was somewhat pleased with himself. He wrote his first ticket and survived to tell about it. Certainly not fun, but good enough for now.

As they sat down in the patrol car, Don asked him, "How did it go?"

Andy was in the middle of giving Don the blow by blow when he looked down and realized that the lady's driver's license was still on his clipboard; he had also forgotten to give her a copy of the ticket. He looked up just in time to see her drive away. He quickly told Don. "Great," Don replied condescendingly. Don quickly put the vehicle in drive and drove in pursuit.

Andy was mortified about screwing up, and Don's comment certainly didn't help. Don didn't say another word as they tried to catch up with her. Andy could only assume Don was thinking the worst, and he felt terrible about it.

Don quickly caught up to the woman's vehicle as she pulled into a bank drive-thru lane. She was oblivious to the police car behind her again as Andy got out and walked up again to the vehicle. To make matters worse, he could see the bank teller in the window, and he knew that she would be able to hear his apology.

The older woman was startled to see Andy again at her window. Andy proceeded to explain his mistake and handed her the ticket and driver's license. She was apologetic about the expired inspection, which made Andy feel even worse. Andy sulked back to the patrol car, and they drove off. Observing Andy's body language, Don could tell how bad he felt, so he never mentioned the mistake again, and Andy didn't bring it up either.

The following traffic stop went much better, and the butterflies in Andy's stomach began to subside as the realization that every stop wasn't certain death sunk in. Andy and Don were becoming more comfortable with one another, and Andy had the feeling that he was going to survive his first day of police work after all.

For the remainder of their shift, they made routine traffic stops and responded to calls for service. Andy was mentally exhausted from an overwhelming first day. He was learning so much, but the pressure was also excruciating.

While walking out of the Substation for the night at 11:05 pm, Andy said goodnight to Don. He collapsed on his bed following his quick drive home, thinking about the day. Thankful to have that one under his belt, but tomorrow would be no easier.

Gone Too Soon

The next day Andy drove to the station a couple of hours early to grab a workout. Since there was a weight set in the locker room, he brought his uniform and showered there. Before anyone from his shift arrived, Andy was ready and sitting in the roll-call room. Being early was becoming a habit, and he figured it was a good one.

When Don walked in, they shook hands and shared small talk while the rest of the officers for the shift slowly assembled. After Mattis read off the daily bulletins and handed out assignments, Andy and Don loaded their equipment into the shop and headed out toward their patrol beat. Because it was the same beat as yesterday, Andy began familiarizing himself with the major avenues. As they turned southbound on Clay Road, the dispatcher broke the silence by radioing a major accident alert. The accident occurred further down Clay Road, so Don picked up the mic and volunteered to take the call. Considering this would be Andy's first major accident, it would be a good experience. Don accelerated towards the scene after turning on his overhead lights and siren. As Andy witnessed his first run hot, he was enthralled with the way other cars were jockeying to get out of their way and let them through.

Up ahead, Andy spotted a commotion with people in the road waving their arms. As the patrol car approached, he could see smoke billowing from a vehicle overturned in a deep ditch on the side of the road. Don was barking out instructions as they arrived on the scene, so Andy understood beforehand what was expected.

The vehicle sustained massive damage to the front end, causing thick, black smoke to rise into the air from the engine. 'That must have been one hell of an impact. I hope the car doesn't catch on fire. I'm not ready for that,' thought Andy. The other vehicle involved in the collision was across the street and had sustained severe damage to the front end, too, so he assumed a head-on collision had taken place. However, with no one standing near the other vehicle, they focused on the overturned car first.

Don turned the siren off, leaving his overhead blue and red lights flashing, and stopped just short of the overturned vehicle. After pushing the button on the dashboard to open the trunk, Don went to grab the fire extinguisher. Completely calm and composed, Don instructed Andy to bring his baton so they could break a window if needed. Ecstatic, he was finally in a situation where he could put his training to use, but Andy was also somewhat surprised by how Don acted like this was an everyday occurrence. While yelling for everyone to get back, they hurried toward the smoke engulfed vehicle.

Don ran to the passenger side with the fire extinguisher in hand and crouched down on his knees to peer inside. "Andy, get everyone back. There is a chance this car might explode!"

Andy was trying to absorb the entire situation and still effectively do his job even though it was his first time dealing with a major wreck. With the thick, toxic smoke building inside the vehicle, anyone inhaling the fumes wouldn't be able to survive for long. So he knew they needed to get the window open for ventilation.

"Break the window!" Don yelled to Andy.

With the baton locked tightly in both hands, Andy swung, repeatedly hitting the glass. The Departmental issued straight stick rod was about 30-inches long and constructed from solid oak. The wand was rounded on both ends and kept bouncing off the glass, but Andy was undeterred. With all of his strength, he continued striking the driver's window.

"HURRY!" Don yelled as flames began flickering from the engine. Don quickly pulled the pin from the fire extinguisher and started spraying directly at the engine block. After only four or five short bursts on the fire, the canister was empty, and the flames were expanding. Tossing the extinguisher down in disgust, Don ran around to help Andy with the window. The pungent smell of gasoline wafted through the air as the steady drip of fuel hit the ground. The expanding crowd was creeping closer as they watched the officers frantically trying to get the window open.

"Get back," ordered Don.

Finally, the tempered glass shattered during one of Andy's strikes. A resounding cheer rang out from the crowd. As the smoke poured out of the broken window, Andy dropped to his knees to see inside. Don pulled a handkerchief from his back pocket, placed it over his mouth, and crawled down next to him. Andy called out to the woman inside, but she didn't move or respond. Andy reached in and felt the women's arm as the flames spread to the dashboard. With all of his might, he yanked her arm, and her lifeless body slid toward the window. Don grabbed the arm as well, and within a few seconds, they had her out of the window.

"Pull her out of here, Andy. I'm going to check if anyone else is inside."

A couple of bystanders jumped in the ditch and assisted Andy in picking her up so that they could get out of harm's way more quickly. Next, Andy guided the group around a parked vehicle to shield them if the burning car exploded. They gently laid her down, and Andy started evaluating her condition. In the distance, an ambulance siren was sounding, so he knew that medical help was almost there.

There were no visible signs of trauma, but she remained unconscious. The smoke inhalation and toxic fumes shallowed her breathing; her eyes rolled back in her head. Adrenaline was pumping through Andy's body as he attempted to feel for a pulse, but he shook too badly to find one. He was overwhelmed with feelings of helplessness. Although he considered conducting CPR his training told him he should leave well enough alone if she was breathing.

Finally, the ambulance arrived, and the EMTs grabbed their equipment and hurried over to help. Andy stood back and looked on as the EMTs worked on the woman. Still unresponsive, Andy was concerned she might not make it. However, medical assistance wasn't his expertise, and he was just a spectator now, so he looked up to see what Don was doing. He started heading back toward the burning vehicle, but Don met him halfway and told him the car was empty. "She's still unconscious. It doesn't look good," said Andy.

"OK, we've done all we can for her. Let's clear these cars for the firetruck," replied Don.

And with that, it was back to business. Andy couldn't help but glance back at the EMTs as he directed cars to turn around and clear a lane for the firetruck. Once the pumper truck arrived, they quickly put out the burning car. The next time Andy turned around, he noticed one of the EMTs performing CPR on the woman while the other EMT ran toward the ambulance to get a stretcher. Never once pausing in their chest compressions, they quickly loaded her in the ambulance and forced oxygen into her face mask.

Andy's heart sank; he knew it wasn't good. Then, more police units started arriving to redirect traffic.

"Get your clipboard and start taking names of witnesses," advised Don. "I'll get the information on the other vehicle."

Andy nodded his head in agreement but couldn't stop thinking about the lady he had pulled from the car. Attempting to focus on the task at hand as he walked to the patrol car, Andy's emotions were getting the best of him while he watched the ambulance drive away with its lights flashing and sirens blaring. He had a job to do, and Don counted on him, so he grabbed his clipboard and started taking statements.

Don discovered the two people in the other car were shaken, but OK. Then, he radioed the dispatcher and requested an accident unit on the scene due to the possible fatality. When a crash involves serious injuries, it was standard protocol to have an accident unit investigate and provide their expertise.

Once Andy and Don were relieved by the accident unit and the scene was cleared, they drove to the hospital to check on the young woman they had pulled from the car. The emergency room staff informed them that she did not survive. It was a massive, emotional blow for Andy because it was the first time someone had died on his watch. And sadly, it would not be the last.

On the drive home that evening, all Andy could think about was the young lady who died horrifically in a smoke-filled coffin. Unable to stop his thoughts, he pondered what could have come of her life and how quickly it was taken from her. Andy feared he was becoming too emotionally attached, and he needed to find that place in the depths of his mind where he used to store burdensome memories. So, he tucked her away and didn't think of her except when reminiscing with Don. But, Andy had to concede there would be many more just like her throughout his career.

Blood Chase

The next day with the memory of the young lady's death safely tucked away, Andy moved on. He couldn't wait to get back to patrol and find out what today's shift had in store for him. A beautiful spring day in Houston, and Andy was loving every minute of his new career. According to Don's weekly reports, Andy was progressing nicely as Don continued to mentor him on the finer points of policing.

The shift began with your typical patrol calls, but Andy was eager to see some action. With the sun setting, darkness fell upon the city for the night as they patrolled down Campbell Road. Andy was panning the area, hoping to find something that appeared to be a crime in progress. Then, out of seemingly nowhere, a red Plymouth Charger whipped out directly in front of them. The tires spun, and rubber burned as the car accelerated to getaway. Don immediately flipped on the emergency lights and siren as Andy radioed the details of the chase. The Charger and police car quickly gained speed, driving through the suburban street while all surrounding vehicles hurried to get out of their path. Worried about the increasing speeds, Don glanced down at the speedometer and noticed they were approaching 70 miles an hour. An unsafe rate of speed for a city street. Additional units responded over the police radio they were en route to cut off the fleeing vehicle.

Flying through the intersection of Hammerly Drive, the Charger nearly clipped another vehicle. Don and Andy were in close pursuit with their siren blaring and emergency lights flashing through the darkness. They were approaching Clay Road, and motor vehicles were required to make either a left-hand or right-hand turn or face the bar ditch straight ahead. The Charger was driving too quickly to handle the turn, and then, it didn't. The driver slammed on the brakes causing the Charger to skid through the intersection and fly to the other side. The underbelly of the Charger slammed into the opposite bank and came to an abrupt stop. The impact sent sparks and smoke plumes from beneath the car.

"OH SHIT!" Andy and Don yelled in unison as they witnessed the impact. Don firmly and smoothly pressed his foot on the shop's brakes, trying to bring the vehicle to a stop before they hit the ditch as well. The shop came to a stop at the edge of the bar ditch. Don exhaled a long sigh of relief, picked up the mic, informed the dispatcher that the vehicle had crashed, and immediately asked for an ambulance. There had to be injuries. No one could make it through a crash like that completely unscathed.

Andy jumped out and ran toward the vehicle wreckage, flashlight shining through the tall grass and into the bottom of the ditch. Seeing the extent of the damage, Andy wasn't worried about the suspects being a danger to his safety. They had to be badly hurt or even possibly dead. Shining his flashlight inside the Charger, blood coated the entire interior of the windows. To his horror, blood was everywhere, and he spotted two young males slumped over, motionless. Andy was in shock at the amount of blood; he had never in his life seen anything so gruesome. It was everywhere! The engine had died on impact, and smoke continued to pour out from under the car. Andy yanked on the door handle to the passenger door, but it wouldn't budge. Andy cried out to Don, "Oh my God, look at all the blood!"

After radioing for assistance, Don made it to the driver's window and shined his flashlight inside. The driver's window shattered on impact. Don observed the two unconscious teens and the back seat was empty. Immediately he recognized the heavy, familiar odor of automatic transmission fluid. On impact, the car's transmission had been forced up through the floorboard, causing the pressure lines to rupture and drenching the entire interior in the red liquid.

Andy was still in hyper-drive as he circled behind the car to get a better look.

Don grabbed him and said, "Calm down, it's not blood!"

"What do you mean?" Andy asked in a panic.

Don calmly explained what the red fluid was, and Andy felt like an idiot. The two young men were severely injured, but they were not bleeding. Both occupants sustained internal blunt force trauma injuries from the vehicle's sudden stop. "Don't move them. They may have spinal cord damage; let the EMTs do that," Don advised Andy.

The car wasn't burning, so they just waited for the ambulance to arrive. Slowly, Andy calmed down but was pretty embarrassed as Don tried to console him. Luckily no one else was present, and Don never said a word about it to anyone. Don was empathetic throughout the entire ordeal, and Andy admired him for it. Someday, Andy hoped to exude the same calmness, coolness, and intelligence as Don. He was improving with each shift but still had a long way to go.

Three Amigos Moving In

Andy's days off were finally here, and it was time for John and Doug to move into the three-bedroom apartment that Andy had found in his complex. It was an easy move for Andy, but John and Doug were relocating from another part of the city. None of them owned many possessions in the early throes of adulthood, so the move was fast, and soon they were sitting around toasting their new place.

After combining their meager furniture pieces, the apartment looked surprisingly good with most of the comforts of home. The three of them were getting along well now, but time would tell how this new arrangement would work out.

The following day, Andy called home to check on his Mom and Dad and catch up on the rest of the family. Andy was excited to share some of his patrol stories and brag about his new apartment. But, disappointingly, all his Mom wanted to talk about was the new house Mike purchased. To focus all of his time and energy on the gym business, he quit his job at the chemical plant. He also bought a new boat, and tonight he was going to take everyone out to eat in celebration.

Andy silently wondered if Mike was over-extending himself but didn't dare bring it up. He just listened and chimed in from time to time about how happy he was for him. After hanging up the phone, he was a little worried, but Mike's previous business ventures had always been successful, and there was no reason to doubt him this time.

His days off flew by before he knew it, and Andy was driving to work, looking forward to whatever new adventures awaited him this week. With every shift, Andy was gaining more confidence and making fewer mistakes. He and Don were becoming close friends, making the job even more enjoyable.

Andy was still longing for the type of call that he could go home and brag to John and Doug about. Both of his roommates were working in a much higher crime rate area, so their stories were more interesting than Andy's, and honestly, he was starting to get a little jealous. Each of them had already been in several car chases and John had even chased down a suspect on foot. Thus far, Andy had only been involved in one short car chase, and he was hoping to up the ante.

The Fall From Grace

Andy loved to drive, and it tickled the shit out of him on Sunday afternoon when Don asked him to take the wheel. As an officer, he hadn't been involved in a good chase yet, and if he was driving, he might finally get a chance to try out his skills from the Academy.

While heading westbound on Hempstead Highway, a call rang out over the radio, "Attention all officers clear and close to 43rd and 290. A shooting just occurred at the Afternooner's Bar. The suspect is described as a white male and is reported to still be at the location."

Don quickly grabbed the mic and informed the dispatcher they were down the road and en route. Several units responded they would be checking by for support. Andy flipped on the emergency lights, Don turned on the siren, and they sped toward the shooting. Granted, it wasn't the car chase he was hoping for, but Andy was finally getting some excitement, maybe more than he bargained for.

Turning onto 43rd, Don feared the possibility that the suspect might be waiting for them. To avoid driving into a possible ambush, he calmly told Andy to pull in short of the bar. The road was clear, and they were close, so Don turned off the siren. "Kill the overhead lights and park over there. More discreet," advised Don while he reached down between the seats and grabbed the 12-gauge pump shotgun.

Considering this was the first time Andy had witnessed him pull his shotgun, he knew shit was getting real. They quickly and quietly exited the car and headed toward the bar entrance, maneuvering between parked vehicles, and scanning their surroundings for the shooter. Don held his shotgun at the low ready; Andy's hand was on his gun, still holstered.

At the doorway, they were startled by a drunk woman staggering out. "Does anyone in there have a gun?" Don asked.

The woman turned and nonchalantly pointed over her shoulder as she stumbled and walked away. She was the least of their worries, so Don pushed open the door. Andy's heart pounded as he drew his pistol. The music was ear piercingly loud, and it wasn't easy to see inside the establishment.

Don silently stepped to his left so that Andy could enter while their vision adjusted to the darkness. Searching for anyone with a gun, they scanned the smoke-filled bar. Several patrons were sitting still at the tables, almost as though they were waiting for the police to arrive. The situation was so eerie Andy wondered if they were even at the right place.

Everyone turned to look at Don as he yelled, "KEEP YOUR HANDS ON THE TABLE!"

Although it was difficult to hear over the music, everyone seemed to get the message. A female bartender leaned back, away from the bar; she didn't want trouble. The smell of cigarette smoke and burnt gunpowder hung in the air; a jukebox played a country song in the background.

At the back of the room, a middle-aged woman was on her knees and bent over someone lying on the floor. The individual on the floor was unconscious, and the woman appeared to be crying. She didn't hear Don and Andy enter the bar with the music blaring. Don started moving toward her, and Andy followed. To protect Don's back, Andy continuously scanned the room as they moved between the tables and patrons of the beer joint.

When Andy and Don had walked past the bartender, she made a slight gesture towards a man sitting on a stool at the bar. Andy carefully observed the older man with long salt and pepper hair pulled back in a ponytail. He was dressed in an oversized coat, both of his hands on a beer. The man appeared oblivious to everything happening around him as he stared straight ahead, smoking a cigarette.

Communication between Don and the woman failed as he attempted to yell at her over the loud music. Finally, exasperated from not being heard, he pointed his shotgun at the jukebox and yelled, "UNPLUG THAT THING!"

A man quickly reached behind the jukebox, pulled the plug, and sat back down in silence. No one moved, and every eye in the bar was fixed on Andy and Don. When the music stopped, the lady on the floor turned around and saw the two uniformed officers. Abruptly, she jumped up and pointed at the long-haired man seated at the bar and yelled, "THAT SON-OF-A-BITCH SHOT HIM!"

Don pivoted toward the man with the ponytail who was still staring across the bar at himself in the mirror. "PUT YOUR HANDS IN THE AIR!" Don shouted at the man.

The man slowly leaned back from the counter and raised his hands as he continued to stare at his reflection. Then, as his hands slowly lifted into the air, Andy spotted a revolver on the bar his folded arms had been concealing. Don aimed the shotgun directly at the suspect and yelled, "DON'T MOVE," and motioned for Andy to move over and seize the pistol.

Andy walked behind the suspect, reached around, and grabbed the revolver. After safely tucking the pistol in his gun belt, he started handcuffing him. Once he was cuffed, Andy pat-down searched him for additional weapons.

Don looked back at the bartender and asked, "Anyone else?" The bartender shook her head no, and her posture relaxed, knowing the whole ordeal was finally over. The crying woman ran toward the handcuffed suspect. Slurring obscenities in his direction, she took a swing at the suspect, but Don grabbed her with one hand as he held the shotgun steady with the other. "Calm down, or you'll be going to jail too," Don demanded.

"I don't care," she screamed as Don pushed her back toward the injured man.

The handcuffed suspect was stoic and continued looking straight ahead at the mirror as Andy had him stand for a complete search. Responding officers began pouring into the bar, and an ambulance arrived on the scene. Andy focused his attention on the prisoner and was astonished at his calm demeanor. The suspect was so matter of fact as though he had anticipated this entire series of events. Making eye contact with him in the mirror, he smiled at Andy with the butt of the cigarette still hanging from his mouth.

Andy suddenly realized that the man had been watching them through the reflection of the mirror the entire time. He had a gun in his hand and could have easily spun on them with the element of surprise. Even with a two-to-one advantage, it would have been bad. Andy almost wanted to thank him for not going there, but he tried to act like he didn't notice.

One of the older responding officers, Jim Zorn, walked over to the suspect and said, "Frank?"

The man calmly looked up at the officer, smiled, and said, "Hi Jim."

"What the fuck?" Jim asked. The handcuffed suspect didn't answer as he dropped his head and shrugged his shoulders.

"You know him?" Andy asked.

"Yeah, that's Frank Porter," Jim replied. "He was in my academy class. But, until now, I hadn't seen him in years."

Andy pulled out the suspect's .357-caliber revolver, searching for a silver butt plate on the handle. Commonly, officers would have a silver butt plate made, engraved with their badge number, and screwed to the flat bottom of the pistol handle. Sure enough, the plate had an HPD emblem with a badge number. All of the pieces were starting to fit together now, but why would he shoot that guy?

The EMTs worked on the victim for a few seconds but quickly pronounced him. The victim was subjected to a single gunshot to the center of his chest and died within seconds. One of the female bar patrons consoled the grieving woman in the corner of the bar. In full investigative mode, Don huddled the witnesses to one side of the bar, away from where the shooting had taken place to prevent crime scene contamination. All witnesses were advised to remain quiet and refrain from discussing what they had seen until the Homicide Detectives could interview them. The five or six uniformed officers inside the bar controlled the scene while everyone waited for the Detectives to arrive.

Don directed Andy to take the suspect out to the patrol car. As part of Andy's training, it was vital for him to experience a homicide investigation. Always excited for some hands-on experience, Andy was looking forward to learning the whole process, but he was also curious to know more about the prisoner. In particular, he was intrigued by how a former police officer could have ended up committing such a horrendous crime and was now being arrested for murder.

"That guy had the drop on us but didn't want it," Andy commented to Zorn while they waited for Homicide.

"Probably so," Jim replied. "Frank was a great cop back in the day."

"What happened to him?" Andy asked.

Several years ago, while working in the Narcotics Division, Frank was fired. He was involved in a controversial shooting where he killed two male criminals and wounded a third. Although there wasn't anything wrong with the shooting, he wasn't supposed to be there, to begin with. He met a criminal informant (CI) by himself which was a big no-no by Departmental policy. Narcotics officers were required to have a partner with them anytime they met informants. Frank didn't want a partner there because he was having an affair with the CI. The woman was running with the Bandidos outlaw motorcycle gang and was snitching on them simultaneously.

Frank met up with her at a bar on the southeast side of town, and when they were walking out to the parking lot for the night, three Banditos jumped them. It was unclear whether or not the Banditos knew Frank was a cop, but Frank was armed, and when he pulled his gun, they pulled theirs. It was over in a flash, and three Banditos were lying on the pavement in the parking lot: two dying and one suffering from a serious gunshot wound. Shit hit the fan when the cops arrived, and once the news media had the scoop on the story, it blew up everywhere. Everyone found out that Frank was having an affair with the CI; Frank's wife left him and took the two kids. Jim heard through the grapevine that Frank married the informant, but he didn't know if it was true. Even though the Grand Jury cleared the shooting, he would never be HPD again.

"He lost it all over that snitch and now look at him," said Jim.

Andy thought back to a crude comment Hurley made at the Academy. They were in the men's locker room, and someone convinced Hurley to tell a war story. After enthusiastically telling his tale, he commented on how women love a uniform. Then, he pointed to his badge and said, "Just remember, boys, this badge will get you a lot of pussy, but it only takes one pussy to take this badge."

Andy remembered being unsettled by the crude comment, but now he understood what Hurley meant. Homicide Detectives finally arrived, and the scene was processed in standard fashion. Don and Andy were asked to transport the prisoner downtown for additional questioning. Throughout the 20-minute drive, Frank was stark silent in the back seat. Andy would glance back now and then, but it seemed as though Frank's mind was a thousand miles away.

Later on, Don and Andy learned the grieving woman in the bar was Frank's former snitch and current wife. She was having an affair with the dead man, and Frank walked into the bar to confront them. The deceased man was an off-duty Fire Department Captain cheating on his spouse. Andy thought it felt like a story out of a dime-store novel.

Once again, Frank would make headlines with his exploits when this hit the news. Andy couldn't believe how a cop could fall from grace so quickly. But maybe Hurley had a point. It would not be the last time Andy would witness such a fall.

Roommates

When Andy got home that evening, John was stretched out on the couch watching TV. John was working Central patrol on what was commonly called the early side of the evening shift from 2 to 10 pm. To ensure only half of any shift was changing at any given time, all three shifts of the patrol division had an early side and a late side.

After work, they typically sat around the apartment, sharing war stories about the escapades that occurred throughout their shifts. Both Andy and Doug were working the late side of the evening shift, but his commute home from downtown took quite a bit longer than Andy's. So as soon as he arrived, they decided to grab a bite to eat at a restaurant down the road.

Andy and John threw their uniforms on their beds and changed into street clothes. Doug, however, had an entire process he followed from start to finish once he got home. First, Doug would take off his badge and nameplate, neatly place them on his dresser, shower, and completely put his uniform away. The longer Andy and John had to wait while Doug took his time arranging everything, the more their impatience grew.

"What, is he expecting a surprise inspection by Hurley or something?" Andy joked.

Except for Doug's excessive cleanliness and impeccable hygiene, everyone in the apartment was getting along well. Somehow, they managed to look past their differences and enjoyed one another's company. Then, at last, Doug appeared from his back bedroom, and off they went.

Andy's parents owned a cabin on the coast, and the group discussed possibly making a trip down there. A small place, right on the water, and not far from where Andy's parents lived. It was just a weekender kind of cabin, but it had all the comforts of home. They could fish or waterski during the daytime and hang out and drink a couple of beers once the sun went down. Also, it would be good to get out of the city for their days off and let loose a little.

Andy and John were scheduled off on Tuesday and Wednesday, and Doug had Wednesday and Thursday off. So they decided that Andy and John would drive to the coast after their shift on Monday night, and Doug would make the trip down after his shift Tuesday night. It was only a couple of hour's drive to the cabin, and they would all travel home together on Wednesday.

The meal was alright, but the company and camaraderie were everything. Sharing their stories, and venting their feelings and frustrations was therapy for them. Only those who had been through similar situations could genuinely relate. Of course, some of the stories were crude, and other patrons sitting close enough to overhear them often thought they were callused from their work. But, in actuality, it was a coping mechanism for them.

Northwest Houston was predominately middle-class with a melting pot of ethnicities, although most of Andy's patrol calls were generated from a few ghetto areas. John worked the northside of downtown, home to a large Hispanic population with fluctuating income levels from poverty to middle-class. Doug worked in an area west of downtown called Montrose, primarily white, where a large concentration of the gay community resided. The income class of Montrose varied greatly from the homeless to the very wealthy. The residents and socioeconomic statuses in these three areas were vastly different, and as a result, each had different ways of policing.

The days seemed to breeze by, and before they knew it, it was already Monday evening. Every shift was different and filled with new experiences; they were learning so much. Coming home to the apartment and sharing their stories allowed them to relive them over and over again.

Once Andy and John made it home from their shifts, they hurried to get ready for their trip to the coast. Doug wasn't home yet, but Andy and John were already packed. The two of them took one last look around to make sure they hadn't forgotten anything.

"John, look at how neat Doug's bedroom is compared to ours."

"How do you think he would respond if his room did look like ours for once?" John asked. It irritated them that Doug could be that much of a clean freak about his room. Doug would even unload his service revolver and neatly stack his bullets in a row each night. So they decided to have some fun and mess with his room a little.

They pulled the bedspread and sheets from the bed and threw them in a heap in the corner. His pillows were tossed in the opposite direction, and Andy emptied his dirty laundry hamper on the floor. Doug kept his shoes neatly organized in their respective shoe boxes and stacked, perfectly aligned. John kicked the stack of shoes over and scattered the boxes around the room. While wreaking havoc on Doug's room, they couldn't help but laugh hysterically.

After closing his bedroom door, they quickly headed to Andy's car before Doug arrived. They laughed halfway to the coast about how Doug would react when he got home. Andy and John were curious if he would get revenge on their rooms, but there wasn't much he could do to make them worse. And, of course, that made them laugh even harder as they drove on through the darkness.

Knowing it would be late by the time they arrived at the cabin, Woody and Poodle left the lights on for them. An assortment of snacks was laid out on the kitchen counter, and the refrigerator was recently stocked with plenty of beer and other refreshments. Andy's parents had gone home for the night, so Andy and John sat on the back porch drinking beer, looking at the stars, and enjoying the quiet of the country.

The following evening, Doug arrived at the cabin, and he was pissed about his room but took it in stride. They enjoyed some much-needed reprieve the next day and spent the day on the water: a relaxing day off and a good break from the stress of patrolling the streets of Houston. Poodle made enormous, home-cooked meals for them, and Woody ensured the boat was gassed up. Andy's parents enjoyed being hosts and having the guys around as much as they enjoyed the hospitality. Life was good, and they took full advantage of it.

On the way back to Houston, Andy took John and Doug by his big brother's state-of-the-art gym. Decked out with all the latest gym equipment and impeccably clean, the place was quite impressive, but Mike wasn't there. Instead, the on-duty gym supervisor informed Andy that Mike was out of town buying gym equipment. A bit strange considering Andy's parents hadn't mentioned Mike was out of town, but last-minute trips probably occurred frequently when running a business.

They headed toward Houston and the start of a new week of adventures. They felt rejuvenated from the carefree life of the country, but everyone was excited about the dangers that lay ahead in their chosen careers. Eventually, the risks of their job would catch up with them and reinforce the stark reality of police work in the big city.

FIVE

Death in a Closet

A slow day on patrol, and Andy was getting a little bored as Don casually drove down Gessner Drive. Thus far, they had answered a few calls but nothing of significance. A little excitement ensued when the dispatcher radioed them with a holdup alarm, but it turned out to be nothing. Cops typically called those false alarms, a windy, but no one knew where the saying originated. Other than that, Andy had taken some prints at a burglary call and checked out a couple of suspicious persons, but nothing to write home about.

Don had put Andy out on a few traffic stops to fill in the gaps between calls, but he hadn't written a ticket yet. Every stop so far was either an old lady or a genuinely nice person with a seemingly reasonable excuse, so Andy couldn't bring himself to write a citation. Each one was let go with nothing more than a verbal warning.

After at least his third verbal warning, Don explained, "You can exercise discretion, but you also need to realize that everyone has an excuse. So quit being such a softy."

Just the same, Andy hated to write a ticket to older people. In all honesty, he usually wrote citations based on the driver's attitude. If they were argumentative or appeared to be pissed off that they were being pulled over, they were going to get a ticket but so far, that hadn't happened.

Then the dispatcher broke the silence with a possible DOA (Dead On Arrival) at a residence in Memorial Village, an affluent area of town with million-dollar homes and hardly any crime. The few calls the police received from that area were typically non-emergency or something of little significance, such as a stolen bicycle. Something as serious as a DOA was particularly unusual. Don responded to the dispatcher that they were en route.

When Don pulled into the driveway, two cars were parked in front of the garage, and everything appeared as expected for that neighborhood. Andy was surprised that no one was outside and re-checked the address to ensure they were at the right house. It was rather peculiar that no one was waiting outside for them; not even an ambulance was present.

They walked to the front door and rang the doorbell. A well-dressed, middle-aged white man answered the door and invited them inside. Although it was evident that he was expecting them, he didn't appear upset or distressed. Instead, he was somewhat solemn and rather matter of fact when he said, "she's in there," pointing towards the master bedroom.

Considering it was still daylight, the house was astonishingly dark, with the curtains drawn. The place was eerily quiet, with no conversation or background noise from a TV or radio. Don headed toward the bedroom, and Andy followed. As they walked through the enormous house towards the room, Andy cautiously scanned his surroundings. Something about the entire situation didn't seem right to him, but he could not put his finger on precisely what. The hair on the back of his neck stood straight up, and Andy remained vigilant.

Upon entering the master bedroom, the man pointed at a closet door over to the right. The door was slightly ajar, with the light shining inside. The man calmly explained his wife had committed suicide in the closet. Although the door opened inward, it would only open about 10 inches because the woman's body was partially blocking it. Nevertheless, the opening was just large enough for Don and Andy to take turns sticking their heads in the closet to get a glimpse of the interior. Inside, a fully dressed woman was lying in the middle of the closet on her right side, in a fetal position. Her head was against the far wall, with her feet pressed against the door. Her body was splattered in blood from head to toe, and the entire closet floor was coated in a thick layer of coagulated blood. However, the remainder of the closet appeared to be in order, with clothes neatly hanging on both sides. No signs of a struggle and nothing was out of place. An ambulance arrived, and two EMTs entered the home carrying a medical case, but Don waved them off. The woman had been dead for some time, but he encouraged them to look in the closet door and confirm his opinion.

If they forced the door open, they would disturb the scene, so Don asked the dispatcher to send for the fire department to pry it open. To cover all technical areas, Don also requested homicide to make the scene, accompanied by the Medical Examiner's office and a crime scene unit. Although he wasn't sure what had happened yet, this was not your typical DOA.

"Sidney, I'm sorry for your loss. Can you please explain to me any details that you know about how your wife died?" Don asked the man.

Andy was still looking around, trying to take everything in while the man recounted what he knew. Sidney's wife suffered from depression for years and attempted suicide twice before. Once, she overdosed by taking an abundance of pills, and most recently, she attempted suicide by inhaling carbon monoxide from the car exhaust in their enclosed garage. She was under the care of both a physician and a psychiatrist.

Andy noticed several prescription bottles on the nightstand, but that didn't explain the blood.

"Did your wife own a gun?" Don asked Sidney.

"No, we don't own a gun," Sidney replied.

"And who else lives in the home?"

"It was just the two of us; there is no one else."

Neither Andy nor Don could tell what trauma caused all the blood, but she suffered severe wounds. When the fire department arrives to remove the closet door, they would know more. As of right now, there wasn't anything else they could do for her but conduct a thorough investigation.

While waiting on the homicide detectives and fire department, Don asked Sidney to sit in the kitchen. Andy began taking notes as Don questioned Sidney about the day's events. The man said he had been at work all day, and sometime around the middle of his shift, his wife left a cryptic voice message on his work phone, but he didn't receive it until he was about to leave for the day. Immediately, he thought that she might be suicidal again, so he tried to call her back before he left the office, but she didn't answer. Quickly he drove home, and when he saw her car in the driveway, and the house was locked, he assumed the worst.

Andy was irked by how nonchalant Sidney was. Displaying no signs of emotion while he described the pain his wife had been living with throughout her battle with depression. It was almost as if he was relieved that it was over. Quite possibly, too unconcerned for Andy's taste, he started to wonder if he had something to do with her death.

Neighbors began to gather outside the home as more emergency vehicles arrived. Several neighbors wondered what could have happened as a fire truck drove up and parked. Don spoke to the Fire Captain and asked if they would wait for the crime scene unit to take pictures before taking the door off.

The Captain agreed but told Don, "If we get a call for service, we have to go, but we will come back as soon as we are finished."

Soon, the crime scene unit arrived and started taking pictures. The detectives first met with Don and collected all information he had gathered thus far; then, they interviewed Sidney. After the crime scene unit and detectives finished looking around, the firefighters used their pry tools on the hinges and carefully removed the door. Andy feared he was watching a homicide investigation unfold, and he was impressed by the detectives' systematic approach of peeling away the scene, one layer at a time.

The investigator from the Medical Examiner's Office assisted the detectives in analyzing the scene with minimal disruption to the evidence. Ingeniously, they used a broom handle to maneuver clothes out of the way to provide them with a better visual without stepping into the closet. Trying to stay out of the way, Andy was in the back of the bedroom, but curiosity was eating away at him.

"Where is Sidney?" Andy asked Don.

"He's in the kitchen having hot tea," he replied.

"That's weird," Andy commented.

"One of the detectives is with him, but Sidney is looking out of the window and staring off into space."

The detectives were now ready to remove the body, so they instructed the funeral home body car employees to pull her out as gently as possible. The body was stiff as a board when they rolled her halfway onto her back and carefully placed her into a body bag. Several large lacerations were on her hands and wrist. Andy thought they must have been defensive wounds, and his suspicion of the husband grew.

The body bag was structurally designed to contain bodily fluids and any evidence on the corpse. Before zipping the bag closed, the detectives inspected her body with flashlights, examining the slashes on her hands, wrists, and the left side of her neck. Their initial evaluation indicated the neck wound severed her jugular vein, causing her to bleed out. After sealing the bag, they lifted her body onto the gurney, covered it with a sheet, and rolled her out to the waiting car.

Returning their attention to the closet where the body was discovered, the detectives searched every square inch with shining flashlights. A large butcher knife was found lying on the floor, previously concealed by her body. Several large towels were spread out on the floor, directly under where her body had been. At least three or four large bath towels had been neatly stacked, one on top of the other underneath her. Lastly, they spotted a notepad on top of a shoebox; a detective directed the crime scene officer to photograph it.

The Detective stretched his arm to reach the pad and slowly pulled it out without disturbing the surrounding area. Dated today was a handwritten suicide letter, in cursive script, written to Sidney. Andy thought it must have been a women's handwriting to have such pretty penmanship. The letter explained she felt that there was no way to overcome her depression. Andy's suspicions were starting to fade as the Detective noted she must have laid out the towels to soak up the blood because she didn't want to make a mess. 'How could anyone cut themselves that many times?' wondered Andy. How anyone could wish to die so badly was inconceivable to him.

One of the detectives returned to the kitchen to question Sidney where he sat solemnly sipping his tea. Andy walked with the Detective, interested in hearing the line of questioning and Sidney's responses. Sidney was willing to answer all questions and didn't appear nervous. "Sidney, was your wife right-handed or left-handed?" the Detective asked.

"Left-handed," Sidney replied without hesitation.

The woman was found lying on her right arm, the wounds on the left side of her neck. 'That would make sense,' Andy thought. Although he could envision her switching hands to slash both wrists, she would most likely use her strong hand to cut her own throat. She probably laid down on her right side and started slashing with the butcher knife. With everything in the closet tidy, a struggle did not occur. An attacker would have been unable to place those towels neatly under her body while still alive and bleeding. Between Sidney's statement and the evidence, Andy was starting to visualize how this could have happened.

The detectives completed the crime scene investigation, so Don and Andy got back in service. Driving away, they discussed what happened, and they were both equally troubled by what they had seen. They kept asking themselves, 'What could bring a person to so violently kill themself?' Andy needed to put that call behind him and move on. His focus was to learn as much from Don as he could and be ready for the next call.

The Medical Examiner ruled the death a suicide after their investigation. The writing analysis concluded the suicide letter was her handwriting. The wounds to her hands, wrists, and throat were in a trajectory away from her body, consistent with someone cutting themselves. When she didn't bleed out from the wounds she had inflicted on her wrists, she started cutting her throat.

Andy needed to move on and tuck the memory of another dead body away. Opening the secluded department in his mind, he safely tucked the image of her inside the box. Like the old saying, out of sight, out of mind.

John's One-Night Stand

Saturday morning, Andy climbed out of bed and knocked on John's door to see if he wanted to grab a workout. They recently joined a nearby gym, and they had gotten into the habit of eating breakfast together and then getting their exercise in. Unfortunately, that's about all they had time for now that Andy moved to the early shift side, 2 to 10 pm. Doug was a runner, so he was more apt to jog around the neighborhood.

There was no answer from John's room, so Andy opened the door, and his bed was empty. 'Did John even come home last night?' he wondered. Andy and Doug were up watching TV together in the living room until midnight, and John wasn't home yet. Then, assuming he was working overtime and would be in later, they turned in. It was somewhat unusual for John not to come home without saying anything, but Andy didn't overthink it as he left to grab a protein shake on the way to the gym.

After an intense weight training session, Andy went to pick up a burger on his way home.

When John finally walked into the apartment, Andy was in the process of getting ready for work. Still dressed in his uniform from the night before, he looked like hell. "Where have you been, asshole?" Andy asked John in a disdainful tone.

As he walked to his bedroom, John just waved him off.

The vague answer would not suffice; Andy followed him to his bedroom. "What the fuck?" Andy asked. Plus, he was curious about what had kept him out all night.

As John took off his shirt, he glanced up at Andy and smirked.

"Do you have anything to say for yourself, young man?" Andy scolded John, impersonating a parental figure, but John continued taking off his uniform. Then, deciding to have some fun with the situation at the discomfort of his roommate, Andy went off in a rant, "I was up all night, just sick to my stomach with worry! I walked the parking lot half the night and called all of your friends. Young man, you are grounded for a week!" With no response from John whatsoever, Andy said in a stern tone, "Seriously, what the fuck happened?"

"Well, you know that cute blonde in Captain Milan's office at the Academy?" John finally replied with a smile on his face.

"NO! You're shitting me!" Andy replied instantly, knowing what John was insinuating. She was so intimidatingly beautiful that no cadet had the nerve to speak to her, much less score. And now John was implying he had spent the night with her. "Well, ass-wipe, what's her name?"

"Mary," John replied as he continued to get undressed.

"How the fuck did that happen?" Andy asked with immense anticipation.

Naked, John pushed past Andy and walked into the hallway bathroom. John pulled the faucet handle to the shower and responded, "You remember Ray Simons from the Academy?"

Ray was a real pretty boy type, but everyone liked him. "Yeah, of course, I know, Ray," Andy admitted.

"Well, he works District 17, and I ran into him at the front desk last night when I was turning in my reports. He said that he was having a party at his place and invited me to come by."

On the north side of town, Ray was renting a trailer home. John stopped by, and after a few beers, Mary walked in. She was drunk and flirting with everyone, and John started flirting back. One thing led to another, and Ray told John they could sleep it off in the guest bedroom. John nodded, walked to the guest room, and she followed.

Hurrying to the bedroom and shutting the door behind them, John and Mary quickly undressed, passionately had sex, and within a few minutes, she was out. He was tired as well, so he rolled over and went to sleep.

Suddenly, she awoke as the sunlight started shining through the bedroom window. It was about 6:30 am; she jumped up and yelled, "Oh my God! I have to go!"

John tried to get her to stay, but nearly panicking, she started grabbing her things and kept repeating, "Oh my God." While John was making small talk with her about maybe getting together again sometime, Mary rushed to get dressed, making it painfully apparent this was a one-night stand and nothing more. "She finished putting on her clothes, ran out without saying goodbye, kiss my ass or nothing. So, I just rolled over and went back to sleep until I woke up and drove home."

"Oh my God! You lucky asshole," Andy exclaimed as he walked away, shaking his head in disbelief. John smiled and stepped into the shower. Andy was still chuckling about John's exploits while he dressed for work. When he was heading out the front door, John was retelling the story to Doug. Andy grinned, thinking it was never a dull moment with three cops living together.

That evening's patrol shift consisted of your ordinary traffic stops and calls for service. Andy was the first one home. So, he took the opportunity to stretch out on the couch and watch some TV. When John walked in, he headed straight to his bedroom without saying a word, which was rather unusual.

"Hey, asshole! Just walk by without saying shit!" Andy called out. John still didn't reply, so Andy got off the couch to see what was wrong. John was taking his uniform off when Andy stepped into his bedroom and asked, "What's up?"

With a distressed look on his face, John stopped undressing and solemnly looked at Andy, "You're not gonna believe it."

Andy asked, "What?"

"Let me get a beer, and I'll tell you.

Beyond intrigued, Andy eagerly followed John into the kitchen. John grabbed a beer from the fridge and sat down on the couch. Nothing typically bothered John; he was always happy-go-lucky. But something was dreadfully wrong. "You know my Senior Officer Arnie Cavazos, right?"

Andy replied, "Yeah, sure."

John explained, "Well, it was around 4 o'clock, so we decided to eat at the Luby's on Buffalo Speedway."

Luby's was a cafeteria-style restaurant with reasonable pricing, where police often dined. John explained that Arnie spotted two HPD officers sitting in the back once they were through the serving line. Recognizing Arnie, they motioned for them to join them. Once they sat down, Arnie introduced his rookie, and they started sharing small talk while they ate lunch. John continued, "Well, the conversation eventually got around to women."

"Go figure," Andy replied with a chuckle.

Considering Arnie was the only married person at the table, he was vicariously living the single life through their stories. The other two officers were real players, sharing one story about their sexual exploits after another. With each tale, the table would erupt into hysterical laughter until, eventually, there was a moment of awkward silence. Then, feeling compelled to add to the discussion with at least one story, John thought about last night with Mary.

"So, I said, hey, you guys know Mary in Captain Milan's office? And they abruptly stopped eating and stared at me with wide eyes like I said something wrong. Arnie pointed at one of them and said, 'KNOW HER? He's ENGAGED to her!' I almost shit myself. Thank God Arnie interrupted me."

"Oh my God! Then what the hell happened?" Andy interjected.

"In shock, I looked at the guy, and he was staring back at me! Unable to come up with anything witty to say, I just looked down at my plate and said, 'Oh, OK,' and acted as though nothing happened."

"OH MY GOD!" Andy exclaimed again, "WHAT THE FUCK DID HE DO?"

John replied, "I don't think another word was said the rest of the meal. I couldn't eat. If looks could kill, his eyes were throwing daggers at me. So I just picked at my food, and Arnie finally said, 'Well, it's time to go.'" Awkwardly, Arnie and John stood up and walked away from the table. Fearful the guy would follow him outside to demand more of that story, John avoided making eye contact.

"Did they?" Andy asked.

"No, but as soon as we got in the car, Arnie turned to me and asked, 'What the fuck was that?' so I told him the story, and he couldn't believe it."

Andy leaned back in his chair and looked up at the ceiling, amused and astonished at John's luck. "What are the chances?" Andy blurted aloud.

Once Doug came home, John had to tell the story again, and Andy enjoyed hearing it just as much the second time around. Doug knew all of them, so he was especially floored. Later on, Doug found out that they called off the engagement, and Andy presumed it was for the best.

John's luck was terrible, and it had never been more apparent than when Andy and Doug were giving him a hard time about a TV he ordered from Sears during a cold snap. The salesperson continually informed John the TV was back-ordered due to the frozen roads up north. Still, Andy and Doug decided to have some fun with John by saying the salesperson was playing him with excuses.

"You're a softy, and you're letting that son-of-a-bitch run all over you," Andy exclaimed.

"Yeah, you are a putz, and he knows it," added Doug. "You'll be the last in line to get a TV because you won't stand up to him!"

"I am not," John demanded. "They just don't have the TVs in yet!"

"I'll bet if you just called that asshole right now and demanded a TV, you'd get one," Andy proclaimed.

"You don't think I will?" John challenged them.

"I know you won't," answered Andy.

"Well, just watch this," John said as he stormed into the kitchen to use the phone.

Andy and Doug just sat in the living room waiting to hear whatever John said when he called the store.

"Yes, can I speak to Mark James in electronics?" John sounded business-like, and Doug and Andy just smiled at each other, knowing John didn't have a mean bone in his body. Then, suddenly John's voice changed, "Yes, Mark, this is John Frost, the guy that has been waiting for a back-ordered TV, and I've had enough!"

Andy and Doug's eyes widened as they looked at each other and listened to John's voice become authoritative.

"Yeah, I know! I've been hearing the same shit for days, and I'm sick and tired of it!" I want my damn television, right NOW!"

Andy and Doug were shocked. Never before had they witnessed John giving anyone such a rash of shit! Suddenly the phone started ringing. The entire time John was holding his finger down on the receiver button of the phone to make it appear as though he was making a phone call.

"OH SHIT!" John exclaimed as the phone kept ringing, and Doug and Andy fell out laughing. Finally, John just hung up the phone and walked past them to his bedroom without saying anything. He slammed the bedroom door shut behind him, and the phone kept ringing. It took several minutes for Andy and Doug to regain their composure from the fits of laughter.

The following day Andy awoke to the phone ringing. It was only 8 am as Andy stumbled to the living room to answer it. Andy's Mom was hysterical on the other end of the line because the Feds arrested Mike and subsequently charged him with conspiracy to import drugs from Mexico. He was held under a $50,000 bond at the Corpus Christi jail. Andy was floored as he stood there listening to his Mom explain what she knew. It was difficult to fathom his big brother being mixed up in anything like that. But, to Andy's knowledge, he had never known Mike to be involved with drugs, so maybe it was for the money. Perhaps that's how he was financing this new lifestyle.

Andy asked his Mom if she needed anything or if he could help somehow.

She said, "No. I just wanted you to know before you heard it from someone else. I'll let you know more when I know."

Andy thanked her, and they exchanged small talk for a few minutes with the promise to call again soon. Andy hung up the phone, staring at the wall as he thought about what his brother must be going through. 'Hopefully, this is something he just got caught up in and not something he was indeed a part of,' thought Andy. Unfortunately, with nothing he could do about it, he had to focus on the task at hand. He would continue to support his Mom and Dad in any way that he could, and he was getting on with his career.

Keystone Cops

Later that morning, Don Barber called Andy and said he was taking the day off to go to Galveston with his wife. The two of them liked to go for long drives on the beach in his Corvette. Andy thanked Don for the call and wished him an enjoyable day off. Andy was incredibly fortunate to have such a great guy as his first Senior Officer. He had learned so much from him. In addition to learning how to become a good police officer, Don also taught him how to be a good man.

When Andy arrived at the station, he was assigned JJ Cousy as his replacement partner. JJ was a new officer who had only been off probation a few months. He was an intelligent man and also an aggressive crime fighter. Sergeant Mattis trusted him to fill in for Don to be Andy's training officer for the day. Andy was familiar with JJ from roll-call meetings and around the station, so thankfully, it wasn't as though he was starting over with someone brand new.

They were assigned a patrol beat close to Acres Homes, a slum area of northwest Houston. It was a high-crime district, and there was no telling what trouble they might find if they were looking for it. JJ was a go-getter, always in hyperdrive, and Andy thought it would be a nice change of pace from Don's calm, cool, and collected personality. JJ chose to drive first, which was OK with Andy because he didn't know that part of town well.

Their patrol car was a piece of shit and would barely start. With more than 60,000 hard miles, the vehicle was on its last leg as a line car. The station mechanic was doing his best to keep it running before it was junked and sold at auction. The battery nearly drained when JJ was trying to start it. On the rare occasion, it did start; the vehicle would stall unless he kept his foot on the accelerator. Anytime they stopped at a red light, JJ had to keep one foot on the gas pedal and the other on the brake to keep it idling. Although JJ asked for a different vehicle, none were available, and considering he was the low man on the totem pole, he was given whatever car was left. They drove the clunker out of the station toward their beat with an attitude to make the best of the situation.

Due to Andy's intense workout schedule, he was always hungry. As Andy increased his weights during his strength training routine, his physique grew, and eventually, he had to go up a size in his uniform shirts. Even though JJ was a tall, slim guy with a slight build, Andy trusted him to be there if shit ever hit the fan. Andy's stomach was growling, and knowing that officers received free hamburgers at the McDonalds on Wirt Road, he asked JJ if he would swing by. "Sure, I could use some fries anyway," replied JJ.

After cruising through the drive-thru, they drove across the street to a shopping center to eat. JJ parked the patrol car, facing to view Wirt Road and Longpoint. The intersection was a busy four-lane Avenue and the major thoroughfare for that part of the city. They parked in a position that would prevent anyone from walking up behind them unnoticed. Also, they could monitor traffic from this spot while they ate and waited for a call.

Andy devoured his entire burger in just a few bites while JJ was still squeezing multiple ketchup packets on his fries. One of the packets ruptured sideways and shot ketchup onto his uniform trousers. Cursing like a sailor, he jumped out of the car, tossing fries everywhere. He threw whatever was left of the packets on the pavement and attempted to clean up with napkins. Unable to help himself, Andy laughed when JJ reached in to grab another stack of napkins, and JJ wiped off what he could. "Do you want to go back to the station?" Andy asked.

"No, I'll just find a filling station restroom and clean up," JJ replied. He got back into the driver's seat, and once again, the car didn't want to start. The battery was nearly drained again before the vehicle finally started. JJ shifted the car into drive, his right foot on the gas pedal and left foot on the brake, hoping it wouldn't die again as they eased out of the parking lot toward Longpoint and waited on traffic.

A long-haired biker dude and his old lady pulled up and stopped at the red light riding a fully chopped Harley. The man was covered from head to toe in tattoos and dressed in full biker regalia. The Harley was upgraded to a straight pipe exhaust system, so the motorcycle was especially loud without a muffler. Coincidentally, that's a traffic violation, and bikers frequently amassed numerous violations with each traffic stop, such as traffic warrants, driver's license suspensions, drugs, and who knows what else. They were stopped at the light, a couple of lanes over, and neither would look at the police car—a dead giveaway.

The light turned green, and the biker pulled away as quietly as possible, which was irrelevant because JJ had already honed his sights on them, and Andy was radioing the license plate number into the dispatcher. Pulling onto Longpoint, the police car almost stalled, but JJ revved the engine and got it going again. Waiting for the dispatcher to return with warrants on the plate number, they followed the bike traveling eastbound toward Hempstead Highway. When JJ couldn't stand waiting a moment longer, he turned on the overhead lights.

The bike turned left onto a residential street to clear the busy boulevard before stopping, then as the motorcycle nearly slowed to a halt, the biker gunned it! A massive ball of smoke bellowed out of the Harley's pipes as the biker twisted the throttle, and the chase was on.

Andy radioed they had a police pursuit in progress and provided the dispatcher with their direction of travel and the description of the bike.

As he flipped on the siren, JJ was cursing like a sailor, "Motherfucker! We've got a chase going, and I got this piece of shit to drive!"

But they were in luck because the bike was a piece of shit as well. The motorcycle smoked like a chimney as it sped down the residential street. As the Harley turned left, the biker leaned and stuck out his left leg to catch the bike if they lost traction during the quick turn. The woman rider on the back leaned with him and glanced over her shoulder at the approaching police car.

Andy continued to relay directions over the radio to the dispatcher. Several police units were heading towards their location to assist in the pursuit. As JJ slowed the police car to turn, the engine died. The steering wheel stiffened, and it took all of his might to turn the wheel without the assistance of the power steering pump. "Start the fucking car," screamed Andy.

"I'm trying," JJ yelled back as they rolled around the corner.

To their amazement, the Harley died too; the biker was desperately cranking the kick bar, trying to get it started. He was approximately 50 yards ahead, stalled in the middle of the road, looking behind him wondering why the police car stopped. JJ pumped the gas pedal, cursing at the patrol car, "start, you bastard!"

As Andy's impatience grew, he figured he could do better on his feet, so without saying a word, he opened the door and bolted out. JJ looked up in surprise and watched Andy sprint toward the stalled bike. The engine hit a few cylinders, and it almost started, so JJ kept at it.

Andy was closing in fast.

"He's coming," the woman screamed to her old man.

While approaching the motorcycle, Andy planned to slam his body into them and knock the bike over. Although this may turn into a physical altercation, at least they wouldn't be able to ride away. However, when Andy was within 10 yards of the Harley, the bike finally turned over and took off. Stretching out his arm, he almost caught the woman's ponytail as the motorcycle sped away in a cloud of smoke.

Andy stopped in his tracks and looked over his shoulder; JJ was speeding toward him in the police car. He had it running again, at least for now, and slowed down just enough for Andy to jump in. JJ reached over, pushed the passenger door open for Andy, and off they went again, profusely cursing as they tried to catch up.

As they approached the following intersection, the bike started leaning to make another lefthand turn. Andy tried to catch his breath as he radioed the direction of the pursuit. JJ desperately tried to slow the car for the turn without killing the engine. Sure enough, as JJ veered left, the patrol car stalled again. Struggling to turn the wheel without the power steering, he cursed the vehicle. Once again, to their astonishment, the Harley stalled too.

They were roughly the same distance as before from the biker, and this time Andy wasn't waiting. He jumped out and screamed, "freeze motherfucker," as he sprinted toward the bike.

The woman was terrified as she yelled to the driver, "he's coming!"

The biker glanced behind him as he continued to thrust down on the kickstart, and at the last second, it roared to life. In disbelief, Andy watched as they took off again in a cloud of smoke. Standing there for a second, he couldn't help but think how silly this was becoming. Then, suddenly, he heard the police car start. Again, JJ floored the gas pedal, the vehicle surged forward, and once again, JJ slowed the car for Andy to jump in, screaming every obscenity he could think of at his vehicle and the bikers.

They were approaching Longpoint Drive again, and the motorcycle was traveling at least 50 mph, but the police car was slowly gaining. As the bike closed the distance on the intersection, Andy knew they were driving too quickly to make a left or right turn. 'How can he make it across Longpoint without slowing for traffic?' thought Andy, and sure enough, he couldn't. The bike cleared the first two lanes from the left, but several vehicles were approaching from the right. Knowing they were about to collide, the biker laid the Harley down on its left side and started to slide. The two riders fell off the bike as it slid through the intersection and collided with the left front wheel of an oncoming car. Both bikers bounced off the car and landed in the middle of the street.

As the police car approached the intersection, JJ slammed on the brakes. To their amazement, the biker jumped up and started running. Disoriented, the female struggled to get to her feet.

The traffic from both directions screeched to a halt as Andy yelled into the mic, "He cracked up on Longpoint!" Then, tossing the mic down, he jumped out, yelling to JJ, "I got him, you get the girl!" Andy considered himself a sprinter, and he knew he could catch up to a biker weighed down in heavy leather, high-top boots, and chains.

JJ turned off the siren and got out as he waved off the traffic. The female was back on her feet; she grabbed her purse and started limping toward the pawnshop across the street. JJ yelled for her to stop and had to dodge around several cars to give chase. People in their cars watched the scene unfolding in front of them, their mouths ajar, attempting to comprehend what they were witnessing.

JJ was closing in fast when she entered the store, fumbling with her hand inside her purse. JJ caught her, slapped the bag out of her hand, and pushed her to the floor. She screamed in pain, evident that she was injured from the crash. When the woman's purse landed on the floor, it made a heavy thud sound. Immediately after he had her cuffed, he looked inside and found a pistol. He was grateful that he got to her when he did.

Andy gained on the biker as they entered an open field behind some houses. They were running toward an apartment complex surrounded by a parking lot. The parking lot was full, and their cars faced the open area. As the biker approached one of the cars, Andy grabbed him from behind and pushed him onto the parked car's hood. Andy's high school football coach would have been proud of that hit. Andy was on the man's back, trying to gain control of the situation.

He slid off the hood, planted his feet on the pavement, and pulled the suspect with him. With his thick boot, the biker kicked Andy's leg. Andy's temper got the best of him; he reached up, grabbed the biker's ponytail, and slammed him, face first, into the hood of the car with all of his strength. Blood splattered from the biker's nose, which appeared to take a little of the fight out of him. Andy managed to get one cuff on, but the biker refused to release his other hand from under him. He screamed, "Stop it motherfucker!" then the struggle continued for a few more seconds until Andy slammed the biker's face into the hood again. The biker finally gave in, relaxed his arm, and Andy finished cuffing him.

They were both exhausted and gasping for air as Andy pulled the biker off the hood and yelled, "Let's go motherfucker!" and turned to start the long walk back to the crash site.

Just then, a slight movement caught Andy's attention, and he looked into the car's front windshield. An older woman with grey hair, who appeared to be about his mother's age, was behind the vehicle's steering wheel. She had been there the entire time, and the woman was in shock as she sat there, silent, with her mouth open. Andy wasn't sure whether she had just pulled in or was about to leave, but he didn't want to stick around to explain. So instead, he took his hand and tried to wipe away some of the blood and saliva left on the hood of her car. He squeamishly smiled as if to say, 'I'm sorry' and turned to walk away with the suspect.

When Andy returned to Longpoint, several units were on the scene, and everything was under control. Come to find out, both the bike and the pistol in the woman's purse were stolen. Andy and JJ exchanged stories, and each of them had a good laugh. Andy figured the older woman in the parked car would file a complaint against him. After the altercation on the top of her hood, there had to be all sorts of scratches and dents from the metal chains the biker wore. Surprisingly, Andy never heard a peep from her, so he must have dodged a bullet on that one.

To add insult to injury, their police car wouldn't start when they were ready to transport their prisoners. JJ asked another unit to transport the two suspects downtown as they waited for the police wrecker to tow them in. The patrol car had made its final run, and now it was being forced into retirement. Andy felt a tad bit sentimental about the old car. Like the cowboy from the old westerns who had to put his horse down after giving it all. If nothing else, Andy had a great story to tell John and Doug when he got home.

That evening, they sat around the living room and listened to Andy tell the chase story. Several times he recounted the tale, and everyone laughed. Then, John and Doug chimed in with their funny but dangerous escapades. It was easy to turn a blind eye to the dangers of the job and only focus on the excitement when times were going so well for the three of them.

Silently, Andy worried about his older brother. Slightly embarrassed that his brother was arrested, he didn't mention Mike's legal issues to John and Doug. He hoped everything would work out or go away on its own, so he tucked it away in his mind, like he did all his bad memories, at least for the time being.

A couple of days later, Andy called home and found out that Mike had turned state's evidence against the others indicted, and he was getting off with a slap on the wrist. Once Mike pleaded guilty, he would be placed on probation and receive credit for time already served in jail. He, too, had dodged a bullet and wholeheartedly promised Mom and Dad that he had learned his lesson. Although he never actually admitted guilt and described the charges as "just a big misunderstanding."

Andy wanted to talk to his brother but he feared Mike would start making excuses like the suspects Andy arrested every day. Everyone had a reason, and it was very seldom that anyone admitted guilt. So unless Mike made some positive changes in his life, Andy assumed he was headed for trouble again.

Dead Men Tell No Tales

Andy's time with Don was ending, and he was moving on to work with a different training officer. Although the next Senior Officer was not the mentor Don had been, he was a good guy. After another month, he moved on again. Andy earned high marks on his evaluations, and Sergeant Mattis was happy with his development. He was eager for his probationary period to be over and be able to ride by himself. He was looking forward to the freedom to patrol his way without being in the shadow of a Senior Officer. Although probation was getting old, the job wasn't. Andy enjoyed constantly meeting new officers, and every new, unknown call presented its own set of challenges. He had been involved in several foot chases now, and even more, vehicle chases. Some of those had taken him to parts of the city he hadn't explored before, and the excitement was exactly what he craved.

During his fourth month of probation, Andy was partnered with Arnie Savage. Arnie was a profoundly religious man who was always quoting the scripture. To Arnie, every call was somehow related to the bible and what God wanted. Andy didn't particularly appreciate how Arnie was always preaching to him, but he didn't dare say anything. As the rookie, he had to go along to get along. So Andy merely nodded his head in agreement with everything Arnie said.

Arnie was disgusted with homosexuals. He referred to them as an abomination and quoted pieces of the scripture to reinforce his beliefs. In northwest Houston, it was rare to make a call involving gay citizens, but from time to time, it did happen. Andy could feel Arnie's contempt anytime they responded to a call involving a gay couple, especially men. Typically, Arnie let Andy take the lead, keeping his distance. Andy found it amusing because the gay community offered little resistance to police authority, and the responding calls were typically simplistic to resolve. Generally speaking, gay couples' homes were tidy, and they provided little to no confrontation with police officers. On the other hand, calls involving rednecks were frequently more challenging to handle.

Arnie would quote scripture in one breath, and in the next, he would throw out a 'Motherfucker'. Andy found his complex personality amusing as Arnie instantly changed from holy roller to the disgruntled cop when something pissed him off. Mainly if the situation involved gay people, or as Arnie referred to them, "fucking queers." Although he wasn't a proponent of suicide, the same rules did not apply in his mind to individuals who were gay. Then, he would somehow justify it as being God's will.

Andy tried not to let his frustration show and would nod his head to whatever nonsense Arnie spewed. This close to the end of his probationary period, the last thing he wanted now was a bad evaluation.

Finally, the month with Arnie was over, and Andy was grateful to move on to his last Senior Officer. If he could just get through this last month, he would be a civil service employee and no longer the lowest man on the totem pole.

Andy was assigned to Ray Gonzales as his final partner, and he was elated. Ray was a great guy with a friendly personality and loved a good joke, and Andy knew him from around the station. He was constantly kidding around with fellow officers and always seemed to have a smile on his face. Ray was in excellent shape and loved to box as part of his workout routine. His father had been a professional boxer, and Ray had participated in some golden glove boxing during his youth. Andy knew his last month working with Ray was going to be great.

The first week went by, and things were humming along as usual. They even kicked around the idea of becoming regular partners once Andy's probation was over, then they would permanently be assigned to ride together. Finally, Andy could see the finish line of his probationary period, and riding with Ray for the rest of his patrol career would be OK with him.

While they were driving down Hammerly Boulevard, they received a call for a citizen wellness check. A man had not heard from his friend all day and was concerned, so he requested a police unit to meet him at his friend's apartment. Since they were just down the street, they arrived within seconds.

Walking up to the apartment, Andy spotted a white male, in his mid-20s, standing at the front door. Nervously, he introduced himself as Jim and said his partner lived here. Andy couldn't help but think how interesting this call would have been with Arnie instead of Ray.

Jim told them his partner, Bruce Johnson, worked with him at Steinman's funeral home as a mortician. Over the last few days, they had been fighting over stupid stuff, and Bruce didn't show up for work today. Jim had been calling his apartment with no answer throughout his entire workday, so he drove over here to check on him. His car was parked in the lot and was his only means of transportation. Previously, Jim had a key, but Bruce had taken it back during a recent argument. Because he wasn't on the lease, the complex manager wouldn't open the door.

Ray knocked on the door and called out with a loud voice, "police officers, we need to talk to you." With no answer, he looked at Andy and said, "stay here, and I'll go check with the manager."

Andy exchanged small talk with Jim as Ray walked off toward the apartment complex office. As they chatted, Andy looked over the windows, and there was no sign of forced entry. All of the windows were locked, and the curtains were drawn shut. The A/C unit was running, so he walked around to the bedroom window, knocked on the glass, and announced, "POLICE." Still no response from inside.

"Oh my God, I hope he hasn't hurt himself," Jim said.

"Do you think he would?" Andy asked.

"Yes, he's tried a few times over the years. He's just so depressed," Jim replied.

"How has he tried to hurt himself before?" Andy asked.

Jim replied, "Well, just a few days ago, he took a bunch of pills. I called the ambulance, and they took him to the hospital and pumped his stomach. After that, the police were called."

There was an awkward silence as they waited for Ray. Andy couldn't help but think of Arnie and how he would grimace at this situation.

Ray arrived with the manager, who carried the set of master keys. She knocked loudly on the front door and announced, "manager" as she opened the door. Ray and Andy eased by her and slowly entered the apartment, declaring, "police officers." Jim and the apartment manager waited outside while they searched the apartment. The inside was immaculate; nothing appeared out of place, and there wasn't even a speck of dust on the furniture. They walked through the apartment, calling out for anyone inside as they scrutinized their surroundings for anything out of place.

Ray opened the bedroom door and said, "Andy, in here."

A young white male, fully dressed, was lying on top of the neatly made bed with a gunshot wound to the head inside the bedroom. He must have died instantly because there was no exit wound and very little blood. The small revolver was in his right hand, and he seemed almost peaceful. A men's suit was delicately laid out on the opposite side of the bed as if he was about to get dressed.

Everything seemed undisturbed as they scanned the rest of the bedroom for clues. The pistol's blue box packaging was sitting on the nightstand with a box of ammunition, and there was one round missing. A receipt showed the purchase of a .38 revolver and one box of ammo.

Ray noticed a handwritten note by the bed and began reading it aloud: "Hello officers. My name is Bruce Johnson, and I hate that you had to see me like this, but there was no other way. Please do not let my friends inside my apartment; I don't want them to remember me like this. Ask the body car to take me to Steinman's funeral home on Westpark, where I work. I want John Simon to process my body, and I have laid out the suit that I wish to be buried in. It was my father's, and it has sentimental value to me. All other wishes are described in my will on the kitchen table in a sealed envelope. Thank you for respecting my final wishes. Bruce Johnson."

Ray advised Andy to radio the dispatcher for an ambulance to check by and pronounce the victim. He was going to walk outside to explain to Jim what had happened. Also, they needed a body car and were required to notify homicide, although he doubted they would come out for a discernible suicide.

When Ray broke the news to Jim, he wasn't surprised. Ray kindly informed him this was now considered a crime scene, and no one would be allowed inside the apartment until the investigation was complete. Jim understood and sadly walked away.

The ambulance soon arrived, and one of the EMTs mentioned they responded to an overdose call here just a few days ago. Once they walked into the bedroom, the EMT said, "Well, he did it right this time. He shot himself in the head just like the officer told him to."

"What?" asked Ray.

The EMT explained that the officer who responded to the first call was disgusted with the situation and cruel to the man. "He told him, why don't you shoot yourself? He was pretty homophobic." The EMT didn't recall the officer's name, but he remembered the officer telling the guy to buy a gun and shoot himself in the head. "I guess he took the advice to heart," the EMT added.

Just then, Arnie walked in to check by with Ray and Andy. "Well, I'll be damned; I made this call a few days ago," Arnie exclaimed. "Did the queer try it again?"

Ray decided to have a little fun with Arnie and teach him a lesson at the same time, so he replied, "Yes, but this time, he took your advice and shot himself in the head, just like you told him to." Then, Ray held up the letter, "He says right here how you were the one who instructed him how to kill himself properly."

Arnie's face turned pale white, and his mouth dropped open, "give me that letter," he demanded as he tried to grab it from Ray.

Ray held the letter back from Arnie as he chuckled a little, but Arnie was dead serious as he yelled, "I mean it, give it here," and reached for the letter again. Ray moved back into the living room, keeping the letter away from Arnie.

Finally, Ray gave in and said, "I'm just kidding. There's nothing in here about you."

Arnie was relieved but still worried because the EMTs overheard everything. "You better be more careful who you advise, Arnie," said Ray.

The EMT just shook his head and said, "We're getting back in service."

"Me too," Arnie replied as he turned to walk out.

"Come back any time," Ray yelled to Arnie, chuckling under his breath.

Andy watched the entire discussion from the bedroom door. It was nice to see Arnie finally get a little taste of his own medicine.

The following day Andy called to check on Mom and Dad and learned that Mike had laid it on thick with them. He had them convinced that the drug case was a big misunderstanding and that the cops just jumped to conclusions. They were confident that Mike wasn't guilty of anything, and he took a plea to get the situation over with. It reminded Andy of the crooks he was going to court on every week. Every defendant had a story, and the cops were always wrong to accuse them. Andy was infuriated that the big brother he idolized growing up was now pulling the same stunt, but he wasn't going to try to change his parents' minds. They were relieved that their son was not a criminal, and Andy decided to let them have their closure.

SIX

I'd Rather Be Lucky Than Good

Ray was on vacation that week, and it was a crapshoot as to whom Andy would be partnered with. He checked the shift assignment logbook and noticed Bubba Long's name next to his. Andy didn't know him well besides the casual pleasantries and hello as they walked past each other in the hallway. Bubba recently transferred from Central Nights, so no one had gotten to know him yet. The rumors were that he was involved in several shootings there, but no one knew for sure. Central had a reputation for being a rough area, and if you worked there long enough, eventually, trouble was going to find you. Particularly the officers who worked the night shift on downtown's north and east side, where Bubba patrolled.

Bubba was a burly man. Although he only stood about 5'10," he was at least 230 lbs of lean muscle with little fat. He had a broad chest and a naturally thick neck. His strength didn't come from weightlifting but from working hard his entire life on the family farm. Bubba was a quiet man who wasn't much for small talk and always had a dip of tobacco tucked under his lower lip; he was constantly spitting.

Andy intentionally overlooked the habit and focused on his opportunity to find out about policing in the higher crime areas of the city. Once roll-call was finished, they got into their patrol car and began situating their equipment. Bubba positioned a short double-barreled shotgun between the front seats. Andy was impressed with his choice of a weapon and how Bubba prepared his firearm. Andy did his best to watch Bubba and learn everything possible from him.

Driving toward their patrol beat, they engaged in small talk to learn more about each other. Eventually, the topic of guns came up, and Bubba mentioned that he had stopped by a gun show on his way to work. "While I was there, I purchased a Smith & Wesson 44 Magnum revolver. Do you want to see it?" Bubba asked excitedly.

"Absolutely," Andy replied. Even though he had never personally handled a 44 Magnum, he had always wanted to ever since he watched Clint Eastwood famously handle the weapon in Dirty Harry.

Bubba pulled over into a parking lot, positioning the car so bystanders could not see the vehicle's rear. He peered around, grinning like an excited child, exposing a little bit of tobacco stuck to his teeth. Andy was dreadfully trying not to stare at it.

"Come on," Bubba said as he pushed the button on the dashboard to open the trunk. They walked around to the back; Bubba reached into an equipment bag inside the trunk, pulled out a blue gun box, and opened it. There it was! A brand-new shiny 44 Magnum with a 6" barrel.

"Here you go," Bubba said and handed the gun to Andy.

Andy was mesmerized by the weapon. The weight and feel of it were pretty impressive.

Then, Bubba asked, "Do you want to shoot it?"

"You bet," replied Andy. "But where?"

"If the calls are slow at the end of our shift, we might be able to slide out to Patterson Road. We can shoot a few cans out there, and no one would be the wiser."

Patterson Road was a desolate part of the city located on the far western edge of town. No one lived in the area, and thick woods surrounded it. Often, teenagers would go there to hang out and drink. Young lovers used it as a place to park and make out. A lot of illegal trash dumping occurred in that area, and even an occasional body was dumped.

"Sounds like a plan to me," said Andy. He could hardly wait to feel what it was like to shoot a 44 Magnum.

As they put the pistol back, the radio sounded in the background, "Attention all officers, clear and close to the 8800 block of Longpoint, an attempted rape just occurred." They looked at each other realizing they weren't far from that location. Bubba hurried back to the driver's seat and reached for the radio mic. He was about to answer the call when he heard another unit take it. Bubba radioed the dispatcher that they would be checking by.

They were nearly there when the assigned unit radioed the suspect's description. "All units near Longpoint and Gessner be on the lookout for a white male, late 20s, short brown hair wearing a grey jumpsuit. The suspect left the scene going westbound on Longpoint, toward Gessner, driving an old white Pontiac Bonneville. It's a four-door, no hood over the engine and a large doghouse sticking out of the trunk."

They could hardly believe what they were hearing. "Well, that should be easy to spot!"

Bubba spun the vehicle around and headed westbound in the direction they assumed the suspect would travel. Intensely, they scanned the streets, driveways, parking lots, and any other areas where the suspect might have dumped the car. Considering that Bonneville would stand out, he wouldn't be able to stay in that vehicle for any length of time.

After searching for thirty minutes, they realized their effort was growing futile. With every additional street they turned down, the anticipation that this might be the one started to fade. Finally, they decided to go back to the scene to obtain more information.

The responding officer was finished interviewing the complainant and had taken a few prints. He wrote his report in the vehicle with the AC blaring to stay cool. Bubba drove up beside him and rolled down his window to find out the details.

This was their first time meeting the officer since he was from the Accident Division, so they exchanged greetings and small talk about the brutal heat before getting to the subject at hand. The victim lived in the apartment complex and was thankfully uninjured from the attempted rape. Because it was the middle of a workday, most residents were still at work or indoors to escape the heat, and no one was around during the attack.

While the woman was washing her clothes in the small laundry room in the apartment complex, and when the wash cycle was nearly finished, the suspect walked in. He wore a grey jumpsuit with 'Harvey' embroidered on the chest pocket, had dirty hands and fingernails, and smelled heavily of gasoline. After pulling a small, compact knife from his pocket, the man ordered her to undress. Sobbing, she repeatedly pleaded with him not to do this.

"Hurry up and take off your clothes, or I'll just kill you," the man threatened.

Attempting to stall for additional time, she asked to put her clothes in the dryer first. Reluctantly, he agreed and nervously looked around. Slowly, she opened the door to the washing machine, took out one garment at a time, and slowly put each item into the dryer as she tried to find a solution.

"Hurry up bitch, or I'll stab you!"

As she kept delaying, he became more and more agitated until he finally forced her to the floor. She struggled to free herself from under the force of his weight as he attempted to unzip the front of his jumpsuit; his zipper was stuck. He had to sit up using both hands. While he was fumbling to get the zipper working correctly and pulling his penis out of his jumpsuit, she used the opportunity to break free from under him. As fast as her legs would carry her, she ran out of the door, around the corner of the laundry mat, and towards her apartment.

She glanced back over her shoulder while she was running and didn't see him following her, so she paused a moment to determine where her attacker went. Cautiously, she walked back toward the laundry mat to confirm he was gone. Then, she walked around to the other side of the building and spotted him driving out of the parking lot. He looked in her direction with his driver's window down, making eye contact. Finally, he gunned the engine, spun his rear tires, and drove away.

The woman thought the vehicle was a 60's model Pontiac Bonneville similar to the one her father used to own. She described the car as rough, with the hood over the engine missing and a white doghouse sticking out of the trunk.

Given all the precise details, they couldn't help but chuckle at what an idiot this man was and figured that he would be quickly apprehended. The officers discussed what was left to be completed in the investigation and how they might search during the remainder of their shift. Lastly, they parted ways and promised to stay in touch should they find any new information.

The rest of the shift was typical, with nothing of significance. As they continued to get to know each other better, they responded to a few calls and made a few traffic stops. Every time they spotted an old white car, they couldn't help but strain their necks to get a good look, but nothing came close to what they were looking for.

Before they knew it, It was already 9 pm, and Bubba asked, "Do you want to swing by Patterson Road on the way to the station?"

Andy anxiously replied, "You bet. Not much is going on right now anyway."

Driving down Patterson Road, it was pitch black outside. They stopped the patrol car near a small bridge where they could see both directions. Bubba opened the truck, picked up his pistol, and loaded it. Andy walked around searching for and picking up cans they could use as targets. Andy aligned all the aluminum cans in a row on the bridge's guard rail and shined his flashlight into the woods to ensure nothing was downrange.

Bubba looked at Andy and said, "You ready for this?"

Andy replied, "Yep!"

Just then, headlights from an approaching vehicle appeared. Bubba said, "Let the car go by first," so they started shining their flashlights into the ditch to pretend there was something they were investigating.

As the vehicle passed, they glanced at it and then suddenly looked at each other with their mouths dropped open and their eyes wide. Then, in unison, they yelled, "OH SHIT!" and started running for the police car. A white 1966 Pontiac Bonneville without a hood and a doghouse sticking out of the trunk casually passed by them, down Patterson Road and off into the darkness.

Bubba started the engine, spun the police car around, and burned rubber driving after the Bonneville. The emergency lights were flashing in all directions as they kept repeating, "Holy shit, can you believe it? I can't believe this shit!"

The Bonneville pulled over to the right, and Bubba stopped the patrol car approximately two vehicle lengths behind. Andy radioed the vehicle's description and advised that the car was wanted for an attempted rape earlier in the day. At the same time, Bubba announced to the suspect over the loudspeaker to slowly step out and show his hands. Andy stepped out of the passenger side and drew his handgun. Bubba had his shotgun at the ready.

As Bubba directed, the suspect got out with his hands in the air. In the beam of the headlights, Andy could tell he matched the general description of the man wanted for attempted rape. Bubba advised him to walk towards the patrol vehicle, and as he got closer, Andy noticed 'Harvey' embroidered on his chest.

They cuffed him, searched him, and found a pocketknife matching the description of the one they were looking for. When Andy searched the Bonneville, it was completely covered in trash and contained nothing significant except the identifiable doghouse. When Bubba asked the suspect where he had been, the man explained he works as a mechanic at a nearby oil-change garage. Both of his hands were greasy, as the victim described. "What's your name?" Bubba asked.

"Harvey," he replied.

"What's your full name?" Bubba asked again.

"Harvey Hackberry," he replied.

"Harvey, were you around Longpoint and Gessner today?" questioned Bubba.

"No."

With Harvey safely tucked in the back seat, they waited for a tow truck. Bubba looked at Andy and said in a voice low enough that only Andy could hear, "You know what this means, don't you?"

"What?"

Bubba smiled and said, "Those cans will live to fight another day."

Andy smiled back and said that he was OK with that. Even if it was just by chance, getting someone like Harvey off of the street felt fantastic. Andy replied, "Wow! Was that lucky or what?"

Bubba smiled as he stared out the windshield into the darkness and said, "Sometimes I'd rather be lucky than good!"

Bubba then started talking in a much louder voice to ensure Harvey intentionally overheard him. He bragged about how their cunning intuition helped them set a trap, and this was perfectly executed police work.

Andy glanced at Harvey, with his head hanging down in the back seat, looking dejected. As Andy listened to Bubba touting their talents, he smiled and wondered if riding with a seasoned crime fighter was always like this. Soon, he would see another side of Bubba that was quite different.

The End Justifies the Means

The next day, Andy was again assigned to ride with Bubba. Andy was hopeful that Bubba might open up more about some of the shootings he had been involved in. The Northwest District bordering Acres Homes was a rougher area, home to predominantly low-income, minority citizens. Good people lived there, but they were continually plagued with a criminal element of drug dealers and gangs ruling the streets. As a result, the neighborhood was more dangerous than the average in the city, and Andy and Bubba were assigned there.

After responding to a few standard calls, the dispatcher sent them to check on an assault victim. The location was a residential address, more than likely indicating family violence. Those calls were particularly dangerous for police officers because of the escalated emotions. Bubba forewarned Andy to remain vigilant and always follow his lead. Bubba's voice was seething in anger, in a way Andy had never heard before, as he gritted his teeth and mumbled, "I fucking hate a wife-beater."

When Andy drove to the front of the small, two-bedroom house and began to park, Bubba directed him to continue driving forward and park further down the street. The driveway wound along the side of the house, back to the detached garage behind it. Bubba exited the vehicle and approached the residence from the sideyard instead of the walkway. Andy followed closely at his heels, intently watching Bubba use an abundance of caution, advancing towards the front of the house.

Bubba knocked on the front door and stepped off to one side, outside of the direct view of the front door. The uncanny silence seemed to extend forever, and with each additional second, Andy's anxiety grew as he began scanning his surroundings in all directions. Bubba's extreme cautiousness was making him uneasy, almost as though they should anticipate an ambush or something.

"Who is it?" a squeamish female voice asked from within the house.

"Police," Bubba replied in a firm tone. The woman immediately opened the door to let them in. Bubba guardedly entered the doorway, glancing right and then left. The woman had been beaten pretty badly. Her left eye was swollen nearly shut, and her lower lip split open with dried blood on the wound. "What's your name?" asked Bubba.

"Mary."

"What happened?"

"He beat me," she replied, lowering her head in shame.

Andy carefully watched all of the doors leading to other parts of the house; the suspect might still be there.

Bubba asked, "Who beat you?"

"Mike," she replied.

"Where is Mike?"

"He left."

"Where to?" questioned Bubba.

"To his place," she answered.

"Do you mind if I have a look around?"

"Sure," Mary replied.

As Andy relaxed a little, he realized Bubba wasn't sure if he believed Mary. Of course, they always had to consider the possibility that the suspect could still be there, making her say he left the scene so the officers would leave. Cautiously, they cleared the house. When they found no one else in the home, Andy breathed a sigh of relief.

Bubba concernedly asked Mary if she needed to go to a hospital to have her injuries checked out, but she declined. He asked her calmly and politely to sit on the couch, and he began to ask more questions. For the past three months following Mike's release from prison, he resided with his common-law wife, Mary. Occasionally, when they got into arguments, Mike would stay at his parent's house for the night, which was about 15 minutes away. She didn't know the address.

The phone rang, and Mary, visibly startled, looked to Bubba for advice. Bubba nodded his head in approval, and she picked it up and answered, "Hello?" A look of terror washed over her face, and as she was about to say something, the person on the other end of the line hung up. Slowly, she lowered the phone to her right side, still latched in her hand, and looked at them. "That was him," Mary said, voice trembling, dropping the phone on the floor. Frightened and meekly, she whimpered, "He's coming." In defeat, she lowered her face into both hands and wept.

"What did he say?" Bubba asked.

In between sobs, she mumbled, "He said he's coming to kill me and then hung up."

"Does Mike own a gun?" inquired Bubba.

"He's a felon, so he ain't supposed to have one, but I think his parents do. So, he may have got one from them," said Mary.

Bubba got up, walked over to the couch Mary was sitting on and sat down next to her. Then, comfortingly, he put his arm around her shoulder and said, "He's not going to kill anyone."

Andy was impressed watching Bubba's compassion for this woman and how he could so calmingly assure her that Mike would not hurt her again.

Bubba turned his head in Andy's direction, and suddenly, his expression changed. He appeared detached, cold, and calculating when he said, "Go park the patrol car around the back of the house and bring in my shotgun. Make sure the car can't be seen from the road."

Andy anticipated instructions to call for backup or radio the dispatcher the suspect's description. Instead, at the strange request, Andy stood there for a second, attempting to comprehend Bubba's implications, when Bubba interrupted his train of thought and firmly said, "Do it now!" Hurriedly, Andy ran outside to the police car and drove it around back. He parked the vehicle directly behind the house, grabbed Bubba's shotgun, and entered the house through the back door.

Walking into the living room, Andy heard Bubba coaching Mary on what to do if Mike showed up. Repeatedly, he reassured her that Mike wouldn't hurt anyone if she did exactly as he instructed. She seemed in shock, but she still intently listened to Bubba. Finally, he told her to sit by the window, watch for Mike's car, and tell him everything she saw.

Bubba backed out of the living room into the kitchen where Andy was standing. He took the shotgun and checked the chamber to ensure it was loaded. He looked at Andy and said, "Just follow my lead." The threshold concealed part of his body, and he was standing to the right of the doorway. His stance indicated he was taking up a barricaded fighting position. After scoping his surroundings, he pointed at the hallway entrance leading toward the bedrooms and said, "You go over there." Then he returned his attention to Mary in the living room.

Bubba's eyes were blazing in a blind rage; it was unlike anything Andy had seen before. Based on how Bubba was prepping and positioning everyone, he was preparing for a confrontation. Andy found it eerie how calm and calculating he acted. 'There has to be another way; there has to be another way...' thought Andy; this was not what he had been taught in the Academy. Of course, this wasn't HPD policy either, but he was a rookie, Bubba was his Senior Officer, and unable to come up with another solution, he did what he was told and hoped for the best.

Andy took up a concealed position at the entrance to the hallway, pondering if he should draw his weapon. Bubba was steely-eyed as he continued to speak softly to Mary and assure her that she would be fine. He asked her several times if she could see anything, but she kept saying, "No, nothing yet."

Occasionally Bubba glanced over at Andy to ensure he hadn't wandered off. Standing there perplexed, Andy couldn't believe what was happening. The seconds felt like hours, slowly ticking by as Andy considered the situation and wondered if he should protest what Bubba was doing. Nervously, Andy shifted his weight from one foot to the other as he waited and worried.

Suddenly, Mary leaped to her feet as she glared out the window. "HE'S HERE!" she yelled.

"Shush," Bubba replied in a low voice. "He'll hear you."

She slowly backed away from the window, eyes continuing to stare outside.

"What's he doing?" Bubba asked in a low, deliberate tone.

"He's getting out of the car," she said.

"Does he have a gun?" asked Bubba.

"Yes," she said in a trembling voice.

"OK, now go back into your bedroom as we talked about." She turned and hurried past Andy toward the back bedroom. She was holding her face in her hands and weeping. Andy, like a spectator, stood by watching a scene from a movie he couldn't stop.

Albeit somewhat muffled, Andy could tell the man was furious, yelling threats and calling her a bitch as he walked closer to the house. Bubba backed slightly away from the threshold and raised the shotgun into a combat-ready position. Andy's heart was pounding through his chest as he drew his handgun. Acknowledging this was happening, he might as well be ready to defend himself. Instinctually, Andy felt like he wanted to warn Mike, but that was out of the question.

Mike assumed the front door was locked because he didn't even try the knob. Instead, he reared back and kicked it with his foot. A loud boom erupted as the front door flexed from the impact, but it didn't open. Mike raised his leg back and kicked, then kicked it again, and this time the door split and flew open. "YOU FUCKING BITCH! I TOLD YOU!" Mike screamed, stepping through the threshold.

Bubba raised his shotgun, aimed it at Mike, looked him directly in the eyes, and then pulled the trigger. There was a massive flash of light, and a thundering sound as the gun recoiled upward. Bubba immediately readied the gun for another shot, but Mike was gone. He had fallen out of the front door with a massive wound to his chest.

Andy had witnessed the entire thing unfold before him but never squeezed a shot. Everything happened so quickly he didn't have time to think. He started leaning into the room from his position in the hallway, looking for Mike, but he was gone. Slowly, he walked toward the front door with his handgun at the ready, and Bubba came up alongside him. Peering outside, they saw Mike lying on the front lawn shifting back and forth, writhing in pain. Bright pink blood pooled through his shirt and onto the ground below him.

Calmly, Bubba told Andy to call for an ambulance and tell the dispatcher that they had been involved in a shooting. Bubba walked outside and kicked the handgun out of Mike's reach. The shotgun was still in Bubba's right hand; the barrel pointed toward the ground in a relaxed position. Standing there a second, Bubba smugly watched Mike struggling to breathe and overcome with immense pain. Over the walkie-talkie, Andy radioed the dispatcher while walking outside.

Stern and through gritted teeth, Bubba threatened, "I'll bet you won't beat another woman, will you asshole?"

Suddenly they heard a scream from behind them. Mary was standing in the front door frame, hands over her mouth, with a look of terror on her face. She started to run toward Mike, but Bubba stopped her and gently coaxed her back inside. This was a crime scene now; he needed to preserve it, but much more pressing on Bubba's mind, he wanted to make sure she would not turn on him. So, kindly but sternly, he reminded Mary that he had saved her life because Mike would have killed her. This was the only way to stop him.

Several units, an ambulance, and news media were heading toward them now. Sergeant Mattis heard the call from the station and headed to the scene too. Homicide and the Medical Examiner's office had both been notified and were en route. Bubba sat Mary down on the couch, the same spot as before, just inside the front door, and asked, "What do you think would have happened if we weren't here?"

Mary had her elbows on her knees with her face in her hands as she sobbed uncontrollably. She mumbled through her hands, "He... he... he would have killed me."

"That's right," replied Bubba. "Now, you and I are connected for the rest of our lives. I will always be here for you, and you will be here for me. Right?"

Mary stopped sobbing, raised her head from her hands, and stared into Bubba's dark brown eyes for a long time. "Yes, I will be here for you," replied Mary.

"The first time we knew Mike was here, he started kicking on the door. You ran to the bedroom and didn't see a thing. Right?"

Slowly, she nodded her head in agreement.

Bubba smiled at her warmly and hugged her tight. "It's gonna be alright," Bubba whispered. They both sat there for a minute; then Bubba got up and walked outside to Andy.

"OK, here is how it happened," said Bubba matter-of-factly. "I asked you to park the car behind the house and get my shotgun in the event he came back while we were taking the report. We wanted to have a chance to arrest him rather than scare him off. But, instead, he surprised us when he kicked the door open."

Andy looked at Bubba and asked about the phone call.

"We just wanted to arrest him. But, instead, he forced the confrontation," Bubba said as he pointed down at Mike.

Andy looked down at Mike; he was no longer moving. Andy wasn't sure if he was dead or alive, but they could do nothing for him now.

"He's a piece of shit!" Bubba said, laced in a tone of disgust. "The world is a better place without him and people like him. He will never beat another woman."

Andy stood there taking it all in as Bubba glared at him. Finally, Andy nodded his head in agreement even though he felt sick about it.

The ambulance made the scene and pronounced Mike dead. 'He was dead the second he kicked in that front door. Bubba was going to make sure of that,' Andy thought to himself. He felt terrible about the whole thing, but in a way, Bubba's misguided logic also made sense. Mike was the piece of shit who kicked in the door and entered the house with a gun in his hand. This was lawful, but it was awful. Andy felt queasy but knew he had to be strong when the investigators came. He was merely Bubba's rookie, nothing more.

Homicide, the Medical Examiner's office, and Sergeant Mattis were all skeptical of how the scene was described to them. They interviewed Mary, and her story was consistent with Bubba and Andy's. Suddenly, Mike appeared at the front door and started kicking it in. Bubba grabbed the shotgun that Andy had brought in for protection and defended himself. The investigators were suspicious but decided to let it go.

Mary seemed to be in a better place now, and the reports all reflected an act of self-defense, which was how it would be presented to the Grand Jury. They would later no bill Bubba, and he now had another notch on his gun. Another side of policing. 'The end justifies the means,' 'Stick to your story,' and 'All's well that ends well.'

Andy got home late that evening after writing his statement at Homicide. John and Doug had already gone to bed for the night, so no one was up to hear his story. He wanted desperately to tell someone about his day, but he was alone with his thoughts. He considered calling home, but it was after 1 am, so it would have to wait. He poured himself a stiff drink, sat in the darkness of the living room, and dwelled on the day. It would become something he did a lot, maybe too much.

The following day Doug had court, so he left the apartment early. John wanted to go to the gym, and Andy shared his story with him on the way there. Andy followed John around the gym to finish his story while they worked out. John was shocked Bubba got away with shooting the guy, but he wasn't going to lose any sleep over another turd off the streets. After they finished their workout, they grabbed a burger on the way back to the apartment and then hurried to put their uniforms on for the day.

When Bubba arrived at the station, Sergeant Mattis was waiting for him. Mattis asked him to step into his office and close the door behind him. Mattis told him that he disapproved of how that shooting went down yesterday. He went on to say, "I don't know how you guys did things at Central Nights, but this ain't Central Nights."

Bubba looked at Mattis and kept his mouth shut. He wasn't sure where Mattis was heading with this.

He continued, "Andy's got the makings of a good cop, and we don't police like that here. So I want you to look for a new home. Are you good with that?"

Bubba nodded his head in agreement.

"You can ride one man until you find a home." Mattis had done his share of killing in Vietnam; he wasn't impressed or intimidated by Bubba.

Bubba sensed that the best thing he could do was let this go, so he got up and asked, "Anything else, Sarg?"

Mattis looked back down at the paperwork on his desk and said, "That's all." Bubba turned and walked out without saying a word.

When Andy arrived for his shift, Mattis called him into his office and broke the news. Andy understood and said he was OK with it, but deep down, he was troubled. Part of him hated that he wouldn't be able to learn more from Bubba, a guy who he genuinely liked. Another aspect of him was deeply troubled by how cold Bubba could be at the same time. Maybe it was because of his time policing in a part of the city where life wasn't valued, and he had grown numb to taking a life. Andy feared the same thing could happen to him if he transferred to a high-crime area. Northwest patrol appeared much more inviting now. He had been involved in his first shooting and survived. Thankfully, he didn't have to pull the trigger, but he did see how quickly taking a life could happen, which scared him. Andy's metamorphosis was just beginning.

John's Helicopter Ride

Andy and John planned a trip back to the cabin on the coast for several days. With the stress of the job, they were looking forward to getting away from the city and decompressing. The fishing was ideal this time of year, and the thought of Mom's cooking made their mouths water.

Doug was up for the trip too, and this week worked best with everyone's schedules for the trip. The weather was warm and sunny, with little chance of rain for the next few days, so they prepared to leave directly after work on Saturday night and make the drive to the cabin. They requested Sunday off to have a long weekend, and then they had their typical Monday and Tuesday off days.

With each day nearing Saturday, their excitement for the trip grew. Andy coached John and Doug on all the equipment necessary to fish correctly on that part of the coast. Then, the three of them shopped together at their local sporting goods store in preparation and bought everything they could need and more.

Andy's parents were thrilled to have the company, and his mother was planning a menu for each day. Andy's Dad wanted the guys to make the most out of their trip, so he would have the boat fueled and in the water before they arrived. First thing Sunday morning, they could just jump in and go.

Friday night, when John got home from work, he was ecstatic to tell Andy about a girl he had just met. She worked at a local restaurant that he frequented, and they had been making eyes at each other for a while now. John finally got the nerve to talk to her, and they instantly hit it off. When he gained enough courage to ask her to a movie or something, he couldn't believe it when she said yes. Before she had a chance to change her mind, John blurted out that he was off on Monday and Tuesday, and she said that either one worked for her. John wasn't going to the coast.

Andy was looking forward to this, and everything was planned for the three of them. He couldn't believe John decided to put a monkey wrench on the trip because of a girl he met at work. "Can't you take her out next week?" Andy asked.

"No, I've already asked her out, and she said yes! I am not backing out now. You guys go without me," John replied.

"Ugh! I can't believe it," Andy exclaimed, turning away in disgust.

When Doug walked into the apartment, he immediately sensed the tension and knew they were arguing. "What the hell is going on?" he asked.

Andy stood up from the couch, pointed at John, and said, "He met some bitch at work, and now he is backing out of our trip!"

Doug shook his head and walked to his bedroom; he didn't mind either way. John stood there, shocked about how badly Andy had taken the news. Enough so that he was rethinking his decision, but he couldn't back out of his date. The trip was off for him, and Andy would have to get over it.

Saturday was uneventful for the three of them. Andy was still brooding over John's decision, so he woke up early and went to the gym without him. He didn't want to spend any time in the apartment that he didn't have to.

After Andy and Doug arrived home from work Saturday night, they loaded Andy's car with all their newly purchased fishing gear and anything else they could possibly need. John reached home before they did and was sitting on the couch watching TV while they scurried around the apartment, gathering everything for the coast. Finally, they took one last look around to make sure they didn't miss anything. Andy paused on their way out the door, "Well, I hope you enjoy your date, asshole!" Andy said to John, jokingly, with a smile. But he meant it too.

"I will," John replied with a smile, "You two lovers enjoy sleeping together in that cozy cabin down there."

Doug enjoyed being the bystander to their bickering and couldn't stop laughing at the two of them going at each other.

"Whatever bitch! You're just jealous!" Andy said and slammed the door behind him.

John stood up and walked to the window to watch them leave. Although he didn't particularly enjoy letting down his friends, he just had to get through his shift tomorrow, and then he would have two days to enjoy with his new girlfriend. He couldn't wait.

After midnight, Andy and Doug made it to the cabin and unloaded their gear. The two of them were exhausted from a long day of work, so they didn't bother to unpack. Emma left snacks for them with a note that she would be there in the morning to cook breakfast.

The following day Andy awoke to the smell of coffee wafting from the kitchen. He rushed out of bed, hurried into the room, and greeted his Mom with a big hug.

"I've missed you! It is so good to see you. It looks like we are down one guest. Who didn't make it?" asked Emma.

"John couldn't get the time off of work." He didn't want to disappoint her by saying he decided not to come because of a date.

She didn't seem to mind and said, "Well, I'll just cut back on the amount of food a bit."

Woody walked into the cabin and greeted Andy with a firm handshake and a smile. "I got the boat ready for you if you wanna go fishing."

"Thanks, Dad. Maybe later. I want to eat some of this deliciously smelling breakfast Mom is making and hang out for a bit." Andy asked about Mike, and Woody said everything seemed to be normal. Both of his parents were convinced Mike had been naive, got caught up in something, and believed they could now put this entire ordeal behind them.

When Doug crawled out of bed, he came out and said good morning. Andy shared some of his funnier stories from work with his parents, and they loved hearing them. Since neither of them knew much about the craziness of police work, they were sitting on the edge of their seats.

Doug and Andy hung out for the remainder of the day. The yard needed to be mowed, and a few repairs needed to be done to the dock, so Andy and Doug made themselves worthwhile as Woody and Poodle looked on.

Shortly before dinner, they grabbed a couple of beers and hopped on the boat for a ride. Andy wanted to scope out a good fishing spot for tomorrow morning. They cruised down the creek, toasted their beers to the good life, and joked about how John had missed out.

After cooking a fabulous dinner that evening, Woody and Poodle left the cabin for their short ride home. Andy and Doug watched TV for a while, still joking about John patrolling as they enjoyed their vacation. Andy toasted, "Here's to those who could have and should have come along." They laughed, sipped their beers, and smiled.

The countryside was quiet, and the fresh, cool air drifted through the open windows in the cabin while they watched TV. Suddenly, they heard a car speeding down the gravel road. Unable to imagine why anyone would be in such a hurry, Andy decided to walk outside to see who was driving so recklessly in the middle of nowhere. His Dad's car pulled into their driveway and abruptly slid to a stop. Although Woody was prone to speeding, he never sped down the road leading toward the creek.

When Woody jumped out, Andy knew something was dreadfully wrong. "What's up, Dad?" Andy asked.

"John's been shot," he answered.

Andy's heart sank; he was terrified he was about to hear his biggest fear come true. "Please, Dad... please... tell me not he's dead!" Andy exclaimed. Doug walked out of the cabin and stood alongside Andy.

"No, he's alive, but it's bad," Woody replied.

"How did you find out?" asked Andy.

"Your Uncle called me just as we walked into the house. The story aired on the evening news in Houston."

"What happened?" asked Andy.

"I don't know the details, but some guy shot him in the chest during a traffic stop," Woody replied.

Everyone stood for a few seconds in silence, thinking about John and what could have happened. Andy couldn't help but think that if John had stuck to the plan, he would be here right now and wouldn't have been shot. Woody didn't have any other information, and the cabin didn't have a phone, so they couldn't call anyone. Because of the cabin's remote location, they could only receive one TV channel. Unfortunately, it was from a local station that didn't broadcast Houston news. So they were in the dark, and the only way to get more information was to drive back to Houston.

Quickly, they walked back into the cabin and started packing their belongings.

Woody told them not to worry about the cabin or getting the boat out of the water; he would take care of everything in the morning. He told Andy to lock up when they left.

Andy said, "OK, I'll call you as soon as I find out anything, Dad."

Woody replied, "Thanks, son. We will be thinking of John and hoping he is alright. I am sorry that your trip was cut short."

"Me too, Dad," Andy replied.

Woody got in his car and headed home to Poodle. The clean-up at the cabin could wait until the morning.

The trip back to Houston was deathly quiet, both too worried about John to say much. Doug continually searched the radio stations for a Houston channel that might broadcast any news regarding the shooting. But unfortunately, it was useless because there were mainly syndicated talk shows on the news channels on Sunday night.

Driving into Houston, they decided to go directly to the hospital and check on John. If he had been life-flighted, they would have taken him to Hermann Hospital in the Medical Center. When they pulled into the parking lot, dozens of police cars and news media trucks were already there. They were at the right hospital.

By the time Andy parked, it was about 1 am. Still dressed in their T-shirts and shorts, they jumped out and headed toward the entrance. When they inquired about John's condition at the receptionist's desk, she told them he was in emergency surgery, but she didn't have any other information. After ID'ing themselves as police officers and John's roommates, Andy asked, "Is there a waiting area officers are being directed to? Family members, possibly?"

"Yes, if you go to the emergency waiting room, you will see several officers there."

They thanked her and quickly headed down the hall. As they rounded the last corner to the emergency waiting room, Andy immediately spotted James Hurley. He was standing in a group of several officers, pretending to care about John. Considering this was neither the time nor the place to rehash old wounds, Andy decided to ignore him. Hurley was still harboring resentment giving Andy a cold stare as he walked past.

Andy spotted Paul Gaye, his old Academy class President, within the crowd. Paul was working Northeast Night Shift and had called out of service to check on his old classmate. "Paul, what happened?" Andy asked as he walked up and shook his hand.

"Where have you been?" Paul asked. "It's been all over the news!"

Andy replied, "We were out of town visiting my folks. We jumped in the car and drove straight here the moment we heard. How is he?"

Paul replied, "He was shot in the chest. Right now, he's in surgery. It isn't good."

"From a pistol round?" Doug asked.

"A .380, I think," Paul replied. "John was on patrol with Arnie Cavazos when they pulled over a couple of Hispanic males near Moody Park. I heard they were brothers, and one of them was wanted in San Antonio."

Andy interrupted, "Do they have them?"

"Yes, the man that shot John was shot as well. He's next door at Ben Taub."

Ben Taub was the county hospital, and it was famous for its emergency room and not much else. Cops would often joke, saying that if you get shot, go to Ben Taub only until you're stable and then get the hell out of there and go to a real hospital.

Paul continued, "The other suspect wasn't involved in the shooting and surrendered. He's at Homicide right now being interviewed."

Andy and Doug glanced around the room, there must have been at least thirty uniforms jammed into that emergency room area. Most worked with John at North Central Patrol, and a few they knew from their days at the Academy. Although it partly felt like a reunion, this was no time for reminiscing.

Hurley had been biding his time, watching Andy and Doug from across the hallway, and couldn't wait a moment longer. Everyone else was dressed in uniform except for them and Hurley had to comment. He walked over with his usual cocky swagger and degrading tone, "Well, look what the cat dragged in. You boys didn't have to get all dressed up for us."

With Herman's death still fresh on his mind, Andy could no longer contain his anger. Hurley had gotten away with his role in Herman's suicide, with zero repercussions, and Andy lost it. He lunged toward Hurley and gripped his throat pushing him across the hallway with his arm fully extended. "YOU SON OF A BITCH!" Andy yelled, tightening his grip on Hurley's throat. Hurley's eyes widened, his mouth open, struggling to breathe. Andy's eyes were blood red with rage; hate washed over his face. Even with both of Hurley's hands on Andy's grip, he still couldn't break free. He was in shock and disbelief that a former cadet had attacked him.

For a second, everyone just watched, unable to believe what was happening. Both Doug and Paul knew their history, but it appeared as though a civilian in shorts attacked a police officer. Suddenly the entire room jumped in to break up the fight. Andy continued gripping Hurley's neck with all his might, and it took a few seconds before they could release his grip. Finally, Andy was getting his just rewards for the abuse he endured from Hurley, and he was punishing him for Herman too. His eyes were fixated on Hurley's flush face as every vein in his head bulged.

Paul peeled Andy's hand away from Hurley's throat, and they were pulled apart. Although he couldn't stop taking his eyes off Hurley, Andy stopped struggling. He was still mad as hell, but he began grinning in satisfaction from being feared by the man he used to fear. Weirdly, Andy never felt better.

Hurley turned away, rubbing his throat and trying to regain his composure. Several officers offered their assistance, but he shoved them off, trying to save face. Hurley was more embarrassed than hurt because a former cadet got the best of him, making him feel small. Another officer attempted to put his arm over Hurley's shoulder consolingly, but he shrugged it off. Hurley walked off alone, with his hand still on his neck.

Paul and Doug had Andy pressed against the opposite wall. Paul yelled in his face, "What the fuck is wrong with you?"

"You know! That son of a bitch got away with it!" Andy blurted out. Paul didn't answer, but he understood the implication. Slowly, Doug and Paul loosened their grip, and Andy relaxed.

Sergeant Wilkerson from North Central Command hurried in to see where the commotion was coming from. "What's going on?"

"Nothing, sir. Just a little disagreement," Paul responded as he continued to grip Andy's shoulder.

Even though Wilkerson didn't know exactly what happened, he could tell there had been a scuffle. With nothing more to go on, he looked at Paul and said, "You guys get a grip and show some respect for the family. They are right down the hall."

That got Andy's attention as he looked in the direction Wilkerson had pointed. He knew John's Mom and Dad, and he wanted to see them. "Can we go visit them, Sarg?" Andy asked.

"Not now," Wilkerson replied sternly. "Right now, the best thing you can do is pray for John and get ahold of yourself. You got that?"

"Yes, sir," Andy responded as he looked down at the floor in humility.

With everyone around the room whispering in hushed tones, Andy knew that he had become a distraction. At this point, the best thing to do was head home and let things quiet down. He gave Paul his phone number and asked him to call if there were any changes or if they began allowing visitors. Paul agreed and said he would stay there until they had an update on his condition. Andy and Doug walked out of the hospital, wondering what tomorrow would bring.

The moment they unlocked the door to the apartment and walked inside, the phone rang. Andy hurried to pick it up.

Paul was already calling from the hospital. "John is out of surgery and stable. He's still in intensive care, and it's gonna be a long road back, but they think he is out of the woods."

Andy thanked him and said to go home and get some rest.

"Are you OK?" Paul asked.

Andy replied, "Yeah, I just lost it for a second. Hurley pushed my buttons, and after everything that happened with him at the Academy, I lost my temper. I'm sorry I caused such a scene."

"Don't worry about it. Let's get together for lunch or something." Andy agreed and said he would call him soon. Lastly, Paul said, "You watch out for Hurley. He is a snake in the grass, and I think he is capable of almost anything."

Andy agreed and hung up.

That night, Andy didn't sleep at all. The combination of worrying about John, being pissed at Hurley, and feeling terrible about the scene he caused at the hospital kept him awake. It was done now and he needed to let it go.

He called home to update his parents on John's condition and promised to call them should anything change. Then, he and Doug grabbed some breakfast and headed to the hospital. Several uniformed officers were sitting with the family when they walked into the ICU waiting room. Right away, Andy recognized John's Mom and Dad, and they looked like they had been through the wringer. However, when he introduced himself again, they remembered him.

A short time later, a doctor walked into the waiting area and asked to speak privately with Mr. and Mrs. Frost. Mr. Frost kindly told the Doctor that his fellow officers should hear whatever he has to say. He added, "These are the guy's John risks his life with. They deserve to know what's going on."

The Doctor nodded his head in agreement, "OK, well, John has lost a lot of blood, so we will be giving him a couple more blood transfusion units to replenish what he lost. I know the police department started a blood drive; that helps. Currently, John is heavily sedated, but he is stable. Although his injuries are serious, he was fortunate. If the bullet were a couple of inches up, there would have been too much damage to fix. Unfortunately, we did have to remove his spleen and a few feet of intestines. Also, he had a puncture to his left lung, but it will heal over time."

Mr. Frost asked, "Will he fully recover?"

"Yes, but it will take a while. With proper care and physical therapy, John will be as good as new," the Doctor replied.

The entire room breathed a sigh of relief. This was the best outcome they could have hoped for. Everyone in the room started hugging. The Frosts were overcome with gratitude, and the Doctor politely excused himself. 'If anyone could live through something like that, it was John,' thought Andy.

Two homicide detectives arrived and introduced themselves to the Frosts. One of the detectives, Jim Bond, was famous around the department because he had managed to solve a homicide case that everyone else had given up on. His tireless efforts were so admirable; that they even wrote a book about him. Mr. Frost asked, "How did John get shot?"

Bond was hesitant to provide details because the investigation was ongoing, but Frost looked desperate to know. So finally, Bond said, "Well, this is off the record, and anything I tell you now may change as we gather more information, but I think we have a pretty good idea of what happened." Bond glanced around the room to make sure no one else would overhear the details of the homicide investigation. "You have every reason to be incredibly proud of John." Bond said, "He did the best he could, given the situation he had to deal with."

Mr. and Mrs. Frost smiled and hugged each other. Then, they started to tear up, and after everyone saw the tears well up for the Frosts, there wasn't a dry eye in the room.

Bond continued, "So, John and officer Cavazos were patrolling north of downtown and stopped at a fast-food restaurant for chicken. Under the shady tree near Moody Park, they pulled over to eat their lunch and watch the traffic on Fulton Street. When they were nearly finished with their food, a car spun its tires and sped off from Moody Park. They put their meals away and followed the vehicle."

John's parents' listened intently to Bond retelling the story and nodded their heads from time to time to indicate that they understood.

"John was driving, and Arnie was on the passenger side." Bond took a deep breath as if to gather his thoughts. Then, he quickly glanced around the room again to make sure no one but cops and John's parents could hear him. "What they didn't know was that these two turds were brothers. The driver's name is Rico Sanchez, and the passenger's name is Alberto Sanchez. Alberto is wanted for murder and shooting a San Antonio cop. He escaped about a year ago from a San Antonio hospital jail ward, and he was running the streets of Houston until John and Arnie pulled him over. Rico isn't the criminal his brother is, but he runs around with him."

The cops in the room are on pins and needles, waiting to hear the rest of the story. "So, John walks up to the driver's side to write a ticket. He briefly speaks with Rico, and Arnie approaches the passenger side to question Alberto. Arnie and Alberto's conversation in Spanish quickly escalated into an argument."

Bond stopped again and looked around the room nervously, "We're not sure what was said, but we think Arnie told Alberto to get out of the car. Right when he stepped out, he punched Arnie. Arnie fell back, and John ran around to help. As John rounded the vehicle, Alberto pulled his gun, so John pulled his too. That's when the shooting started. We think John was hit first in the abdomen. After that, he fired his revolver at Alberto as he fell backward but missed. Then, Alberto shot Arnie in the hip, and Arnie returned fire, hitting Alberto in the leg. At that point, Alberto ran off."

Bond stopped and looked at the Frosts and asked, "This is a lot to absorb. Are you sure you want me to continue?"

"Yes, please," Mrs. Frost said through tears. Mr. Frost was in a daze, envisioning what his son must have gone through.

Bond continued, "John emptied his revolver as he was falling. We know that he tried to reload but wasn't successful."

Mr. Frost then asked Bond, "But how did Alberto get arrested?"

"Ronnie Johnson," Bond answered. "Ronnie was working an extra job, directing traffic at the church down the road when he heard gunfire. Immediately, he ran to investigate and saw Alberto limping away with a gun in his hand. Arnie yelled at Ronnie to get that guy because he had just shot him. John was laying on his back in the street, trying to breathe."

Bond took a breath and continued, "Ronnie Johnson gave chase as Alberto ran around a house on Patton Street. The homeowner was doing dishes in her kitchen when she spotted Alberto running behind her garage. When she spotted the uniformed officer, she assumed he must be chasing the man. Silently, she waved her arms to get Ronnie's attention and pointed to her garage. Ronnie understood and approached the garage from the other side."

"Instead of walking into Alberto's ambush, Ronnie approached him from behind. We don't know the specifics of how that shooting went down yet, but Alberto is in the hospital, and Ronnie's not." Bond slightly grinned as the Frost's sank back in their chairs, relieved.

Mr. Frost was prouder than ever of his son, realizing John did everything he could. Bond thanked the Frost's for their son's service and promised justice would be served. He left his card and advised them to call if they needed anything.

Understanding they wouldn't be able to see John today, Andy and Doug said goodbye as well. When he was ready for visitors, they would come back. They talked about John's shooting on the drive home, knowing that it could happen to them. Each time they walked up to a vehicle during a traffic stop, they were taking a chance. It wasn't the idea of death that scared Andy; he just hoped he would do the right thing if that moment came. He certainly didn't relish the thought of his parents seeing him in a hospital, or worse, in a funeral home. Yet, in his mind, it would be far worse if the detective told them he screwed up and was shot as a result. It wasn't about being killed; it was about doing what was right and honorable.

A couple of days later, John was moved to a private room, so they stopped by on their way to work. They saw an attractive young lady sitting across John's hospital bed as they walked in. Surprised to see visitors, she jumped up and excused herself from the room. Andy and Doug barely had the chance to utter the word "Hi" as she hurried past them and out the door. John was heavily sedated, lying on his side, but he recognized them. He didn't show much emotion other than to raise one of his fingers as if to say, "hey."

Andy couldn't help but point at the door and ask, "Is that her? The girl you missed the creek trip for?"

Even under the influence of the pain medication, he knew what Andy was asking. At least he was able to see the humor in the situation, and he sluggishly chuckled. John then grimaced as the laughter caused stabbing pain in his chest. Doug tugged on Andy's arm to silently gesture to cool it.

With a breathing tube down John's throat, he could only shrug. Then, suddenly, a nurse bustled into the room, concerned that John's heart monitor had increased, and she needed to check his vitals. Andy wondered if his comment was the cause but shut his mouth.

They decided to leave and let John rest. Andy didn't get any satisfaction from messing with a guy who couldn't defend himself anyway. They said their goodbyes and told John they would be back to see him soon. While Andy was walking out the door, the young woman narrowed her gaze and tightened her lips in a go-to-hell look. She must have heard his comments, but he let it go. Eventually, she would get over it, or she wouldn't. Either way, he was only joking and wasn't going to apologize.

Andy and Doug tried to get back into a routine at home, but it wasn't the same without John. Today, he was supposed to get off the ventilator, so they decided to visit him on their way to work. They would drive their own cars and go their separate ways after the hospital.

As they walked into the hospital room, John's parents and one of his brothers were there. Thankfully, John was off the ventilator and much more alert. After exchanging greetings and small talk, Andy finally asked him what he remembered about the shooting. Besides the helicopter ride, John's memory is completely blank until he awoke in the hospital the next day.

The Doctor walked in for a routine visit, and Mr. Frost introduced him to everyone. He politely nodded and asked John how he was feeling. John replied, "I've been better."

The room filled with laughter. Next, the Doctor checked John's wounds, and John asked about the large incision from his rib cage to his navel. The Doctor replied, "Well, I had to remove your spleen and some of your intestines, so I needed room to work."

John then asked, "How long was I under Doc?"

"About four and a half hours," the Doctor replied.

"Wow! That long, huh?" John answered.

The Doctor smiled and said, "Well, I only needed about forty-five minutes to repair everything, but I spent two hours getting all that chicken out of your stomach. My god! How much did you eat?"

Again, the room erupted into laughter, knowing how much food John could put away. Even John chuckled, grimacing in pain. He was healing well, but a bullet was still lodged in his back. "It's located near the surface of your skin, so the surgery to remove it will be relatively minor." The Doctor continued, "It was a good thing that your stomach was so full because it moved a lot of your other organs out of the bullet's path." He finished his exam and politely left the room with a promise to come back tomorrow.

The time had come for Andy and Doug to leave, so they said their goodbyes and headed to work. As they walked out of the hospital, Doug said, "You didn't give John any shit!"

Andy smiled and replied, "His time is coming. I didn't want to embarrass him with his parents in the room."

Doug shook his head and said, "Let it go, Andy."

Andy stopped and yelled, "HEY!" Doug stopped and looked back as Andy said, "Be careful out there. I don't want to have to visit two roommates." Although Andy had a slight grin, he was dead serious. Doug smiled and walked away. Andy couldn't believe he was starting to worry about his buddies, but the realization that none of them were invincible had finally sunk in.

SEVEN

Clean Underwear

With his probationary period finally over, Andy drove to work feeling ten feet tall. He completed six months of supervised patrol with six different Senior Officers, and each one gave him a glowing review. After meeting every task required of him, it was time to reap his just rewards. He was now a civil service employee; therefore, he was guaranteed due process before being disciplined or terminated. As a probationary officer, he was an at-will employee and could be fired or punished without recourse.

More significantly, he was now allowed to ride by himself. He had never been on his own in a patrol car, and the freedom to go and do as you please sounded incredible. For safety reasons, most police units assigned two officers to a vehicle, but typically at least one patrol car in every district contained only a single officer. Even after what happened to John, Andy didn't fear the additional danger of riding alone. He simply blocked it out of his mind.

John was rehabbing around the apartment, getting back to his old self again. Now that he was strong enough to work out again, his strength returned, and he was eating everything in sight. John got a pass on his last month of probation, so he was also finished. No one in their right mind would hold a guy back who lost his spleen on duty.

As Andy walked into the station, his first stop was to check the roll-call roster. His heart leaped in excitement when he noticed he was assigned as a one-man unit, Sergeant Mattis must have a lot of trust in him. "You ready for this?" Mattis asked.

"Yes, sir," Andy replied with a grin, "I will make you proud."

Mattis smiled and said, "Just be careful out there." He turned and walked toward the roll-call room, and Andy followed, still grinning from ear to ear.

While they waited, the guys laughed and jabbed at one another, as friends do. The conversation jumped around between current events, sports, and work. Eventually, word spread that Andy was off probation and would also be riding by himself. Of course, this drew a special kind of jest, but Andy took it well.

Since there wasn't a formal ceremony for a rookie completing probation, friendly ribbing was the norm. Andy wanted to get through his first few days on his own without doing anything embarrassing and be seen as just one of the guys. The title rookie insinuated he was less than capable; he wanted to be their equal. Now to get out there and prove that he could do the job.

Mattis read the alert bulletins to start roll-call, then announced North Shepherd District was shorthanded while officers took time off to attend a funeral for one of their own. As a result, some northwest units would be assigned to run calls there this afternoon. Since North Shepherd bordered Northwest District, and both districts were under the same Captain, it made sense to assist.

Andy was assigned to the 6th District, just east of where he had patrolled previously. Although he didn't know the area, he was familiar with the major streets. Thoroughly exhilarated for his first shift by himself, he wasn't bothered that he would be in unfamiliar territory. He was up for the challenge.

The guys took a few more jabs at Andy walking out of the station. He smiled and waved them off as he nervously looked for his patrol car. Once he located the vehicle, he loaded his equipment and placed his shotgun on the roof. When riding with Bubba, he learned to always pack his shotgun last so it would be easiest to grab.

Driving out of the parking lot, Andy turned right onto Hempstead Highway. The forgotten shotgun made a scratching noise as it slid down the vehicle's roof. Instantly, he realized his mistake, 'Oh my God' he thought. Immediately, he stopped the car, jumped out, and grabbed the gun, hopefully before anyone noticed.

To make matters worse, he jumped out so quickly that he forgot to put the car in park. As a result, the car started rolling forward, so Andy had to jump back in and slam on the brakes. The vehicle came to a sudden stop, still rocking back and forth. He threw it into park, and the radio chattered from the guys behind him. Everyone had witnessed the entire ordeal and was repeatedly clicking their microphones. It was their way of silently laughing over the radio.

'Ugh, unbelievable! Could this shift have started any worse?' he thought. But, at least no one was injured, and he recovered his shotgun. It had a few new dings and scratches but was still functional. Mortified, he drove away, wondering how he would ever live that down.

Once he pulled onto highway 290, he notified the dispatcher he was on duty. Right away, he was assigned to a burglary in progress at 6455 Sherwood Way. Andy responded he was en route.

As luck would have it, he was familiar with Sherwood Way because he passed it several times when driving down Pinemont Street. The dispatcher described the suspect as a black male, about six feet tall, with a slim build. He was last seen running southbound from the reported location wearing a white T-shirt and blue jean shorts. Andy was at least 15 minutes away, so he headed that way in a hurry. Of course, he figured any self-respecting burglar would be long gone by the time he got there. He was comforted when the dispatcher assigned a North Shepherd unit to check by with him.

Driving across the northwest district and turning onto Sherwood took Andy about 10 minutes. He scanned the block numbers and determined he was headed in the right direction, so he sped up until he reached the 6400 block. There was a white wood frame house with the number '6453' written on the curb, but the next residence on that side of the street was 6457, which appeared abandoned.

Set back from the road was a trailer home, not numbered. Andy thought that must be 6455, and the North Shepherd unit pulled up alongside him. He looked around for whoever called them, but the street was vacant.

The North Shepherd officer introduced himself, "Hi, I'm AJ Morris," and extended his hand. AJ was a tall, lean, black officer.

From time to time, Andy had seen AJ and recognized him. "Are you familiar with this area?"

"No, sorry," AJ replied, "I've never worked this side of the district."

"Neither have I," but, just the same, Andy felt good about having him there. Andy pointed to the trailer home, "I think that must be it, but I haven't seen anyone."

"Well, let's have a closer look," AJ suggested. So they started walking toward the trailer, Andy on the left side while AJ walked around the right. They were looking for anyone or any signs of forced entry to confirm they were at the correct house.

Suddenly, a black male jumped out a window and hit the ground running. In hand, he had a white sack resembling a pillowcase, and he matched the suspect's description perfectly; Andy yelled, "POLICE! STOP! AJ, over here," then he started giving chase. Presumably, the sack contained stolen items, and his running only confirmed that they were at the right place.

The suspect ignored Andy's commands to stop and sprinted toward the rear of the property. Andy loved a good foot chase, and he found one. However, he feared this guy might be a faster sprinter, especially wearing shorts and a t-shirt. On the other hand, Andy was dressed in a full police officer's uniform, gun belt carrying his loaded firearm, a radio, handcuffs, and flashlight. If he could keep the suspect in sight long enough, he might wear him down and outdistance him. Generally speaking, most criminals didn't do much to stay in shape. Although they may be fast for a short distance, they usually tired quickly.

Andy couldn't believe his luck. He was in a foot chase on the first call of his first day off probation. He had a chance to prove himself and understood that chasing a thief could be dangerous, so he was grateful AJ was there. AJ was right behind him, calling the dispatcher on the handheld radio, "Suspect is a black male, white t-shirt, and shorts. Running southbound from Sherwood."

A 6-foot chain-link fence enclosed the backyard directly ahead. The suspect dropped the bag to use both hands to get over the fence. Andy was within a few feet of the suspect when he flipped over the top and landed on the other side. He made eye contact, drew his pistol, and yelled, "STOP! YOU SON-OF-A-BITCH," but it had no effect; the suspect jumped up and ran. He holstered his pistol and started climbing. Unfortunately, he lost grip and fell to the other side as he cleared the top. Andy hit the ground so hard the air was knocked from his lungs, but he rolled and sprang to his feet and continued running. Behind him, he heard the clanging sounds of AJ climbing the fence and then the loud thud when he also hit the ground. AJ was breathing heavily now, and Andy wondered how long they could keep up.

Running through residential backyards, Andy noticed they were approaching another fence. It was a shorter one, only about waist high. The suspect didn't even slow down as he leaped and cleared it with one hand in a smooth athletic move. Closing in on the fence, he heard a large dog barking on the other side. A German Shepherd, defending his territory, chased the suspect and closed in fast. Andy took his chances and hopped the fence as well.

When the suspect reached the opposite fence, the dog caught up with him and clipped at his feet. The dog missed by an inch, and the suspect cleared the fence in the same fluid leap. Luckily, the shepherd didn't notice Andy coming behind him, momentarily startling the dog. Surprised, the shepherd yelped and spun around while Andy sprinted past and cleared the fence.

Unfortunately, AJ wasn't going to be quite as fortunate. The shepherd was on high alert now, looking for a new target. AJ saw the dog, and the dog was ready for him, so AJ ran along the fence to avoid it. It was worth taking more time, not to get bit.

The suspect ran across the street, and Andy started to close distance. At this point, they weren't more than fifteen yards apart. Then, in a panic, the suspect glanced back over his shoulder, and Andy knew it was only a matter of time. The suspect was tiring, and all he had to do was keep him within sight.

Andy spotted another 6-foot chain link fence ahead, running through the next yard. A massive brick building was on the other side. As the suspect started climbing, Andy stretched out his arm and grabbed his shoe. Andy had the suspect's shoe in his hand as the man flipped over and landed flat on his back. He raised his head to look at Andy, his chest heaving; exhausted. Andy threw the shoe down, drew his revolver again, and yelled, "I'll kill you motherfucker!" The suspect paid zero attention to Andy's idle threat, jumped up, and sprinted off to the left side of the building.

Andy cursed, holstered his pistol again, and started climbing. Finally, he topped the fence and jumped to the ground as the suspect rounded the corner of the building. Andy looked back, but AJ was nowhere in sight. The building was huge, and now he had lost sight of the suspect, the one thing he didn't want to happen. He spotted the man running toward a side entrance as he rounded the corner. Just then, Andy realized he had entered the hospital's emergency entrance. If the suspect made it inside, it would be easy to lose him.

As he sprinted toward the entrance, Andy's lungs were screaming for oxygen. He didn't have much energy left, but he desperately needed to close the distance before he lost him in the building. Two nurses were pushing a gurney when the suspect bolted past, shoving the stretcher out of the way. The nurses struggled to keep the patient from falling off the ramp, and the suspect paid them no mind.

The suspect paused for the automatic glass doors to open, giving Andy a chance to close the gap. Finally, the doors opened, and the suspect ran in. Andy yelled, "WATCH OUT!" to the two nurses as the chase barreled past them. With the automatic doors still open, Andy didn't break stride. The suspect ran erratically down the corridor, clutching trays and pieces of equipment, tossing them in Andy's path. The suspect turned right through double swing doors as Andy maneuvered the makeshift obstacle course.

The double doors were still swinging when Andy ran through and straight into an operating room. Doctors and nurses dressed in full masks and gowns hovered over a patient in the middle of a surgical procedure. Andy yelled, "Sorry, sorry, sorry..." and continued running through in hot pursuit.

The suspect ran into the adjoining washroom; sinks lined the walls on both sides. A few hospital staff members pressed up against the wall, attempting to stay clear of the mayhem. As the chase entered the women's locker room, several doctors and nurses were screaming, currently in various stages of undress. Everyone covered up with towels and ran out of the way. The suspect slipped on the wet floor, and Andy saw his opportunity, but instead also became a victim of the slippery floor. He reached out, trying to grab the suspect, but missed as the suspect got to his feet and took off again. Andy yelled, "Sorry," to the medical staff, got to his feet, and continued to give chase. He had come too far and gone through too much to stop now.

The suspect pushed the next door open, with Andy only a few steps behind. They entered a large cafeteria dining hall with long tables lined perpendicularly from end to end. People jumped to their feet to get out of the way as the suspect leaped from one table to another with Andy on his heels.

The man ran into the kitchen and came to a dead end. Andy hoped that AJ was not far behind if this turned into a physical fight. The suspect turned around, frantic, like a caged animal trying to dash past. But Andy grabbed him, and they tumbled to the floor.

The suspect started swinging wild punches and screaming, "LET ME GO." Andy attempted an armbar technique taught in the Academy, but it failed. At this point, he was trying to hang on long enough for AJ to find them. As they rolled around on the floor, Andy finally gained control of his arms, preventing him from punching.

The man continued squirming, trying to break free, yelling, "Let me go, man! I didn't do nothing!"

In the distance, AJ yelled, "Make way," in a commanding tone.

Those words were music to Andy's ears; help was almost there.

AJ pushed through the crowd of onlookers to get to the struggle and immediately fell into the melee like a linebacker. He was blessed with upper body strength and was able to overpower the suspect quickly. With the situation finally under control, AJ started handcuffing him. Even though it was apparent the struggle was over, the suspect was still running his mouth.

"Stop beating me! I didn't do nothing!" the suspect yelled and pleaded.

Andy was exhausted and grateful to AJ for taking control while he got to his knees to catch his breath. Unfortunately, the crowd of onlookers was encroaching. So, he yelled, "Get back," mustering as much bravado as possible.

He suddenly realized he was the only white person there. The room was predominately filled with kitchen staff, and although no one was interfering, they weren't supportive of the arrest either. The suspect antagonized the situation by continuing to scream, "I didn't do nothing!"

AJ searched the suspect's pants for weapons and evidence, unconcerned by the gathering crowd.

Andy radioed the dispatcher to provide an update. When the dispatcher asked for the address, Andy didn't know what to say other than, "We're in a hospital." So, Andy asked the crowd, "What's the name of this hospital?"

A large black woman stepped forward, ignored Andy's question, and asked, "Why y'all beating on him?"

No officer enjoys hearing when a bystander is sympathetic to the suspect. Andy could sense a gathering storm. He asked again, "What is the name of this hospital?"

Finally, the lady yelled, "Why don't you let him up?"

AJ looked up and told the lady in no uncertain terms, "Shut up and get back," he wasn't intimidated by the crowd.

The suspect took full advantage of the situation by sadly saying to the woman, "I didn't do nothing, ma'am. They just jumped me on the street and started beating me, so I ran in here!"

The situation became increasingly volatile, and Andy began to feel a new kind of fear. The crowd was closing in, mumbling amongst themselves, deciding what to do.

AJ announced loudly and sternly, "This asshole just burglarized a house! It might be yours. Where do you live?"

"I didn't burglarize nothing," the suspect chimed in.

"Well, y'all don't have to beat on him," she responded.

AJ lost it and yelled, "Bitch, I ain't beating him! Now, back up!"

AJ's comment further fueled the crowd's agitation, and the woman was enraged. Finally, several uniformed security officers pushed their way through the group. Hospital security had been dispatched to the disturbance.

Security advised the crowd to get back as they positioned themselves between the kitchen staff and the officers. AJ and the woman continued arguing back and forth, exchanging insults, while the security officers remained between them. The suspect was escalating the encounter with his constant declarations of innocence. Andy was anxious to get out of there. The security staff helped him up and ushered the officers toward an exit.

AJ and Andy controlled the handcuffed suspect, and the security staff relocated them to a private office. The crowd remained in the kitchen, their agitated voices fading in the distance. Since they finally had the crisis under control, Andy could relax and take a deep breath. It was an excellent time to get back on the radio and contact the person who made the original call. The dispatcher replied that the complainant was on the phone but said no one had been to her house yet. She was still waiting outside for someone to respond. Andy's heart dropped, wondering, 'Then who the hell have we been chasing?' For an instant, he worried the suspect's claims of innocence might be true. AJ and Andy's eyes met as they tried to piece everything together. 'If he wasn't guilty, why did he run?' Andy thought.

While searching the suspect's pockets, AJ found several pieces of jewelry. The items were consistent with what a burglar would take, so they were confident this man must have burglarized the trailer if nothing else. Then he noticed a sizeable antique pocket watch engraved with David Anderson. Andy asked the dispatcher, "What's the complainant's name?"

"Susan Anderson," the dispatcher replied.

"Is she missing a pocket watch with the name David Anderson on it?" asked Andy.

The dispatcher returned after a short pause, "Yes, that was her father's!"

Andy breathed an enormous sigh of relief, looked at AJ, and said, "We got him."

"You ain't got shit motherfucker," the suspect yelled out.

AJ and Andy grabbed his arm, yanked him to his feet, and thanked the security staff for their help. "How do we get out of here?" asked Andy.

The security supervisor replied, "Right this way," and walked them to the front of the hospital building. Andy promised to come back and collect their names for his report but thought it was more important that they get out of there first.

AJ looked up at the name on the building and radioed the dispatcher, "Can you have a patrol unit meet us in front of St. Christopher hospital?"

"I have one en route," the dispatcher replied.

For the first time, they finally knew the name of the hospital. For some reason, it felt good to know where this calamity had occurred.

Looking themselves over to ensure they hadn't lost anything; Andy suddenly realized his pants were ripped from zipper to back beltloop. Bending over to get a better look, he could see his bright white underwear. He finally realized why his mother had often warned him, 'Always wear clean underwear. You never know when something could happen.' He recalled hearing a loud rip hurdling a short fence during the chase. He continued running, remembering having more freedom to move. Andy smiled, thinking about how the tear must have helped his stride and how the kitchen staff must have seen his underwear during the struggle on the floor.

A patrol car pulled in, and to Andy's surprise, it was Arnie Savage. Although it was ordinarily nice to see a familiar face, Arnie would not have been his choice. Andy was impressed with AJ, and he didn't want Arnie to do or say something that might embarrass him. As Arnie got out of the car, he noticed Andy's pants and said laughingly, "You ripped your pants, Andy."

"I can't believe you noticed," Andy replied sarcastically. Andy glanced over at AJ and grinned as they put the suspect between them in the back seat.

Andy gave Arnie directions to the trailer and mentioned the address was 6455 Sherwood Way. Arnie used to patrol the North Shepherd area and replied, "I know where that is." Andy was amazed, looking out the car window at how many backyards and streets they crossed during the chase. All of it went by in a flash, and although he didn't remember it being that far, there was no denying the distance driving toward the trailer.

Andy pointed to the right and blurted out, "turn here," as they approached the street.

"That's not Sherwood Way; that's Sherwood Drive," Arnie replied.

"What?" Andy asked.

Arnie replied, "I'll take you to Sherwood Way." He continued driving north for two more streets while Andy sat there with his mouth open, peering around at street signs. Sure enough, as they turned right, he saw the street sign read 'Sherwood Way.' Andy never paid attention to the second name on the street sign. Reality set in that he had never been on the right street. He was starting to feel stupid, but his saving grace was that he had his man.

As they pulled up to the correct address, the complainant came out of her house in a hurry, waving her hands in the air. She was visibly upset when Andy got out to talk to her. "Where have you guys been? I called almost an hour ago," she said.

Andy thought that he could defuse her anger by handing her stuff back, "I'm sorry, ma'am, but is this your stuff?"

"Yes," she said excitedly.

Andy reluctantly said, "I'm sorry, ma'am, but I will need those back to document for evidence. I promise you will get everything back as soon as I have the items accounted for in my report."

The complainant was a little worried, but she nodded her head in agreement. "So, is this the guy?" she asked as she walked to the back window of the patrol car.

"You tell me," Andy replied. AJ opened the rear door and pulled the handcuffed suspect out so she could have a good look. State law allowed a witness to identify a suspect immediately after the offense. As she stared at him, the suspect dropped his head because he couldn't stand to be paraded around like this.

"That's him," she exclaimed. Andy felt vindicated, but now he needed to recover the suspect's bag dropped during the chase. The other pressing question was, 'Who the hell owned that trailer home?'

Arnie brought the suspect down to central for booking while Andy and AJ finished their investigation. Upon recovering the pillowcase, they found several more stolen items. The trailer home was vacant, but some neighbors offered to secure the premise and notify the owners.

Eventually, they gathered everything they needed for the report, and Andy thanked AJ for his help. After everything they had experienced together over the last hour, they felt a special kinship. They agreed to stay in touch and would hopefully see each other in court.

Andy sat down in his patrol car, cranked the AC, and waited for a crime scene unit to take photos and prints. As he cooled off, he couldn't help but laugh about his first day off probation. Between ripped pants, the infamous chase, and a forgotten shotgun, it was a day he wouldn't soon forget. It was unbelievable that he drove to the wrong address but still managed to get the right guy. He couldn't help but think back to what Bubba had said, 'I'd rather be lucky than good!' He also made a promise to himself to always wear clean underwear.

When he finally got off work, he couldn't wait to tell the guys about the first day riding by himself. He could finally match one of Doug's chases, and John could use a good story. So, they sat around drinking beer, laughing at Andy's luck, and shared stories late into the night.

Andy called his Mom the following morning to tell her about his first day riding solo, but she had terrible news again about Mike. After many years of marriage, he and his wife were getting a divorce, and Mike needed to sell the gym to cover the expenses. 'What would he do now?' wondered Andy. Although Mike's plans of grandeur weren't working out, Dad always said that somehow Mike managed to come out of every shitty situation smelling like a rose. Andy said goodbye and hung up without telling her the story. It just wasn't the time.

Just His Luck

As Andy walked into the station for his afternoon shift, Sergeant Rain called him into his office, "Well, I hope you didn't like it too much around here because you're going to be reporting to the jail for six months." Andy's heart sank; he feared this might happen and just when he was starting to get the hang of the job.

Being assigned a six-month stint in jail was like getting drafted. They needed fresh bodies to fill the workstations from time to time because very few officers worked there full-time. The names of all officers coming off probation would be put in a hat, and if your name came up, you were going without recourse. The only consolation was you would be transferred back to your original division after six months.

"When do I start?" asked Andy.

"Tomorrow, 3 pm. You'll be working the 3 to 11 pm shift." Clearly, the topic was not up for negotiation; Sergeant Rain barely looked up to acknowledge Andy's reaction. "Good luck, and we'll see you in six months," Rain commented.

"Thanks, Sarg," Andy responded dejectedly as he turned to walk out into the hall. Even though he understood it was the luck of the draw, he still felt like someone had sucker-punched him. Andy's crime-fighting days were over for the next six months, which seemed like a lifetime. But, curiously, he wondered if the stories he heard about the jail were true. 'Guess I'm about to find out,' he thought.

He walked into roll-call and sat down beside Ray. "You look like you just saw a ghost," Ray commented.

"I did, the ghost of my crime-fighting career going out the window," Andy said.

"What are you talking about?" asked Ray.

"I'll be working at the jail starting tomorrow," Andy said with a sigh.

"Oh shit. That sucks," Ray said. He was almost as bummed as Andy. Their hopes of becoming regular partners would have to be put on hold for at least six months.

The shift was somewhat uneventful, and it seemed to drag on as Andy daydreamed about the twist in his life. As Ray tried to make small talk to pass the time, he had two things to ponder. What would the jail be like, and what was happening to Mike? He didn't share his concerns with Ray; he just tried to get through the shift and start this new job.

The following day, Andy called home and broke the news to Mom and Dad. His exciting career of policing in the Houston metroplex would be on hold. He thought there wouldn't be as many stories as the excitement of patrol. He would be wrong.

The First Day in Jail

Driving downtown for his first day in the hole had Andy filled with anxiety. Beginning with his first days at the Academy, he heard numerous tales about the escapades within those concrete walls. Then, his first time taking a prisoner to central, he witnessed a fight break out between a prisoner and two jail intake officers. Now, it was Andy's turn to find out what fighting for a living was like.

Entering the jail, Andy was greeted by a giant of a man named Sergeant Cook. While shaking hands, Andy was amazed when he noticed Cook's hands were twice his size. He couldn't help but wonder how many times his fists had been used to bring a prisoner to his knees. Cook was strictly business and a career jail guy, so he worked there full time. Andy couldn't understand why anyone would prefer working in the jail instead of patrolling the streets, but Cook wasn't alone. Several officers and supervisors were assigned to the jail full time. Andy saw them more as glorified security officers than real cops, and now he was one of them. Cook directed Andy to take his gun belt off, secure it behind the front counter, and report to the Lieutenant's office.

Lieutenant Lehia was a soft-spoken, intelligent man with impeccable English who didn't use southern slang. Although he was a rather large man, he wasn't intimidating. By the way, he carried and presented himself; you knew he was educated. Andy's initial impression was that he reminded him more of an English professor than a jail Lieutenant. Lehia invested time in getting to know all the officers who worked for him and inquired about Andy's background.

After exchanging small talk for a few minutes, Lehia got around to the real reason for the meeting. "I know what you have heard about the jail, but it's not true. We don't kick ass and take names down here. If you have that attitude, you will not last long."

Even though the speech seemed like something he recited to all the new guys, Andy nodded in agreement. Andy assumed this formality was their attempt to dial back young officers so that the Lieutenant could say, "I tried."

Then, Lehia said something that stuck, "Many of the wino's in the drunk tank are Vietnam veterans. They have been fighting all their lives and are still proud people. When they arrive here in a drunken state, they are combative. All of them have been wounded in the war in one way or another, and some even have metal plates in their heads. One good punch from a young man like you, and they're dead. You kill one of them, and you'll be brought up on charges like those HPD officers you've been reading about."

He was referring to the five Houston officers arrested and charged for brutalizing a prisoner in their custody. The body of prisoner Joe Campos Torres, a former Marine, was found floating in Buffalo Bayou. The idea of being accused of murder sent chills down Andy's spine.

Suddenly they heard a loud commotion. "FIGHT!" Lehia sprang to his feet and sprinted past Andy like a gifted athlete without saying a word. Witnessing him run out the door in a flash, Andy was startled by the quickness of such a large man. Although he was unsure of precisely what, Andy figured he should do something, so he got up and followed. Down the narrow corridor, a stack of blue uniforms on the concrete floor struggled with a prisoner at the bottom of the pile. The struggle was beginning to become violent. Someone from within the pile screamed, "LET

GO!" Fellow prisoners in the drunk tank were shouting encouragement to the inmate.

Now that they knew a fight was underway, Andy expected Lehia to slow down, but he continued full blast into the pile of humanity. Andy was impressed by how the Lieutenant engaged without hesitation. Lehia ran straight into the physical altercation and started pulling their arms and legs apart to get to the core of the melee. However, the prisoner was not giving up, and he continued cursing and kicking. When more jail officers hurried passed Andy to help, he felt like a spectator to a barroom brawl. Even though he wanted to jump in and help, he remembered the speech that Lehia had just given him moments ago. This situation only added to the confusion because Lehia had just said there would be no kicking ass, yet he was in the middle of an enormous ass-kicking contest.

The fight lasted about 30 seconds, and they had the suspect cuffed. Lehia stood up, brushed off his pants, and walked past Andy without saying a word while adjusting his hair back in place. The prisoner was ushered off to a single-holding cell, bleeding from a head wound and cursing as though he was still looking for a fight.

Andy quietly followed Lehia back to his office, still shocked. Lehia stood at his desk for a few seconds, gathering himself. Waiting for Lehia to address what they had just witnessed, Andy sat down without saying anything. Lehia stood there long enough to catch his breath, sat down, and started telling Andy about his assignment. He reviewed the daily expectations, but Andy was having difficulty focusing. His mind drifted back to Lehia telling him they don't fight in the jail, then, seconds later, he jumped into a massive brawl. Once Lehia finished his orientation, he asked if he had any questions.

"No, sir," Andy replied.

Lehia never mentioned the fight. Instead, he stood up, shook Andy's hand, and said, "Welcome aboard." Andy returned the smile and realized this would be an interesting six months.

Learning the Ropes

Sergeant Cook spotted Andy walking out of the Lieutenant's office and signaled him over. Cook's expressions rarely changed. He always appeared serious, he didn't particularly like anyone, and he was always pissed off. They walked back toward the location where the fight had erupted. The holding cell was referred to as the 'Drunk Tank' because most prisoners inside were inebriated. The large room could hold at least thirty men, and this was where police officers initially dropped off their prisoners before they were processed into the system.

The other prisoners mixed with the drunks were arrested for anything from trespassing to murder.

Bill Hooks and Donnie Parker were searching prisoners when Sergeant Cook introduced Andy and advised them to show him how to shake jakes. A term they used to describe searching prisoners after they were pulled out of the holding cell.

Donnie was a funny guy who enjoyed making people laugh by telling a good joke or doing something amusing. He was a short-timer and about to rotate back to patrol. He completed his six-month tour and was waiting for word on his last day. Hooks was a full-time jailer who had no intention of leaving. Bill was endowed with a good sense of humor, and he avoided confrontations with prisoners.

The day-to-day work in the jail was both monotonous and dangerous. The repetitious routine and constant exposure to dangerous inmates made it easy to become too comfortable with the threat. Their escape from the daily grind was the good-natured pranks played on one another. Typically, the inmates and trustees were the recipients of their shenanigans, but dangerous inmates were exempt.

The drunks fell for damn near anything. Sadly, most of them were full-time alcoholics, revolving in and out of the jail system. They served their time, only to be arrested for the same thing again. Sometimes they wouldn't even last twenty-four hours outside the jail walls. Their minds were fried from years of alcohol abuse, and they made the perfect stooges for a good joke.

One of Donnie's favorite pranks was bringing loaded cigarettes to work. Even though he didn't smoke, he would buy a pack. Then, before his shift, he would carefully load each cigarette so that once the drunk lit it and dragged on the cigarette a few times, it exploded. Wino's would incessantly ask for a cigarette, and Donnie would grin and gladly give them one. Then he stepped back and eagerly watched the drunk light it, take a drag or two, and POW! The wino would look at it with an astonished expression, and then, it was gone, with pieces of tobacco everywhere while Donnie rolled with laughter.

They exchanged small talk with Andy, getting to know him a little. While they chatted, they pulled prisoners out of the tank, one by one, and searched them. Everything was removed from their pockets, including belts, and the incoming property officer inventoried every item. Finally, the property was sealed and locked in a room until the prisoner's release.

The incoming officer was a career guy named Frank Desmuke, who had been working there for two years and didn't intend to leave. Frank loved messing with prisoners' minds, particularly the drunk ones. During the property inventory process, he would ask unnecessary questions that had nothing to do with their incarceration. Then, he would feed off their responses and instigate a confrontation to draw a reaction. Anytime he found a gullible prisoner, he would have some fun at their expense. For example, one night, a man who wasn't especially intelligent was there on a trespassing charge; Frank asked him who he killed.

"What?" asked the prisoner, confused.

Frank pointed at the paperwork and said, "It says that you are charged with murder right here." The prisoner immediately started panicking and denied he had killed anyone.

Frank would antagonize the prisoner for as long as he could until they had enough and began shouting obscenities like, "Fuck you man! I don't have to take this shit," or "I don't have to answer your stupid questions!"

Then, Frank diverted to his most frequent tag line, "Have you always known you are a homosexual?"

After that, shit always hit the fan. While the shakers dragged them off to the elevator, they would continue screaming, "I'm not gay!"

Frank merely grinned, held up the paper, and said, "Well, it says right here you are." Of course, the report said no such thing, but Frank didn't care. It was his way of amusing himself as he called for the next prisoner.

Andy was starting to catch on to the shaking routine, and more importantly, he was learning how to deal with being assigned to work at the jail. You could be angry for the duration of your shift, hating your job, or creatively think of ways to have fun and make the best of a thoroughly depressing place.

The jail was disgusting, smelled, and filled predominately with people of little redeeming value. Diseases were everywhere, and in those days, they weren't equipped with essential protective products like latex gloves. Alcoholics were covered in urine, vomit, and sometimes feces. There was no telling what diseases they had—a cold, the flu, Tuberculosis, Hepatitis, on and on. And now, a new threatening illness, HIV, which they had very little information about, scared the hell out of them.

Then you had your more apparent hazards of the job, such as the danger from prisoners. Many inmates knew that the seriousness of the crimes they committed would keep them incarcerated for the duration of their lives. Therefore, many of those individuals were particularly dangerous and would hurt you in a seconds chance. Plus, there was always a possibility the arresting officer missed a weapon, which is why they searched them again.

Shakers needed to persistently evaluate who they were dealing with. If a prisoner appeared dangerous, the shaker would check the paperwork to see their charged crime before opening the cage. For protection and security, there were always two shakers.

Anytime a fight broke out between prisoners in the drunk tank, the shakers were required to break it up. Moving through a mass of prisoners in tight quarters was especially treacherous. In that environment, anything could happen, but they had to do it.

Unfortunately, some jailers used their bravado attitudes, the threat of force, or actual physical force to deal with prisoners. If a prisoner refused to comply with a command, they responded by taking them to the ground, and the fight was on. This usually resulted in several other officers having to jump in and help. If supervision was constantly having to investigate you for excessive force complaints, you wouldn't last long working at the jail. That required paperwork and additional reports, so the officer was quickly transferred elsewhere.

Civilian employees were also employed at the jail, and they performed mundane functions such as administrative work and running the elevator. The permanent elevator operator, Jessie Garcia, took prisoners to their respective floors. The women's cells were located on the 6th floor of the building, and the men's cells were on the 5th. A jail cell was built into the elevator to prevent a prisoner from attacking the operator and taking control. Instead, the jailers placed the prisoners into the elevator holding cell, and it could only be opened from the operator's side. Then, Jessie escorted the prisoner to where they needed to go. Male and female prisoners were never transported together.

Jessie was an older gentleman and well-liked by all. He frequently made it known to the female prisoners that he was not married. Rumor had it that Jessie hit on the prostitutes who revolved in and out of jail.

Andy was learning the work and how to cope with working there. There would be many more lessons ahead, especially dealing with people. He had a choice; Andy could make prisoners comply by force or use his wits and talk them into compliance. The result was usually the same, but Andy preferred the path of least resistance.

EIGHT

John Goes to Jail

John was now fully recovered and had returned to patrol, but he was having difficulty adjusting to his position again. Every time he pulled someone over for a traffic violation, he had butterflies in the pit of his stomach. Even riding with a partner, he was nervous as a cat whenever they were outside their patrol car. He couldn't wait for the stop to be over. So, when John's name came up for a transfer to the jail, he welcomed the change.

Andy was delighted when he found out that John would soon be joining him at the jail. Adding to the excitement, they were assigned the same shift and days off. In preparation for the new position, Andy began instructing John on the do's and don'ts and what goes on at the jail. Of course, everything was a little different away from the free world.

On John's first day, he sat through Lehia's orientation speech, and Cook walked him down to start learning the ropes. Andy and Billy McDonald were shaking that day, with Bill Hooks working as the incoming property officer. When Andy spotted John walking toward him, he started smiling ear to ear. John returned the smile as Cook began introducing them. Mid introduction, Andy interrupted, "Wait a minute Sarg. I heard this guy is a homosexual."

Cook stopped and looked at John, unsure of what to say.

"Don't listen to that fag Sarg. He's just jealous," replied John.

Realization set in for Cook that he was the butt of the joke, "Awe shit, you know what to do," and walked away shaking his head.

"Just stand there bitch and watch a couple of professionals work," Andy told John, pointing toward the wall. John tried to keep a straight face, but he knew Andy was fucking with him. They often called each other a bitch, but they considered it a term of endearment in jest.

Billy introduced himself to John and pointed at the incoming property window, "That's Bill Hooks. He's fucking crazy."

Bill smiled and waved with an arrow going through his head. One of those trick arrow headbands that made it look like an arrow pierced your skull. "Sorry, John, but I've got a splitting headache today," Hooks said as they all chuckled.

McDonald was a take no shit kind of jailer. Endowed with a serious demeanor, he blew up like a pit bull if an inmate gave him a reason. Although he wasn't a big guy, he acted like King Kong. John intently watched Andy and Billy search prisoners while Hooks inventoried their property. Lastly, a photo was taken of the prisoner, and they were ushered off to the holding area to wait for the elevator ride upstairs.

The next prisoner out of the holding tank was a real winner. He was completely covered in tattoos from head to toe and pierced everywhere. The man had numerous piercings in both ears and more in his nose, eyebrows, lips, tongue, and even nipples. In amazement, McDonald stepped back and reviewed the prisoner's paperwork.

"What the fuck are you in here for?" Billy barked at the prisoner. The prisoner was in his early twenties with a slight build. He wasn't threatened, appeared calm, and avoided eye contact. "Just where else are you pierced, son?" Billy asked the prisoner.

Hooks was grinning from ear to ear because he knew this would be good.

"Excuse me?" the prisoner timidly asked, unsure precisely what Billy was asking.

"What the fuck is up with all of these metal spikes coming out of your body?" Billy asked.

"I don't know," the prisoner responded squeamishly.

"I asked you where else you're pierced, BOY!" Billy demanded.

There was a short pause as if the prisoner wasn't sure what to say. Then he said in a low voice, "Well, my penis and testicles."

"YOUR WHAT?" Billy shouted at him as he continued, "Something ain't right with you, boy! What the fuck is your problem?"

The prisoner paused for a moment and then replied in a low voice, "Well, I guess...I guess I'm just into pain."

Billy stood back and thought about the situation, then leaned forward and whispered into the prisoner's ear. "Well, you fuck up while you're here, boy, and I will make you cum. Now get over there and sit down."

The prisoner did exactly what Billy said as Andy shook his head in bewilderment and glanced at John. John was grinning and looking around to see who else heard. Andy then clapped his hands and said in a condescending tone, "Bravo, Billy! You really know how to handle those types."

Defiantly, Billy responded, "Well, that shit just ain't right! What the fuck is this world coming to?" he asked rhetorically as he opened the cage to call out for the next prisoner.

Female prisoners were in a separate holding area and searched by female officers in a private room. Occasionally, a transgender woman came through, and it wasn't always apparent that they were changing their gender. Often, the trans person didn't disclose they were transitioning in hopes that they would be kept with their gender identity. During their search, the female officers were required to have the female inmate bend over and spread her butt cheeks to check for a penis, but occasionally one made it through.

Kasey Burroughs was a brute of a woman and an officer on the 6th floor. She spoke with a strong southern drawl, her appearance looked like a bulldyke, but if she was gay, she never let on that she was. On the contrary, she often joked and flirted with the guys in the basement, insinuating she wanted to hook up. She would tell the crudest joke of any man, and she just wanted to be one of the guys. Rumor had it that she was a widower with a couple of grown kids, although she never talked about them. On the northeast side of town, Kasey owned a small ranch where she raised cattle and horses. She would even dip tobacco while she hung out with the guys in the basement on break from time to time.

Andy respected her bravado and how she ran the women's floor with an iron fist. In a heartbeat, she would stick up for a female prisoner when justified and, just as quickly, slap one down if they got out of line. Even the supervisors treated her with kid gloves because of her personality and running such a tight ship. They rarely had to supervise her or anyone on the 6th floor, which meant less paperwork. When she spoke to him, Andy was courteous, responding, "yes ma'am" and "no ma'am," and stayed out of her way.

A few weeks earlier, a trans woman came in on a prostitution charge. She failed to disclose she had not completed gender reassignment surgery yet because she wanted to remain on the women's floor. The departmental policy indicated that if a prisoner had a penis, they were a man and would be housed with the male inmates. The trans woman was about six feet tall, which should have been a clue, but she was pretty attractive, donning a large pair of fake breasts. Everyone noticed her walking through processing wearing a very revealing tight dress.

When it was time to be searched, the female jailer brought the trans woman into a private room for a one-on-one frisk. The jailer patted her down, and asked her to pull up her dress and drop her panties. After she complied, the female jailer shined a flashlight between her legs. With nothing hanging down and no indication of stored contraband, she told the prisoner to get dressed. Then the jailer advised, "Take a seat on the women's bench and wait for the elevator." Unfortunately, the jailer didn't spot the trans woman's taped penis between her butt cheeks. The jailer should have had her turn around and conduct the same procedure, but complacency let it slide.

The catcalls immediately started from the drunk tank once the trans woman walked out and sat down to wait for the elevator. After Jessie motioned for her to get in, she walked provocatively toward the elevator, and the jeers roared; she was thriving on the attention glancing back and smiling as the door closed.

Once she arrived on the 6th floor, Kasey directed the trans woman to a cell where another prisoner was fast asleep in her bunk. She sat on the other bunk and started taking off her shoes, then stood up to take a piss and removed the tape holding up the penis.

The female cellmate woke up to a penis urinating in her cell and immediately began screaming bloody murder, "HE'S A MAN! HE'S A MAN!"

This immediately drew a response from Kasey, and she stormed down to see what the commotion was. Then, she opened the cell door while the transgender woman tried to quiet her cellmate.

"He's a man," the cellmate shrieked, and once Kasey caught a glimpse of the penis, that was all it took.

Kasey grabbed the trans woman by the hair and dragged her from the cell toward the elevator. "Police brutality," the trans person screamed.

But Kasey didn't care and continued pulling her at a fast clip. Finally, she rolled over and got to her feet once they reached the elevator. Unfortunately, that was a mistake, Kasey punched her in the face, and she fell. Blood splattered from the trans woman's nose as she screamed, "You hit me!"

Kasey yelled back, "Yeah bitch, and I'll hit you again if you get up!" She rang for the elevator as she prepared for a response, but the trans woman thought it best to stay down and applied pressure to the bloody nose.

Once the elevator doors opened, Kasey grabbed the trans woman's hair again and drug her into the elevator. "Take us down to the basement!" she ordered Jessie. Jessie didn't say a word; he closed the doors and looked straight ahead. The transgender woman didn't struggle and just lay there holding her hair while Kasey refused to release her grip.

Andy was searching a prisoner and glanced up to see the elevator door open and Kasey dragging the trans woman out by her hair. She released her grip and pointed in Andy's direction, yelling, "DON'T EVER SEND A MAN UP TO MY FLOOR!" Then, she stepped back inside and demanded, "Take me back up," and the elevator door closed.

They helped the transgender woman up and escorted her to the male side of the hallway to wait for the elevator ride to the 5th floor. Segregated from the general population, they placed her in a single cell typically reserved for special prisoners, including law enforcement and celebrities. Andy never heard another word about the incident. He thought that if any of the other jailers had acted in such a way, there would be an investigation, but not Kasey. That was Andy's only brush with her fury, but he never forgot it.

Later that night, John and Andy sat in their living room telling Doug the stories about their day in the jail. Doug loved to listen but rarely contributed with his own, partly because he knew it would make them miss patrol.

The following day, Andy called home to check on Mom and Dad, but he only continued to hear about Mike, and everything was even more alarming than before. He was regularly traveling to Mexico on business. But, of course, Andy didn't ask what kind of business, and he didn't want to know. Andy didn't care to hear about whatever trouble Mike was mixed up in now. He decided that it was best that he not know. Instead, he chose to remember the admirable qualities about the big brother he always looked up to and hoped that he wasn't involved in more than he could get out of this time.

Roscoe's Big Adventure

Jail trustees were Municipal prisoners who were allowed to work off their fines by performing chores such as emptying trash or mopping floors. They provided the Police Department a free labor workforce for menial tasks on all three 8-hour shifts. In their downtime, trustees could work for tips shining officers' shoes or washing cars. In a two-week sentence, an ambitious trustee could make up to $100 cash. Upon their release, they would hit the street to buy a bottle of the cheapest wine they could find.

With money in their pocket, they walked to the east side of downtown and bought wine for all their friends. Once they were passed out in an alley, their good buddies would rummage through their pockets for any leftover cash. Eventually, a police unit or Patty Wagon would pick them up for public intoxication. They would end up back in jail until they slept it off.

Once they were sober, they would be brought in front of a municipal judge, where they would plead guilty, and the judge would fine them up to $200. Since they had no money to pay the fine, they would work it off as a trustee at the rate of $8 a day. This vicious cycle repeated itself over and over, but in an odd way, it kept these alcoholics alive. If not for the two weeks where they could dry out, and get regular meals and medical care, they would be dead in a relatively short period of time.

Jailers interacted with trustees their entire shift and got to know them well. Andy was especially fond of a tall, lanky wino named Roscoe Murphy. He was from Tennessee, and Andy learned that he had moved to Houston as a young man. He was now in his mid-40s, but he looked much older. He had been a drunk for several years and lost his wife and family to alcoholism. His life consisted of the same vicious cycle, so his only address was the trustee dorm across the street from the main police station. He received three square meals and a shower plus any toiletries he needed to stay somewhat groomed.

One day, in casual conversation, Andy learned that Roscoe had never seen the ocean. Andy was struck by that as he realized what a limited life Roscoe had led. Andy felt sorry for him because he seemed hopelessly caught up in this disease of addiction with no way out. Roscoe didn't seem to mind, though. He seemed very content with his life, or at least it appeared so. Andy got an idea to include Roscoe on a fishing trip to Galveston that he, John, and Bill Hooks had been talking about. He thought that it would be cool to take Roscoe with them and show him the ocean, but how?

Later that shift, Andy, Bill, and John drove over to a nearby restaurant on their lunch break. Andy started talking about the fishing trip and asked, "Why don't we go next Tuesday? We are all off that day."

Bill responded, "That works for me. I'll even drive!"

Andy then posed the question, "Hey, why don't we take Roscoe with us?"

"What? Are you crazy?" Bill responded.

Andy explained how Roscoe had never seen the ocean and how cool it would be to see his reaction to the surf. John then asked, "What the fuck are you talking about, Andy? He's a trustee! We can't take him anywhere!"

Andy responded, "Why not?"

Bill just listened as Andy and John continued to argue. "Because HE's A FUCKING TRUSTEE!" John shouted back at Andy.

Andy kept explaining his plan and how he could check him out of the trustee dorm for the day. "How the hell are you going to check him out?" John asked while making quotation mark gestures with his fingers, "He's working off a sentence imposed by a Judge! DON'T YOU NOT GET THAT?"

Andy explained how Frank Desmuke was supervising the trustee dorm next week. "Frank won't care. We'll have Roscoe back before his shift is over, and no one will be the wiser!"

Bill commented, "That won't give us much time to fish. It's an hour's drive to the surf."

Andy replied, "That's OK. We won't want to be in that sun any longer than that anyway."

John looked at Bill and asked, "Are you really considering this?"

Bill replied, "Well, it would be cool to see his expression. I mean, Roscoe is a good guy."

John couldn't believe it as Andy pleaded with him, "Come on! This is gonna be fun!" John looked back at Bill but said nothing. Andy could tell that they were starting to buy into the notion, so he added, "Look, if Desmuke won't go along, all bets are off." Bill nodded his head in agreement, but John said nothing as they finished their meal. Once they got back to the jail, Andy couldn't wait to tell Roscoe. He spotted him emptying cans and shouted, "Roscoe!"

"Yes, sir, officer Andy?" Roscoe asked.

Andy walked to him and asked in a low voice, "How would you like to go and see the ocean?"

Roscoe leaned backward and responded with a puzzled look on his face, "No, officer Andy, I ain't going to the ocean."

Andy explained their plan, but Roscoe still looked puzzled and just turned and walked away. It was as if he was somewhat scared to even answer that question. Andy called him back and explained, "Look, it's OK. It's just for the morning."

Roscoe looked astonished and confused at the same time as he said, "OK, officer Andy. OK." Roscoe started emptying trash cans again as if nothing was said. Andy knew that he would have to stay on Roscoe to make sure he would remember. Roscoe's short-term memory was diminished from alcoholism, so it would take a day-to-day reminder from now until Tuesday.

Andy walked over to the trustee dorm the next day and bounced the idea off Frank Desmuke. Frank thought they were crazy, but if they had him back in the dorm before 3 pm, he didn't care. "I ain't taking no heat for you boys. Especially not for a wino!" Desmuke told Andy.

Andy assured Desmuke that he would be back in time and walked away with a grin of satisfaction. Desmuke went back to his desk work, shaking his head and chuckling to himself.

Tuesday came before they knew it, and Bill picked up John and Andy at the central police parking lot early that morning. It was about 6:30 am, so it was still dark as they loaded a couple of ice chests and their fishing gear in the bed of Bill's pickup and jumped in the cab. Bill's truck was a two-door cab with only one bench seat, so Andy slid in the middle, and John was riding shotgun. "Drive around back to the dorm," Andy said excitedly.

"Are you sure you want to go through with this?" Bill asked.

"Yes, he should be there waiting on us! It's all set," Andy replied. Bill just shook his head as if he wasn't sure about this idea. As they turned toward the trustee dorm, Andy could hardly believe his eyes. Roscoe was sitting on the curb, dressed in blue jeans, tennis shoes, and a white t-shirt. He even had a brown paper sack lunch packed. Andy grinned from ear to ear and pointed as he exclaimed, "There he is!" Bill pulled up next to the curb and let Andy out. "You ready, Roscoe?" Andy asked.

"Yes, sir, officer Andy," Roscoe replied with a toothless grin.

It was the first time Andy ever saw Roscoe smile, and he was struck by it. He knew he was doing a good thing, even if it was technically wrong. Andy looked in the window of the trustee dorm and saw Desmuke standing there, looking back. Andy gave him a thumbs up sign, and Frank smiled and shook his head.

"You're in the back, Roscoe," Bill said.

"Yes, sir, officer Bill," Roscoe replied as he crawled up in the bed of the pickup and sat down with his back against the cab. Roscoe seemed right at home amongst the ice chests and fishing gear as they pulled away. They entered the freeway ramp on I45 South, and Andy opened the sliding back window of the cab, asking Roscoe, "You OK back there?"

"Yes, sir!" Roscoe shouted as he gazed over the city skyline with amazement.

The outbound traffic was light that morning, so they got to the beachfront in less than an hour. They stopped at a part of the beach south of town, with only a few tourists and a handful of fishers wading in the surf. Bill backed his truck as close to the water as he dared so that they could use the tailgate to rest their gear on. Andy couldn't help but notice the look of amazement on Roscoe's face as he stared toward the surf. Andy nudged Bill and John and asked Roscoe, "What do ya think?"

"How far out there does that water go?" Roscoe asked.

"All the way to Europe I guess," Andy answered.

"Man, oh man!" was all Roscoe could say.

They finished setting up their spot with lawn chairs and ice chests. Andy had brought a bottle of Boone's Farm Strawberry Hill wine for Roscoe. John saw the bottle and asked, "Do you think that's a good idea?"

Andy replied, "Well, I couldn't have him just watch us drink beer and not have anything for him."

John shook his head in disagreement while Andy watched Roscoe at the surf's edge. Andy called for Roscoe to come back. "Yes, sir, officer Andy?" Andy pointed at the bottle of wine and said with a stern voice, "Roscoe, you cannot get drunk today! I brought you a bottle of wine, but we are going to ration it, so you must ask every time you want a sip.

OK?" Roscoe nodded his head and replied, "Yes, sir, officer Andy. Can I have one now?"

"Not yet," Andy replied.

Roscoe said, "OK," as he turned to run back to the water.

"I still think that is a mistake," John commented. Andy didn't reply.

They waded out in the surf and cast their fishing lines past the breakers. Roscoe followed closely as he struggled to stay upright from the waves rolling in. He had lost a lot of his balance and coordination from years of alcohol abuse. Yet, everyone couldn't help but be entertained by a grown man playing in the surf like a kid.

Roscoe watched in amazement as Bill caught the first fish and threw it in the ice chest. Andy opened a beer and sat back to enjoy the Texas sun, so John and Bill joined him. They were becoming comfortable with how things were going, so when Roscoe walked up with a sheepish grin and asked Andy if he could have a sip of wine, he said, "Sure!" Andy opened the bottle, and Roscoe quickly drank down several large gulps. "Woah, big fella!" Andy shouted as he stood up to grab the bottle back from Roscoe. "It's gonna be a long day. You have to pace yourself." Roscoe smiled and wiped his lips. He had a grin as Andy had never seen before. Andy thought that even with all the risk, it was worth it to see Roscoe having the time of his life.

Hours passed, and Roscoe kept coming back for another sip of wine, but each time it was nothing like a sip. Andy would scold him about drinking too much, but Roscoe would just smile and say, "Yes, sir, officer Andy." Andy looked at the bottle, and it was about two-thirds empty. He knew he had to cut Roscoe back, but it was too late. Roscoe was losing his balance and starting to slur his speech. He was getting loud and obnoxious, just like the drunks that came into the drunk tank. The alcohol had a maximum effect because of Roscoe's damaged liver. He had only consumed enough for a normal person to be a little tipsy, but Roscoe was getting worse by the minute. He was singing loudly and dancing around like a drunk teenager.

People on the beach were starting to notice, and it was about time to leave, so they decided to break camp and head back before Roscoe did something stupid. They loaded up the truck, and Andy told Roscoe to stay out of the water and dry off. Roscoe started cursing and becoming belligerent, just like he did when he got arrested. His whole demeanor changed in just 30 minutes, and the situation was quickly going south for them.

All John could say was, "I told you, goddammit!" as they loaded the truck. Andy yelled at Roscoe to get a grip, but it had no effect. Roscoe didn't want to leave, and he physically struggled with Andy and Bill trying to get him in the pickup's bed. John shook his head as he watched the shit show. Everyone around them was watching as well, and they were starting to draw a crowd.

Andy threatened to whip Roscoe's ass if he didn't sit down in the bed and shut up. Totally disgusted, Andy grabbed what was left of the wine bottle and put it in the pickup cab. Driving away from the beach, Roscoe was singing his heart out while people on the beach watched them drive away. John asked, "Now what? We can't take him back to the trustee dorm like this!"

Andy replied, "He's got an hour to sober up. Maybe we should make him eat something."

Bill drove toward I-45 with a worried look on his face. It was already about 1:30 pm, and they didn't have any time to lose if they were going to make it back before Desmuke's shift ended. Andy turned around to check on Roscoe, and he saw him chugging beer out of the ice chest. "PULL OVER!" Andy yelled. The truck rolled to a stop on the side of the road, but by that time, Roscoe had finished that beer and started on another one. Andy jumped out and yelled at Roscoe, "Give me that, you son-of-a-bitch," as he reached out for the beer Roscoe was drinking. Roscoe looked surprised that Andy was so pissed off.

"What?" Roscoe asked.

Andy jumped up in the truck's bed and grabbed the remaining beers out of the ice chest. He put them in the cab and got inside. Opening the rear window, he yelled back at Roscoe, "Shut the fuck up, Roscoe! Do you hear me?" Roscoe just waved him off as if he was carefree. John was furious as they pulled back onto the freeway. He wouldn't look at Andy or say a word. Bill was more concerned than mad as he sped northbound on I-45 toward Houston.

Roscoe was now pointing and yelling at the other cars in the northbound lanes. He was getting a lot of looks from people in the cars on either side of them, and then Bill looked in the rear-view mirror and said, "Oh shit!" It was a Texas DPS

Trooper pulling them over. He looked down, and he was doing every bit of 80 in a 55-mph zone. "That's just great!" Bill exclaimed.

Andy opened the sliding window and yelled, "ROSCOE! YOU SHUT THE FUCK UP, OR WE'RE ALL GOING TO JAIL! YOU HERE ME?"

Roscoe replied, "Whatever. I live in the jail!" Andy slammed the rear window shut as he couldn't believe their luck.

Bill pulled off the freeway, mumbling, "I knew it. I knew it. I just fucking knew it." Andy struggled to get the beer cans and wine bottle under the seat and out of view as the Trooper walked up to Bill's truck.

He passed Roscoe sitting in the bed as Roscoe politely said, "Howdy!" and gave him a half-hearted salute. The Trooper could instantly see that Roscoe was plastered as he asked for Bill's driver's license.

"Afternoon, sir!" Bill replied as he handed his license to the Trooper.

"Do you know why I stopped you?" the Trooper asked.

"Was I speeding?" asked Bill in a squeamishly.

"80 in a 55," the Trooper responded as Bill could hear Roscoe singing in the background. "What's his deal?" the Trooper asked.

"Well, sir, we are all Houston Police officers and...."

The Trooper interrupted, "HE'S A HOUSTON POLICE OFFICER?"

"No, sir, he's a trustee from our jail, and we were just taking him down to the gulf for a little getaway. Kind of a good behavior reward."

"Say what?" the Trooper asked.

Bill thought he did not put that well and probably gave more information than he should have. "Well, he's not a trustee right now, but that's how we know him. He had a little too much fun on the beach, so we are taking him back home to sleep it off."

The Trooper looked at Bill and then at John and Andy. "Do you boys have IDs?" the Trooper asked.

"Yes, sir," they all answered in unison as they hurried to get their IDs.

Bill handed all three Police IDs to the Trooper, and he backed away from the cab and asked Roscoe, "Do you have any ID?" John cringed as he wondered what Roscoe was going to say next.

"No, sir," Roscoe answered. "I lost mine, but my name is Roscoe Murphy, and I am from Tennessee. These officers showed me a great time today, and I really appreciate it." Roscoe's comments were slurred a bit, but he got the message out just fine. John could not believe his ears as Roscoe sounded rational.

The Trooper stood there for a second as if he was thinking the situation over. He then gave Bill the IDs back and said, "You boys need to slow down and get Roscoe home. You hear now?"

"Yes, sir," Bill answered as he started the pickup. "Be safe out there," Bill said as he started driving away. The Trooper turned and walked back to his police car, shaking his head. Roscoe gave a hearty thumbs up to the Trooper as they drove off. Bill looked at his wristwatch and thought if they hurried, they had just enough time to get Roscoe back before 3 pm. A few miles down the road, Bill looked ahead and saw nothing but taillights. There was a monster traffic jam, and no one was going anywhere fast. "Now what?" Bill asked.

"Don't ask me," John replied. "Ask Mr. Genius over here," as he pointed at Andy. Andy didn't reply because he figured he deserved that. He realized this was a bad idea, and things were only getting worse. They slowly crept through traffic, bumper to bumper, and Roscoe kept singing and pointing at cars in other lanes. The truck finally exited the freeway and entered downtown at 4 pm. They didn't know who the evening shift trustee dorm officer was, so they couldn't take a chance and go there with Roscoe. Andy said, "Let's just take him where he always goes to get drunk."

John asked, "How will he get back to the dorm?"

Andy responded, "A unit will pick him up in no time. They'll just think that he just got drunk and wandered off. It's not the first time that's happened." That was the only idea they had, so Bill turned toward Commerce Street, where all the winos hung out.

Bill pulled up to the corner of Leland and Jackson Street and told Roscoe to get out. Roscoe had passed out in the pickup bed and didn't budge. Andy motioned for John to let him out, and he jumped up in the bed of the pickup and started shaking Roscoe. He eventually started coming to and looking around, and Andy helped him out of the pickup. They watched Roscoe as he staggered off toward several winos that were sitting under a tree.

Roscoe was home now, but it was not as Andy had imagined. This day had turned into a nightmare, and Andy felt stupid and disappointed at the same time. No one said a thing as they drove to the Central Police parking lot and stopped at Andy's car. Bill said, "Keep your fingers crossed! See you tomorrow." Andy nodded as Bill drove away. John was still fuming and didn't say a word the entire way home. Andy was still beating himself up inside, so he appreciated the silence.

The next day the three of them showed up for work as usual. Andy was as nervous as a cat when he walked in to get his assignment. He wondered what had happened to Roscoe and if anyone was the wiser. They soon learned that Roscoe had missed his bed check and was counted as an escapee. A patrol car brought him in for public intoxication, and he was charged with leaving a correctional facility. That meant that he couldn't be a trustee until he served his time for the escape. He was sentenced to 30 days and transferred to the City Prison farm. P-farm was a long-term facility that housed municipal prisoners not eligible for trustee status. Andy knew the arresting officer and spotted him dropping off another prisoner. Andy flagged him down and asked, "Hey Mike, did you pick up Roscoe yesterday?"

"Yeah, he was staggering around on Leland Street, drunk as a skunk." The officer replied.

Andy asked, "I heard he escaped from the trustee dorm?"

"I guess. He kept mumbling something about going to the beach. I told him there was no beach anywhere near here. I don't know where he got the booze from, but you know these drunks, where there's a will, there's a way."

Andy smiled and said, "Good point," as he waved and walked away.

Desmuke wouldn't even talk to Andy, Bill, or John for at least a week. He hadn't got in trouble for Roscoe not making bed check, but it never looked good when a trustee walked off. Andy was worried that if push came to shove, Desmuke would crack and tell what really happened, but he never did. The entire incident was forgotten in a day or two.

Roscoe served his 30 days at the P-farm and got out, only to be arrested the next day for public intoxication. He was now eligible to be a trustee again, and when Andy spotted Roscoe mopping floors, he asked how he'd been doing. "Just fine, officer," Roscoe replied. He had forgotten Andy's name.

"How did you like the beach trip?" Andy asked.

Roscoe stopped mopping and looked up at Andy with a puzzled expression and asked, "What
beach trip, officer?"

Andy paused as he looked at Roscoe for a few seconds. He was shocked that Roscoe had no memory of the trip. "Nothing Roscoe. Never mind." Andy replied as he turned and walked away.

Andy was disappointed and relieved all at the same time. He had learned a valuable lesson about human nature and the disease of addiction. He had come to learn that some people just cannot be helped and that he had risked far too much to try that again. He had dragged John and Bill into this, and it could have been disastrous for them as well. His skin was getting thicker all the time with the lessons of life. He needed to stick to the path of least resistance, and life would be much easier.

Life on the 5th floor

Most of the complaints generated in the jail originated from the men's 5th floor. Three officers were on duty at a time, without supervisors because of the limited workforce. Most of the time, things ran smoothly, however, the lack of supervision occasionally facilitated the officer's mishandling of unruly prisoners.

One of the officers assigned to the men's floor on the evening shift was Arnold Stagger. He was a tall man with a lean figure and rugged features. He was quiet and didn't engage with prisoners if he didn't have to, but his temper quickly rose when one was disobedient. Typically, Arnold waltzed into work 10 minutes late and promptly sat behind the desk in the main hallway with his feet propped up. The area was his lounge with whichever newspaper or magazine in hand that he brought from home. From that desk, he could see all prisoners exiting the elevator, and he yelled and directed the inmate toward a jail cell while one of the other jailers remotely opened the cell door. Arnold preferred to keep his interaction with the prisoners to a minimum.

Andy rarely had to work the 5th floor, but occasionally he drew the short straw and was stuck there for a shift. Today was one of those days, so as the elevator opened, he stepped in and said in a low voice, "5th floor, Jessie. Wish me luck."

Jessie smiled, "Working with Arnold?"

"Yeah, I guess so."

"You'll need all the luck you can get," Jessie said with a chuckle.

The remaining officer working the 5th floor was an old head, HD Newsome. No one knew what HD stood for, but the standing joke was Heavy Duty, so that's what everyone called him. Without the uniform, he looked more like a trustee than an officer, in his late 50s, with long, grey hair that was greasy and rarely combed and about a two-day growth of whiskers. A cigarette was always dangling from his mouth, and he smoked them down to the filter. Sometimes the cigarette would have at least an inch of ashes hanging on the end because HD couldn't be bothered to flick them off. So instead, he let the ashes fall, and sometimes they landed on his uniform. As a result, small burn holes littered the front of his shirt, and when he smiled, which was infrequently, he was missing several teeth. He was a likable guy with a quiet and easy disposition if you could overlook his appearance. For most of his 30-years, HD worked on the 5th floor and was happy to be there for the remainder of his career.

Immediately when the elevator doors opened, Andy smelled the stench of HD's cigarettes, and a grey haze lingered in the air. He stepped out and Jessie chuckled while closing the doors. HD stood at the end of the hallway, reviewing the roster of prisoners. He intently read each name on the roster every shift, but no one knew why. The rumor was HD disowned his son because of a life of crime, and he assumed one day, he'd show up in jail.

"Hey, HD!" Andy yelled out in a cheerful voice.

As he glanced up, his eyes were squinting from the rising cigarette smoke, and he mumbled, "Hey." He resumed reading, and the long stream of ashes from his cigarette fell onto the roster. "Seen Arnold?" HD asked, brushing the ashes off before they burned a hole in the paper.

"Not yet" replied Andy, "but it's only 3 o'clock; he still has 10 minutes."

"Hmmm," HD grumbled. Although he disapproved of Arnold always arriving late, he wasn't one to rock the boat. Once he finished reading the list, he walked toward cellblock C to conduct a wellness check. The first responsibility of a cell block officer is to complete a headcount to ensure all prisoners are alive and accounted for. With only bars across the front of the cells, it was easy to peer inside while walking down the cellblock corridor.

Since Arnold always took cellblock B, Andy started working A. He was only a short distance into his wellness checks when he noticed a prisoner standing in his cell, completely naked, with something smeared all over his body. Pieces of food from his last meal covered the floor, and the cell was in disarray. Andy stopped and carefully observed the prisoner while the man continued to stand uncannily still, barely blinking. Unnerved by the prisoner's lack of response to his presence, Andy asked, "Hey man, are you OK?" The man remained silent and never met Andy's eyes to acknowledge he knew he was there. "What's your name?" Andy asked, with no response. "HD," Andy yelled out, "Come take a look at this one!"

"On my way," HD responded.

"What are you in here for?" Once again, the prisoner didn't answer.

HD walked up with the roster and said, "It says here, Mr. James Dawson. He's in here on hold for homicide."

"Why do you have food all over you, and why are you naked?" Andy asked inquisitively.

Finally, a question compelling enough to elicit a response from Dawson, he looked at Andy and spoke in a low, monotone voice, "Well, I thought that I could slide between the bars if I got slippery enough."

Andy asked HD, "What do we do now?'

HD lit another cigarette and mumbled, "Well, he ain't a wizard, is he?"

When Arnold finally walked in for his shift, he noticed them down cellblock A, so he yelled out, "What's going on?"

"We got a live one here," HD responded. "Open up cell door number four. We need to move this one to the padded cell."

Who knows why they call it a padded cell because it was anything but padded. Instead, it was a tiny, 4' X 4' cell that stood 8 feet tall and was constructed with concrete walls and a solid steel door. A recessed light was in the ceiling, and a drain hole was in the floor. Once inside, there was no way for a prisoner to hurt themself short of beating their body against the walls, which sometimes happened.

"If we're gonna have to fight this motherfucker, I'm taking my watch and rings off," Arnold said. "I've already had to replace one watch, and I ain't gonna buy another one."

"Should we call a supervisor?" Andy asked.

"Fuck no!" Arnold replied, "We'd have them up here every 5 minutes if we called them for something like this."

Andy nodded as they headed back toward the desk and started taking off their watches, badges, name tags, and anything that could be ripped off. HD removed the cigarette from his mouth, and he set the filter on the edge of the desk while the burning end hung off.

Arnold said, "OK, I'll open the door from the control panel and call him out. Once he exits the cell, we'll walk him back to the desk and cuff him here. Once he is contained in the padded cell, we can take the cuffs off. If shit hits the fan, let's get him to the ground and control him."

HD and Andy nodded in agreement, and Arnold pulled the lever and opened the cell. The door slid open, and Arnold yelled, "Prisoner in cell number 4, step out." In eager anticipation, they stood waiting for a few seconds, then the prisoner bolted out the cell door and started running away from them at a full sprint. At the end of the long corridor were more bars, and with every cell door closed, there was nowhere to run.

Still running at full force, the prisoner ran directly into the bars at the end of the hallway. And he did not attempt to slow down or protect himself before impact. His face hit first and recoiled off the bars, landing on the concrete floor, moaning and writhing in pain. Blood was streaming from his face as he lay there semi-consciously.

Arnold and HD glanced at each other unable to believe what they had just witnessed and hurried down the hall to the prisoner. For a moment, they stood over him, trying to grasp the extent of his injuries and determine how to proceed, when they suddenly heard an authoritative voice, "ARNOLD!!" Sergeant Cook was standing at the end of the hallway with disapproval, as though he had just caught his kids doing something wrong. "What the fuck is going on?" Cook demanded, marching toward them.

Nervously, Andy immediately began explaining what had occurred. Throughout the entire recall of events, Cook stood with his arms folded across his chest, glaring.

As Andy was finishing up, a prisoner yelled out from a cell over Cook's shoulder, "That's right, Sarg! That crazy motherfucker ran right into those bars. It was like he didn't even see them!"

Cook turned around to glance at the prisoner who offered his account and then looked back. He stood there for a few seconds looking at each of them and then looked down at the naked moaning prisoner. Cook ordered, "Get that crazy fucker into the padded cell! I'll have the jail doctor look at him." Cook turned and walked away, shaking his head and instructing, "I want a letter from all three of you...AND GET THE NAME OF THAT WITNESS!"

They grabbed the arms of the bloody prisoner and started dragging him toward the tiny cell. He slid easily across the smooth concrete floor with the food still caked on his body.

For the next hour, they wrote their statements and processed prisoners when they got off the elevator. Once finished, Andy volunteered to take the letters down to Cook. When the elevator opened, he stepped in, and Jessie asked, "How is life on the 5th floor?"

"Get me out of here, Jessie, please," Andy replied, knowing there was never a dull moment.

Stop, Drop, and Roll

For the last two days, Andy worked as the incoming property officer. Grateful he wasn't working on the 5th floor, he hoped this work assignment continued. Sadly, when he checked the roster for the day, he saw his name assigned to the 5th floor, so much for his short-lived good fortune. Reluctantly, he stowed his gear and headed to the elevator. The door was already open; Jessie was sitting in his swivel chair and waiting for the next passenger to take up. Jessie gave a knowing grin when Andy stepped on.

"Another day in the barrel?" asked Jessie.

"Oh boy, lucky me," Andy replied sarcastically. They both enjoyed a good laugh at Andy's expense as they rode up.

Jessie offered thoughtfully, "Hey, if you need help today...? Don't call me." Once again, they burst into laughter as the doors opened to the familiar stench of cigarette smoke. "Good luck," Jessie said behind him.

HD was at the end of the hallway, leaning over Arnold's desk, reading the prisoners' roster again. "Hey, HD," Andy greeted cheerfully.

HD glanced up through a thick haze of smoke and replied, "Hey," then returned to reading names.

"See anyone you know?" Andy asked with no response. He considered asking HD about the rumor swirling around but thought better of it. Still determined to strike up a conversation, Andy asked, "So I guess I have cellblock A?"

"Guess so," HD responded, not bothering to look up.

"Do anything fun before work?" Andy asked. HD stood up and looked at him skeptically with his cigarette dangled precariously between his lips. Awkwardly, Andy mustered a smile to break the tension while they stared at each other for a second. Then, HD hung the roster up and walked to cellblock C to start his headcount, not saying a word.

As he watched HD walk away, Andy was disheartened. He wondered if he should say something, but he understood HD was a man living out his existence, and only the work kept him going.

Arnold walked off the elevator when Andy made it back from his cellblock check. Andy noticed he was his quintessential 10 minutes late, peering at the clock. "Hey, Arnold. How are you?"

"Fair to midland," Arnold replied in a monotone voice. He dropped his gear and headed off to check cellblock B. Sitting next to Arnold's desk, Andy snickered at Arnold's typical, cheery self.

The two mandatory requirements included feeding the prisoners and allowing them a phone call during a shift. When the officers had time, they allowed the inmates their phone calls. Five phones were mounted on the wall in the main hallway, each strategically placed at eye level, so the prisoners had to stand to use them. More than two prisoners at a time were never allowed to congregate in the hallway.

They brought the prisoners out individually for safety reasons. Each one searched before using the phone. Generally, they allowed 5 minutes, but that fluctuated depending on what was going on and what kind of a mood the jailer was in.

After Andy finished allowing phone calls from his cellblock, he returned to the desk in the main hall, where Arnold sat reading the paper. HD was downstairs grabbing a bite to eat, so Andy asked Arnold, "Do you want to get your phone calls out of the way?" Arnold merely grunted while he continued reading his newspaper article. Andy shrugged his shoulders and sat down to relax before lunch break.

Once Arnold finished his paper, he said, "Alright, I'll do my phone run, but then I'm going to lunch."

"Knock yourself out! My lunch can wait," Andy sarcastically replied.

Arnold walked to the control panel for cellblock B. One at a time, he remotely opened the cell doors and yelled for the prisoner to exit the cell and walk to him. He conducted each search and advised the prisoner he had 5 minutes to make a phone call.

Things were progressing as usual until Arnold reached cell number 8. The inmate in that cell was a tall, lean, black male with an attitude who had a generous amount of Jheri curl cream in his hair. He stepped out of the cell with a swagger and walked toward Arnold, not in a hurry to go anywhere quickly. "You want a phone call, or not?" Arnold asked.

"Yes sir, officer sir," the prisoner replied snarkily.

Arnold was unimpressed when he found a small butane lighter on his person during the search. "Where did you get this?"

"I've had it the whole time," The prisoner responded. Occasionally a lighter was missed during the intake search, so Arnold confiscated it and informed the prisoner he had 5 minutes to use the phone. "Cool, brother," he replied.

"I ain't your brother. Just make your call," Arnold barked out, pointing toward the phones.

Andy overheard Arnold's conversation, but he didn't pay much attention as those interactions were common. Instead, he sat at Arnold's desk reading an article while Arnold leaned back against the phone bank wall playing with the confiscated lighter. He passed the time flicking the lighter as the prisoner called his mother. Frustrated that she had failed to bail him out, the inmate yelled, "What the fuck, Momma! Did you get me an Attorney?"

That drew Arnold's attention, and he scolded the prisoner, "Hey! Keep it down, and you got one minute, finish up."

The prisoner gave Arnold a dismissive glance over his shoulder while he continued to argue with his mother.

Arnold wondered how much longer he should put up with this asshole when he noticed the Jheri curl product was applied so thickly that it was nearly dripping. Unable to help himself, he flicked the lighter and passed the flame by the prisoner's head. Suddenly, a blue flame shot up the back of the prisoner's head and quickly went out. His hair was so thick and long that the man didn't notice. Arnold was mesmerized by the flame and turned to Andy, "Andy, watch this!"

Andy looked up from his paper and saw Arnold wave the lighter past the prisoner's head as another flame blazed up and then went out. Oblivious to Arnold's shenanigans, the inmate continued screaming at his mother.

Amused by the singeing of the prisoner's hair, Arnold looked at Andy and did it again. Andy's eyes widened in terror as he sat up and pointed at the prisoner. Arnold turned back to see a large blue flame had climbed 6 inches above the man's head, and the prisoner was still unaware he was on fire. To smother the fire, Arnold slapped the back of his head, but some of the flammable product rubbed off on Arnold's hand, catching it on fire. He quickly slapped it against his pants and put the flame out as the prisoner yelled, "What the fuck!" and turned to see who hit him. The flames were now too large for Arnold to put out with his hands. He grabbed the prisoner and forced him to the floor, hurrying to stomp out the fire. The entire back of his head was engulfed as he screamed and desperately clasped onto the phone. With the phone cord stretched as far as allowed, he yelled, "MOMMA! They're kicking my ass!"

Andy grabbed a fire extinguisher and ran to help. Arnold held the prisoner to the floor, desperately trying to stomp out the flames. Andy pulled the safety pin, aimed, and squeezed the handle, releasing a massive plume of white powder. The prisoner's head was completely engulfed, putting the fire out. Arnold pulled the phone from the prisoner's hand and hung it up. He could hear his mother's voice screaming, "WHAT'S HAPPENING?" right before he disconnected the line. The prisoner was in the fetal position, covered in white powder, holding the back of his head. With a bit of smoke still coming from his hair, Andy grabbed wet paper towels and tried to blot out the remaining smolder.

Arnold instantly diverted blame, "What the fuck happened?"

The prisoner replied, "I don't know, man! I was just talking to my Momma when you hit me on the head. The next thing I knew, you was stomping my head, and my hair was on fire."

"I saved your life, asshole!" Arnold barked at the prisoner. "That shit in your hair can spontaneously combust. Now get up and get the fuck back in your cell. I should have let you burn!" Arnold helped the prisoner to his feet and led him towards his cell. Anxiously, the prisoner asked about his phone call and if he should see a doctor about his head. "You're fine," Arnold barked at the prisoner.

"Just get your ass back in there and wash up in your sink. You should stop wearing that shit on your hair. It's dangerous!"

After Arnold locked the inmate back in his cell, he advised the rest of the prisoner's phone liberty was over. He walked back to his desk and plopped his head down, exhausted from what just happened.

Andy sat down next to Arnold, "Do we call a supervisor about this?"

"Fuck no," Arnold responded, "Do you want to write another letter?"

Andy shook his head no and leaned back in his chair. They sat there for a minute, and then Andy said, "You know, I have heard that Jheri curl shit can reignite on its own."

Concerned, Arnold's head popped up, and he looked at Andy, "What are you talking about?"

"That's just what I've heard."

Arnold jumped to his feet and ran to the restroom. He grabbed a trash can and started filling it with water, yelling at Andy to get ready to open cell number 8. Arnold turned off the faucet and shuffled down the hall to cellblock B with a trash can full of water. Stopping in front of the prisoner's cell, he yelled, "OPEN UP 8!" Andy opened the cell door from the control panel.

"NO!" the prisoner screamed as Arnold entered the cell and threw the can of water on him.

"There! Saved your life again!" Arnold yelled. He casually instructed, "Close number 8," and walked back carrying the empty trash can.

"Mother fucker," the prisoner mumbled.

While Arnold put the trash can away, he said, "Son of a bitch ain't burning up on my watch."

Andy sat back down and tried to absorb what happened when the elevator suddenly opened, and HD walked out. He calmly asked, "What's that nasty smell?"

"It's your cigarette," Arnold replied condescendingly.

"What happened while I was gone?" HD asked. Something seemed off to him.

"Nothing," Arnold replied quickly and glared at Andy. Andy nodded his head in agreeance and looked away; this could blow up in their faces.

At the end of his shift, Andy was relieved to press the elevator buzzer. Hopefully, that would be his last time working on the 5th floor. Initially, he anticipated finding an easy path to complete his rotation at the jail, but the 5th floor certainly wasn't it.

He called home the following day to check on the family, and eventually, the conversation turned to Mike. Due to his business travels, they hadn't seen him much lately. Although they weren't sure what specifics the business entailed, Andy had his suspicions. So he decided to change the subject and told them a few jail stories and promised to make a trip home soon.

Christmas was coming, and Andy knew he would see Mike there. Since his arrest in Corpus Christi, Andy hadn't spoken to him, but he wouldn't be able to avoid him during the holidays. His parent's home wasn't particularly large, and the entire family usually attended. Regardless of how everything played out, it would be nice to have everyone together again.

NINE

Shaking with the Chief

With only a month left on his assignment at the jail, Andy couldn't wait to get back to patrol. In a short amount of time, he forged many new friendships and learned how to deal with prisoners. However, the world on the outside seemed so distant when he was working there. One couldn't escape the feeling of being in a dungeon, barricaded behind solid steel doors and bars. Without windows, he didn't know if it was day or night without checking the time.

The place was always as noisy as a train station, except for one moment. A small transistor radio was kept near the ceiling of the property room, where it could get the slightest reception. Mostly they aired music, with the occasional news broadcast. While working on incoming property, the DJ broke in with a newsflash that afternoon, "Ladies and Gentlemen, I have just received word that Elvis Presley has died." Andy couldn't believe his ears; he yelled for the guys to quiet down and listen. Then, he turned up the volume while the DJ recounted the current details available regarding Elvis's death.

The entire jail basement became starkly silent. The drunks were typically the noisiest of the bunch, and they were even pressed against the wire cage, trying to hear as much as they could. However, it didn't take long for the chatter to start back up and slowly build into a dull roar as everyone exchanged stories about when they saw Elvis perform or their favorite song or movie. Andy was amazed at how a single event like the death of Elvis Presley could merge people from all walks of life, even if only for a moment.

As the winter cold settled in southeast Texas, new jailers arrived, and others returned to their previous postings after serving their 6-month stint. Now that Andy had seniority at the jail, he had settled into two regular assignments. Unless they were shorthanded, he didn't have to shake jakes. Usually, he worked his preferred assignments as an incoming or outgoing property officer. Both were desk jobs that didn't require handling prisoners, making those positions much cleaner and less dangerous.

That winter was ferocious, with a few nights getting into the 20s. One night when temperatures were below freezing, a wino started beating on the jail entrance door, begging to surrender. "You can't surrender. You have to get arrested," Andy told him.

"Then arrest me," the drunk man pleaded.

Andy pointed into the dark, "You need to go find a patrol officer to arrest you."

In defeat, the man looked down, shook his head, turned, and stumbled off into the cold darkness. About 30 minutes later, the man got his wish as a patrol officer escorted the same alcoholic into the drunk tank. As he walked through, the wino made eye contact with Andy and grinned, pointing to the arresting officer.

On Christmas Eve, the jail staffed a skeleton crew to allow as many officers as possible to be with their families. Andy was assigned to work as a shaker and incoming property. Although it was more work, he didn't mind because it meant that someone else could be home. Plus, the fast pace would make the night go by quickly. Rumor had it, that the Chief of Police traditionally came to the jail and worked a position that day of the year to allow another officer to be home with family.

The Chief was like a God; Andy had only seen him on television or passing in the hallway with his entourage. Around 6 pm, Andy heard a commotion in the direction of the front desk; sure enough, there was the Chief. He was a tall, imposing man with a deep voice commanding attention. He was shaking hands with the employees, dressed in a coat and tie. He took off his jacket and worked his way down to incoming property with an entourage of jail supervisors in tow.

That night, Andy worked with a new officer who had only been at the jail for about a month. Both men stood in reverence, waiting for the Chief to speak. The Chief introduced himself, shook Andy's hand, and asked if he was married. "No, sir, I'm single."

The Chief nodded and then looked at the other officer and asked, "How about you, son?"

The officer replied, "Yes, sir. I have a wife and baby girl."

"Good for you," the Chief replied. "Go home and be with them. I got your shift the rest of the night."

The officer replied, "Yes, sir. Thank you, sir," and hurried off.

The Chief turned to Andy, "Just line me out, son, and don't hold back if I screw up."

Andy replied, "Yes, sir. No problem! I'll pull them out one at a time and go from there." The Chief nodded in agreement.

Andy searched prisoners with the Chief of Police for the remainder of the shift, making his Christmas incredibly special. At the end of the shift, Andy was proud to shake the Chief's hand and thank him for what he did. The Chief replied, "No, thank YOU! Have a Merry Christmas, young man."

The next morning Andy packed the car with Christmas presents and headed home. Although he was a little worried about seeing Mike, he didn't focus on it. He missed his Mom and Dad and looked forward to sharing memories with his older brothers.

When Andy arrived, he was somewhat relieved to discover that Mike visited his parents last night and wouldn't be coming back for Christmas Day. The holiday was filled with food, football, and a few of Andy's war stories. They feasted, watched games, and passed around the eggnog until it was empty. Andy missed Mike and wanted to see him, but the timing didn't feel right.

John's Elevator Ride from Hell

Andy became so comfortable with the monotonous work that he was bored unless he found something to occupy his time. So, he played pranks on his fellow jailers and trustees for entertainment. The planning part was almost as fun as the execution. First, he picked up loading cigarettes from Donnie Parker, and now he was buying them on the way to work. Carefully, he'd load each one and then hold onto them until an unsuspecting drunk asked for a smoke and became his next victim.

The basement level was the incoming property area, and outgoing property was directly above it. The two floors were connected by a steel box (i.e., dumb waiter) which slid up and down a pole to transport prisoners' property. A continuous looped rope operated the system with pulleys at each end, and the container slid up and down from either end as needed.

Andy saw it as an excellent opportunity to mess with whoever was working on the other end, especially if it was John Frost. If he were up on the first floor, he'd ask a trustee to bring him a bucket of water. Then, he'd fill the dumb waiter and yell down to John to stand by for some property. Once he knew John was directly below, he released the box, and from the weight, it went flying down the pole. When it slammed on the rubber stop, the water splashed everywhere, including all over John. Andy jumped back to his workstation as if nothing had happened, listening to John curse below.

When he was working in the basement and John was upstairs, he'd think of a creative way to pull something. Once, he filled the container with toilet paper and lit it on fire. Quickly, he hoisted up the dumb waiter and looked up as pandemonium broke out above, with John trying to battle the blaze. Cursing and with minimal options, John threw his cup of coffee on the fire, but it didn't help. Next, he used the fire extinguisher in the room to blast the container, extinguishing the flames. John then looked down the chase, simultaneously cursing Andy and coughing.

After finding pepper spray in a prisoner's property envelope, Andy loaded the dumb waiter with tissues and saturated them. While holding his breath, Andy quickly hoisted the container up to John. After a few seconds, John started coughing profusely. Once he realized Andy doused the tissues in pepper spray, he burst into a cursing tirade. He attempted to lower the dumb waiter, but Andy held onto the rope. In the end, John had to evacuate the outgoing property room, and the tissues had to be removed. Sergeant Cook wasn't particularly pleased with Andy over that escapade and yelled at him, "CUT THE CRAP!"

Those kinds of pranks were a daily occurrence, and Andy loved playing them on anyone, especially John. Mainly because they were such good friends and John was a good sport, but he was such an easy target. Even when John tried to fire back, it always seemed to backfire on him.

On one of Jessie's days off, John was assigned elevator duty. While Andy and Bill were in the middle of searching prisoners, a woman arrested for prostitution came through wearing a provocative dress. Her huge boobs were bulging over the top of her tight dress, evoking catcalls galore from the drunk tank while she walked down to the female bench, waiting to go upstairs. She ate up the attention, flirting with anyone and everyone. John eventually came down and took her up to the 6th floor in the elevator.

Before long, her pimp bonded her out, so John rode to the 6th floor to take her down to outgoing property. As she walked into the cage, she immediately began flirting with John, and he suddenly came up with a prank of his own. He asked if she would be willing to flash her breasts at the officers in the basement.

"Sure, baby! Anything for you," she said.

"Cool," John responded and opened the cage. "Stand out here so they can see!" About that time, the buzzer rang, which typically meant they had prisoners waiting in the basement to be picked up. "Great, they are waiting on us," John said. "Now, when the door opens, flash your tits, and then I'll close the elevator doors and take you up to the first floor."

"Sure thing, sweetie!" she replied with a smile.

John was grinning in anticipation of Andy's expression when the doors opened. Finally, some retaliation for all the pranks he had endured. The buzzer rang again, which meant to come directly to the basement. That was unusual, but John figured they must be busy down there.

Just as the elevator stopped, John said, "Here we go!"

Right on cue, she opened her blouse and exposed her breasts as the doors opened to Lieutenant Leiha and three jail Sergeants. They were ringing the bell because they needed to go up to the 5th floor to investigate an excessive force complaint. Instantly, John realized his practical joke had gone horribly wrong. He screamed at the whore, "Get back in the cage! What the fuck are you doing?" Then, he pushed her back into the cage and slammed the door shut.

She yelled back, "But you told me...."

John interrupted her, "I didn't tell you shit!"

Without saying a word, Lehia stepped onto the elevator.

"Where to Lieutenant?" John asked.

"Well, first, drop this young lady off, and then take us to the 5th floor."

John replied, "Yes, sir," and closed the door, staring straight ahead. Andy and Bill stood there, mouths ajar as the door shut and then erupted into laughter once everyone was out of sight.

Nothing else was said on the elevator ride up. John stopped on the first floor and walked the woman to outgoing property, and she said, "I just did what you...."

John interrupted again, "Just shut up!" He got back in the elevator and closed the door for what felt like the longest trip ever to the 5th floor. The awkward silence lasted the duration of the ride. It seemed like an eternity before the door opened, and they stepped off.

The last person to step off the elevator was Sergeant Cook, and he momentarily stopped and glared at John, "What the fuck was that?"

John didn't know what to say, so he innocently shrugged his shoulders and closed the elevator door. He sat there leaning his head against the elevator wall for the next few minutes, wondering why his prank had backfired so horrifically.

In typical Lieutenant Lehia style, he never said a word about it. John had already suffered enough, and no other action was necessary.

Rotten Raymond

The next day, John was over the elevator fiasco and seemed almost giddy on the drive to work.

"What are you so happy about?" asked Andy.

John replied, grinning, "You know the hot blonde that works in ID on the 4th floor? I have a date with her tonight after work."

"No way!" Andy exclaimed. Considering no one had even spoken to her, Andy was shocked.

As they pulled into the parking lot, Andy pointed, "That's her yellow Corvette, isn't it?"

John said, "Yeah, she said we can take it tonight. She's going to pick me up at the apartment. It'll be my first time riding in a Vet!"

"Cool," Andy replied, "I'm not waiting up, so let me know how it goes in the morning."

Andy was assigned to work the front desk, so he would be processing paperwork. Once officers entered the jail, Andy accepted their booking forms (i.e., blotters) before placing the prisoner in the drunk tank. What he enjoyed most about that assignment was the interaction with the cops who worked patrol. He spotted guys he didn't normally see, even from Northwest patrol and some of his old Academy class.

Andy had only processed a few blotters when he looked up in time to see James Hurley walking in with a prisoner. Initially, they were surprised to see one another, but then Hurley cocked a slight grin. Even though Andy always felt like less of a cop assigned to the jail, Hurley only intensified the feeling. Andy hated that Hurley was on the street while he was stuck working here.

Hurley turned in his booking paperwork and commented condescendingly, "I see the cream has risen to the top."

"Whatever, Hurley," Andy responded and took the blotter from him.

Hurley agonizingly added, "Maybe you have finally found your calling. Enjoy!"

Andy glared while Hurley arrogantly walked out the door. He couldn't subside his feelings of inadequacy seeing Hurley, and he was more anxious than ever to go back to patrol. 'Just a few more days,' he thought.

Lieutenant Lehia walked by during the afternoon and asked Andy, "Aren't you about at the end of your tour here?"

"Yes, sir," Andy responded, standing in respect.

"Any chance you have decided to change your mind and stay on full time?" Lehia asked.

"Thank you, sir, but I want to get back out there and chase bad guys." In understanding, Lehia smiled and walked away. Andy liked Lehia, and he would do anything for him except sign up for another tour in the jail.

Raymond Johnson walked into the jail with a couple of drunks in tow he picked up for public intoxication. Raymond was a funny character who drove the patty wagon downtown. The police van contained two front seats and a cage separating them from the rest of the empty van. No seats or carpet were in the back, making it easier to wash out after picking up filthy winos. Every night, at the end of his shift, Raymond used a water hose to spray the vomit, urine, and sometimes feces left behind. Quite frankly, the job was disgusting, and as a result, his nickname became Rotten Raymond. Raymond was anything but rotten. He was a kind and jolly soul who didn't even mind the nickname. Out of respect for a Senior Officer, Andy never called him that.

Raymond gave Andy a nod and said, "Hey, Bud." He referred to everyone as Bud; Andy was no exception.

"Hey, Raymond," Andy responded.

"Got a couple of winners for your collection," he said, tilting his head towards his prisoners.

"Thanks, Raymond. We can always use more customers," Andy replied jokingly.

"You may not see me the rest of the afternoon. I have to drop off my van for an oil change. I don't know if they have another one for me to drive today."

"What will the winos do without you?" Andy asked, chuckling.

"Oh, they'll get by," he replied, dropped off his blotters, and walked out.

After Raymond dropped off his van at the police garage, he called the desk Sergeant to check-in. "Sign out one of the patrol cars while your van is in the shop," he advised.

Raymond was a little disappointed because he had been looking forward to a bit of reprieve from the drunks while waiting for the maintenance to be completed. "Where do you want me to put the winos, Sarg?" Raymond asked.

"In the back seat like everyone else," the desk Sergeant replied.

Although it didn't make much sense to ruin a perfectly good patrol unit, Raymond wasn't one to complain, "Sure thing Sarg," he replied and checked out a car.

Raymond headed his usual route toward the busy downtown streets, admiring the clean vehicle he was temporarily issued. He monitored the radio for any wagon call reports from officers needing assistance. Sometimes, he'd spot a belligerent drunk harassing a pedestrian. And anytime an alcoholic was found passed out on the sidewalk, you can bet that Raymond hauled them off.

The dispatcher radioed Raymond to meet an officer with a drunk at the corner of Crawford and San Jacinto. Raymond hoped the drunk wasn't too nasty; he didn't want him messing up his new patrol car. Quickly, he spotted an officer standing over someone laid out at the end of an alley. Thankfully, the passage was wide enough to drive down, so Raymond backed his car up to the officer and got out. "Looks like you have a winner," Raymond said cheerfully.

"Unfortunately, that's true," the officer replied. "This gem threw up all over himself."

"That's not all!" Raymond said, making a thoroughly disgusted face. The man also had pissed and shit himself, and God knows what diseases he's carrying. At least he was breathing normally, and there were no signs of trauma, so Raymond decided to wake him up. Raymond squatted down next to him and, with his knuckles, started rubbing the drunk's chest, "Hey, wake up!"

Briefly, the semi-conscious drunk opened his eyes and groaned, "Fuck you," then he rolled over and passed out again.

"Where is the patty wagon?" the officer asked.

"I'm afraid the wagon is out of commission today," Raymond replied.

"I would hate to get this car on my next shift," the officer commented.

After looking back down at the man covered in bodily fluids, Raymond glanced around to ensure there were no witnesses in sight; then said, "You know...I think I'm just gonna roll him into the trunk. It's only a 5-minute drive to the jail."

"Really?" the patrolman asked.

"Why not? Better than the back seat." It was a cool day, so the heat wouldn't be a problem, and the man was so intoxicated that he probably wouldn't even wake up. He opened the trunk and asked, "Hey Bud, can you give me a hand here?"

The officer grimaced; the last thing he wanted to do was touch that guy.

"Come on! I can't lift him by myself," Raymond reasoned.

"Alright, I guess," the officer replied and grabbed his legs. They rolled him in, and once the intoxicated man hit the floor of the trunk, he let out a moan. They laughed at the situation, and Raymond slammed the trunk lid.

They waved and parted ways, and Raymond radioed the dispatcher he was en route to central with one prisoner. He turned toward San Jacinto Street and had only traveled a couple of blocks when he saw a disturbance on the sidewalk. Immediately, he slowed down and peered through the windshield, spotting a patrol officer struggling with two suspects.

The dispatcher radioed, "I have an assist officer in the 300 block of San Jacinto."

With the struggle occurring directly in front of him, Raymond quickly turned on his emergency lights and hit the siren for a short burst. Then, he slammed the brakes, threw the vehicle in park, and jumped out as one of the suspects broke loose and darted past him on the sidewalk, bumping and knocking over pedestrians in his path.

The officer now had the upper hand with the other suspect, and a couple of citizens had jumped in to help. Although it had been years since Raymond's last foot chase, he instinctually took off after the fleeing suspect as fast as he could run.

The suspect rounded the corner at Crawford Street and headed northbound toward Buffalo Bayou in a full sprint. The bayou was a thick brushy area notorious for crime and transients. If the suspect made it down the bank, Raymond knew it would be hard to keep up in that terrain.

No longer used to running, Raymond tired quickly, his heart pounding, and completely winded. He wasn't going to be able to keep that pace for much longer when he spotted two construction workers ahead. "STOP HIM!" Raymond yelled.

The workers sprang to action, jumping in the suspect's path. Allowing just enough time for Raymond to catch up, he tackled the man from behind, and they tumbled onto the street. A brief struggle ensued, but the workers stepped in again and helped Raymond cuff the suspect. Breathing heavily, Raymond slowly got to his knees, his chest heaving in and out.

"Hey officer, are you OK?" asked one of the concerned construction workers.

Even though Raymond was exhausted and gasping for air, it felt good to be involved again in an actual foot chase. Slowly, he stood back up, grinned, and answered, "Never better." As the suspect pleaded his innocence, Raymond pulled him to his feet and said, "Tell it to the judge." He thanked the two construction workers for their assistance and walked the suspect back to the other officer.

Raymond turned the prisoner over to the patrolman and agreed to write a supplemental report when he got to the station. He radioed the dispatcher that he had made an arrest and was headed back to central. The channel lit up with chatter from units in congratulations as Raymond grinned with pride. "Way to go, Raymond!" cheered over the speaker, followed by a long string of mic clicks.

As he drove to the station, all Raymond could think about was how he couldn't wait to tell his wife about the chase. After parking the patrol car in the lot, he turned in the keys for the next shift. Word about the pursuit rapidly spread around the station. While writing his report, several officers came by to slap him on the back and offer their congratulations. He had to tell the story a few times but finally got out of there for the 45-minute drive home.

All the while, the drunk remained forgotten in the trunk, sleeping it off in the police garage. The next shift, another officer, was assigned the same patrol car. He drove the vehicle to the employee parking lot to load his gear. Suddenly, a loud banging came from the trunk, startling the unsuspecting officer. Immediately, he pulled over and hit the trunk release button. He hopped out and found a man reeking of alcohol and feces, squinting from the bright sunlight in his trunk. "Fuck, man," the drunk yelled. Confused, he was trying to piece together where he was.

"What the fuck?" the officer asked, wondering the same thing.

"Who the hell are you?" the drunk asked.

"What the hell are you doing in my trunk?" the officer asked.

"Oh shit, man, I need a drink," the man said exasperated, rolled over, and went back to sleep. The officer immediately radioed for a supervisor. The entire event began to unravel when they reviewed the vehicle log and found that Raymond had last driven the car.

At this point, Raymond was home retelling his heroic foot chase story to his wife. She was so proud and hanging onto her husband's every word when the phone rang. "Hello," Raymond answered.

"RAYMOND! Captain Simmons here. Did you put a wino in the trunk of your patrol car?"

"OH SHIT! I'm sorry, Captain. I forgot!"

"No shit, you forgot! I want you in my office in 30 minutes!" the Captain commanded.

"But Captain, it's at least 45-minutes to central from my house," Raymond replied.

"I SAID 30 MINUTES!" Simmons shouted and slammed down the phone.

Raymond stood there for a second, trying to think, as he slowly turned to his wife with a look of embarrassment. 'How did this happen?' he thought.

"What's wrong, honey?" his wife asked.

With the receiver still in hand, Raymond responded quietly with disbelief, "I have to go back to work," as he hung up the phone and walked to the door.

"But why?" his wife asked.

"I'll explain it when I get back," Raymond said, discouraged, and left.

After what felt like an incredibly long drive, Raymond reported to the Captain's office and took his ass, chewing like a man. To the best of his ability, he tried to explain his actions in his report and waited to be reprimanded. In the end, they didn't do much to Raymond other than a written warning. Raymond already had the shittiest job at Central Patrol, and no one wanted it. If they punished him too severely, they feared he might resign, and they'd be in a real fix.

Word about Raymond's blunder quickly spread, and it wasn't long before Andy heard about it in the jail. Most people found it funny, but no one held it against Raymond. On the contrary, everyone found it amusing at Raymond's expense. It was going to take a while for him to live it down.

That night Andy was eager to hear about John's date, so even though he said he wouldn't, he decided to stay up and wait for him. Before long, John silently walked in and headed straight to his room. "What the fuck? Why are you home so early?" Andy asked, rising from the couch, and following John into his bedroom.

John looked down and shook his head. He didn't want to talk.

"What the fuck happened? I know you didn't get lucky. You're back too early for that."

John flopped on his bed and stared at the ceiling.

Andy sat down beside him, "Was it that bad?"

"Worse," moaned John.

"Well, tell me," demanded Andy.

After a few seconds, John gave in, "Well, it didn't go well from the start. We went to TGI Fridays, but nothing clicked. We didn't have a single thing in common, and the entire meal was unbelievably awkward."

Andy broke in, "So? That happens. What's the big deal?"

John answered, "Well, as soon as we finished eating, we decided to call it a night. The drive home was brutal. Neither of us said a word. I didn't even enjoy the ride in the Vet."

Andy broke in, "Get over it."

"You haven't heard the worst part yet," whined John. Andy waited so John could continue, "We pulled into the apartment complex and parked. She turned the radio down, and there was this awkward silence when I thought about kissing her. I swear, I had no warning. I don't even know where it came from!"

"What?"

"I ripped a huge fart."

Andy stood up, exclaiming, "Oh my God! NO! Tell me; you didn't!"

"Yes, I was mortified. I apologized, and she said, 'What? I didn't hear anything.'"

In hysterics, Andy fell back onto the bed, laughing. "What then?" he asked in anticipation.

"I just said goodnight and got out. She didn't say a thing. I glanced back while she was driving away, and she was rolling her windows down. How do I face her at work tomorrow?"

Andy tried to regain his composure and replied, "You're fucked, and you didn't even get to first base." Andy stood up, walked out of the bedroom, and closed John's door behind him, still laughing.

"Fuck you, asshole," John yelled.

Andy went to bed thinking how the day had started out so well for John and Raymond, and yet they both had suffered a tragic turn of events. As he began to drift off to sleep, it was apparent to him that there are no guarantees in life or love.

Getting Out of Jail

On Andy's last day at the jail, he was assigned to the front desk, but he spent a lot of his shift saying goodbye to everyone he had met during his six-month stint. Even though he never wanted a rotation at the jail, he would miss it. Several officers tried to convince him to stay on, but Andy was ready to head back to patrol. A beat on the street was where he felt the actual work of policing was done.

John decided to stick with it at the jail. He felt more comfortable with the predictability of a jailer's routine. Now that Andy was going to be reporting to the Northwest station, John would be riding to work by himself. Their paths would cross much less, but they always remained close.

The last shift flew by, and when Andy and John drove home together for the last time, they decided to take another trip to Andy's parents. A few weeks had passed since their previous trip, and they could use some home cooking. Since they were off for the next two days, they decided to start packing as soon as they walked into the apartment.

Now that Doug had a girlfriend, he spent a lot of his time with her. Andy and John rarely saw him around the place except when he stopped by for a shower and a change of clothes. Later, that same girlfriend became his wife, and they would spend the rest of their lives together.

The following morning, Andy and John hit the road and two hours later, pulled up to the cabin. Delighted and hungry, they could smell the glorious scent of his Mom's cooking.

Over breakfast, Andy's parents shared an embarrassing story from the past week. With Woody staying on the road, he called Poodle to check on things at the end of each day. During one of their chats, Woody asked if she saw a news story about President Reagan sending Marines into Grenada to rescue some students. "NO! Oh my god! What about the Janecks?" Poodle exclaimed.

"What about the Janecks?" Woody asked.

Poodle was having difficulty understanding why the Marines would invade the small town of Ganado, Texas. She was worried for the safety of her friends who lived there.

"NOT Ganado, Grenada!" Woody explained.

"Where is Grenada?" she asked, still clearly confused.

"It's an island in the Caribbean," Woody informed her.

"OH MY GOD!" Poodle exclaimed in relief, "I don't care anything about that. I thought you were talking about Ganado. You scared me half to death!"

Everyone around the table enjoyed a good laugh.

Andy couldn't help but ask about Mike, but all they said was he was traveling a lot for business. Sometimes to Mexico or the Caribbean, but they never asked for specifics. Like Andy, they didn't really want to know.

Andy and John went on to have a fantastic weekend fishing and meeting up with old friends around town. Andy introduced John to a girl he grew up with, and they instantly hit it off. As their relationship flourished, Andy found himself alone in the apartment more and more.

Mary's

Andy was ecstatic about what his first day back on the streets would bring, like his first day out of the Academy—again assigned to ride with Ray, which was nice because they enjoyed each other's company. However, like most officers with several years of experience in patrol, Ray was happy to answer calls from the dispatcher and write a few tickets. After a few days of riding together, Andy was looking to partner with someone who still hungered for the thrill of the chase.

During his rotation at the jail, Northwest station added a new officer, Dave Carroll. Dave recently transferred from Northeast Division, a known heavy crime district. Andy and Dave were the same age and had similar interests, so they started riding together. They were constantly on the hunt for burglars, hijackers, and car thieves throughout their shift. Of course, supervision was satisfied if you answered calls and wrote your share of tickets, but Andy and Dave aimed for felony arrests and enjoyed the excitement of a good chase.

They were patrolling the Spring Branch area when the desk officer radioed Andy to call the station. There was an opportunity to work an extra job that night, and Andy had never worked one before, so he said, "Sure. Where and when?" The desk officer explained that near the north side of downtown, a nightclub called Mary's had a cash job.

"The job starts at 10 pm, so you will need to take an hour off to make it there in time."

Andy wrote down the address and asked, "Who am I working with?"

"A central officer named Arnold Stagger. Do you know him?"

Surprised, Andy answered, "Yes, I worked the jail with him."

"Good. He works there a lot, so he will show you the ropes," the desk officer responded.

Although Andy was apprehensive about working with Arnold, he had already committed and could use the extra cash.

At the end of the shift, Andy turned in his paperwork and headed to Mary's. The nightclub was located on a busy street in a predominately Hispanic community and was a hopping place for Hispanic nightlife, with a 24-hour café across the street. Unfortunately, the location was known for its high crime rate, and it wasn't far from where John had been shot.

When Andy pulled up, he spotted Arnold standing on the sidewalk in front of Mary's and waved. Arnold motioned him to park directly in front of the nightclub. He had been saving space for Andy and was excited to see him pull in. Arnold jumped in the front seat and asked, "Hey Andy, how's life back on the streets?"

"Good," Andy replied, "Are you still at the jail?"

"Yeah, but I get out soon. Have you worked here before?"

"No."

"Well, this is easy," Arnold said. "We sit here in the car, and if Mary needs us, she comes out and signals. She pays us in cash at the night's end, and we're done." Andy asked why Mary didn't want them inside. "It's a dance club, and mostly wetbacks come here," Arnold said. "They get nervous with police inside, so Mary wants us out here. If a fight breaks out or she needs someone escorted out, she'll let us know. Do you have a slapper?"

"No," Andy replied.

Arnold pulled out his slapper and said, "If you are gonna work here regularly, you might want to invest in one of these."

Andy was starting to rethink this as an easy job, but he was already there. Even though he'd seen a slapper before, he had never thought about buying one. The handheld impact weapon was a thick leather strap containing a piece of lead in the middle for weight. It could fit neatly in a back pocket for quick access during a fight. It was a devastating weapon in a close-quarter altercation.

The following two hours passed by without incident. Mary hadn't come out, so Andy thought Arnold might be right about this being an easy gig. They sat there listening to the radio and chatting while watching people pass by. On the opposite side of the street, Andy noticed a man walking toward them. He appeared a bit nervous, glancing around in all directions, possibly lost or looking for someone. Unfortunately, the intersection was dark with only one streetlight, so it wasn't easy to see.

The man started to cross the street when a car pulled in front of him and stopped. That must have been who he was looking for because he started talking to the driver. Suddenly, they heard a loud pop! It sounded like a small-caliber handgun. "WHAT WAS THAT?" asked Arnold.

"I don't know," replied Andy. They looked around, trying to decipher where the noise came from. The man was still standing casually next to the car as it slowly drove away. The man walked to the café and went inside. Andy and Arnold gave up trying to find the source of the sound. A vehicle might have backfired, or someone may have lit some firecrackers. However, gunshots were not uncommon in that part of town.

A few minutes later, an ambulance approached with red lights flashing and a siren blaring. EMTs rushed inside the café with their equipment. Curious if it had anything to do with the pop they heard, Andy and Arnold crossed the street and entered to investigate. The same man they had watched walk into the café was on the floor, and the EMTs were working on him.

He had been shot in the abdomen, and the paramedics needed to get him to a hospital. "Who shot him?" asked Andy.

"He came in here like that," a man at a table said. "He got shot outside!"

Andy suddenly realized that they had witnessed him being shot in the street. He tried to remember the car, but all he could recall was a dark-colored, two-door sedan.

Two patrol officers arrived as paramedics carried the victim out on a stretcher to the ambulance. They asked Arnold if it was their call, and he said, "No, we're working an extra job across the street at Mary's, and when we saw the ambulance pull up, we walked over to see what was happening."

The patrol officer asked, "Who did the shooting?" And they had to admit they most likely witnessed it. The officers understood and took the information. "I don't see homicide making this scene. There's not much to investigate here. We'll take some statements and check the road to see if there are any bullet casings."

Andy and Arnold walked the officers to the location of the shooting. They searched the area with their flashlights but didn't find anything, so the assigned officers headed to the hospital to check on the victim. Andy and Arnold were left behind, feeling inadequate as crime fighters for letting a shooting happen right under their noses.

Suddenly, Mary came running out and yelled, "Fight! Come in quick!" Arnold sprinted up the stairs toward the entrance, with Andy hurrying to catch up. Mary jumped out of Arnold's path as he rushed inside. Arnold pushed people out of the way, heading to the center of the dance floor.

The club was packed with at least forty or fifty people on the dance floor, and Mexican music was blaring. Most people couldn't hear Arnold yelling, "GET OUT OF THE WAY," as he pushed toward the fight. Andy spotted Arnold pulling the slapper from his back pocket and thought, 'Uh-Oh, this ain't gonna be good.'

Two Hispanic males were locked in combat in the middle of the dance floor. They were too consumed throwing punches at one another to notice Arnold approaching at breakneck speed. One of the combatants had his back to Arnold as they swung wildly at each other. Arnold reared the slapper back and struck him on the back of the head. The impact sounded like bones crushing as the man dropped to the floor. The other man watched him fall and looked up in time to see Arnold swinging the slapper again. Arnold hit him dead center in the forehead, and he too crumbled.

The fight was over before Andy could do anything. Both men were lying on the floor, bleeding profusely from head wounds. Andy didn't know if they were even alive as Arnold turned toward the crowd and started yelling for them to get back. Everyone quickly backed up, fearful they would be struck next.

The DJ finally turned off the music, and the lights came on. Andy gawked at the two men lying motionless on the dance floor and thought they would need an ambulance. Arnold had another approach in mind to resolve the situation. "GET UP MOTHERFUCKER!" he yelled at one of the men, kicking him in the rib cage. The man rolled to one side, moaning in pain. Arnold kicked him again, this time in the ass, "I SAID GET UP MOTHERFUCKER!"

In dismay, Andy could only watch like everyone else as the man held his head to stop the bleeding, struggling to get to his feet. Then, Arnold started in on the second man, "YOU TOO, MOTHERFUCKER! GET UP!" repeatedly kicking him. The man tried to get to his feet, but not quickly enough because Arnold kicked him again. "OUT THE DOOR WITH BOTH OF YOU!" Both men staggered, blood trickling down their heads and dripping onto the floor. The crowd parted ways as the two men made their way toward the door. Arnold was right on their heels, yelling, "DON'T STOP ASSHOLES! KEEP GOING!"

They made it out the door, stumbled down the sidewalk, and walked off into the darkness together. Arnold and Andy followed them until they disappeared in the night. Whatever differences they had earlier were no longer critical. "Are you going to make a report?" Andy asked Arnold.

"What for?" Arnold replied. "They are lucky I didn't put them in jail!"

Andy shook his head disbelievingly while they sat down in his car to wait for this night to end.

Arnold wasn't phased in the slightest by the entire evening; it was just another night for him. Andy would never again believe a desk officer offering an easy extra job. He never wanted to work with Arnold again, and he hoped that was the last time he ever had to walk into Mary's Cantina.

Eventually, Mary paid them, and Andy quickly headed out of there. He gave a half-hearted goodbye, waving and speeding off toward his apartment and the hell away from Arnold. This would be a story that would rival anything his roommates could come up with.

The following day Andy received a call from two Texas Rangers investigating a counterfeit Rolex watch operation. Someone was importing the watches into Texas and selling them as originals. Somehow Mike's name came up in their investigation, and after interviewing him, they found Andy's name and phone number in his wallet. Because he was a Houston police officer, they decided to call Andy and see what he knew about the smuggling ring.

Andy was unbelievably embarrassed and explained he had no clue what this was about. However, he had always had his suspicions that Mike was up to something. After a short interview, the Rangers were convinced Andy was oblivious to Mike's business dealings.

It devastated him to know the big brother he had admired and respected was still involved in criminal activity. Part of him wanted to know more, and another part wanted nothing to do with it. He considered calling Mike and confronting him but assumed Mike would only have an excuse and deny everything.

Like so many things before, Andy tucked the thoughts away in hopes they would disappear. He had his own life and chose to ignore the building storm around his brother; hopefully, it wouldn't come his way.

Moody Park

Dave Carroll took the day off, so Andy patrolled as a one-man Sunday afternoon. For most citizens of Houston, it was a lazy summer day, but Andy was already getting his share of calls when he spotted a drunk driver swerving in heavy traffic. Due to the extra paperwork involved and having to take them downtown for booking, he hated working DWIs, but this guy was too dangerous to overlook. So, reluctantly, he turned on his overheads and pulled him over.

People under the influence were notorious for lying about how much alcohol they had consumed. The standard answer was, "A couple of beers," but this guy was brutally honest and replied, "About a case!" Andy appreciated the man's honesty and smiled, walking the drunk back to his patrol car. He figured this would be the extent of his crime-fighting for the evening.

After booking the drunk and filing the appropriate paperwork with the traffic division, Andy headed out I-10 just as the sun was setting. Hopefully, there was still enough time to find some trouble before the end of his shift.

Up ahead, several vehicles were changing lanes, trying to maneuver around something. Once he worked his way through traffic, he discovered another obvious drunk traveling 40 mph in the middle lane of a high-speed freeway. Andy couldn't believe his luck, but it was another driver far too intoxicated to be on the road; he couldn't pass by.

Eventually, he pulled the driver over at the Washington Street exit, stopping on the narrow shoulder. With the freeway drivers speeding past him, Andy hated to exit his car here, so he grabbed the PA speaker, "HEY! You, in the car! This is the police. Drive up the exit ramp to the service road and stop!" The drunk waved in understanding and started up the ramp but stopped in the middle of the service road. Again, Andy yelled through the PA, "PULL THROUGH THE INTERSECTION AND STOP!" The man waved as if they were old friends.

The traffic light on Washington Street was red, so Andy pulled in front with the emergency lights flashing to stop oncoming cars. Once they were safely through the intersection, they came to a rest on the shoulder of the road, and Andy breathed a sigh of relief. It was nearly dusk when Andy got the drunk out of his car. "How much have you had to drink?"

"Just a couple of beers," the man responded. Andy knowingly grinned at his answer and turned him around to be handcuffed. "Come on, officer," he pleaded.

But Andy ignored him as he tucked him into the patrol car's back seat.

Andy picked up his mic to check if a DWI unit could take his prisoner, but the dispatcher interrupted, "ATTENTION ALL OFFICERS, THIS IS A CITYWIDE ASSIST! ALL UNITS AVAILABLE RESPOND TO THE 3700 BLOCK OF FULTON DRIVE AT MOODY PARK. THIS IS A CITYWIDE ASSIST THE OFFICER. PLEASE RESPOND WITH YOUR RADIO NUMBERS IF YOU ARE EN ROUTE!"

As Andy listened to the number of officers responding, he was stunned. 'What the hell is going on?' he wondered. Then he suddenly realized that it was only a few blocks from where he worked at Mary's nightclub the other night. During a citywide assist, all officers were requested to respond, no matter what their typical assignment was.

He couldn't stand by and not go, but he was stuck on the side of the road with a drunk, and this guy would kill someone behind the wheel. He switched his radio to the central patrol channel and listened to officers shouting about a riot. When Andy heard his fellow officers in trouble, that did it, he had to find a way to get there.

Andy got out of the patrol vehicle, opened the back door, and yelled, "GET OUT!" Quizzically, the drunk looked at Andy, wondering what was going on. Andy pulled his legs out and helped him to his feet to expedite the process. Then they walked to the back of his car while traffic passed by, oblivious to what was happening.

An empty field was next to where they were parked, covered with waist-high Johnson grass that probably hadn't been mowed in months. Johnson grass was native to Texas, and it grew thick that time of year. "Stay right here," Andy ordered. Then, quickly, he grabbed the man's keys from the ignition and locked the doors to his car. He hurried back and held the keys in front of the drunk's eyes, "You see these?" Andy asked.

"Yeah," he answered, trying to focus his vision on the key ring.

Andy reared back and threw them as far as he could into the field of tall grass.

The drunk watched the keys disappear and yelled, "What the hell?"

Sternly, Andy looked the man in the eyes and pointed at the field, "By the time you find those keys, you'll be sober enough to drive." Then he pointed to the gas station across the street and said, "I suggest you go to that station and call someone to come get you. You can find those keys in the morning."

The drunk nodded his head in agreement.

"Don't come back here and try to drive that car until you are sober. You hear me?" Andy demanded. He continued to nod yes while Andy removed the handcuffs. Andy jumped in his police car and quickly sped off toward Moody Park with red lights flashing and his siren blaring. The intoxicated man leaned against his car, watching Andy drive away.

Attentively, Andy listened to the radio and quickly accelerated, entering the freeway. Officers described the chaos. A violent crowd was hurling rocks and bottles at the officers, hijacking police vehicles, overturning cars, and setting them on fire. The dispatcher announced the department's riot vans were en route to the scene. Those vans were equipped for these situations, filled with riot helmets and large ballistic vests. The vans were staged at central because the department had anticipated something like this. Then, most officers shrugged their shoulders and thought of them as a waste of money but now, not so much.

Laser-focused, Andy weaved in and out of traffic at a high rate of speed. Previously, he was under the impression that riots only occurred in large cities up north, not Houston, Texas. Lately, the Hispanic community has been on edge because of the Joe Campos Torres incident. As a result, activists were publicly speaking and organizing marches. It appeared emotions were boiling over now, and the hot summer weather combined with copious amounts of alcohol from the Cinco de Mayo fiesta didn't help.

After Andy turned onto Fulton Street, he pulled into the makeshift parking area for arriving police vehicles. At least fifty police cars were already there, with more pouring in every second. Andy grabbed his wooden baton and headed toward the sounds of shouting in the distance.

He merged with a growing stream of arriving officers as he jogged down Fulton Street toward Moody Park. In the distance, Andy could see the glow of fires and hear chanting coming from the rioters banned together in the park. Moody Park was always a quiet and beautiful park that he drove by to visit his uncle, loaded with beautiful large live oak trees. But now, it was a scene of violence with an angry mob.

Once Andy made it to the rally point, he joined the makeshift line of officers hurriedly grabbing helmets and vests from the riot vans. The helmets donned face shields, and although the vests were two sizes too large, he didn't mind. He strapped his helmet on, adjusted the vest to the best of his ability, and headed toward the makeshift skirmish line.

Sergeant Mattis was there barking out orders, trying to organize a group of arriving officers. Andy nudged toward them and spotted several northwest officers, including Ray Gonzales. After he shifted positions down the line to stand next to Ray, he felt a sense of easiness being with guys he knew. "Move up!" Mattis yelled, motioning the group forward. Slowly, they walked on toward the chaos with their batons ready. Although there wasn't an effort to march or stay in step, they were taking shape and starting to look like a cohesive unit.

They were now within a block of the fires, and Andy struggled to see the rioters beyond the flames. Curiously, he wondered how large the crowd was. By the sound of the chants, they numbered in the hundreds. Every time a rioter stepped forward to throw something at the officers, the excitement in the crowd grew. A loud cheer erupted when a lit bottle was heaved toward the officers and ignited on the pavement.

Just short of the busting glass, Mattis halted the line to re-evaluate. From a closer vantage point, Andy could now see the faces of the angry mob. The entire situation was surreal; it felt like a scene from a movie with the overturned police cars burning in the street. Nothing a country boy from south Texas ever thought he would witness. Suddenly a rioter jumped on top of an ambulance hijacked earlier in the riot. He used it as a pulpit to incite the crowd, yelling obscenities and chanting. The news crew abandoned their Channel 2 truck, and the team ran to safety. During the confrontation, their police beat reporter, Jack Hunt, was injured and suffered a head wound. He was well respected among the rank-and-file police officers as a trustworthy news reporter. Arriving officers were incensed by his injury as if they harmed a fellow cop.

Mattis listened to the police radio for direction while watching over the crowd. No one of significant rank was taking charge. Either they weren't there or chose to dodge the responsibility if this all went terribly wrong. Mattis was not that kind of a guy, though. He was always the take-charge type who saw a problem and did something about it, come what may.

"CLOSE RANKS," Mattis ordered and motioned everyone to pull their face shields down. Mattis waved his arm forward; they needed to push the crowd back from the burning cars for the fire department to have access to them. Another volley of rocks and bottles hit the pavement directly in front of the officers. They continued forward in as much of a line as they could maintain. The police officers were dangerously close to the range of projectiles now.

Several feet past the flames was an abandoned police car. It was still upright and relatively unharmed until one of the rioters suddenly jumped onto the roof, and with a hand full of chains, he started pounding the windows while the sound of bursting glass echoed in the night. That was a bridge too far as Mattis responded with a resounding, "CHARGE!"

Forty riot police bolted forward in an impressive show of force. The line must have been too intimidating for the crowd to withstand; they instantly turned, running in all directions. Andy expected a physical altercation with the rioters, but they scattered quickly.

Mattis lost control of the police force; there was no calling them back once they passed the burning vehicles. It was too loud to hear anything, especially wearing a riot helmet. Reverting to basic instincts from patrol, when a suspect ran, they gave chase until they got their man.

Andy was running alongside Ray, and he was a great guy to have with you if it came down to a fight. With the crowd scattering in all directions, there was no way to catch everyone involved, but they hoped to arrest at least one rioter.

The park was far behind them as they ran toward Irvington Village, a government housing project. They had zero intentions of coming back empty-handed; someone was going to jail. It was only a matter of whom.

The minimal streetlights were the only illumination as they hurdled curbs and ditches, closing in on one rioter. As he glanced back over his shoulder at the officers chasing him, he was terrified. Andy was surprised how quickly this punk changed from an angry rioter into a scared kid running for his life.

He ran alongside the apartment building, hoping the cops would pass him by. But that was not happening, with Andy and Ray locked on like a couple of hawks going after prey.

When they were within arm's length, Andy leaned forward and gave him a slight push. That was all it took for the man to tumble to the ground. Ray landed on top of him, used his baton to pin him down, and quickly cuffed him for the long walk back to the park.

Suddenly, the suspect defiantly started yelling at his fellow rioters. "Fuck these pigs! Viva la resistance! Viva la Joe Torres!" His transformation incensed Andy because he was scared to death seconds earlier, and now he was the revolution leader. Andy wanted to bust him in the mouth, but he knew he couldn't, so he tried to ignore the insults.

When they arrived at the skirmish line, the fire department put out the burning cars, with officers providing a safe perimeter around them. Most of the crowd had been dispersed, and only a handful of the protester's arrested. Andy was proud he and Ray were one of the few officers to catch one. They turned him over to a temporary booking station for processing and transport to jail.

Mattis made sure his guys were accounted for and congratulated everyone on a job well done. Then, he instructed them to standby until the night shift could replace them with fresh troops. Nothing else significant happened that night, although the incident sparked several days of unrest. The department deployed extra patrol, including the SWAT team, to provide overwatch with their snipers. He thought that would be a cool assignment and wondered if he could ever make it there.

Once the night shift started arriving, Mattis released his guys for the night, and Andy headed back to Northwest, reflecting on what he thought would be a lazy

Sunday shift. He wondered what happened to the drunk he left on the freeway. Andy feared that decision might come back to haunt him, but he would do it again given the same situation. Andy was starting to believe sometimes you do what you have to, even if it's not what they taught in the Academy.

TEN

NARCOTICS

For the next few months, Andy continued riding the streets of northwest Houston with Dave, but the challenge he yearned for wasn't there. He kept an eye on the bulletin board at the office, hoping to find something exciting and new. Openings around the department were posted on the board, and he figured a change would do him good, but where?

Every week, Andy loved to watch a popular TV show starring two undercover police officers, Miami Vice. The entire premise seemed like an incredible job. Don Johnson and his partner always pulled off a big dope bust and then got the girl to boot. So maybe, doing undercover dope deals would be just the ticket. As luck would have it, he noticed narcotics had an opening, so he filled out an application, and they scheduled an interview.

The interview went well, and shortly after, he received a notice to report to the Narcotics Division on Monday. But, of course, he hated to say goodbye to his buddies again. They promised to stay in touch, but that rarely happened. HPD was so massive that you seldom ran into anyone you didn't work with.

"Officer Parker!"

'What the hell does a Narc wear?' Andy nervously pondered, trying to get dressed for his first day. Still unsure, he settled on a casual look, similar to what most narcotic officers seemed to wear around the station. A simple t-shirt and jeans would suffice, but where would he hide a pistol? More than likely, he wouldn't need it on his first day, so he could leave it in his car. Ideally, he wanted to fit in and get through the day without screwing up.

He thought about the stories he heard on the drive downtown and wondered if they were exaggerated. During his short career, a few narcotic officers had been shot in the line of duty, and one of them had died.

Walking to the elevator at central, Andy spotted Donnie Parker, a familiar face from his days at the jail, but he hadn't seen him since. Although they only worked together for a few shifts, Andy could tell right away that he liked him. They shook hands, chatted while waiting for the elevator, and stepped in for the trip to the 6th floor. It turns out it was Donnie's first day in Narcotics as well. "Do you know anyone there?" Andy asked.

"Not a soul," Donnie replied.

"Me either," Andy said. "Maybe we can work together. Like partners or however, they do it."

"Yeah, that would be cool."

The elevator stopped on the second floor, and the blonde woman from the ID section got in. She briefly glanced at Andy, making eye contact as she turned to push the button to the 4th-floor. She was her typical all-business self with no expression. Standing behind her, Donnie looked at Andy and wiggled his eyebrows questioningly. Andy shook his head to wave him off. The doors opened on the 4th floor, and she got off without a word. As soon as the doors closed, Donnie asked, "You know her?"

"Long story, so I'll have to tell you that one when we have more time."

"Did you hook up?" Donnie asked eagerly.

"No, but my roommate tried," Andy replied, "As I said, it's a long story but a good one. Remind me later, and I'll tell you all about it."

"Doesn't she drive a yellow Vet?"

Andy busted out laughing, the doors opened to the 6th floor, and they stepped off.

"What? Tell me!" Donnie demanded.

Andy laughed and waved him off as they walked to the front desk. Marvin Gentry immediately greeted them, he had worked the front desk for years, and everyone knew him. "Hi, Marvin," Andy said, walking up and gesturing toward Donnie, "We're your recruits, reporting for duty, sir," Andy said, saluting.

"Oh, brother. Fresh meat," replied Marvin. "You guys can go down and talk to Sergeant McCain. I think he's expecting you."

"Thanks, Marvin," Andy replied and walked toward the entrance. For security, the door remained locked until Marvin unlocked it remotely from his desk. For the first time, Andy was finally going to be behind that door, an entirely new experience for him.

The Narcotics Division was run by Captain Johnny Jones, a well-respected and extraordinarily likable man. Under him worked two shifts worth of narcotics officers. Each shift was under the command of a Lieutenant and three Sergeants. Andy was assigned to the day shift under the management of Lieutenant Riley. Riley had a demanding, complex personality and a reputation for running his shift with an iron fist; some thought he was bipolar. Donnie was assigned to an entirely different set of supervisors on the night shift.

Sergeant McCain stepped out of his office as they headed down the hallway and yelled, "Down here, guys!" They walked in and introduced themselves. For years, McCain worked in the Narcotics Division. He was a fair and accommodating guy who loved to chat about fishing and hunting. But when it came to supervising officers under his command, McCain was all business.

Andy and Donnie listened intently as he quickly ran through the day-to-day operations and the dos and don'ts. "Do you guys know anyone up here?" McCain asked.

"No, sir," they both replied.

"OK," McCain said, "I'll walk you around and introduce you. Then, you can spend the rest of the day getting to know everyone, and we'll start first thing tomorrow."

"Yes, sir," Andy replied.

"And stop calling me, sir," McCain demanded. "Just Sarg is fine."

"You bet, Sarg," replied Donnie.

McCain showed them the dayroom, a large open area with a vast table capable of seating twenty people. There were approximately ten phones on the table for officers to conduct business. "Andy, you're gonna be partnered with Mark Kiley for the time being," McCain said. "He'll be in later, and I'll introduce you."

"Sure thing, Sarg," Andy replied.

"Donnie, you're gonna be with Jack Spencer on the night shift; may God help you," McCain said.

"OK, Sarg," Donnie replied, chuckling, but McCain wasn't laughing. Donnie and Andy looked at each other as he walked away, wondering if McCain was joking.

Over his shoulder, McCain yelled, "Jack's on vacation, so just hang out in the dayroom and help out as needed for the remainder of the week."

"Got it," Donnie replied and turned to Andy, "What do you think?"

Andy shrugged his shoulders and sat down, trying to take it all in. "Are you going to grow your hair long and do the beard thing?"

"I guess so," Donnie replied.

"I'm not unless I have to. I mean a little maybe, but nothing like down to my shoulders or whatever," Andy said.

"I work a bank extra bank in uniform, so I'll have to give that up, I guess," Donnie commented. "I don't think they would appreciate a long-haired uniformed officer."

"Ha, no, I don't think so," Andy replied. "Where is it?"

"Sharpstown Bank off the Southwest Freeway. I work in the lobby until 4 o'clock, and then I go to the drive-through and walk the tellers in with their cash boxes."

Donnie went on to tell Andy that one of the tellers is gay and speaks with a lisp in a feminine voice. "His name is Bruce, and you can't help but like the guy. He's nice enough, and he's always asking about my day. You know, like what I did on patrol and stuff like that. But I just can't get past the flaming queer thing." Donnie imitated the teller's speech, "He's so flamboyant! And that lisp. Oh my God!"

Andy laughed at Donnie's impeccable imitation.

"Officer Parker! How was your day? Did you arrest anyone today?" Donnie said in his fake femme voice, waving his hands dramatically in the air. Andy was bent over, laughing.

Mark Kiley walked in and introduced himself. He was tall, lean, and roughly Andy's age. He typically dressed in casual street clothes, although he always carried a briefcase. Years ago, his older brother was a narcotic officer and was killed on duty. Everyone respected Mark for following in his brother's footsteps and the bravery it must have taken to do the very thing that cost his brother his life.

After chatting for a few minutes, Mark asked Andy, "Hey, you wanna go with me on a drive-by? I need to check a location that I have a clue on."

"Sure," Andy replied. Anytime a narcotics officer went to collect a tip from an informant, they referred to it as a clue. The information could pertain to a person or a location they need to investigate. "Do I need anything?"

"Just your gun," Mark replied.

"OK, I need to stop by my vehicle and get it. I didn't bring it up here," Andy said.

"No worries," Mark replied.

Donnie tried to introduce himself to some of the other narcotics officers coming in and out of the dayroom, but with no one to make formal introductions, it was incredibly awkward. Narcs were suspicious by nature, particularly the jaded, older ones. Generally speaking, they rarely got close to anyone; and occasionally, they even had to bust fellow narcs, although that was rare. Everyone was polite, but Donnie could sense the mistrust.

Mark and Andy walked down to the police garage and got into Mark's black Chevrolet pickup, his assigned cool car. His undercover truck was seized during a drug deal a couple of years earlier, and now Mark used it as a take-home vehicle.

Half of the vehicles used in the Narcotics Division were seized during previous drug deals, and as long as you didn't come across the former owner, they worked great. The Chevy was like any other pickup except for the police radio mounted in the glove compartment and the covert antenna hidden between the cab and the bed. On their way out of the police garage, they stopped by Andy's car to grab his pistol, then headed toward the southwest part of town.

On the Southwest freeway, they were crawling in bumper-to-bumper traffic. Andy nervously looked around at the surrounding vehicles. Since it was his first time out of uniform on duty, it felt weird that no one around them knew they were cops. The windows were rolled down for Mark's cigarette smoke to waft out, and Andy tried his best to act cool.

They exited the freeway and stopped at a red light on the service road. Andy made eye contact with the driver in the lane next to them. An old four-door Pontiac with three other guys in the vehicle had their windows down, music blaring, and looked like dope heads. Unable to stop himself, Andy stared at them.

The driver assumed Andy was looking for drugs, so he asked, "Hey dude, you looking to score?"

Andy tried to keep his composure as Mark leaned forward and said, "Yeah, man! What ya got?"

"Hooch," the driver replied.

"Cool, man. Let's do this," Mark said, and the driver motioned to follow them.

Andy couldn't believe it was that easy. Finally, the light turned green, and they slowly pulled forward.

"We'll see what they have and blow the deal off. Then we'll get a uniformed unit to pull them over when they leave," Mark said calmly. The Pontiac pulled ahead and turned into a grocery store parking lot.

Andy realized this was really happening as Mark drove in behind them. They were already doing a drug deal on his first drive-by on his first day. He didn't have the foggiest idea what he should do or what Mark had planned. With zero training as an undercover officer, he had no time to work this out. There were four against two, and he wasn't sure Mark was armed.

Andy's pistol was tucked in his pants, but his t-shirt was tucked too, exposing the weapon. Quickly, he pulled his shirttail out but feared it wasn't long enough to conceal it. "Are we staying in the truck?" Andy asked.

"Yeah, we'll just drive up next to them," Mark replied.

Andy decided to take his pistol out and tuck it in the seat next to him for quick access. The Pontiac stopped in an open area of the parking lot, and Andy's heart was hammering in his chest, thinking about other narcs who died doing deals like this. Andy didn't appreciate that they were flying by the seat of their pants, but he had to trust Mark.

Mark pulled the passenger side of his truck alongside the dealer's driver's side. With several feet still between the two vehicles, Andy tried to scan the Pontiac for anything potentially threatening. Mark opened his door and walked around to the front of the truck. 'What the hell? We were supposed to stay in the truck!' Andy thought anxiously. Mark took a drag from his cigarette and casually walked to their car like he did this every day. Resting his forearms on the bottom of the window opening, he leaned in the driver's window and asked, "Whatcha got, man?" Andy was thoroughly impressed by how calm Mark was. Here was a man who lost his brother during a drug deal gone sour, so he knew how dangerous this was, but he was chatting with these guys like they were old friends.

Andy scrambled to decide if he should stay in the truck near his pistol or get out and be closer to Mark? Sweat started to bead on his brow. He couldn't tuck the gun back in his pants without being seen. But, on the other hand, he felt compelled to position himself closer to Mark to cover him, so he settled on splitting the difference between his gun and the drug deal. He opened his door and stood close enough to reach his pistol should he need it.

The driver showed Mark a large bag of marijuana. "This is good shit, man," the driver said.

Mark reached in the car, picked up a bud, and smelled it. He dropped it back in the bag and said, "Yeah, man. That smells like sweet stuff." Andy started to relax because this was where Mark would blow the deal off.

Acting as though he was grabbing his wallet to make a purchase, Mark naturally reached around his belt line and pulled his pistol out, pointing it directly at the driver. Andy couldn't believe what he was seeing, 'THIS WAS NOT THE PLAN!' Andy screamed internally. The dealer's eyes widened in terror, looking down at Mark's 9mm barrel. "Just be cool. I'm a cop, and you're under arrest," Mark calmly explained as though he was introducing himself to a new friend.

To Andy, it felt like he was watching everything in slow motion, even though his mind was racing. Was it safe to momentarily take his eyes off what was happening to grab his gun? Or should he stay and watch for signs of someone doing something stupid? Andy grabbed his pistol and ran to the suspect's car, and started yelling at everyone in the vehicle, "Don't move motherfucker!" Mark looked at Andy as if to say, 'Dude, calm down. It's cool.'

No one in the car offered resistance as Andy's barked out commands. Mark took another drag on his cigarette and told Andy, "Cover them while I radio for a patrol car." Andy nodded his head as he nervously continued to scan the suspects.

Mark tossed his cigarette on the pavement, stomped it out with his shoe, and leisurely walked back to the truck to use the radio in the glove compartment. When the patrol cars arrived, the suspects were cuffed, and Andy was relieved to find out they didn't have a gun. Once the patrol units drove away to central with the prisoners, Andy and Mark followed to file the charges. "What about the drive-by?" Andy asked.

"We'll do it tomorrow. I couldn't help but take advantage of a bird in the hand," Mark replied.

"I gotta tell you, man; you scared the shit out of me when you got out of the truck," Andy said.

"Yeah, you have to roll with these things sometimes. There ain't no script," Mark replied, lighting another cigarette. Andy nodded and figured that was the nature of the beast and the way things were done. He finally found the excitement he had been craving and possibly more danger than he bargained for.

Meanwhile, a search warrant for ecstasy was being drawn up at the office. The new drug was becoming increasingly popular in the nightclubs around Houston, and it had particularly taken root in Montrose, the typically gay area of town. The Montrose area was named for the major street running through it, and the majority of the stores, restaurants, and nightclubs in that part of the town catered to the gay community.

Tom Woods was the case agent on the warrant, and he had five guys lined up, but he needed one more. He asked Donnie if he would come along and help handcuff suspects. "I have no idea how many people will be in there. It's one of those flophouses where queers go to have sex and do drugs," said Tom.

"Sure thing," Donnie replied. He was grateful to be included and hoped to have a chance at being accepted into the group. Tom handed Donnie a narcotics raid jacket and said, "Here, you'll need this." Houston Police Narcotics was written in bold yellow letters across the back, and the windbreaker was adorned with police patches. It was intended to be worn over a ballistic vest to identify themselves as narcotic officers. Everyone executing the warrant had long hair and varying degrees of facial hair, from full beards to long mustaches. They didn't look like cops, so identifying themselves was a challenge.

In the dayroom, they briefed the details of the warrant and the location. Tom explained who the primary suspect was and what the house looked like. They would knock, announce themselves at the front door, and then Tom would kick it open. That was the extent of their limited planning. Finally, everyone agreed to park their cars at a business nearby and jump in the bed of a pickup to drive to the house. They would use a uniform patrol car to cover the back and provide added police identification.

Once they finished the briefing, everyone headed directly to the meet location. Donnie rode with Tom and started to feel good about being included, although he could tell that some guys were still a little suspicious of the new guy. Nevertheless, Donnie was determined to win them over and do whatever it took to fit in. "You got a pistol on you?" Tom asked.

"Yep, but I need to stop by my car and get my vest," Donnie replied. After grabbing Donnie's vest, they headed out for his first warrant. Tom called a uniformed patrol unit over to meet everyone when they arrived behind the business. They quickly reviewed what was about to happen and jumped in the pickup's bed with the patrol car close behind.

People stared at the truck driving down Montrose, loaded with five scruffy-looking guys in the back. Everyone was dressed in their Houston Narcotic Raid Jackets with their long hair waving in the wind. Donnie was thrilled it was his first day, and he was in the bed of a pickup about to hit a drug house.

They pulled into the driveway, and everyone jumped out of the bed and hurried to the front door with the uniformed cop behind them. Donnie stayed back and planned to fill in where needed.

Tom pounded, "POLICE, SEARCH WARRANT! OPEN THE DOOR!" He turned the doorknob, but it was locked, so he reared back and kicked the door with all his might. The door gave way, flew open with a violent thud, and slammed against the far wall. They hurried through the entranceway, yelling, "POLICE!"

A bloodcurdling scream came from the back of the house. Then, Donnie heard someone yelling, "Get your hands up!" Donnie walked toward the screaming and saw a couple of officers pointing their weapons at two guys in bed. Both men were naked and trying to grab sheets to cover themselves. "Show me your hands, motherfucker," one of the narcs yelled.

"Get out of that fucking bed," a narc officer demanded.

Then one of the men spotted Donnie and yelled, "OFFICER PARKER!" Donnie's mouth dropped open. He couldn't believe his luck; it was Bruce from the bank.

"I said get the fuck out...." then, mid-sentence, the narc stopped, looked at Donnie, and asked, "Did he just say your name?"

Donnie's efforts to fit in with the guys were at stake. He was done if they thought he had a relationship with a dope using queer. Abruptly, Donnie pointed his pistol at Bruce and yelled, "Shut up! You don't know me!"

"But I'm..." Bruce tried to talk.

Donnie interrupted him, "I SAID SHUT UP!"

The two narcs in the bedroom looked at each other, and one said, "He knows Donnie! Hey Tom. Better get in here. We've arrested one of Donnie's friends!"

Donnie lowered his weapon and walked out of the room to avoid the controversy, with Bruce yelling in the distance, "Officer Parker, please!"

The team finished their investigation and arrested two people. Since Bruce was not listed on the search warrant and no drugs were found near him, he was released. It was a pretty safe assumption that he was just there for the sex. Donnie tried to avoid being anywhere near Bruce and stayed outside until everything was concluded. Donnie was mortified, and it was an embarrassment that he would not soon live down.

The first day in Narcotics had been memorable for both Andy and Donnie. They got a taste of what Narcotics work was like and could only hope the rest of their careers would be more predictable.

HL & P

When Andy arrived at the Narcotics office the next day, Marvin Gentry was on the mail run. One of Marvin's jobs was to gather up the mail each day and deliver it around the office. The addressees were predominately supervisors and administration secretaries, but with two shifts of employees, sometimes he had an armful.

"Afternoon, Marvin," Andy said.

"Huh?" Marvin replied.

"I said AFTERNOON," Andy repeated loudly. Andy realized Marvin was hard of hearing and in one of his grumpy moods. The older he got, the less patience he had. Marvin said his hearing impairment was due to the bombing and gunfire he experienced serving in World War II. Although he was old enough to have been in the war, many of the narcs on the 6th floor doubted some of his stories. No matter what anyone talked about, Marvin did the same thing, only bigger and better.

Sergeant Houseman, the Administration Sergeant for the day shift, also had a nasty disposition. His mood could be as bad as Marvin's, if not worse. To complicate things, he was also hard of hearing and suffered a stroke several years ago, which diminished his reasoning skills. Houseman's ailing health was why Captain Jones kept him in the office and away from any situation involving hands-on police work.

Andy followed him down the hallway leading to the Sergeant's office while Marvin continued dropping off mail. Marvin walked past Sergeant Houseman's desk, dropping several letters. "Morning, Houseman," Marvin said low and grumpily.

Houseman was concentrating on some paperwork and barely heard him. Then, finally, he looked up and asked, "What?"

"I said morning," Marvin replied as he continued to walk around desks, dropping off mail. Andy wasn't going to miss this encounter, so stood there watching from the doorway.

Houseman put his pen down and spun around in his chair to give his full, undivided attention, "What did you say?"

"Nothing," Marvin replied, disgusted, and waved Houseman off.

"NOTHING?" Houseman said in a raised voice, demanding to know what Marvin said.

"Fuck it! It doesn't matter," Marvin snarled, glaring at Houseman.

"Well, fuck you too! And get out of my office!" Houseman shouted, pointing to the door.

"Asshole," Marvin replied, turned, and walked out. He was finished with the mail run, and it wasn't worth staying there and arguing. Houseman sat there watching Marvin walk out of the office and slowly turned around to continue working.

Andy shook his head, chuckling on the walk to the dayroom. A mutual hearing deficit turned a morning greeting into a confrontation, with both men now pissed off at each other. 'Never a dull moment on the 6th floor,' he thought. Andy was in the middle of pouring his cup of coffee when Mark walked in.

"Hey Andy, want to do another drive-by?"

"Sure," Andy replied cheerfully.

"We'll need some help for this one. Let's wait until after roll-call," Mark suggested. Andy agreed. Mark had a clue on a meth lab in a trailer home complex located in far northeast Harris County. He was trying to gather more intel, but he knew who the cook was and which trailer he lived in. The cook was the person responsible for making the methamphetamine. The complex chemical process could be hazardous if the cook didn't know what they were doing. The location was commonly called a lab because the equipment needed to make meth was remarkably similar to what you would see in a chemist's laboratory.

"This guy is real hinky," Mark told Andy. Hinky was police jargon used to describe someone suspicious of everything and everyone. "He's staying up 24 hours a day to cook and shooting dope to stay awake. My informant tells me that he's constantly looking out the windows, paranoid of law enforcement. I checked the utilities, but Houston Lighting & Power (HL&P) has already cut his electricity off, so no one is paying the bills there. I think he is cooking using propane tanks and possibly lanterns for lighting. I need to get a good look at the front door to see the numbers on that trailer, but there is just no way of getting close enough."

Andy sat intently, listening and absorbing as much information as possible. He was learning so much, but he didn't want to ask a stupid question and let Mark know how uninformed he was.

Soon a few more of the day shift crew arrived, and Mark started recruiting help for his drive-by. Finally, Sergeant McCain walked in and asked, "What was the big meeting about?"

Mark explained the possible lab and his problem with getting more information on the trailer home. Mark said, "As far as I know, the entire complex is full of crooks. I don't know anything about them, so I will base this on the worst-case scenario."

Sergeant McCain asked, "Why don't we use the HL&P uniform?"

Mark smiled, "That's a great idea, Sarg!" The HL&P uniform was a bright orange jumpsuit with bold black letters 'HL&P' printed on the front and back. The light company used them to identify their employees who walked house to house, reading meters each month. After the meter numbers were turned in, the bill was calculated by how much electricity was consumed. It was common to see the brightly orange-dressed meter readers in the neighborhood. No one would think twice about one of them walking through a subdivision or trailer park complex.

The Narcotics Division just happened to have one of the jumpsuits, and it was Andy's size. Sergeant McCain smiled and turned to Andy, "Let the new guy try it on. I think it'll fit him perfectly." Everyone seemed amused that it was Andy's turn in the barrel to wear the orange suit. Andy just smiled. At this point, he had no clue what they were asking of him, but he was all in.

Mark reviewed the plan with the guys, and McCain showed Andy the back closet where the suit was kept. "Just put this over your clothes," McCain said and handed it to Andy.

"Can I carry my pistol?" Andy asked.

"Sure, but you won't be able to access it quickly," McCain replied.

"That's OK. I feel better knowing I have one," Andy said.

McCain then said, "Tuck a walkie-talkie in there too and use a remote mic so that we can communicate with you."

Andy finished suiting up and stuck the handheld radio in his back pocket. He ran the earpiece up under his shirt to his ear to monitor the radio and call for help if necessary. McCain handed Andy a clipboard, smiled, and said, "Here, this completes the ensemble. Go get 'em, tiger!" McCain slapped Andy on the back as they walked into the briefing room and everyone had a laugh, but deep down, everyone knew this was serious business.

After finishing the briefing, they headed to their assigned locations around the trailer park. Andy rode with Mark, and they reviewed the plan several more times so that Andy knew exactly what to do. The guys had strategically picked their positions to respond quickly in the event Andy was in trouble, and they would warn him by radio if anyone were walking around.

Once the perimeter was set, Mark dropped Andy off to start his route. "May the force be with you, my son," Mark said with a smile as he let Andy out of the pickup. Andy returned the smile and shut the door as he started toward the first trailer.

While walking down the street, the realization that Andy was entirely alone came rushing over him. The suspects in this trailer park could be capable of anything. Andy conducted a radio check with Mark as he made it to the first trailer.

"Gotcha, loud and clear," Mark replied. Andy relaxed a little, knowing that the guys were only a radio call away. There were roughly about six trailers to go before he reached the cook's house, so he did his best to imitate the meter readers he had seen in the past. One by one, he moved down the street, pretending to record numbers on his clipboard until he finally reached the target location.

He took his time, making mental notes of all windows and the front door. Andy jotted down the numbers posted to the right of the glass storm door.

The radio cracked, "The crook is coming out the back door!" Andy shuttered with questions immediately racing through his mind, 'Is he looking for me? Did he make me? How could he have known?' Silently, he looked and listened. "Crook is walking toward you, Andy." Andy cautiously walked to the end of the trailer and turned back to look. "Get out of there, Andy!" Mark shouted over the radio.

Suddenly Andy spotted the suspect at the other end of the trailer. The moment their eyes met, the man made a break for it and ran toward the back of the complex. Andy figured the gig was up, and he was trying to escape. He wasn't sure if he was doing the right thing, but his patrol instincts took over, and Andy gave chase.

Several officers screamed over the radio that he was in foot pursuit. Once Andy knew the team was closing in and help was on its way, he no longer felt alone. In case the crook was armed, Andy unzipped his suit as he ran, awkwardly stumbling and trying to reach his pistol. Andy realized what Sergeant McCain meant by not being able to get to it quickly.

The suspect repeatedly glanced back, panicking, as he ran between the trailers. "STOP MOTHERFUCKER!" Andy screamed. Terrified, the crook kept running. Andy was closing distance quickly as the suspect stumbled, maneuvering around lawnmowers, AC compressors, and children's playground equipment. Dogs were barking, but luckily none of them were giving chase. "STOP MOTHERFUCKER!" Andy screamed again. He was within arm's reach as they rounded a trailer and ran across a small lawn. Andy gave him a good shove in the back, sending him tumbling end over end. The crook stopped, flat on his back with Andy standing over him, pointing his pistol directly at his face. "I'LL SHOOT YOU, ASSHOLE!"

The suspect raised his hands, "OK! OK! I'll pay the bill!"

"WHAT? What the fuck are you talking about? I'm the POLICE!" Andy said, standing there, pistol in hand, as the other team members quickly closed in.

"Oh, thank God! I thought you were HL&P!"

Puzzled, Andy lowered his gun a bit, trying to understand what the crook was talking about.

They cuffed and searched him. Apparently, he was getting threatening letters from HL&P about the money he owed them from his unpaid electrical bill. When Andy came around in the meter reader uniform, the suspect thought he was there to collect a payment, so he decided to slip out the back. When Andy started chasing him with a pistol, he figured they were serious this time.

They all laughed about the calamity on the way back to the office. All except the crook anyway. They found some methamphetamine in his pocket, so they were able to get a search warrant on the trailer. The lab team dismantled the lab, and the cook was charged with manufacturing a controlled substance. He still seemed somewhat relieved that it was a legal matter he faced rather than a bill collector with a gun.

The Grand Jury

The following day Andy called home to tell Mom and Dad about his new adventures in the Narcotics Division and check on things. His parents got a kick out of his stories about life on the narco beat. Eventually, his Mom mentioned that Mike had moved to Houston. "He has a business opportunity there, so he moved into an apartment on the southwest side." She didn't elaborate, and Andy didn't ask. He could only imagine and assumed Mike must have skated on the Rolex investigation. Mike had a knack for getting out of trouble, but things were different in the big city, and the people here played for keeps.

Andy continued worrying about Mike and his illegal endeavors on the drive to work. But soon, his mind drifted to what may be in store for him today. So far, each day had been filled with the excitement he had yearned for, but would it last? Over three days, he had already seen more action than he had anticipated in a year.

Sure enough, when he walked into the dayroom, they were planning another warrant. Rico Gonzales had a search warrant to execute for heroin and needed assistance, and Mark had already volunteered them. Rico was one of the more experienced narcs on the day shift, and when he put a deal together, it was well planned and usually produced results.

So that everyone could follow along as he explained the specifics, Rico had the plan drawn up on a grease board. Once he had recruited enough help, he began explaining who the suspect was. Throughout Rico's presentation, Andy couldn't help but be impressed by his attention to detail. He had thought of everything.

The apartment complex was located on the east side of downtown, an area notorious for heroin. The one-bedroom apartment was on the bottom floor of a two-story building. According to Rico, this drug dealer was responsible for supplying a significant amount of black tar heroin to that part of town. Black tar heroin was brought into the country from Mexico, whereas white heroin originated overseas. Also, black tar was less expensive and more prevalent in the Houston area.

At the end of the briefing, Rico indicated that he didn't have information about the suspect being armed, but he had been known to carry a pistol in the past. This would be a simple knock and announce, then breach the door by kicking it open. He told everyone, "Let's just be careful! There's no reason to get hurt by forcing this deal; if things don't go as planned, follow my lead." After that last comment, Andy had some pre-game jitters.

They left the office and drove to the rear of the suspect's apartment complex, parked, and put on their raid jackets. Rico's partner, Frank Barnes, was the only one who carried a short-barreled shotgun and his pistol. Everyone else carried one handgun and a couple of extra magazines. The team lined up and headed toward the apartment. Andy and Mark were at the end of the stack for containment and cuffing prisoners.

Stack was the tactical term used to describe an entry team lined up to go through a doorway. Because Andy was still the new guy, he was placed at the very end, and he was fine with that. Rico was in front, quietly leading them toward an open gate and patio.

The patio was relatively small, and there was an Old Smokey BBQ pit obstructing their way as the team tried to fit in. Sure enough, one of the team members bumped it, and the lid fell off, crashing to the concrete patio with a loud clang.

Rico hastily turned to see what had caused the noise, and that was the first time Andy noticed he looked worried. Surely the suspect heard it too, and now they had most likely lost the element of surprise and its advantages.

Now they were left with two options, back out and call the whole thing off or go ahead and do this thing. Rico chose the latter, yelling "POLICE," and kicking the door. Unfortunately, his boot landed next to the doorknob and deadbolt, yielding no results. He kicked the solid door again and continued yelling, "POLICE."

Everything seemed to unfold in slow motion for Andy as he watched from the back of the patio. He didn't like being in such a small, enclosed area with no way out, but he stuck to the plan.

On the second kick, the door flew open, and Rico pointed his pistol toward the open doorway. "POLICE MOTHERFUCKER," Rico yelled, and then a single gunshot rang out from within the apartment. The entire stack flinched as if to dodge the bullet, but only Rico knew where it came from. Rico aimed and fired three consecutive shots through the threshold while the rest of the team could only watch. Rico continued yelling "POLICE," while he backed out of the gate and fired a fourth round.

When Frank attempted to peer into the doorway with his shotgun at the ready, he couldn't see anyone. Everyone else ducked to avoid being hit by a stray bullet while watching Rico screaming demands to someone inside. Then, unexpectedly a voice from within the apartment yelled out, "ALRIGHT! I GIVE UP!"

Rico yelled, "CRAWL TO ME MOTHERFUCKER! DO IT NOW!" Rico was entirely off the patio but still aligned to see inside the apartment.

Glancing around the enclosed yard, Andy felt trapped and considered leaping the fence, but he thought that cowardly, so he just hunkered down and waited.

"ALRIGHT, DON'T SHOOT! I'M COMING OUT!" the voice from the apartment yelled.

Rico yelled back, "Come to me motherfucker! Get your ass out here, NOW!"

"Don't shoot," he pleaded again.

"I ain't gonna shoot!" Rico replied, "Just keep coming with your hands in the air!"

A pair of hands appeared in the doorway, and the suspect crawled out on his knees. Several team members grabbed him and pulled him to the side. He was handcuffed and searched, then Frank asked, "Where's the fucking gun, asshole?"

"Inside on the kitchen counter," the man replied. "I swear, I didn't know you were cops!"

"Fuck you! Is anyone else in there?" asked Frank.

"No, sir," the suspect said, ashamedly dropping his head.

Rico stood him up and walked the suspect in front of him in case of an ambush. He looked over the suspect's shoulder with one hand on the suspect's handcuffs and the other on his pistol.

Everything ended as quickly as it started. The team strategically entered the apartment and found no one inside. They began searching the premise for narcotics, and Rico radioed for a supervisor and homicide to respond. Although no one was hit, homicide and internal affairs would be required to investigate the scene.

Andy was fascinated by Rico's ability to remain calm throughout the situation. Even during the gunfire, he never seemed to get rattled. Instead, he appeared to be more angry than excited. Andy figured that his years of doing this line of work must have hardened his nerves.

Homicide, IAD, and the DA's office soon arrived, along with the news media. It turned into a massive spectacle since they planned to file attempted capital murder charges on the suspect for shooting at police officers. The crime scene unit took pictures of the bullet holes scattered throughout the apartment walls. All the rounds went through the sheetrock and stopped in the exterior brick. Thankfully, as it turned out, the crook's gun jammed. Curiously, they wondered if he was forced to surrender because of the jammed weapon or if he wanted to surrender.

Several ounces of uncut heroin was found hidden in an old shoebox, an awful lot for a low-level street dealer. This crook would go to prison for a long time, especially with the attempted capital murder charge. The suspect continued to claim he never heard anyone announce police, so he assumed a rival drug dealer was trying to rip him off.

A few weeks later, subpoenas arrived for them to appear before a grand jury investigating the charges. Andy had never testified at a grand jury hearing before, so he was nervous even though he had never fired a shot.

On the day of the hearing, they gathered in a small waiting room while the grand jury questioned witnesses. The only cop they called in was Rico. After testifying, he told them, "The crook is still claiming that we never said police."

"That motherfucker," Mark exclaimed. "We all heard you!"

"I know, but that's all he's got," Rico replied. "He's sticking to his story."

Soon the DA came out of the grand jury chambers chuckling, "You guys can go. The grand jury is going to true bill him for the attempted capital murder. He's done!"

"OK, thanks, but what's so funny?" Rico asked.

The DA had to pause to regain his composure, "You know the lady that lived in the apartment next door?"

"Yeah? So?" Rico asked.

"Well, the Grand Jury Foreman wanted to question her, so he asked me to subpoena her too." He broke out laughing again.

"Well...what?" asked Rico.

Still chuckling, the DA continued, "The Foreman asked her what she heard before the shooting started. She paused for a moment and then said, 'Well, I heard a loud boom like someone kicking the wall, and then I heard POLICE MOTHERFUCKER! and that's when the shooting started.' I swear, I almost lost it right there."

The guys busted out laughing, and several slapped Rico on the back. He smiled and said, "Thanks! Let's go, guys," he waved and walked out.

When they got off the elevator at the office, Gentry asked, "How did it go, boys?"

Rico waved and said, "Good," and continued walking, but Andy couldn't help himself. He stopped to tell Marvin what the neighbor lady said to the grand jury. For the next ten minutes, Marvin went into a story about a shooting he was involved in back in the good ole days. Andy then understood what everyone meant about Marvin always one-upping the story. As Andy stood there, annoyed and forced to listen to Marvin's tale, he realized he should have just kept walking as Rico did. Next time, he would know better.

IAD Traffic Stop

Andy dropped his fitness membership and started working out at the old Academy gym. The gym at central was free, and he could use the extra cash at the end of the month. As a bonus, he made new friends from all over the department while he worked out. Everyone there had a similar mindset and enjoyed staying in shape. Andy figured that someday, being in shape could save his life.

He showered in the same locker room he used as a cadet, which brought back good and bad memories of his time there. He missed his old classmates, and his thoughts eventually drifted to Herman. 'What would have become of Herman if Hurley hadn't tormented him?' he wondered. These days, he rarely saw Hurley except in passing around the station or at the credit union. He noticed Hurley was promoted to Sergeant and felt sorry for whoever had to work for that bastard.

After his morning workout, Andy headed to the 6th floor for another day of the unpredictable. As he walked past the front desk, Marvin Gentry yelled, "The Captain wants to see you and Kiley in his office."

Andy stopped dead in his tracks. The last time he had been called into a Captain's office was in his old Academy days, and it hadn't gone well. "Do you know what he wants?" Andy asked.

"Not a clue," Marvin replied, "but it seemed important."

Andy continued toward the dayroom, and he found Mark kicked back with his boots on the desk, reading the paper. "Mark, the Captain wants to see us!" Andy said urgently.

"Yeah, I know," Mark replied, unconcerned. "I was waiting for you to get through with your workout. Let's go see what the old man wants." Mark got up and casually strolled past him as Andy followed like a nervous cat. First, they stopped at Sergeant McCain's office to see if he knew what was up. "Hey, Sarg," greeted Mark.

McCain interrupted, "Come with me." McCain got up from his desk and walked out into the hallway toward the Captain's office. Finally, he stopped and knocked on the door, "Come in," announced the Captain. Andy felt as if they were walking into the oval office. The walls were covered with rich wood paneling, and it had a warm, business-like feel to it. The Captain was seated at his desk in a business suit, reading over some paperwork. Lieutenant Riley sat on the couch across the room. And Andy was still struggling to imagine what could have brought them together.

Captain Jones stood up from his desk and shook McCain's hand, although Riley didn't bother. Instead, he nodded at McCain while Jones shook hands with Mark and Andy and thanked them for coming. Even though he knew they weren't there for a friendly chat, Andy felt a bit better that Jones was cordial.

Jones invited them to sit down as they engaged in small talk. Once everyone was seated, and the idle chit-chat quieted, Jones pulled a folder from his desk drawer and laid it in front of him. A serious look came over his face as he said, "What I am about to show you is top secret. You cannot breathe a word of it to anyone. If I as much as hear a rumor that you told anyone about this case, I will have your ass. Understood?" Andy swallowed nervously and nodded his head in agreement.

"No problem, Captain," Mark agreed. Lieutenant Riley carefully studied those in the room. Andy assumed the Lieutenant was just trying to read their reactions, so he continued paying close attention.

Jones continued, "You will take no notes, and this folder will not leave my office. I need you to memorize this information and then do as you're told, and nothing more. Understood?"

"Yes, sir," Mark and Andy replied in unison.

The Captain opened the folder and spun it around so the contents faced Andy and Mark. They looked down, and it was immediately clear why the secrecy. An IAD investigation report with a picture of an HPD officer in full uniform is stapled to the complaint form. Internal Affairs Division, IAD, was newly formed and made up of several supervisors whose job was to investigate complaints and illegal activity conducted by Houston Police Officers. The Captain asked, "First, do either one of you know this officer?"

"No, sir," they both replied.

"He works Sunnyside, on day shift patrol." Sunnyside was an area of town known for a high crime rate. "IAD has an informant, and she claims he is dealing dope out of his patrol car. They don't have undercover officers at IAD, so they have asked us to help by following him and seeing if he meets anyone. They want to know who he meets, license plates, descriptions, etc."

Andy and Mark both agreed.

The Captain added, "Just tail him from a distance and make mental notes on his travels. Especially anything out of the norm. I want to know where he stops, especially if he talks to anyone."

"When do we start?" asked Mark.

"Right now," replied Jones. "He's working today, so drive out to Sunnyside and see if you can locate him. His radio number is 15A23. Monitor the channel and see if he gets a call or conducts a traffic stop. Then, you should be able to locate him and start your surveillance. Understood?"

"Who do we report back to?" confirmed Mark.

Captain Jones stood up and stuck his hand, "Directly to me. I want to hear from you at the end of each day."

They shook the Captain's hand, and Mark responded, "You got it!"

Mark walked to the dayroom to get his briefcase, and Andy stood at the elevators waiting. "You boys in trouble?" Gentry asked.

"No, just helping the Captain with something," Andy replied.

"Hmmm," Marvin replied.

When they got on the elevator, they looked at each other, shocked by their assignment, but didn't say anything. Andy presumed the elevator was bugged, and the moment anything was said, the Captain would instantly know. So, silently, they rode down to the 1st floor and headed for Mark's truck.

Once they got in the pickup and shut the doors, Andy turned to Mark and said, "Holy SHIT! Can you fucking believe this?"

"Yeah, it's serious shit," Mark replied. As they drove out of the parking garage and onto the freeway toward Sunnyside, they chatted about how to do this. They turned the radio to the patrol channel and headed toward the most significant assignment they ever had.

Once they exited MLK boulevard, they began looking for marked police vehicles. Units were radioing their traffic stops and responding to calls, but they hadn't heard 15A23 yet. Andy was astounded by how busy the day shift channel was and how calls for service were going out every few minutes. Although it made him miss patrol a little, he had moved on and felt empowered by this top-secret mission.

Finally, they heard the call they had been waiting for, "15A23 out on traffic, 8700 MLK. Red pickup occupied two times." Andy couldn't believe his ears! They were only about eight blocks away and headed in the right direction. Then, in the distance, they glimpsed the flashing police lights. Andy's heart began to race.

Tailing a fellow police officer made it almost surreal. "Don't stare. We'll cruise past and pull over down the road," said Mark.

"Got it," Andy replied.

Mark slowed down so that they would have more time to get a good look. Standing by a red pickup, the officer was speaking with the driver. Andy tried to note as much as possible without being too conspicuous. They pulled into a vacant parking lot down the street, and Mark asked, "Did you get a look at his face? Is it him?"

"Yep, that's him," replied Andy.

Mark said, "Cool, let's just wait here until he pulls out."

It seemed like forever as they sat nervously watching the rear-view mirror. Finally, the officer got back in his patrol car and pulled out onto MLK. On the radio, Andy heard the officer's voice report, "15A23 back in service." While the unit drove past them, they tried to act like they were reading. Fortunately, it didn't appear as though he was paying any attention to them, which is precisely what they were hoping for.

Mark pulled out and followed from several car lengths back. He tried to keep vehicles between him and the patrol unit to appear inconspicuous if the officer looked in his rear-view mirror. Suddenly the patrol car turned around and headed back toward them. Mark said, "Well fuck me! Just be cool, and I'll try to turn around as soon as possible. I don't want to be too obvious."

Andy said nothing, but his eyes were glued to the approaching police car. The officer had his driver's side window down and stared at them as they casually passed each other.

Mark watched the side mirror intently as they passed and said, "SHIT! He's turning around!"

Andy asked, "Do you think he made us?"

"No way," Mark replied, but the patrol car turned around and sped up. He pulled into the traffic lane behind them, and they could do nothing but watch their mirrors. "Just be cool," Mark said. "He's probably after someone else."

Suddenly the police lights came on. "Awe fuck," Mark said, slowed down, and pulled into the nearest parking lot.

Andy was about to shit himself, wondering where they went wrong. The patrol car followed them into the parking lot. Nervous, Andy's heart pounded, and his palms were clammy. He had been looking forward to doing a good job for the Captain, but now their cover was blown before they started. Andy heard the officer call out on traffic, describing their vehicle. Andy quickly turned their police radio off and closed the glove compartment. "Just follow my lead," Mark said.

The officer got out and slowly walked to Mark's window. He was wearing sunglasses, so Mark couldn't see his eyes in the mirror, but he was obviously checking out the truck. There was no time to develop a story, so Andy decided to key off whatever Mark said.

Mark had his window down, smoking a cigarette. After taking one last drag, he flicked the butt onto the ground.

"Afternoon, officer," Mark said cheerfully.

"Afternoon," the cop replied. "Do you know why I stopped you?"

"No, sir."

"Really?" the officer asked skeptically. "You don't have a clue?"

That was all it took for Andy to know the gig was up and this was about to get ugly. 'How would he explain this to the Captain,' he wondered. IAD had trusted narcotics to surveil someone, and they blew it from the get-go.

The officer then pointed at the inspection sticker on the windshield of Mark's pickup. "You didn't notice this little guy?" the officer asked. In disbelief, Andy stared at the inspection sticker in the window and was at least grateful they weren't burned after all. The officer didn't have a clue who they were. Andy wanted to laugh and cry simultaneously, but he contained himself and breathed a sigh of relief. "Sorry, officer," Mark replied, "I must have missed that."

"Well, it's only out a month, so I'll tell you what I'm gonna do. Let me have your driver's license, and I'll check you for warrants. Then, if you're clear, I'll let you off with a warning. Sound fair?" asked the officer.

"Sure thing," Mark replied, giving the officer his license.

"Be right back."

As the officer walked back to his vehicle, Andy glanced at Mark and asked, "You don't have any warrants, do you?"

Mark just grinned and said, "Well, I guess we're about to find out." They both let out a nervous chuckle. They listened to the officer relay Mark's driver's license information to the dispatcher; Andy turned the police radio back on quietly. All Houston narcs were issued an undercover driver's license from the Texas Department of Public Safety. Of course, everything on it was fake, so the officer wouldn't know his true identity. Now they needed to figure out how to break the news to the Captain.

The dispatcher quickly advised Mark's license was clear, so Andy turned the radio off and closed the glove box. The officer got out, gave the driver's license back to Mark, and wished them a good day. The officer was incredibly friendly and professional. Andy had hoped he was a jerk, so he wouldn't feel bad if they busted him later. One thing was for sure; it wouldn't be Mark and Andy doing the surveillance anymore. Their part in this investigation was over.

The long drive back to central was quiet, and the elevator ride up felt like an eternity as they stood there feeling like a couple of losers. When they knocked on the Captain's door, Sergeant Houseman came storming out in a huff. Infuriated, he walked right past them and stomped off toward his office. He'd just finished complaining to the Captain about someone in the office fucking with him, and he wanted it to stop.

Knowing that Houseman has had difficulty with his reasoning skills since his stroke, the night shift guys started jacking with his desk to have some fun at his expense. First, they took a polaroid picture of his desktop and then took everything off. Next, they spun the desk around so that the opening for his legs to fit under was now against the wall, and the solid back of the desk was facing out.

Utilizing the polaroid pictures as a map, they put everything back exactly as before and waited for Houseman to arrive. He sat down and continually tried to slide his legs under the desk, but his knees repeatedly hit the outer partition. He tried again and again, but he kept bumping into the partition each time he attempted to put his legs under the desk. Finally, he stood up, looked down at his desk, and still couldn't figure it out, so he sat back down and tried again. The night shift guys watched through the office window, laughing hysterically at their prank.

To make things worse, Marvin Gentry was on his mail run as he walked into the Sergeant's office with a handful of letters. Already pissed and looking for someone to blame, Houseman started in on Marvin. They started going after each other like two junkyard dogs chained together. The night shift guys had to get between them before it got out of hand.

The Captain was on the phone with Lieutenant Riley when Mark and Andy walked into his office. He motioned for them to sit down as he yelled at Riley, "LOOK, you tell those night shift guys that I said to stop fucking with Houseman! NO...wait... Don't tell them I said it, or they'll start fucking with me. Just tell them to stop!" He was extremely frustrated as he hung up the phone and looked at Mark and Andy. "WHAT?" he asked them. He had already had enough for one day.

They went to great pains to explain what went wrong as they threw themselves on their swords and asked for forgiveness. The Captain seemed to take it well but coupled with Houseman's issues; he had reached a breaking point. He pushed his chair back and opened the bottom drawer of his desk. He pulled out a bottle of Jack Daniels and poured a drink into a shot glass. He downed it like an old pro and asked Mark and Andy if they wanted a hit. Both declined; the Captain shrugged his shoulders and returned the bottle. He looked up and said, "Just like before, if I hear a word about you two telling anyone about this, I will have your ass. That goes for my bottle as well! Now get the HELL out of here and go find some dope."

With that, Andy and Mark stood up and walked out, never to breathe a word to anyone about their assignment or the Captain's whiskey. In a way, Andy had gained even more respect for Captain Jones. Even though he was a figure of authority, he could see past a simple mistake. And yet, he was human and sometimes needed a crutch to help him through the day. Andy hoped that he could take the Captain up on his offer to have a drink with him someday but under more favorable circumstances.

ELEVEN

Here's Jack!

The following week, Andy was in the dayroom waiting on Mark to return from testifying in court when he ran into his old buddy, Donnie Parker. The chance meeting was a lucky one because Donnie and Jack Spencer had been working the evening shift from 6 pm to 2 am. Jack was a good guy and a better-than-average narc who loved putting dope dealers in prison.

Although Andy heard about numerous shootings Jack had been involved in throughout his career, all appeared to be justified, and not even the Grand Jury found an issue. 'Had Jack become a cold-blooded shooter, or had he simply been in the wrong place at the wrong time?' Andy couldn't stop himself from wondering. Just the same, Donnie liked Jack and had grown to trust him, which was good enough for Andy. One thing was for sure; Jack would not back down from a gunfight.

"Hey, Donnie," Andy said as he walked into the dayroom.

"Hey. How's it going, Andy?" Donnie greeted.

They caught up on small talk about work and how they were acclimating to the Narcotics Division so far. Then, mid-conversation, Jack walked in, and Andy finally met the legend he had heard so much about.

The first thing Andy noticed about Jack was his thick Cajun Louisiana accent. They shook hands, and Jack said, "So you're Andy Wallace. Donnie has told me a lot about you."

Andy was proud Donnie mentioned him in conversation. "Don't believe everything you hear. What are you guys up to? Night shift doesn't start for five more hours."

"We've got a deal set for 4 o'clock. It's the only time the crook would do it. We could use some help if you want to come with us," Jack suggested.

Andy said, "Well, my partner is not due back for a while. Hell, he may not even make it back today if he gets hung up in court. So, I'll ask Sarg if it's OK."

"Sure, just let us know," replied Jack.

Andy walked into the Sergeant's office, where he found McCain leaning back in his office chair, reading the newspaper. "Hey, Sarg!" Andy said, "Would it be alright if I go with some night shift guys on a deal? They are shorthanded, and Mark's not due back for at least a couple more hours. So, I don't have anything to work on until then."

McCain lowered his paper enough to peer over it, with his reading glasses slid halfway down his nose. "Which night shift guys?" he asked suspiciously.

"My old buddy Donnie Parker and some others." Andy intentionally didn't mention Jack because he knew McCain was leery of his guys going anywhere with him. Even though McCain didn't have anything against Jack, something always happened when he was involved.

"Isn't Parker working with Spencer?" questioned McCain.

"Yeah, and a bunch of other guys," Andy responded, trying to downplay Jack's involvement.

"Well, if they have a bunch of guys, why do they need you?"

"Come on, Sarg!" Andy pleaded. "I'm just gonna cover the back. I want to see how the night shift guys work. Plus, the experience would do me good."

McCain raised his paper and went back to reading. Andy stood there wondering if that meant yes or no.

"Just cover the back, and that's it," grumbled McCain.

"Right, Sarg," Andy replied.

"AND I WANT YOU TO CALL ME WHEN IT'S OVER!" McCain hollered while Andy rushed out of his office.

Eagerly, Andy hurried back to the dayroom and blurted out, "I'm in!"

"Great," Donnie answered.

"OK, grab your shit and meet us in the parking garage. You can ride out there with us," said Jack.

"Aren't you gonna cut the deal up here?" asked Andy.

"The guys are meeting us out there," Jack replied. "We'll cut it up at the meet location."

Andy could already see the night shift operated much differently. Day shift held mandatory formal briefings before ever assembling at the scene. Their briefings often included diagrams, pictures of the suspect, and detailed assignments were discussed in advance. Andy figured Jack would do the same at a remote location, so he decided to keep an open mind. Although Andy hadn't conducted the planning phase at a remote location before, he wasn't judgmental, and he just wanted to learn and see some action.

Loaded in a plain white van, they headed to the meet location westbound on I-10. While Jack elaborated on the deal, Andy paid close attention. The search warrant was for possession of methamphetamine, and the suspect in question was a biker dude nicknamed Snake. He was residing in an old upstairs apartment in Spring Branch. The area consisted predominately of middle-class neighborhoods. Unfortunately, crime rapidly increased due to a large influx of undesirable residents. After a reliable informant purchased meth from Snake, they were granted a search warrant for the apartment.

Jack parked the van across the street from the apartment behind a 7-Eleven convenience store. Three nightshift narcs were already there. Andy recognized Sam Flores from working out at the gym, but he didn't know the other two.

Jack introduced Andy to the rest of the team, "Hey guys, Andy volunteered to go in first." Completely put on the spot, Andy nearly fainted, staring back wide-eyed in panic at Jack. Jack cracked a smile, busted out laughing, and slapped Andy on the back. Everyone had a quick laugh, and then Jack got down to business, "OK, here's the deal. I will run the informant in there one more time to confirm our crook has dope. Once we know, we'll hit it."

Sam asked, "Won't that burn your informant?"

"Fuck him," Jack answered. "I ain't using that motherfucker anymore anyway. He's getting too pushy, and I'm done with him."

"Sucks to be him," Donnie said, and they all chuckled.

Jack continued, "Well, if we get the green light, I'll lead us upstairs, and Sam will kick the door. I'll go in first with Donnie behind me. The rest of you fall in line behind us."

"Do you want me to cover the back?" asked Andy.

"Hell no!" Jack scoffed. "It's a second-story apartment. That motherfucker can't fly." The guys laughed again, but Andy worried about what he would tell Sergeant McCain. He figured it wouldn't matter anyway because McCain would have no way of knowing where he ended up.

Jack and Donnie left to meet with the informant while Andy stayed behind with Sam and the other guys. Even though he didn't know them well, he was surprisingly comfortable in their presence. While they chatted about other deals they had in the works, they were relaxed and confident, and that's what Andy's perception of being a narc was. However, the day shift was much more stringent, and the supervisors mandated their involvement in all aspects. As a result, Andy thought he should transfer to the night shift at the first available opportunity.

Shortly, Jack and Donnie arrived back at the meet location.

"Let's do this!" Jack said excitedly.

Everyone scattered to gather their gear. Andy put on his vest, pistol rig, and raid jacket. That was one standard operating procedure that hadn't changed, even for the night shift.

They jumped in the van for the short drive across the street.

"I'll park on the side of Snake's building, and we'll unass the van there," Jack advised in his thick Louisiana drawl. Everyone nodded. Just a few minutes ago, they were chatting and cutting it up like schoolboys, but now it was deadly serious on the drive across the busy traffic lanes of Longpoint.

Jack parked the van and turned around to make eye contact with the team. He held up a short-barreled 12-gauge pump shotgun and said, "Old Smokey here will lead us to the stairs, and then Sam is up." Sam nodded his head in agreement, and Jack continued, "It's the door on the right at the top of the stairs, numbered 2214. If anything goes wrong, follow my lead," Jack added.

Andy watched Jack's coolness and confidence in awe. He realized why Jack had such a reputation, and it was hard not to be impressed.

They stepped out of the van, drew their weapons, and formed a single file line as they walked along the sidewalk of Snake's apartment building. Jack led with Old Smokey at the low ready. Andy strained to see what was ahead.

A young mother pushing a baby stroller was walking directly toward them. When she saw a group of longhaired men with guns, she instantly froze, terrified. Jack kindly smiled and motioned with his index finger to his lips for her to keep quiet. Quickly, she pushed the baby stroller in the opposite direction as they continued toward the apartment. Andy glanced back to make sure she was still moving, but she was already gone. She had zero intention of hanging around to see what happened next.

Once Jack led them up the stairs, Sam stepped around and squared off on apartment 2214. He reared back and yelled, "POLICE! SEARCH WARRANT!" and kicked the door with a mighty blow. The door didn't budge at all. It was fully intact.

"POLICE!" yelled Jack. "Get it open, Sam!"

"I'M TRYING!" Sam yelled, and he kicked the door again and again. The more time it took for them to get through the threshold, the more dangerous this became, and the group started to fret.

Just as Sam kicked the door for the fourth time, gunshots rang out. Three rounds in short succession flew out the door past Sam. Then, without a moment's hesitation, Jack stepped forward and fired three rounds into the deadbolt lock with Old Smokey. Another round splintered through the door jam, and Sam was hit in the face.

"I'M HIT!" Sam yelled, stunned, grabbing his face and falling back.

Seeing Sam fall amplified Jack's fury; he turned toward the door, yelling, "YOU MOTHERFUCKER!" Two more bullets flew through the door, just barely missing him. Shaking in rage, Jack kicked the door again, and this time it flew open. Snake was in the hallway attempting to reload a six-shot revolver when he looked up to see Jack in the open threshold. Jack raised his shotgun to a hip fire position and screamed, "YOU MOTHERFUCKER!". He fired two rounds from Old Smokey, just missing Snake by an inch. Snake dropped the revolver and ran; he didn't slow down and dove headfirst out the second-story window falling to the grassy lawn below. Jack ran after him, yelling, "MOTHERFUCKER!" At the open window, Jack looked down and saw Snake get to his feet and hobble away, dragging one leg behind him. He aimed his shotgun, then hesitated. Instead, he turned around and ran out the front door, pushing past his teammates, yelling, "THAT MOTHERFUCKER SHOT SAM!" Sam was lying on his side, covering his face, and screaming for help.

In a flash, Jack sprinted down the stairs after Snake while the rest of the team tried their best to care for Sam and clear what was left of the apartment.

Snake hobbled across the busy lanes on Longpoint. Vehicles honked and swerved, trying to avoid hitting him. Finally, making it to the other side, he glanced back to see Jack rounding the corner of his apartment building with a shotgun in hand. With no chance of outrunning Jack, Snake gasped and limped into the 7-Eleven.

Snake, panicked and scared, yelled at the clerk, "A CRAZY FUCKER'S TRYING TO KILL ME!" Stunned, the clerk stood there with a blank expression and didn't respond. Snake nervously glanced around the store, looking for a way out, and ran to the back to find the door locked. The only unlocked door was the restroom, so he ran inside and locked the door behind him. He sat quivering next to the toilet in the corner, waiting for the worst.

Jack was deranged, sprinting across Longpoint. Now, cars swerved to avoid hitting another pedestrian, a longhaired, bearded man wearing a police raid jacket carrying a shotgun. All the while, Jack screamed, "POLICE," and dodged cars. He ran into the store and looked toward the clerk, who instinctually pointed toward the restroom.

Jack spun and stared at the door; the hunter had finally found his prey. Then, he calmly walked to the restroom, and with one mighty kick, the door flew open. He raised Old Smokey and stepped in to find Snake squatted in the corner with his hands in the air, whimpering, "Please don't kill me!"

Jack grabbed Snake by the hair and drug him out of the restroom. Snake screamed in agony as Jack dragged him to the center of the store and put Old Smokey to his head, pressing the shotgun to his temple. "I'm gonna shoot you like the dirty piece of shit you are. Just like you shot Sam!" Snake was crying, snot dripping down his lips, begging for his life.

The clerk begged, "Please, sir! Not in here." Jack turned and stared at the clerk holding his hand out, motioning him to stop.

Donnie ran into the store yelling, "JACK! STOP! NO! SAM'S ALRIGHT!" Jack didn't believe him; he had seen Sam fall; he was shot in the face. But why was Donnie saying he's OK? Donnie walked over and put his hand on Jack's shoulder in a comforting gesture, "It's OK. Sam's OK." Slowly, Jack started to relax and lowered Old Smokey while he listened. Snake sobbed on the floor, hoping he might live. The clerk leaned back against the wall, took a deep breath, and hoped this nightmare would soon be over.

Donnie handcuffed Snake, apologized to the clerk, and escorted the suspect out. "That's OK! I'm just glad it's over," the clerk responded.

As they approached the apartment complex, Jack spotted Sam standing by the van. Sam waved and smiled as he held a bandage to his face. Jack hurried to him and asked, "What the fuck? I thought you were dead!"

Sam replied, "I know. Me too! The wood fragments from the door hit me in the face, and I thought I was hit. Sorry, Jack!"

Jack lowered his head; all of it made sense now. He almost killed a guy to avenge a shooting that never happened.

As more and more police cars arrived, the place turned into a circus. Andy met up with the apartment manager to call Sergeant McCain. Although he wasn't looking forward to the conversation, he had to tell him before someone else did. Homicide, IAD, and the DA's investigators were en route to the scene, so the team waited to explain what happened.

Sergeant McCain arrived and spotted Andy standing with the other officers. "Where's Jack?" demanded McCain.

"I don't know, Sarg. He left a few minutes ago. I'm not sure where he went," replied Andy.

McCain blew a gasket and started screaming at the top of his lungs, "HE LEFT THE SCENE OF A SHOOTING? WHAT THE FUCK WAS HE THINKING?"

Then Jack walked up carrying a large fountain drink and a bag of chips.

"WHERE THE FUCK HAVE YOU BEEN?" McCain demanded.

Calmly, Jack replied in his Louisiana drawl, "I just walked 'cross the street to get a drink and call my lawyer."

In disgust, McCain threw his hands in the air, shook his head, and walked away. 'How can Jack still be so calm?' pondered Andy. It was just another day at the office for him, which made Jack simultaneously cool and deadly.

Andy got to see some action that day, but it wasn't what he expected. He quickly changed his mind about transferring to the night shift. Although the day shift was a little less exciting, it was much more predictable, and that's what he needed now.

The Other Side of the Bed

At 2 am, Andy's phone woke him from a dead sleep. Any call at that time of night is never good news. Mark Kiley asked if he had heard about the night shift shooting. "No, what happened?"

"While they were executing a warrant on the eastside, four-night shift guys were shot," Mark replied.

"Oh my God! Who?" asked Andy.

"I don't have any names yet."

"Are they OK?" Andy asked.

"I think they will survive, but it ain't good," Mark answered.

"Wow! What hospital?"

"Ben Taub, I think," Mark said.

"Holy shit! It must be bad if they're in the Tub!" The County Hospital was nicknamed the Tub.

After chatting for a while, they agreed to check with each other in the morning. Andy hung up but couldn't fall back to sleep. Instead, he lay awake, worried sick about Donnie and the other guys he knew on night shift. He had only been in Narcotics a short while but had already seen more action than his three years in patrol. The job was dangerous, exciting, and fun simultaneously, the trifecta. Unfortunately, Andy was about to find out just how dangerous.

He didn't sleep a wink the rest of the night, wondering what happened and hoping it wasn't anyone he knew. Four guys getting shot on one deal was unheard of. Although the night shift guys pressed the fight sometimes, they weren't stupid.

Andy gave up on sleep, blew off his morning workout, and instead called the Narcotics desk to get an update on the guys. Marvin Gentry told him one of the officers was David Green, but Andy didn't recognize the other names. From his few interactions with David around the office, he seemed like a nice guy. Unfortunately, Marvin didn't have much information to pass on, except everyone was in stable condition and would likely recover.

Andy and Mark decided to meet up at Ben Taub on their way to work. Every time a police officer was shot, it was like a circling of the wagons. So, when Andy arrived, he wasn't surprised the parking lot was full of police cars. This was a time to take care of their own, and the dangers of the job were genuine.

The desk receptionist advised David Green was moved into a private room on the 5th floor. As they walked to the elevators, Andy unexpectedly came face to face with Hurley. 'What the hell is he doing in a suit and tie, and why is he here?' Andy irritably wondered.

"Well, well, hello, Wallace," Hurley said with a shit-eating grin.

"What the fuck are you doing here, Hurley?" asked Andy.

"Well, not that it's any of your business, but I'm investigating the shooting. I'm working in IAD now. I heard you went to the Narcotics Division. I can't wait for the day I get to investigate you." Hurley smiled, winked, and arrogantly walked away.

Andy didn't say a word. Instead, he angrily glared at Hurley walking down the hallway.

"You know him?" Mark asked.

"Yeah, he's a real sweetheart," Andy replied.

"I would have never known. It seemed like you two were gonna hug for a minute there," Mark replied, chuckling under his breath.

They knocked on David's door, and a woman's voice invited them in. Slowly, they pushed the door open, and there were a bunch of night shift guys standing around to provide their support. David was lying in bed while his wife cared for her injured husband.

"Hey, David," Mark said as they politely eased into the room.

"Hey, guys," David replied.

"You OK?" asked Andy.

"Aww, it's just a flesh wound," David quipped, and all the guy's chuckled.

An awkward silence fell over the room, and Andy and Mark began to soon feel like outsiders, so Mark said, "Hey, we'll come back later and visit."

Andy chimed in, "Yeah, we just wanted to stop by on the way to work and check on you."

David replied, "OK, guys. Thanks for stopping by, but I'm good."

Politely, they nodded to everyone and waved as they clumsily backed out of the room. The day and night shift guys were like two separate families connected by the Captain. They were similar yet different, and neither one let the other in on the family secrets.

Andy was still perplexed about his chance meeting with Hurley. Once again, Hurley held all the cards as the IAD Sergeant, and Andy was left hoping to stay out of his way. When he got off the elevator on the 6th floor, Gentry said Lieutenant Riley would address roll-call with more information about the shooting. "Really?" asked Andy.

"Yep, he wants everyone there," replied Marvin.

Rumors spread like wildfire through the office as the day shift crew slowly arrived, chatting about the shooting over their morning coffee. No one had specific details, but they would soon learn the ugly truth.

Sergeant McCain was the first to have new information from a sergeant on the night shift. Evidently, a 67-year-old drug dealer shot four of the six officers attempting to execute a search warrant at his home. From his vantage point in the hallway, the older man picked the officers off one by one as they entered the front door. Every officer, except Green, fell outside the door, leaving David alone inside with the shooter.

David took a round to a leg and another to his dominant hand. The leg wound forced him to the floor. Then, the second bullet hit his pistol hand, sending his only weapon sprawling. He crawled out of the line of fire to a kitchen corner. Frantically, he looked and felt around with his good hand for his gun in the darkness. Just hoping he would find his weapon before the shooter found him. When the gunfire stopped, his worst fear became a reality as footsteps slowly walked toward him on the hardwood floor.

When the older man spotted David in the corner, he immediately pointed his revolver at him. Seeing his short life pass before his eyes, David pleaded with him, "Please don't do this. I have a family." Mockingly, the shooter tilted his head to the side, smiled, and pulled the trigger anyway. The revolver clicked, and the hammer fell on the spent round. The man had already emptied his chamber, firing all six shots; the gun was empty. The shooter dropped it on the floor, turned around, and walked out the front door with his hands in the air. At last, he was handcuffed and taken into custody.

The entire dayroom erupted into outrage that the son-of-a-bitch who shot four cops didn't get so much as a scratch. The room was buzzing as everyone discussed what might have prevented this tragedy. The roar of voices fell to a low rumble as Lieutenant Riley walked in and yelled above the noise, "All right! Hold it down!" He stood there for a few seconds for dramatic effect, waiting for everyone's undivided attention. He began by reviewing last night's events, but most of his presented information was already known. He said, "This will not happen on day shift." Moving forward, he announced a plan to start the Raid team, which would consist of at least eight full-time officers and one full-time Sergeant. "I'm appointing Sergeant McCain to lead this team. As such, he will be in charge of the selection process." The team's full-time responsibility will be strictly warrant execution. As usual, the case agents will conduct investigations, but from now on, they will be handed over to the Raid team if a search warrant or buy-bust is required.

Whenever the team was not busy with a warrant or covering a buy-bust, they would train. Firearms, breaching, and anything else they may need to master. Riley continued, "No long hair or beards, this team will look like cops, act like cops, and because they only do one thing, they will perfect it."

Riley just described Andy's dream job, and it sounded like music to his ears. Finally, his primary focus could be all the exciting aspects of the job, like kicking doors, and he wouldn't have to keep his hair long or grow a beard like most undercover guys.

He glanced around the room to determine who his competition might be. Mark was more interested in the investigation portion of the job, so Andy assumed he wouldn't be interested. Riley ended with, "If you want to be on this team, I need your name by close of business today. Depending on how many want to sign up, there will be some hard choices, but I want to get this team up and running ASAP." Riley turned and walked out without saying another word. Everyone sat there looking at each other in silence until the chatter started building again.

After roll-call, the conversations returned to last night's shooting, but Andy had his sights set on this new endeavor. He headed straight to McCain's office to be one of the first to sign up. McCain sat at his desk reading his usual newspaper. McCain didn't even have to look up and said, "Let me guess, you want on the team."

"Bingo! How did you know?" Andy replied with a smile.

"Let's just say it was a lucky guess," mumbled McCain.

"Well? What do I need to do?"

"I already wrote your name down," McCain replied. "Nothing else for now." He continued reading, so Andy took the hint and walked back to the dayroom.

"Are you gonna put your name in?" Mark asked.

"Yeah, I think so," Andy replied.

"Bullshit! You can't wait to sign up," Mark said.

"I know. I didn't want to seem too eager. It's not that I don't like what I'm doing, but I think it's a better fit for me," replied Andy.

"I think you'll be perfect for that team," Mark said.

"Thanks, Mark! I hope so," Andy replied. Knowing Mark approved was encouraging.

"Well, for now, you wanna meet a CI with me?"

"Sure, let's do it."

Mark received a phone clue from a female living in the 4th Ward, just west of downtown. An older woman was selling dope, including codeine cough syrup and Quaaludes, out of her home.

They met with a young woman, Tamica, at a local convenience store, and she told them about a woman in her 60s who lived on Arthur Street and was dealing prescription medications out of her house. She lived with her elderly husband, who wasn't involved with the dope business but knew of his wife's dealings. Tamica agreed to make a controlled buy to purchase some codeine syrup from the woman. Mark and Andy would supply her with money and watch while she walked into the house, bought the syrup, and returned with the drugs.

Tamica hopped in the truck, and they drove inconspicuously past the dealer's house. With no one outside, Mark slowed down as Andy took notes. Once the initial reconnaissance was complete, they dropped Tamica off at the convenience store. "Am I gonna get the crime stoppers money?" inquired Tamica.

"Absolutely, as long as we get the drugs," Mark replied. "Call the crime stopper hotline and get an informant ID number. Then, call us back when she has a good supply of dope." Tamica agreed and walked away.

Mark and Andy researched their gathered information and started an informant file on Tamica. As they ran criminal record histories, they determined the suspect's name was Thelma Johnson. She lived with Douglas Johnson, and both had done time for drugs. With Tamica's information verified, they drafted an affidavit for a search warrant and waited for her call.

The next day a message awaited them from late last night; Tamica had called and would call again around 3 pm. Right on time, Gentry's voice came over the intercom, "Phone call for Kiley or Wallace on line 3." Mark answered the phone and spoke with her while all Andy could do was listen with anticipation.

"Uh-huh, how much? Uh-huh, OK, we'll meet you at the same place in about an hour. Does that work?" Mark asked. "Great, see you then." Mark hung up and excitedly looked at Andy, "Let's make a draw and buy some dope!"

A safe in the lieutenant's office contained cash agents would draw for narcotics purchases. Andy had to sign for the $100 and would later account for it with the purchased narcotics. $100 would be enough for Tamica to buy some Quaaludes and a bottle of codeine syrup. They met with Tamica and drove her to a spot several houses away from the suspect's home. They gave her the cash and watched her walk to the dealer's front door and knock. The door opened, and she went inside for about 3 minutes, then walked out and headed down the street.

Mark and Andy let her walk several blocks, watching from a distance to see if anyone was following. Then they picked her up and drove back to the convenience store, where she gave them a syrup bottle and two Quaaludes.

"How much?" asked Andy.

"$75."

"I need the change back," advised Andy.

"I don't get no spending money?" Tamica pouted.

"Sorry, darlin'. I got to account for every penny." Andy inspected the syrup bottle; it was opened and partially used. "Why isn't the bottle full?"

Tamica smiled mischievously and answered, "I had to make sure it was good stuff." Licking her lips.

'Unbelievable,' Andy thought, shaking his head. He wrote down her crime-stopper ID number for her reward, then they dropped Tamica off at the convenience store and headed back to the office to tag the dope and finish the warrant.

"What about the missing syrup?" Andy asked Mark a bit anxiously. He shrugged his shoulders and smiled while he took a drag from his cigarette; it was typical for informants to be users. The old saying, 'It takes one to know one,' rang true. They drove back to the office, formulating their plan and how to put a team together to hit the place. Finally, it occurred to Andy this would be the perfect assignment for the new Raid team, but they would have to execute the warrant while the woman still had a good supply of dope.

After they tagged the drugs, they briefed McCain on their investigation. Then they got to work typing the affidavit and search warrant. Mark left to obtain a judge's signature while Andy briefed the day shift on their deal. Soon, Mark returned with the signed search warrant, and they were ready to go. No one thought about what happened on the night shift a few days ago. Everything was business as usual.

They gathered in the convenience store parking lot for the short drive to Arthur Street with their warrant in hand and wearing their raid jackets. McCain drove the van as the rest of the makeshift team stuffed themselves in the back. Then, turning on Arthur Street, McCain said in eager anticipation, "This is it!" Everyone shuffled to their respective positions.

McCain brought the van to a stop at the house, and they shoved the vehicle doors open. It felt like a race for the front door, with everyone moving at breakneck speed as though they were being shot at. The element of surprise was important, but it was difficult not to make a mistake at this pace as the team jumped the ditch and dodged the shrubs in the front yard.

The first man to the door yelled "POLICE," reared back, and kicked the door in. Of course, not everyone was there yet, but that didn't matter. The door burst open, and they entered yelling "POLICE," pointing guns in all directions. Most of the guys kept moving toward the back of the house, searching for the bathrooms to prevent narcotics from being flushed. Andy was 4th through the door, and the entire situation felt like organized chaos, but at least no one had fired a shot.

Andy ended up in the master bedroom, where an older man was lying on the bed watching TV. Surprised, he offered no resistance; he just put his hands in the air. Andy quickly scanned the rest of the room. Mark came in looking for additional suspects but found none.

Things began to calm down with everything under control, and Mark walked back into the living room in time to see Thelma Johnson being handcuffed. She was stunned when Mark presented her with a copy of the search warrant. He told her she was welcome to read it, but she didn't respond. Then, Andy's voice exclaimed, "Bingo," from the bedroom. Mark and Sergeant McCain hurried to the back in time to see Andy pulling a tray of Quaaludes and codeine bottles out from under the bed. This is what they came for! They smiled at each other, silently acknowledging their job well done. Mark questioned Thelma about the narcotics, but she took zero responsibility for them.

Sitting on the bed, Sergeant McCain questioned Mr. Johnson about the drugs, but he insisted he knew nothing. Finally, frustrated, McCain pointed across the bed and said, "Don't give me that shit! We found the dope under the bed you sleep in, right over there!"

Mr. Johnson looked at McCain seriously and said, "Yes, sir, officer, but I sleep on this side of the bed." McCain stared at him for a second, perplexed by the man's answer, then he turned his head to look at Andy and chuckled. Andy smiled and laughed. Adding to the hilarity, the older man's facial expression indicated he didn't understand why they were laughing.

McCain said, "Let's wrap this up and book them. Then, we'll let the DA figure out who they want to charge."

"Yes, sir," Andy replied, helped Mr. Johnson up, and handcuffed him. Nothing else was found after completing a thorough search of the house.

Andy was proud they wrapped up the investigation quickly, although the execution left a lot to be desired. As the new guy, he wasn't sure how to make a dangerous job safer but hoped the Raid team would find a better way.

Making the Team

Andy finished his workout early the following day and exchanged greetings with Gentry once he exited the elevator on the 6th floor. He poured a coffee and sat down in the dayroom, waiting for the day shift crew to arrive. Stirring his coffee, he noticed a piece of paper pinned to the bulletin board. From distance, he could barely read 'Raid Team Members' on Lieutenant Riley's letterhead. He rushed over to read the names, spilling his coffee. There it was! He wanted to scream with joy, but he kept his composure when he spotted his name. It wasn't first; it was next to last, but that didn't matter, he was on it, and that was good enough.

Andy rushed into the Sergeant's office and spotted McCain reading the morning paper at his desk. "Sarg! Thank you for picking me for the Raid team."

"Not my choice," McCain replied as he read the paper.

"Yeah, I know. But you would have picked me if it were up to you. Right?"

After a moment of silence, McCain lowered his newspaper and looked sternly at Andy, "If it were up to me, I wouldn't be on this damn thing." Puzzled, Andy tried to understand what he meant by that. McCain continued, "Look. You guys are rolling the dice every time you go out on one of these warrants. One of these days, it's gonna come up snake eyes just like it did for those night shift guys. I just don't want to be the one dealing the hand when that happens." That was a sobering comment for Andy. McCain lifted his paper and started reading again.

Stunned, Andy didn't know what to say. McCain was old school and past the point in his career where he was willing to take risks. Andy was the opposite; he was utterly oblivious to the dangers. An adrenaline junky, constantly itching for a fight. Even though deep down he knew his job could cost him his life someday, he didn't care to think about it.

He turned and walked out of the Sergeant's office without saying another word. McCain could be moody, and Andy knew enough to stay out of his way. He was so excited that he didn't even look at the other names, so he hurried back to take a better look. He stood there sipping his coffee and studying the list for a while.

First on the list was Don Hammond, who was no surprise to Andy. Don came to the Narcotics Division from the SWAT Team. A known tactical guy and well respected throughout the Division. Don was always a cool hand in stressful situations, and the peer picked favorite for Team Leader.

Number two was Ron Masterson, a brute of a guy with an attitude to match. Even though he was only 5' 11", he weighed well over 240 lbs and was built like a bulldog. Although he didn't exercise, he was naturally strong and made up for what he lacked in tactics or techniques with a fierce personality. He reminded Andy of a bar bouncer who was willing to take on anyone, no matter their size. As a patrol officer, Ron was involved in several shootings and had proven himself as someone willing to press the fight.

Third on the list was Ron's best friend, Fred Wells. Fred was a likable guy and extremely hard working. He was always energetic and willing to help. At times, he was a little high-strung, but he was brilliant. He was tall, lean, and always looking for a deal. Fred searched the papers and ads for any way to save a buck. He would even go so far as to save sales receipts for everything he purchased, no matter how small, to write off the sales tax at the end of the year.

Next was Tom Fincher, an easy-going guy until someone pushed him past his breaking point. Once that line was crossed, he had a temper like a junkyard dog. Tom didn't have a tactical background but was incredibly athletic and picked things up quickly. Before joining the Police Department, Tom resided in Indiana. After only three years on patrol, he transferred to Narcotics. Andy related to Tom, and their personalities meshed well.

Coming in fifth was Brad Raskey, a big guy with a gruff personality. He didn't say much and usually looked at people as though he wanted to rip their throats out. Andy wasn't sure how to take him most of the time, so he tended to steer clear of him. Sometimes he was surprisingly friendly, but that wasn't the norm. Usually, he acted as if he would rather be somewhere else; he gave the impression that he was there to do a job and nothing more.

Number six was Sam Flores. After Sam was involved in the shooting with Jack Spencer, he transferred to days to get away from the hectic pace and instability of the night shift. Sam was friendly, dependable, and always willing to help; everyone liked him. During high school, he was a star athlete, and he was also deployed for a short term to Vietnam when serving in the Army. Andy thought Sam was an excellent choice because he would be a stabilizing force among a group of extreme personalities.

Andy was number seven, and number eight was Joe Duncan. Joe was well into his 50s, and everyone else on the team was relatively young. He had been a police officer for more than 20 years and knew everyone. As a chain smoker, we would smoke one cigarette after the other and did nothing to stay active. He was naturally thin because his diet consisted of coffee, nicotine, and booze at night.

It was easy to see why the others were picked, but why Joe? He wasn't tactical or athletic, and he never did more than what was required. On the day shift, Joe was infamous for never executing a dope deal of his own. He was always just a helper. Most people thought the Captain kept Joe around for amusement.

On one occasion, Joe initiated a heroin investigation of his own. Everyone on the day shift was surprised and assumed it must be a big deal for Duncan to work it. Some had great anticipation, and others figured it was a phone clue Joe happened to answer. When they executed Joe's warrant and arrested the suspect, the team didn't find a thing searching the house. As he interrogated the handcuffed suspect at his kitchen table, Joe was beginning to get nervous. The searchers started mumbling amongst themselves, and Joe was becoming desperate. "I said, WHERE'S THE FUCKING DOPE, ASSHOLE?" Joe yelled threateningly. Nervously, he smoked one cigarette after the other, the entire kitchen filled in a fog of smoke. Finally, the rest of the team gave up searching; Joe had come up empty. He was leaning over and staring, but the suspect kept his head down and said nothing. McCain was the Sergeant on the deal and stood there watching Joe trying to get something out of this guy.

Everyone was equally annoyed and felt sorry for Joe by this point. Joe felt the glare of everyone's eyes, so he did the only thing he could and continued threatening the suspect with what would happen if he didn't come clean. "You better give up the dope, or I'll burn this fucking house down. You hear me, ASSHOLE?"

In desperation, Joe grabbed the broom leaning against the wall. The handle was a hollow metal tube with a plastic cap. To intimidate the suspect, he slammed the broom down on the table within an inch of him, as hard as he could. The broom made a loud slapping noise, and the plastic cap flew across the room and several foil packets of heroin along with it.

Everyone stood there in disbelief as the crook watched his freedom fly out the end of the handle. Then, finally, he dropped his head as the realization set in that his life was over for the next several years. Joe looked at McCain, took a drag on his cigarette, and arrogantly said, "See? I told you I'd find the dope." Everyone just rolled their eyes and laughed. There were many more Duncan stories, but that was a classic.

Andy was still studying the list when Mark walked in and congratulated him.

"Thanks, Mark."

"I think you're a great fit for that team," Mark replied.

The rest of the day shift slowly started showing up, and the Raid team became the main topic of conversation. Many wondered why Joe was on the list, but most presumed the Captain was taking care of him, and besides, someone needed to drive the van.

After roll-call, McCain called the Raid team into the Sergeant's office. He reviewed the expectations of the team. Next week, they were scheduled for firearms training with Sergeant Pearlman. Pearlman was an Administrative Sergeant and a competitive shooter who agreed to help hone their shooting skills. Then, McCain released the group to finish any open investigations and close them out by the end of the week.

Andy couldn't wait to get home that evening and tell John about his new assignment. First, he called Mom and Dad and told them. They accepted the news with mixed emotions when realizing this was a more dangerous job. Andy tried to calm their fears but knew they were still worried.

Andy celebrated with a cold beer and waited for John to get home. John was still in the jail and had no plans of going anywhere. Andy told him all about the new team when John finally walked in. John looked at him for a second, stunned, and then said, "Do you want to get your ass shot or something? Let me tell you, it ain't fun!"

"Oh, John. Don't be such a downer. I ain't gonna get shot."

"Well, I didn't think I was gonna get shot either, but I did! You can find better ways of getting a helicopter ride than life flight."

Andy just laughed and said, "Come on. I'll buy you a beer. Let's go out tonight and hang one on! I'm buying."

"Well, if you're buying, I'm drinking," John answered. "I might as well get something out of you before you go and get yourself killed." They laughed but deep down, Andy knew there was some truth to John's concerns.

Hard Knocks

Competitive shooting was a hobby for Sergeant Pearlman, and he was eager to pass on his skills to the team. Andy was learning a lot from him, but their tactical training was still a work in progress. Thankfully, their assignments were based on their talents, which was an improvement. Because of their size, Masterson and Raskey typically breached doors. As the Team Leader, Don usually stayed toward the back during entries, overseeing the operation. The rest of the team filled in as needed until they worked out more assignments.

The following Monday, on the southeast side of downtown, a buy-bust was set for 1:00 pm in a shopping center parking lot on Scott Street. During the briefing, Andy was impressed with the precise details and well-vetted plan. Don led the initiative, delegating detailed assignments, and McCain intently watched from the back of the room.

The case agent was Joe Gonzalez. Joe had a regular informant they fondly called 99, a nickname given because of the endless number of deals he made. 99 was a short Cuban refugee who spoke broken English but could wheel and deal in the drug trade and had a knack for attracting big-time drug distributors. It was a full-time job for him, and at one point, crime stoppers owed him so much money for his efforts that they had to give him an IOU.

Gonzales and his partner, Tom Bell, thoroughly researched and investigated the suspect they were targeting. An ex-con from Mexico who served time for selling cocaine and was deported after a short stint in prison. Now back in Houston, he was knee-deep in his former trade. Although he was not known to carry a gun, they could never know for sure.

Gonzales drove a black Trans Am with a giant gold eagle painted on the hood, just like in *Smokey and the Bandit*. The vehicle was seized during a dope deal and had since been assigned to Joe. In an open part of the parking lot, he and 99 would be sitting in the vehicle across from Eckerd's drug store. Drug dealers preferred conducting business in public places to avoid being ripped off or killed by other dealers.

Once Gonzales confirmed the narcotics, he would give the signal by taking his sunglasses off if he was outside or pumping the brake lights if he was in his car. Then, the Raid team would move in and take them down. Gonzales and 99 would be arrested alongside the suspect to preserve their identity. The Raid team would park a short distance from Joe and be prepared to move in quickly once the signal was given.

The raid van was a plain white 3/4-ton Ford with a customized interior containing six captain-style seats mounted in the back for comfort during long stakeouts. They used money seized during drug forfeitures to trick out the van with tinted windows all the way around and curtains that could be drawn for further concealment. Doors were on both sides and the back for a quick exit regardless of their needed direction. The supercharged AC unit delivered cool air to the rear on those hot summer days when they had to sit for hours waiting for a suspect to show up.

Tom Bell would oversee the perimeter by coordinating case agents and uniformed officers. A constant presence was needed for identification purposes. People in the area needed to be informed this was a police operation, especially when longhaired guys with guns jumped out of vehicles. In addition, they wanted to avoid a situation where a citizen might try to get involved.

Once the briefing finished, they drove out to the shopping center and met with the uniformed officers down the street. They were given assignments and a back radio channel for communication. Everyone found a place to park, and they radioed Gonzales that they were ready.

The Raid team parked near the street where they could scan the parking lot for anyone suspicious. Everything appeared normal, with citizens coming and going from their cars as they shopped at the various stores. Somehow, no one noticed several men sitting in parked vehicles throughout the lot with engines idling, observing people come and go. Even when shoppers parked next to the raid van, they still didn't notice anything. They would have been shocked to realize eight men were armed to the teeth inside the idling van with mirrored windows, ready to pounce. Fortunate for them, they were cops and only interested in getting dope dealers off the streets.

30 minutes later, a dark blue Camaro pulled alongside the Trans Am. Joe was speaking to the suspect with the driver-side window down, and the radio came alive with descriptions of what the surveillance team could see. The team intently watched through the mirrored windows, waiting for the signal. Then, Joe, 99, and the suspect got out of their cars and walked toward the rear of the blue Camaro.

The dealer was a Hispanic male in his 20s with short black hair and a goatee. He wore a baseball cap and sunglasses and looked suspiciously around the parking lot before opening his trunk. Once opened, he fumbled with something inside, and that was it; Gonzales took off his sunglasses. "It's a bust," a voice announced excitedly over the radio. Duncan put the van in gear and started easing across the parking lot. Andy's heart was pounding as he struggled to stay calm. It was the first deal on the new Raid team, and he didn't want to make a mistake.

McCain radioed the uniformed vehicle to come in as the perimeter team officers started getting out of their cars. But one of the officers was too close; the suspect spotted him wearing his raid jacket when he exited the vehicle. The suspect slammed the trunk lid down and took off on foot through the parking lot. "He's running," an officer screamed over the radio. Andy peeked out the van's side window and spotted the suspect scurrying between cars a couple of parking rows over. Andy had a good angle on him, so he yelled, "I got him!"

The van was still in motion when Andy opened the side door and took off running at a full sprint. Dressed in full raid gear, he drew his pistol, weaving between parked cars, watching the crook. The van doors opened behind him, and voices were yelling, so Andy knew the team was on the way. He planned to cut the suspect off before reaching the strip center, but the suspect changed direction and turned toward the pharmacy. Andy didn't lose an inch; he remained hot on his tail. Citizens tried to get out of the fray as Narcs with guns jumped out of vehicles and ran toward the chase.

A woman was walking out of Eckerd's Pharmacy with her hands full of bags when the drug dealer collided with her in the doorway. She was knocked to the ground, and the suspect stumbled over her, barely staying on his feet. Andy was now just a few short steps behind. Andy leaped over the woman and narrowly missed kicking her head as he flew through the open doorway in hot pursuit. The woman tried to get to her feet, but when she saw several more team members running toward her, she laid back down and took cover. Shoppers inside the store started screaming as the commotion came barreling through the door.

The crook sprinted down one of the aisles, with Andy right behind him. "POLICE!" Andy loudly announced, he wanted to make sure everyone knew who he was and warn patrons of the chase.

At the end of the aisle, an elderly couple shopped for greeting cards on a freestanding display rack. They were utterly oblivious to the calamity coming toward them. Andy was almost within arm's reach when the crook grabbed the older man and spun the shopper between them. All three of them toppled to the floor in a heap as the woman screamed at the sight of her husband's fall. Andy reached around the older man as he held onto the suspect with one hand. With his other hand, he tried to holster his pistol. He needed both hands to fight, but he had to secure his gun first.

The old man yelled, terrified, while the crook used him as a shield from Andy. His wife lifted her walking cane and beat Andy on the back with it. "Let him up, let him up!" she yelled and then clubbed Andy with several direct hits to the head. The older man continued screaming, covering his face, clueless to what was happening.

Andy hoped the commotion he heard behind him meant help was almost there, so he held on for dear life and endured the beating. He had a death grip on the suspect with one hand, and he used his other arm to shield his head from the blows. She continually shrieked, "Let him go, let him go!" as she struck Andy with her cane.

Tom Fincher was the first to arrive at Andy's aid and seized the woman's cane. Fred Wells piled on the suspect and quickly gained control of him. Tom helped the older man to his feet with one arm as he held on to the cane with his opposite hand. The woman tugged her cane, yelling, "Give me that, you son-of-a-bitch!"

Andy rolled off the pile, flat on his back, trying to catch his breath. Then, casually, McCain walked up, surveying the calamity, looked down, and asked, "Are you taking a break?"

Andy returned a smile and said, "Sorry, Sarg. Just catching my breath."

The store manager arrived and asked if everyone was OK as Andy got to his feet. The older man was shaken but didn't appear hurt. The maddened older woman couldn't care less that they were police officers. She pointed her finger at Andy, determined to give him a piece of her mind, "Young man, you ought to be more careful! You could have hurt someone!" Andy nodded apologetically and walked toward the front door. The drug dealer was led away in handcuffs. Sergeant McCain smoothed the situation over with the elderly couple and collected their information for the report.

When Andy walked outside, he noticed Joe Duncan already had the van parked at the front door. With the engine idling and the AC blasting, Joe smoked his cigarette. He was the only team member who didn't bother to get out of the van and had just followed the foot chase in the vehicle. Joe probably wouldn't have been any good in a foot chase anyway, and Andy appreciated the van being close. "Did you get your exercise?" Joe asked, taking another drag on his cigarette.

"Just stretching my legs," Andy replied with a smile as he flopped down in one of the captain chairs, chest still heaving.

The Raid team's first bust did not go as planned. Narcotics work was notorious for things going sideways due to the unpredictable nature of crooks. Nevertheless, they got their man, the dope, and no one was hurt except for a few bumps on Andy's head. He was proud of chasing down the suspect, but he feared he might be criticized for giving chase by himself during the debriefing.

The next day all was forgiven during the critique, but the perimeter guy that spooked the crook was told to stay back next time and let the Raid team do its job. It was a new concept for case agents, and it would take some time to get used to. But this career was exciting, and he was getting all he asked for.

TWELVE

I Ain't Touching That!

The following morning, everyone was to meet at the Academy for additional firearms training. When Andy arrived, Sergeant Pearlman was preparing targets at the Hogan's Alley range. It was named after the famous Clint Eastwood movie, *Dirty Harry*. Although the range was nothing to brag about, it had a three-sided dirt berm so you could shoot in three directions.

Pearlman was stapling paper targets when Andy asked, "What's up, Sarg?"

"Not much, Andy. You're early," Pearlman replied.

"Yep, a habit I got from my Dad. He says, if you're early, you're on time. If you're on time, you're late. If you're late, it's unacceptable," Andy smiled and said with pride about his father.

"Good saying. I agree," Pearlman said and continued setting up shop.

"Besides, I was late on my first day at the Academy, which didn't work out too well."

"I'll bet not. Did you get the wrath of Hurley?" Pearlman asked.

"Yep! I guess you two have met."

"Who doesn't know that prick."

"Can I help Sarg?" offered Andy.

"Sure, hand me those targets as I staple," replied Pearlman.

As they worked, Andy asked Pearlman about competitive shooting in hopes of learning more and how to sharpen his skills. When Andy inquired if he had any suggestions, Pearlman stopped, looked at him, and said, "Well, first, I think you are relying too much on your pistol. You're a good shooter, but what will you do if your handgun malfunctions?"

"Tap, rack, bang!" Andy replied. The common phrase for the procedure to clear a malfunction for most semi-automatic handguns.

"Sure, and that works most of the time," Pearlman said. "But what if it doesn't?"

"Shit, I don't know," Andy replied, puzzled.

"That's not a good answer in a gunfight."

"What do you suggest?" Andy asked.

"Two guns!" Pearlman said with enthusiasm and a smile.

"One in each hand like the old west?" Andy said part jokingly.

"No, but what about taking a shotgun as a primary weapon and having a handgun as a backup? If something happens to the shotgun, you still have your pistol." Pearlman said, still hanging targets.

Andy nodded his head in understanding, "That makes sense."

"There's an old saying, two is one, and one is none," Pearlman said. Andy knew he would check out a shotgun from the office right then.

While waiting for the rest of the team to arrive, Pearlman started with basic drills, but every course was timed to add stress. Nevertheless, Andy loved the competition, especially when practicing skills that might someday save his life.

McCain's pager went off just before noon, so he left the range to call the office. He instructed the team to break for lunch and be back in an hour. Don Hammond was the van's driver today, so he offered to drive everyone to a BBQ restaurant down the street. They jumped in and started cutting up as old friends would do. The team camaraderie was infectious; Andy knew he'd made the perfect career choice.

Duncan started to light a cigarette, but Masterson gave him a rash of shit about having to breathe his smoke. "Can't you wait to get out before lighting that cancer stick, you old fuck!"

"What, are you on a health kick?" Duncan asked.

"No, I just don't want to die from your bad habit," Masterson countered.

"Gotta die from something," Duncan replied as he reluctantly put the cigarette away. Andy was grateful because he didn't care for the smoke either, but he wasn't brash enough to say anything.

McCain was impatiently waiting for them when they got back from lunch. "We gotta go! We have a briefing at 1 pm in the office," commanded McCain.

"Whose deal is it?" asked Don.

"Dimango's."

"Wow! Really?" He asked, impressed.

McCain nodded his head and walked away. Ben Dimango didn't have deals often. He was assigned to a federal drug task force but considering no one had run a warrant for Ben, this must be good.

Back at the dayroom, Ben was busy drawing up a two-bedroom floorplan on the grease-board. A methamphetamine warrant for a small wood-frame house in the town's Heights area. The area had suffered an economic downturn, and undesirables were moving in. Homes in that part of town were built in the 1930s and 40s and typically constructed with pier and beam foundations. The floors were usually hardwood, so sounds reverberated throughout the house.

As soon as the team arrived, Ben described the suspect as a meth monkey, meaning that he was strung out on methamphetamine most of the time. The suspect had an extensive criminal history but was not known to carry a gun. He was a direct link to a clandestine lab, and he was holding a stash of meth. He lived with his old lady, also a meth freak, but she didn't have a criminal record.

Once Ben finished, Don started outlining the plan, "Raskey will do the breach, and Andy will lead the stack to the door. Once the door is open, Andy will be first in." Andy was shocked because he had never been picked first before. As his mind raced through a barrage of emotions from proud to nervous, he tried to focus on what Don was saying, "Tom and Fred will be two and three, and the rest of us will fill in after that. Joe will drive the van and bring up the rear."

After the briefing, Andy thanked Don for his confidence. Don smiled, "You've earned it. Now make me proud." Andy nodded and walked off to check out a shotgun from the equipment room, but McCain stopped him.

"Where are you going with that?" McCain asked.

"I thought that I would use it today. Sergeant Pearlman suggested taking a second weapon instead of relying on one."

"Have you trained with that shotgun?"

"Well, no, but I have hunted with shotguns all my life. I know how to work a shotgun Sarg," assured Andy.

"Well, you're not risking your life with a gun you have never shot. Once you qualify with it, I'll let you use it." Andy dropped his head in disappointment, but he knew McCain had a valid point. "We'll get you checked out on it this week. Just not today."

Andy turned and smiled at McCain, "Cool. Thanks, Sarg!" And he walked back to return the shotgun.

Joe waited in the van, smoking a cigarette with the engine idling. It was nice and cool with the AC blaring when the team piled into their spots. Andy usually sat in the back, but Don moved him up to the side door seat to make it easier for a quick exit.

The stench of cigarette smoke hung in the van, which only fueled the fire for Masterson to start in on Joe's smoking again. They bantered back and forth, much to the team's amusement, but most of the group agreed with Ron and wished Joe would stop.

A uniformed patrol car met them in the parking lot, and McCain briefed the officers on the plan. Duncan drove the van out of the lot for the short trip to the Heights with a patrol car in tow. After turning onto the target street, the van slowly rolled to a stop. Andy jumped out and quickly started for the front door. The guys filed out and joined to form a stack behind him. Softly, Don cautioned, "Let's be careful, boys." Don's calm demeanor reassured Andy, but this was his first time leading, so he couldn't help but be anxious. His heart was pounding, so he took deep, calming breaths to focus.

With soft steps, Andy walked onto the porch's hardwood planks. The old wooden deck creaked and groaned under the team's weight while they positioned themselves at the door. Andy stood to the right so Raskey could get a good swing with the ram. The steel pipe had two handles and weighed about 30 lbs. If used correctly, the ram delivered a tremendous amount of force. Fortunately, most doors only took one swing unless special measures were taken to reinforce the lock.

The house was quiet except for the faint sound of a TV playing inside. Hopefully, the suspect was busy watching a program and not waiting for them. If

Andy was wrong, the first step inside could bring him face to face in a fight for his life, so he hoped for the best.

"POLICE, SEARCH WARRANT!" Don yelled the signal for Raskey to rear back with all 240 lbs of brawn. The ram slammed directly into the deadbolt lock, and the door flew open with fragments splintering into the room.

Andy was through the door like a shot out of a cannon. So much so that Fincher was at least two steps behind him as they entered the living room. Immediately, Andy spotted a long-haired guy sitting on the couch, and the room smelled strongly of marijuana. The TV was blaring, and the man was terrified when he saw Andy. As he moved cautiously across the room, Andy kept his pistol pointed directly at the suspect, yelling, "FREEZE MOTHERFUCKER!" The man posed no immediate threat, so Andy turned his attention toward a dark hallway directly ahead.

To take advantage of the fleeting element of surprise, he wanted to quickly scan the rest of the house. Fincher moved to the couch and pushed the man to the floor; he didn't offer any resistance and mumbled, "What the fuck?"

"Police motherfucker," Tom yelled, holding the man face down on the wood floor.

The team poured through the door and headed in various directions, searching the residence. As Andy entered the dark hallway, Fred slapped him on the back and said, "Right behind you!" Andy felt reassured a team member had his back as he spotted an open door on his left with a light on inside.

Stepping into the room, he spotted a naked woman lying on the bed. Andy pointed his pistol at her and yelled, "FREEZE! POLICE!" She was wearing headphones, listening to music, and never heard the commotion. Terrified when she spotted Andy, she threw a dildo across the room. As the vibrator sailed through the air, she snatched the bedsheets and tried to cover up. Andy checked to see what was thrown and saw a white dildo hit the wall and fall to the hardwood floor. Still running, it loudly rattled, reverberating around the room.

Fred entered, moved across the room, and cleared the closet and under the bed. As the situation calmed down, it was painfully obvious that the dildo was still vibrating around the hardwood floor. Hammond stepped into the room to check on Fred and Andy and noticed the woman in the bed. "What are you doing?" she asked.

"Search warrant," replied Andy.

"I don't have any dope," the lady exclaimed.

"Doesn't matter. You're under arrest!"

The dildo had vibrated its way to Fred and bumped against his shoe as it continued making the awful sound. Fred glanced down and was disgusted it was touching him, and he kicked it across the room to get away from him. It rattled loudly, skipping across the floor, and stopped between Andy's feet. Andy didn't want it near him either, so he kicked it toward Don, who did a quick high step to prevent the dildo from touching his shoes. "Turn that fucking thing off!" Don yelled.

"I ain't touching that," Andy replied, disgusted and looking to Fred.

"Don't look at me!" Fred replied.

"Get over here and turn this fucking thing off," Don demanded to the woman. Quickly, she got out of bed, wrapped herself in a sheet, and turned it off. Then, she placed the vibrator on the nightstand and sat down on the side of the bed, face in her hands, unable to believe what was happening.

"Get her dressed and bring her into the living room," Don said and turned to walk back toward the front of the house. Andy asked her where her clothes were, and she pointed at a dress hanging in the closet. Fred grabbed it and tossed it to her. Then, suddenly, she stood up, the sheet falling behind her, with no modesty whatsoever as she dressed. Fred and Andy remained to ensure she didn't do anything stupid. Once she was finished, Fred handcuffed her and walked her into the living room. The suspect from the couch was taken out to the police car so they wouldn't be able to communicate with one another.

McCain oversaw the search and asked, "Do we need to get a female officer over here to search her?"

"No need, Sarg, she's clear," replied Fred.

"How do you know?" McCain asked inquisitively.

"Well, let's just say that there was no place we couldn't see when we found her," Fred replied, chuckling.

McCain paused and then nodded his head in understanding, "Well, let's get another police vehicle for her. I don't want these two talking on the way downtown."

"Roger that, Sarg," Fred responded.

They found a trace of meth and a partially smoked marijuana cigarette on the coffee table—nothing else. Ben said the suspect must have already sold most of his stash. Fred and Andy made eye contact and spontaneously busted out laughing as they loaded back into the van. Don chuckled as well. Several guys asked, "What?" Andy and Fred relived the hockey puck dildo story, laughing all the way back to the office.

Andy drove home that evening to an empty apartment. John was spending more time with his girlfriend, and Andy figured it was only a matter of time before they tied the knot. That would leave Andy as the last of the three amigos who hadn't paired up yet. He sat alone in the living room, sipping a beer and recounting the day.

Helicopter Narc

Andy's pager went off while working out at the police gym, and he recognized Sergeant McCain's number on display. When he returned the call to the office, he found out they had a deal brewing. McCain asked if he could be in the office in 30 minutes for a briefing. Unfortunately, Andy's workout would have to wait, so he headed to the showers.

Walking out of the locker room, Andy couldn't help but glance at the basketball court and see the hoop where Herman hung himself. Terrible memories came flooding back of that horrible night; he had Hurley to thank for that.

In the briefing room, Andy poured a cup of coffee and found a seat among the guys, already ribbing each other. The bond had grown immensely amongst the team, and they were becoming close friends. The closer they became, the more commonplace the verbal digs were; whether in the dayroom or raid van, they made fun of each other like old friends.

The jabs sometimes got personal, but everyone had thick skin and took it in stride. The main instigator was Ron Masterson, and he loved to verbally jab everyone, just like a schoolyard bully. Anytime he found someone's weakness or got a reaction, he became the predator honing in on his prey. He liked an audience and relished the attention. Instinctually, he knew how far he could go and usually stopped just short of making someone angry. Then he'd offer a halfhearted apology, so there were no hard feelings.

Masterson's favorite victim was Joe Duncan because he was older and didn't banter well. This morning, however, he focused on Andy. The rest of the team quickly realized Masterson's new target, so they leaned back to enjoy the show. "Morning, Charles Atlas," Masterson shouted loud enough for everyone in the room to hear. Years ago, Charles Atlas was a famous bodybuilder, so this was Masterson's way of making fun of Andy's weightlifting.

Andy answered, "Morning, Ron."

"Where you been?" Masterson asked, already aware of the answer.

"Just grabbed a quick workout," Andy responded, glancing around the room. Then the realization set in that Masterson was targeting him today, which was OK. The attack wasn't personal, so he didn't mind; it was for the entertainment of everyone in the room.

"Do you wear tights when you work out, so you can check yourself out flexing in the mirrors?" Ron asked.

"Every time," Andy responded with a smile. He might as well play along to diffuse some of Ron's jabs.

"Do you guys shower together down there?" teased Masterson.

"I don't think you would appreciate being stuck in that van with me if I didn't shower," Andy replied.

"Yeah, but do you shower TOGETHER? You know. Do you guys posedown with each other in the shower, or what?" All the guys around the table started chuckling and glanced at Andy in anticipation of his reply.

Andy thought it best to continue playing along, "Sure! Do you want to watch? In fact, why don't you come down there sometime? I'll wear those tiger-striped undies that you like so much."

The entire room erupted into laughter, and Ron realized that Andy wouldn't sit there and take it. "I just might do that," Ron answered, pushing back from the table and turning away. He was finished with that round.

Masterson spotted Duncan laughing, so he went after him, "What are you laughing at, you old fuck?"

Duncan took his cue from Andy and attempted a comeback, "Boy! Don't start with me. I was fighting crime when you were still shitting yellow." Then, there was another round of laughter from the guys, and even Masterson couldn't help but chuckle, seeing everyone exchange smiles around the room.

McCain walked in, "Alright, hold it down. Let's brief this deal," just like a schoolteacher trying to get the kids' attention. McCain divulged Rico Gonzales planned to meet a suspect in a parking lot on the northside of downtown. Rico intended to flash a large amount of money, insinuating that he was a big-time player to the drug dealer. It was safer to surprise the drug dealer with the cash instead of telling him in advance to prevent a premeditated rip-off. Of course, anytime an undercover officer was dealing with a suspect, there was a risk, which increased significantly if the crook brought friends.

McCain explained they would park the van at a grocery store and cover Rico. The flash would only take a few minutes, and if all went well, he planned to drive away. However, if the crook did something stupid, the Raid team would protect Rico first and the money second.

They finished the briefing and headed for the van. Soon Joe drove them out of downtown with McCain riding shotgun. Before long, Masterson started his verbal assaults on Joe again. "Hey, listen, you old fuck, don't light that goddamn cigarette in here. I ain't dying from your secondhand smoke." Although Masterson said it as a light-hearted joke, most of the team agreed, especially when trapped inside. Duncan was the only one who smoked, and even with his window rolled down, it didn't help much.

Since they were already on the subject, McCain decided this was an excellent time to address the issue, so he told Duncan not to smoke in the van anymore. Duncan was a heavy smoker, so that was a severe blow because he couldn't step out of the van for fear of being seen by the suspect. In compliance, he just nodded and said nothing, but everyone knew Joe would be in a world of hurt if he couldn't feed his addiction.

They parked near the corner of the grocery store since it provided the perfect vantage point to see in all directions. Once again, Andy enjoyed watching people coming and going, knowing they were oblivious to the raid van with its mirrored windows and idling engine. Curiously, he wondered how often he had done the same thing before becoming suspicious of everything. Sadly, narcotic work drove home the point that crime was everywhere if you knew where to look.

McCain radioed the surveillance team and advised they were set and ready for Rico, scanning the parking lot. The surveillance team observed a long-haired Hispanic male leaning against the grocery store, smoking a cigarette. He was acting nervous, as though he was waiting on someone and drawing everyone's attention. Rico parked on the edge of the lot as surveillance closely watched the man near the store. After observation, they soon realized he was a street dealer, more than likely selling dime bags, the street name for $10 worth of black tar heroin.

The grocery store security guard spotted the dope dealer and ran him off. Begrudgingly, the dealer walked away and headed toward the raid van. Andy urgently whispered, "He's coming over here! What the fuck?" Everyone in the van was silent and watched. Fred Wells drew his pistol in case the suspect did something stupid. "This guy's not part of Rico's deal. He's just a street punk," said McCain reassuringly in a low voice. "Everyone, stay cool."

Andy fixated on the crook as he walked to the van and turned around. For concealment from the security guard, he stood behind the raid van. The dealer accepted cash and handed the customer a small tin foil wrapper. As the two exchanged a few words, Andy could hear muffled Spanish, and then the customer walked away.

The dealer made two transactions right under their noses, and then a third customer started walking toward him. The crook waved him off and pointed toward the sky. Above was the unmistakable sound of a Hughes 500 police helicopter on routine patrol. The customer nodded in understanding and walked away. Andy found it rather amusing that the dealer thought the helicopter was a threat when he stood next to a narcotics raid van full of officers. The entire team laughed when the drug dealer walked away to establish another place to continue his trade.

Rico's dealer arrived, and the money flash went as planned. He was back in his car in no time and safely drove away. Before the raid van pulled out, McCain switched the radio to the local channel and asked for a patrol unit. A unit quickly responded, and McCain relayed a thorough description of the street dealer. "We can't get involved because we're covering our UC, but we know this guy is dealing," McCain added.

"Got it," the patrol unit responded.

"Let's go," McCain told Duncan, and he started to drive away. Duncan intentionally took his time as everyone strained to watch the patrol car turn into the lot. The heroin dealer spotted the unit and started quickly walking away. McCain radioed the officers, "That's him walking southbound along the building."

"Roger that. We see him!" The patrol car accelerated, and the man picked up his pace, nervously looking back. He started running, and the chase was on as everyone in the van started yelling like schoolboys cheering for their home team.

Although the excitement made Andy miss his old patrol days, he loved this job way too much to go back.

Duncan drove off, and the team watched the pursuit fade into the distance. As spectators, they intently listened to the chase on the radio, and when an officer broke the air, "1A23, we have the suspect in custody!" Cheers erupted with everyone high fiving each other as if they had made the arrest themselves, heading toward the office and onto the next deal.

Stick 'em Up!

Even though their first few deals didn't go perfectly, the team was inheriting a lot of work from case agents. At least they hadn't lost any dope, and no one was hurt. Most case agents realized that a specialized unit was the safer way of doing a dangerous job. Pearlman's instruction impacted the team, and they trained with him whenever they weren't running warrants. His unique perspective caused you to think about things differently. "Why is everyone here wearing cowboy boots?" Pearlman asked the men.

"Well, they are in style," Andy replied.

"Sure, I get that, but you aren't going out dancing. You're at work. Why don't you wear something more suited for your job?"

"Like what?" Andy asked.

"Well, when you are running up to houses and across wood floors, is traction important?" Pearlman asked.

"Well, yeah, sure," answered Andy.

"Then why don't you consider wearing tennis shoes?" Pearlman asked. Logically, it made a lot of sense, so Andy wore athletic shoes with rubber soles from that day on. In addition, he convinced Andy to turn in his cool-looking pistol grip for a full stock. "It'll give you better control, and that's more important." Andy was inclined to agree and had no problem with the change.

Usually, Joe didn't attend the training, and because he only drove the van, McCain let him slide. Joe only shot his pistol once a year when the Department made him qualify, usually shooting the minimum score, which was good enough for him. Afterward, he would pay Fred Wells $25 to clean his pistol because he did not want to be bothered. Most of the time, the gun just stayed in his briefcase.

One Friday afternoon, the team was training at the range when McCain received word that Johnny Barbosa had a search warrant for heroin. Johnny didn't work many cases, but it was usually heroin when he did. The warrant location was in a neighborhood off Harrisburg Street, an area of town notorious for black tar heroin and cartel gangs.

Most of the guys were hoping to cut out early for the weekend, but that was no longer an option. Tom Fincher and Ron Masterson had taken a vacation, so McCain was down to only five guys, which was disconcerting.

When the team arrived at the office, Johnny already had the house diagramed on the grease board in preparation for the briefing. Like most in that area, it was a small wood-frame structure. There was a garden behind a couple of storage sheds in the backyard that the crook was known to frequent. Don handed out assignments, and soon they were headed toward Harrisburg Street.

McCain radioed a request for a two-person unit to meet them behind the Fiesta Grocery store near the target location. He needed them to cover the back of the house, but the dispatcher only had a one-person unit available. After thinking about it for a few seconds, McCain looked at Joe, "Joe, I don't want that officer going to the back of the house by himself. Can you go with him?"

"Sure, Sarg," replied Joe. "I was doing this job when these sprouts were...."

McCain interrupted, "Yeah, I know, when they were shitting yellow."

The van pulled behind the grocery store, and the team quickly donned their vests and raid jackets. When the patrol car arrived, McCain and Joe explained the situation to the officer. "I'll follow you around the back of the house, just in case the crook's there," advised Joe.

The officer nodded, "Sure! I got it."

Within a few minutes, Barbosa arrived with verification the suspect was home, and they were good to go. "Let's do this!" McCain announced, and then everyone piled in the van. Don pushed a cassette tape into the deck and cranked up the volume on the drive out to Harrisburg Street. And out of the speakers, the opening song to the movie *Jaws* starts blaring, the infamous piece that always leads up to the inevitable shark attack. The whole van is nodding along to the sound of French horns as they approach the target residence.

Just short of the house, Joe stops the van, the doors fly open, and they bail. McCain looks back at Joe on his way out, "Catch up with that officer!"

Joe nodded, nervously put the van in park, and fumbled to open his door.

Andy paused at the front porch, then felt the reassuring tap on his back, indicating someone was with him. He stepped up toward the front door, and Raskey set up for the breach. After Hammond yelled, "POLICE," Raskey slammed the ram forward with all the strength he could muster. The door burst open, and Andy sprang forward to roll the dice once more.

Joe caught up with the officer at the back of the house and started scouting around the yard. No one came around back when they breached the front door. Don loudly announced "POLICE," and heavy feet stomping throughout the small house sounded like a stampede as the team cleared it.

Considering it was more excitement than usual for Joe, he needed to catch his breath, so he lit up a smoke and took a deep drag. The officer continued to keep a vigil on the back door with his pistol drawn. Assuming the worst was over, Joe meandered over to look at the crook's garden to see what he was growing. As he rounded the corner of the tool shed, he coincidently found the suspect. When the raid van pulled up, the dealer was already in the backyard, so he quickly jumped behind the shed to hide. His plan worked quite well until Joe's curiosity had gotten the best of him, and now they were face to face.

In Joe's haste to get out of the van, he had forgotten to bring his pistol. Unarmed, he instinctually took his cigarette out of his mouth with his left hand, pointed his right hand's index finger in a gesture resembling a gun, and yelled, "Freeze Motherfucker!" The suspect raised his hands in the air as the patrol officer ran over, pointed his pistol at the suspect, and ordered, "Get on the ground." Quickly and without incident, the suspect lay face down, and the officer handcuffed him while Joe continued smoking his cigarette.

McCain heard a commotion from the backyard, so he walked alongside the house in time to see the uniformed officer lifting the suspect from the ground and Joe grinning. "What the fuck happened?" McCain asked.

"I got 'em, Sarg!" Joe replied, proudly smiling from ear to ear. "Took him down with just my finger," Joe said, pointing his make-believe finger gun.

"Where's your pistol, Joe?" McCain asked.

"Well, I guess I forgot it in the van, but as it turns out, I didn't need it. All I needed was my finger to take this motherfucker."

McCain dropped his head in disbelief as he turned to walk back to the front of the house. He had mixed emotions because he wanted to curse Joe out, but at the same time, he blamed himself for putting Joe in the situation to begin with.

As McCain walked back to the front of the house, Hammond walked out of the front door and said, "He must have given us the slip, Sarg. The house is empty."

"I know," replied McCain. "Duncan got him in the backyard, and we're never gonna hear the end of it."

"What? Really?" Don asked. Joe walked into view with the officer and the handcuffed prisoner. Joe looked at Don, raised his index finger to his lips, and blew his fingertip like a smoking gun. "What the fuck is that about?" Don asked Sergeant McCain.

"Joe found the crook hiding in the backyard, but he forgot his gun, so he just pointed his finger at him, and the son-of-a-bitch surrendered," McCain replied shockingly.

"Holy shit!"

When the house was turned over to Johnny, the guys loaded into the van for the short drive back to central. Joe bragged the entire way back about how he didn't need a gun to take down a punk like that. The guys gave Joe a rash of shit about how absent-minded he was and how he was lucky the suspect wasn't armed. McCain didn't say a word as he stared ahead out the windshield. He was ashamed of himself for putting Duncan in a position that could have gotten him hurt.

Rolling the Dice

The team was bustling now, conducting as many as four search warrants a day and often working well into the night. Sometimes they would leave one warrant and go directly to another, violating their rule by omitting a formal briefing. Some case agents grumbled, waiting on the team to run their warrants, but Lieutenant Riley stuck to his guns, and only the team executed forced entries.

Once they finished a search warrant for Mark Kiley, they drove back to central, ready to grab lunch. When pulling into the parking lot, the office radioed Sergeant McCain, advising another briefing was waiting for them in the dayroom. "More work, guys! Let's go!" McCain said as the van rolled to a stop. Some of the guys started complaining, walking toward the station. Everyone was hungry, and no one had eaten yet. When you signed up for the Raid team, you got all that came with it, so McCain didn't want to hear it.

There were only three female narcs on the day shift, and Deanie McDonald was one of them. An excellent investigator who rarely conducted undercover work. She primarily worked with informants and arrested criminals through search warrants; this deal was no different. In a small duplex on Navigation Street, a female CI was turning tricks for her pimp. After she scored some heroin for Deanie, she discovered there was a lot more in her pimp's bedroom.

Since it was a simple deal, the briefing didn't take long, and soon they were riding out to the staging location—this time, a fire station not far from the target house. Deanie drove after them and said the crook was standing outside, so this was their best opportunity to take him down. It is always safer for officers to apprehend a suspect in the open rather than enter a structure searching for them. So they jumped in the van and headed out. As they slowly approached the driveway, Duncan slowed the van, and McCain quickly pointed to a black male and said, "There he is."

Andy opened the side door and, just as the van rolled to a stop, bolted out with his shotgun at the ready. The pimp heard the commotion and turned to see Andy yelling, "POLICE! FREEZE!" Fred Wells was right on Andy's heels while the rest of the team poured out of the van. The suspect took off, running toward his front door. A prostitute jumped in front of Andy to buy the pimp some time. Andy didn't want to lose sight of the suspect, so he stiff-armed her and ran into the open door. The place was pitch black, and when his eyes finally adjusted, he spotted the suspect running down a narrow hallway toward the back of the house. Andy chased the man with Fred right behind him. Then the pimp took a quick turn through a threshold and slammed the door behind him. Andy grabbed the doorknob; it was locked, so he backed up to kick it in. Out of his peripheral, Andy saw Fred with a pistol in hand. It was comforting to know that he wasn't alone regardless of whatever awaited them on the other side of this door. When Andy's foot made contact with the door, it flew open with a great booming sound. The noise was unbelievable; it was as loud as a gunshot. Then Andy realized it was a gunshot. He jumped back, attempting to determine where the shot originated. On impact, the door hit something and was stopped about halfway open. "Who shot?" yelled Andy.

"I don't know," replied Fred.

With the lack of confidence in Fred's tone, Andy wasn't convinced, so he asked more directly, "Did you shoot?"

Not quite sure of himself, Fred glanced at his pistol and then back at Andy, "No, I don't think so."

A rather odd response, so Andy still wasn't convinced Fred didn't shoot. Finally, he pushed the door the rest of the way open, and the suspect was lying on his back in a tub half-full of water. Petrified, he held both hands up, shaking. The door must have hit him and knocked him into the bathtub. Andy was still wondering where the shot came from, though.

"Are you guys OK?" yelled McCain from down the hallway.

"Yeah," Andy answered.

"Did someone shoot?" McCain asked.

"Yeah, we think so!" replied Fred.

"YOU THINK? What do you mean, you think?" McCain asked, unable to believe what he was hearing. Andy caught sight of a layer of smoke suspended in the air, and the smell of burnt gunpowder confirmed his suspicions.

McCain walked over to the suspect in the bathtub and said, "Get him up!"

So Andy stepped inside to ensure the rest of the bathroom was clear. Fred and Sergeant McCain stepped in behind him. Fred reached down, grabbed the crook's arm, and said, "Get up, motherfucker." He stood the suspect up and turned him toward the wall, water dripping from his soaked clothes. McCain reached behind them and closed the bathroom door for more room, and then Andy suddenly spotted it. A black muzzle blast on the inside of the door, starting at eye level and leading to the ceiling. The marking must be from the gunshot they heard. Andy's eyes followed the black soot up the door to a bullet hole in the ceiling. "Oh shit," Andy exclaimed. Fred and McCain turned and spotted the fresh gun residue running up the door. But where was the gun?

Fred turned to the handcuffed pimp, "Where's the gun motherfucker?" The suspect turned his head away, remaining silent. In frustration, Fred shoved the suspect's head against the wall and more forcefully demanded, "Where's the fucking gun, asshole?"

You couldn't see through the murky bathwater, so Fred reached down and searched the filthy tub with his bare hand. McCain held the crook firmly against the wall. Finally, Fred yelled, "I got it!" He held up a dripping wet semi-automatic pistol. When the crook ran into the bathroom, he slammed the door shut and pointed his handgun towards the door, waiting for whoever entered. Unfortunately, he didn't count on Andy kicking the door, so the impact forced the barrel up, and it fired when it flew open. Then, the gun was knocked free and fell into the bathtub, and the crook fell on top of it.

McCain was infuriated that this punk tried to shoot one of his guys. Unable to stop his emotions from getting the best of him, he elbowed the pimp's head into the wall. McCain wasn't normally the type to display that kind of anger. Not once had Andy ever seen him do anything inappropriate, and now he was losing it. "YOU MOTHERFUCKER! YOU SHOOT ONE OF MY MEN, AND I'LL GUT YOU LIKE A FISH!!" McCain screamed and hit the crook a second time; the crook's knees buckled. Fred stepped between them.

Andy grabbed McCain's arm and pulled him back toward the door. "It's OK, Sarg! We got this."

"IT AIN'T OK!" McCain replied, "THAT MOTHERFUCKER..." as he tried to push back into the room.

Don Hammond heard the commotion and hurried down the hall to see if he could help. Andy spotted him and said, "We need to get Sarg out of here!"

"OK," Don answered with understanding. However, McCain continued his threats as Don grabbed his arm and pulled him down the hall.

McCain broke free and said, "I'm OK!" and started to regain composure. McCain pushed his hair back from his face, straightened his shirt, took a deep breath, and walked away.

As Fred walked the crook out, Andy made eye contact with the man that just tried to kill him. And the piece of shit acted like he couldn't care less. Andy decided to have another look around the bathroom. He stared at the black muzzle blast on the white door and slowly followed it up to the hole in the ceiling. If the shooter were a few inches further back, the door would have missed the gun, and things could have ended much differently. Looking at the cheap laminate flooring, he imagined himself lying there, bleeding out. Then, he realized that McCain was right. Every time they kicked a door, they rolled the dice, and no matter how good he thought he was, he knew he just got lucky. Sergeant McCain called Homicide and requested them at the scene. The team was advised to preserve everything, so everyone immediately stopped searching for dope.

Andy walked out to the raid van, stowed his gear, and sat down on the running boards. He leaned over and rested his head in his hands.

"You OK?" asked Don, concerned.

"Sure," Andy replied unconvincingly.

Don took off his vest, dropped it in the van, and said, "Good job in there."

"Thanks, but it didn't feel good. I just got lucky, Don," Andy replied.

Don smiled, 'Sometimes, I'd rather be lucky than good.' It was a familiar phrase, and now it rang true more than Andy wanted to admit.

The homicide detectives arrived, and right behind them, James Hurley from internal affairs. Andy cringed seeing Hurley walk dressed in his suit and tie, with that cocky smirk wiped across his face. Andy walked over to McCain and said quietly, "Sarg, Hurley, and I have bad blood between us. I don't want to talk to him."

"Don't worry about Hurley," McCain replied. "I know that asshole, and it'll be OK. You did your job, and you have nothing to be worried about."

Andy nodded, walked back, and sat down. The investigation was much more detailed than Andy had anticipated. First, a crime scene unit took pictures and measurements. Then, they bagged the suspect's hands so the lab could run a trace metal test. They also tried to retrieve the bullet, but it exited through the roof and couldn't be found.

When the detectives were finished, everyone was asked to go to Homicide and write a statement. Whenever there was an investigation of this magnitude, that was standard protocol. McCain ensured Andy didn't have to speak with Hurley, and he was thankful, but he knew Hurley would be lurking in the distance.

On the ride downtown, the guys shared their accounts of what just happened, and all agreed the piece of shit should be in the morgue right now. As usual, Ron Masterson was the most outspoken of the group. "Why the fuck didn't you shoot that motherfucker?" Ron asked loud and obnoxiously. Andy didn't want to give him the satisfaction of a reaction, so he said nothing. "Seriously, that motherfucker tried to kill you, Andy!"

Andy couldn't let that go, so he turned to Ron and asked, "What the fuck, Ron? Did you want me to murder him in the bathtub?"

Ron said, "I would have shot that motherfucker! That's all I'm saying!" Awkward silence in the van followed; Andy turned away and stared out the window. Even though everyone knew Ron liked to give people a hard time, this was different. Maybe Ron had a point. Maybe Andy should have pulled the trigger, and now the seed of doubt had been planted. Nothing more was said as they silently continued their ride to Homicide.

The long-awaited weekend finally arrived, and Andy couldn't wait to see some of his old friends from home. Everyone would meet up at his apartment and then head out for a night of dancing on the Northside of town. Andy loved to dance, and it had been a while since he had seen anyone from his high school years, so this was a big treat. Plus, he needed to decompress after a challenging day and enjoy a carefree night out.

Right after he finished showering, the doorbell rang. Andy threw on a pair of shorts and a t-shirt and answered the door. His friends came to visit him in the big city, and they had a friend in tow. Terri lived with her Mom and Dad in northwest Houston but attended college in San Marcos, TX. Instantly, Andy was smitten with her and embarrassed his apartment was in disarray. Granted, he didn't care if old friends saw his messy place, but this was different. This was the only first impression he would get to make. He politely invited them in and hurried to pick up clothes and the dirty dishes left on the coffee table. They made small talk as Andy tried to make the place presentable and finish getting dressed. Soon they were headed out for a night of fun that would change Andy's life forever.

Andy couldn't take his eyes off Terri. She was pretty, intelligent, and an excellent dancer to boot. Although they chatted as a group, it was apparent that Andy and Terri were in their own world as the night went on. By the end of the night, Andy knew he had to see her again, and he was elated when she gave him her phone number.

As usual, John was out of town, visiting his sweetheart in Andy's hometown. He stayed with Andy's Mom and Dad when he visited her, so now John saw Andy's parents more than he did. When John finally got home, Andy dominated the conversation, eagerly telling him about Terri and how he couldn't wait to see her again.

In the coming months, Andy and Terri started a romance that would be unlike any they had ever known. To bridge the distance, Andy would drive to San Marcos and stay in a hotel, or she would travel home to Houston for the weekend. Something extraordinary was growing between them, and they both knew it. It would not be long before Andy would pop the question, and they started building their lives together.

To Shoot or Not to Shoot

A week had passed since the shooting incident, and Ron's mumbling about Andy not pulling the trigger was starting to die off. Of course, Ron still brought it up occasionally, but his jabs weren't as pointed, and his signature smile told Andy that he was kidding.

The team returned to their hectic routine of search warrant execution and buy busts all over the city, but nothing of significance. They hoped for a short day and an early start to their weekend by Friday afternoon, but it wasn't in the cards. Sergeant McCain received a call from case agents Darlene White and Lisa Bobbinet, who inquired if the team was available to run a warrant for them. McCain said, "Sure! No problem," even though he knew the guys would be less than enthused.

Lisa and Darlene had obtained information on a Mandrax dealer in far northwest Houston sitting on a large stash of pills. Mandrax was a popular narcotic used in nightclubs around Houston. Their informant divulged the drug dealer was residing in a three-bedroom home with his wife. The couple didn't have kids or dogs, and surprisingly, neither one of them had a criminal record. Furthermore, the informant added he had never seen them with a gun, so it sounded like a simple deal.

During a quick briefing, Don detailed their plan at the office and gave out assignments. Raskey would breach the door, Andy would be first in the stack, and the rest of the team would follow. Finally, they loaded up the van for the long ride to northwest Houston during Friday afternoon rush hour traffic. Still unnerved from the last incident, Andy thought about the similarities between this deal and Deanie's simple warrant the previous week. He couldn't forget how that turned out, but at least lighting doesn't strike twice, right?

As the sun was setting over the neighborhood, the team turned onto the target street. Don made his usual announcement for everyone to get ready and turned up the *Jaws* music. Just short of the suspect's home, Joe stopped the van, and the team quickly exited and started toward the front door. This seemingly ordinary, peaceful middle-class neighborhood was about to be turned upside down. The evening sun cast long shadows across the pristinely landscaped green lawns as the group approached the door. It felt almost eerily quiet; no children were playing, dogs weren't barking, not even a lawnmower could be heard in the distance. Usually, he would be comforted by the silence, but for some reason, it was daunting.

When the team positioned themselves for Raskey's breach, Andy heard a TV blaring inside. Don yelled, "POLICE!" and Brad charged forward with the mighty ram. The violent impact sent the door flying open, and Andy immediately spotted the primary suspect sitting on the couch. Startled, he threw his hands in the air and leaned back to surrender. The team flowed through the house while Fincher and Wells took the primary suspect to the floor, shouting, "POLICE, GET ON THE FLOOR!"

Andy proceeded deeper into the house, approaching a dark hallway to his right. He paused for a moment to check if a peer was with him before entering the hallway. Then, Masterson tapped him on the back and said, "GO!" A few steps into the hallway he noticed a well-lit room at the end of the corridor, glowing in the darkness. A woman sat on the bed, staring at him, frightened. Andy moved toward her in the darkroom, yelling, "POLICE OFFICER! GET ON THE FLOOR!"

Andy remained laser-focused on her as he passed closed doors on his right and left. He assumed they were bedrooms or possibly a bathroom, but he was more concerned with the woman who currently posed the most significant threat.

All of a sudden, the woman reached down, grabbed a pistol from the nightstand, and pointed it directly at Andy. Stunned, he yelled, "PUT THE GUN DOWN!" The way she awkwardly held the gun told Andy that she had probably never held one before, but now it was pointed right at him. Andy stopped in his tracks, and although he wanted to fire his weapon for protection, something about her made him pause. Since Ron was only a step into the hallway, he quickly backed up and took cover. Andy was the only one left in the hallway as he demanded, "PUT THE GUN DOWN!"

"Who are you?" she asked, quivering.

"POLICE! PUT THE FUCKING GUN DOWN!" Andy had already given her more chances than he would have a male in the same situation. Maybe the clumsy way she held the gun or her terrified expression convinced him she didn't know what she was doing. Either way, he couldn't let this go on any longer, so he switched the safety off.

Just out of Andy's view, someone was sitting on the bed with the woman, who said in a feminine voice, "Mary, please put the gun down." The woman acknowledged her and looked back at Andy.

"PUT THE GUN DOWN, OR I'M GONNA KILL YOU!" Andy warned one final time, and he began to apply pressure to the trigger. At that instant, she threw the gun to the floor as though it was suddenly on fire. Andy breathed a deep sigh of relief, released the trigger, and lowered the shotgun. He pushed forward and kicked the pistol away as he scanned the room. The woman on the other side of the bed had her hands in the air with a panicked expression. Ron pushed into the room with Andy, and both women were put on the floor.

Ron cuffed them while Andy covered them. Sergeant McCain rushed in, asking, "What happened?" He had been too far away to hear the verbal exchange but was told Andy nearly shot someone.

"She had a pistol!" Andy said defensively.

"Where is it?" McCain asked.

Andy picked up the pistol from the floor and pulled the magazine out. It was a fully loaded 9mm magazine, but the chamber was empty when he pulled the slide back. She couldn't have fired without racking a round. Andy felt slightly better, knowing that his life was never really in jeopardy.

"You OK?" asked McCain, concerned.

"Yeah," Andy replied, although he wasn't happy about the situation. McCain turned and left the room. When Andy glanced over at Masterson, Ron was glaring at him. "What?" asked Andy. Ron kept his mouth shut, slowly looked away, and went back to searching the room. Andy knew this would spark controversy again because he didn't pull the trigger last week. What would be his excuse this time? Andy knew Ron wasn't going to let this go.

The scene was turned over to Lisa and Darlene, so they loaded into the van for the long ride to the office. Andy was not looking forward to the trip or the awkward silence that stretched forever as they drove inbound on Hwy 290. Tension was thick in the air, so Andy decided to get it over with and blurted out, "OK! Let's have it!"

Ron knew exactly what Andy meant, "What the fuck, Andy? Why didn't you shoot that bitch?"

"She didn't even know how to use that gun," Andy replied heatedly. "I gave her the benefit of the doubt."

"Well, your benefit will get one of us killed someday," Ron shouted.

McCain turned around from the front seat and interrupted, "Hey! Save it for the debrief tomorrow! No one got shot, and that's what matters. There will be plenty of time to do this tomorrow!"

After their verbal altercation, the van fell silent for the rest of the 20-minute ride to central. Andy looked out the window, replaying the events with the woman over and over. Ron had a point; taking chances with his own life was one thing, but this was different. He took a chance with Ron's life and everyone else in that hallway. If she had fired a shot, hitting Ron or anyone else, Andy would have to live with the fact that he could have stopped her and didn't. The thought sickened him because he didn't have the right to take chances with the lives of others.

Upon arrival, McCain instructed everyone to meet in the office tomorrow at 10 am for the debriefing. Andy sulked to his car for the drive home and popped the trunk to stow his gear as Tom Fincher walked by, "Hey Andy, don't let Ron get to you. You know he's a blowhard."

"Yeah, but he's right, Tom. I guess I should have shot that bitch," Andy replied sullenly.

Tom placed his hand on Andy's shoulder, "It turned out OK. That gun wasn't even loaded."

"But I didn't know that," Andy interjected.

Tom stopped and changed the subject, "Wanna grab a beer?"

"No, I'm good. I just need some rest." Andy replied. Tom could see Andy was struggling and needed time to think, so he turned and walked away.

The following day's briefing began with Hammond reviewing details about the reasons for the warrant and what they knew about the residence before the raid. To everyone's surprise, Lieutenant Riley decided to sit in on this one. After hearing about the near shooting, he must have some thoughts to share. Andy just hoped Riley wasn't there to give him more grief. Don explained the routine execution plan; then it was time to get to what everyone was waiting for. Don asked Andy to describe his entry and what led to the confrontation with the woman in the bedroom.

Andy nervously walked up to the grease board. This was his first time addressing the team, which only worsened things. He knew some had doubts about him, and this was their opportunity to let him have it.

He went into excruciatingly precise detail about what he saw and did, entering the hallway. First, Andy tried his best to explain his thoughts when he saw the woman with the pistol. Then, accepting responsibility for his mistake, he apologized for putting Ron and his teammates' lives in jeopardy by not taking the shot. Everyone was shocked by Andy's admission, but he had been up all night replaying the situation, piece by piece. He didn't have the right to put everyone's life at risk that way.

Lieutenant Riley jumped up and firmly announced, "Wait a minute! I disagree!" The entire room quieted, stunned. Riley had never attended a debriefing session before, and now he was taking it over. Confidently, Riley made his way to the front of the room and sternly looked at each of them. Using his index finger to emphasize his point, he thumped it on the table and said, "I put this team together to avoid shootings, not create them!" He momentarily stopped for dramatic effect, then continued, "I don't want another cop to get shot, but I also don't want to bring undue scrutiny on the Department by us shooting people that don't need to be shot. We can always Monday morning quarterback about what we did or didn't do, but only the one at the tip of the spear can make that call, and we should all support that." Then, with his authoritative voice, he emphasized, "This was a good deal, and if it had gone the other way, that woman would be dead for pointing a gun that couldn't fire a shot, which would be a tragedy."

Riley stood there a moment to let them reflect on his words, then said, "I am putting the team in for a Chief's commendation. Not just for yesterday, but for the good work you guys do every day." The room was silent as he walked out and shut the door behind him. Everyone tried to absorb what just happened, and Andy waited for Ron to chime in, but he said nothing. Finally, Don finished the critique, and everyone was released to grab lunch.

As everyone filed out of the room, the guys started chatting amongst themselves. Andy stayed behind, stunned by Riley's speech. He wondered if the lieutenant's comments would quash some of Ron's grumblings, but that wasn't exactly his style. Ron loved to stir the pot, and Andy knew the stew wasn't done yet.

The following day Mark Kiley called Andy before work, asking if he wanted to go for a drive and check on some real estate he had purchased. A 5-acre tract in a large acreage subdivision along the banks of the Brazos River. Located in the country, the acreage was a good 45-minute drive South of town and was considered an excellent place to raise a family. It sounded good and precisely what Andy had been looking for, so he eagerly agreed.

Immediately, he was attracted to the large oak trees and abundant wildlife. He envisioned a cedar home nestled amongst a canopy of trees where he and Terri could raise a family. Even though it would be a long commute to work, having his kids go to a country school and be raised with traditional values was worth it. Andy found a 6-acre lot that looked promising and started making calls to see if it was a dream he could afford.

The Phone Call

Andy was subpoenaed to court for the case where the pimp tried to kill him. It was the first time his case appeared on the court docket, so Andy assumed it was merely procedural, but it was a chance to get a glimpse of the man that nearly shot him. Anxiously, Andy watched the bailiff walk the prisoner before the judge in an orange jumpsuit with shackles around his hands and feet. Andy was pleased to know he couldn't make bail. If nothing else, he was at least going to spend some time behind bars. After a few legal proceedings, the judge set the case for trial in 6 months; Andy was dismissed.

With some time left to kill before roll-call, he went to the office, thinking it would be a good opportunity to have a cup of coffee and read the paper before everyone else showed up. However, once he was on the 6th floor, one of the phones wouldn't stop ringing, so he decided to answer it. Someone asked for Sam Crockett, a Sergeant on the night shift. Andy jotted down a message and paged Sam.

Then within a few minutes, Gentry's voice announced over the PA system, "Wallace, pick up line two."

"Narcotics, this is Wallace," answered Andy.

"Hey Andy, it's Crockett." Andy started telling him about the message, but Sam interrupted, "Hey man, I'm sorry I didn't call you last night, but I didn't want to wake you. I was going to call you first thing this morning, but you beat me to it." Andy was clueless as to what Sam was talking about, so he just listened. "Look, we didn't know he was your brother before this went down." Instantly, Andy's heart sank; he knew exactly who Sam was talking about. Crockett continued, "After we arrested him, your name came up."

Andy interrupted with, "It's OK, Sam. That's not why I was calling. I just answered a phone call for you, so I wanted to give you the guy's number."

Andy gave Sam the information and asked a few questions about Mike's arrest. Crockett couldn't say much because of the conflict of interest but said Mike was caught in an ecstasy lab on the city's southwest side. They had booked him in the city jail under a hold for the Narcotics Division. Because the case agents were still working on the details, Sam didn't know if he would be charged. Although he didn't think Mike was the target of the investigation, he couldn't say more. Andy didn't ask who the agents were; he would be too embarrassed if he knew them. He awkwardly thanked Sam and hung up the phone.

He sat in the dayroom alone in his thoughts and stared at the blank wall for several moments. He was simultaneously mad and worried. Angry that Mike would come to Houston and continue his illegal dealings. It was one thing to be arrested by the Feds in Corpus Christi; Andy didn't know any of them. The Texas Rangers investigation went nowhere, and Andy didn't know them either. But this was different. It was in his backyard and involved guys he worked with. Andy was livid and also worried about the man he idolized growing up.

It meant Mike was processed through the drunk tank where Andy previously worked. Andy wondered if John was working when Mike came through. Even though John didn't know Mike, he probably would have recognized his name. Then, Andy realized his brother was sitting in a jail cell just one floor below him. Although he wanted to go down and see him, he wasn't sure if he would hug him or hit him. So instead, Andy tucked the thoughts of his brother away and focused on the task. He loved his job and worked with guys he trusted, but he wondered, once this news broke, would they still trust him? He could only hope they would understand and see beyond a family member's mistakes.

He decided against mentioning the arrest to his Mom and Dad or anyone else in the family. If they found out, it would be from someone else. He would act surprised and claim to know nothing about it. That was the strategy, and he was going to stick to it.

THIRTEEN

Stairway to Hell

Several weeks passed, and the team ran one warrant after another without incident. They were very good at their job and looking forward to receiving the Chief's Commendation. Usually, that entailed a trip to the Chief's office and a photo op to boot. Duncan took the day off, so Don Hammond was driving the van as they slowly turned onto the target street. This time, they were executing a warrant for cocaine for Mark Kiley, but Andy had an unusual feeling about it. Nervously, he peered out the front windshield, trying to glimpse the dump-out location.

The plan was to off-load on the north side of the 4-plex apartment building where the suspects couldn't see them. The informant said they were always on the lookout, and if they saw anything resembling law enforcement, they would flush the dope. Far more concerning, the CI saw guns in the apartment, including a sawed-off shotgun, which gave Andy pause. Hammond glanced in the rearview mirror to make sure everyone was ready. His eyes met Andy's, and he gave a reassuring wink to gesture, 'It'll be OK.' That helped, but Andy's anxiety was still more heightened than usual. McCain appeared unphased by the seriousness of what they were about to do. He was the calming force with an attitude who never let his men see him sweat.

Andy glanced around the van to see if anyone else was as tense as he was. The quiet uneasiness made him think; deep down inside, everyone knew this one was different. Don radioed the perimeter team that they were on the final approach. Lastly, he pushed the cassette in the deck, which cued the *Jaws* theme music, as he did on every deal.

Andy made eye contact with Masterson, who he discovered was staring at him. Ron would be second through the door, and the calculated look on his face told Andy that if someone needed shooting, he was there to do it. Then, sheepishly, Andy broke eye contact and looked out the window. He didn't need controversy fogging his thoughts. What he needed was to remain sharp and focused on the job.

Don brought the van to a slow stop as they quickly off-loaded and flowed around the front of the building. John Schulte, Kiley's partner, led the team into the entrance of the 4-plex. John was familiar with the floor plan, so he would guide them up the narrow stairway to the correct door. According to the CI, the door was not reinforced, so John would breach with the ram.

As they entered the aging building, Andy smelled the dust, dirt, and filth accumulated throughout the years, and the stench was revolting. They walked to the back of the foyer and turned 180 degrees to enter the stairway with an open landing above them. Unfortunately, the stairs were narrow and dimly lit, causing the building to seem like something out of a cheap horror movie.

Andy never liked going up stairwells, and this one was incredibly creepy. The entire team was funneled into a column with nowhere to go but up or down. Neither option was good for a gunfight. The only positive thing about being shot on a staircase was that hopefully, you would roll back down to your buddies.

As the team eased up the stairs, Andy was directly behind John; the worn boards creaked under the weight of all the men in full gear. The building was eerily silent except for the music from one of the upstairs apartments. As they ascended, no one said a word; weapons pointed in all directions. Then, finally, the crook's door came into view halfway up the stairs. It was just ahead on the left and the music source. The sounds grew louder as they approached the landing, and John stepped past the door and squared up with the ram.

As Andy was about to yell 'POLICE,' the door opened, and an older black man stepped out. He stood startled, with his eyes bulging and mouth open. John dropped the ram and grabbed him, pulling him back. John yelled, "POLICE!" and glanced inside. Someone darted across the room with a shotgun in hand; John screamed, "SHOTGUN!" Then, Andy wondered if he should continue or back up. Since he knew Ron was right behind him, he thought his courage would be questioned again. If he hesitated, the controversy would worsen, and Ron's criticisms would begin again. Andy stepped forward and turned through the threshold to face whatever waited for him.

The room was dimly lit, with loud music playing on the stereo, and he immediately smelled marijuana. As Andy entered and scanned to his left, he noticed it was a corner-fed room. A man was standing in the far corner with his hands down by his side. Andy yelled, "POLICE!" and pointed his shotgun directly at the suspect, and he started raising his hands. Ron entered the doorway, turned left along the wall, and started yelling at the suspect to get on the floor, but he didn't respond. As Ron stepped forward to force the suspect to the floor, Andy turned to cover the two open doors. Andy suddenly spotted someone in the open doorway with a shotgun on his right. Because Ron was focused on the suspect in the corner, he hadn't noticed, but the barrel was pointed directly at him. As a reflex, Andy squeezed the trigger and fired without giving it a second thought. A blast of light went off like a camera flash in the darkroom, and for a split second, Andy couldn't see anything. Then, once his eyes finally regained vision, he realized whoever had been holding that shotgun was gone, and the other suspect in the corner was gone as well. He wondered if he had shot both men for a second because they fell instantaneously.

Ron spun around to see who fired as Andy pointed and yelled, "He's over there! He's got a gun!"

"ARE YOU SURE?" Ron asked incredulously. Tom and Fred entered the room as everyone tried to understand what had happened. "SOMEONE WITH A SHOTGUN WAS IN THAT DOORWAY!" Andy yelled in a commanding voice. He knew he didn't imagine it. Andy began to regain his low light vision, and he presumed the suspect must have fallen behind a couch blocking his view. At that distance, there was no way he could have missed him.

Ron cautiously moved along the far wall; handgun extended as he shined his flashlight behind the couch. "POLICE! DON'T MOVE!" Ron yelled as he spotted the man lying on the floor. The suspect was moaning and curled into a fetal position. Ron continued screaming, "SHOW ME YOUR HANDS MOTHERFUCKER!" The man was too severely injured to comply and just lay there seething in pain.

When Ron spotted the pool of blood under the man's torso, he knew the man wasn't faking. As Ron stepped forward to the injured suspect, Andy covered the two open doorways. "Where's the gun?" Ron asked, shining his flashlight around. Then, he looked at Andy, "I don't see a gun!"

For an instant, shock ran down Andy's spine as he replayed the image of the shotgun barrel pointed at Ron. He clearly saw a gun, so he confidently yelled, "BULLSHIT! He had a shotgun! I SAW IT!"

"I don't see it, Andy," Ron said, still concerned.

Andy replied, "KEEP LOOKING; IT'S THERE!"

Ron holstered his pistol and rolled the man over as he yelled out in pain. Ron replied, "SHUT UP, ASSHOLE! DON'T DEAL, DOPE, AND YOU WON'T GET SHOT!" Then, Ron spotted the pistol-grip shotgun; the suspect had been lying on it and was covered in blood. Ron yelled out, "GOT IT!" and held up the gun. A sense of vindication washed over Andy, and he breathed a sigh of relief. Ron was still in full tactical mode and called for Fred and Tom to help search the remaining rooms, but they were empty.

Sergeant McCain stepped into the apartment to check on everyone, and Fred pointed at the wounded man and said, "We're good, Sarg, but we need an ambulance for this guy." McCain told everyone to get out of the apartment except for Don, and he radioed for an ambulance. Now they needed to preserve the scene for Homicide while he and Don stayed with the wounded suspect.

The ambulance arrived within minutes, and everyone was expecting the wounded suspect to be pronounced DOA. But, to their surprise, he was quickly loaded, and the ambulance sped off with lights and sirens blaring. Later, they learned the thick leather jacket the suspect was wearing slowed the buckshot rounds enough to save his life. Unfortunately, they had to crack his chest at Ben Taub to save him, but he would live to stand trial.

Andy dropped his gear in the raid van and sat down on the back bumper to wait for Homicide. One by one, the guys walked over and asked if he was alright. Then they offered their support for a job well done, which comforted Andy.

Eventually, Ron walked over, sat down beside him, put his hand on his shoulder, and asked, "Hey, man. You OK?"

Andy continued staring at the pavement, "Sure," he answered. "Thanks for asking."

"Listen, I want to thank you for doing what you did. I never saw that son-of-a-bitch! It scared the fuck out of me when you shot that fucker!"

"No worries, Ron. It scared me too!"

"Well, anyway," Ron continued, "for the record, I saw him with that shotgun!"

"What?" Andy asked as he sat up and looked at Ron questioningly.

"You know, right before you shot him," said Ron with a wink. "I saw him coming out of the doorway with that shotgun."

Andy realized Ron was attempting to help with his testimony, so he quickly corrected him, "NO! This is a good shooting, Ron! There's no reason to say anything but what happened. Just tell the truth. That's it. OK?"

Ron nodded in agreement, "OK, man, just trying to help."

Andy looked down and replied, "I know."

Ron dropped his head, a little embarrassed to have offered. He slapped Andy on the back and awkwardly walked away.

It took about 30 minutes for Homicide to show up, the DA investigators, and the news media. Rapidly, the scene turned into a circus, so McCain requested to release his guys to go downtown and start writing their statements. The detectives agreed but wanted Andy and Ron to walk them through the apartment and show them what happened.

Ascending the dark stairway again felt particularly creepy. Andy just wanted to get this over with and get the hell out of there as quickly as possible. They demonstrated how everything played out and covered all the investigator's questions. Ron was honest and told them precisely what happened, "I was dealing with this guy here when I heard Andy shoot. I spun around to see what had happened. I didn't even see that dude. Andy saved my life." He was floored to hear Ron describe it like that, and a feeling of acceptance fell over him as they were released.

The ride to Homicide was quiet for the most part, with a few stories shared. Everyone seemed to have a slightly different perspective on what happened, but Andy only listened. No one doubted him now, but Andy didn't hold grudges.

He needed to call Mom and Dad before the story hit the evening news and let them know he was OK. He thought about Terri and knew she would find out soon. Currently, she was off at college, but her parents would surely call her the minute they saw the story. Their love was growing, and he hoped that the emotions of an event like this wouldn't turn her away and ruin their future together.

The one thing Andy didn't need was Hurley assigned to this case and making trouble for him. To his amazement, he later found out Hurley no longer worked at IAD. He was promoted to lieutenant and transferred to the Records Division. In Andy's mind, that was a perfect place for Hurley. The chances of Andy ever running into him there were about as minuscule as any place he could imagine.

That evening Andy called his Mom and Dad to break the news about the shooting. He tried to downplay the incident as much as possible because he didn't want them to worry. But, they saw through the sugar coating, and he could tell they were concerned. When Andy finally called Terri, he danced around her questions, and she listened carefully. He feared she would think twice about becoming serious with a man who risked his life for a living, but she took it in stride.

With those two chores behind him, he set up a meeting with a mortgage company about buying the acreage in the country. It was a stunning piece of land in the woods, and one night, when Terri least expected it, he drove her there and proposed. She said yes, and their future would be forever intertwined.

The following April, they married and started building their dream home on their small piece of heaven. Terri graduated from Southwest Texas State University and was selected to teach at the local high school. Everything was beginning to fall into place.

Andy realized narcotics officers were either just getting married or divorced, but sadly no one seemed to remain married. So, he figured he could either remain in narcotics or stay married, but the two were not compatible. Then, he wondered where he could find a challenging and exciting job that wasn't as dangerous as kicking in doors.

One of his classmates from the Academy recently made the SWAT team. Bobby McGirt was a good guy but not a physical standout. Andy perceived SWAT team members as Green Berets and 10-feet tall with years of combat experience, but Bobby had none of that. So, he called Bobby to ask about life on SWAT and learned that there was still an opening. However, they were only taking applications from uniformed divisions, which meant Andy would have to transfer out of the Narcotics Division if he wanted to be considered. Although it was a difficult decision, he and Terri discussed it, and they agreed it was worth a try.

Andy transferred to central patrol, evening shift, and said goodbye to his buddies in narcotics. He had risked his life with these guys for the last three years and built several lasting friendships. They developed a bond that only those who risk life and limb together can know. It was a sad goodbye, but he was on to the next adventure.

The New Kid

Andy's nerves were on edge as he drove downtown for his interview at SWAT. Dressed to impress, he had a fresh haircut and wore a neatly pressed class-A uniform with spit-shined shoes. A face-to-face interview was the last stage in the selection process, so he knew he was a finalist. When the opening was posted over a month ago, at least forty officers applied, but now it was down to a handful.

Andy shined in the physical testing, finishing at the top of the list. His personnel record was spotless, with no disciplinary action whatsoever, so the only obstacle was if any of the brass found out about Mike's criminal record. Andy wasn't in control of that, so he focused on the positive. If they asked, he had an answer prepared, 'Due to my brother's actions; I have nothing to do with him anymore. Now, we are only connected by blood.' He hoped they'd understand and not make it an issue.

The SWAT office was in an underground command center from the cold war era. The place was designed to survive a nuclear blast and still function. Yet, as he walked down the narrow stairs leading almost 30 feet below Bagby Street, he heard the rumble of heavy trucks passing overhead. With only recessed lighting illuminating the way that occasionally flickered, the place felt like a dungeon.

The Captain's Secretary told him to wait in the dayroom until he was called for his interview. Andy sat wondering what questions they would ask him as he gazed at his surroundings. It was an impressive complex of offices and large rooms underground equipped with emergency generators that could power the entire place for days. Several detailed maps of the city covered the walls that included power lines and waterways.

Suddenly, voices could be heard coming from down the hall, "Thanks for coming in. We'll be in touch." Andy recognized the young officer leaving his interview, and they waved to each other as if they were old friends. "Wallace?" came a voice from down the corridor.

Andy hastened to his feet and firmly replied, "Yes, sir!" Knowing it was showtime for him as he briskly walked toward what he hoped would be his future.

He stepped into the open door of a small office where three SWAT Sergeants were expecting him. As they stood up to shake hands and introduce themselves, Andy was slightly intimidated. Sergeant Jenson led the interview, with Sergeant Rosekrants and Sergeant Hague chiming in with questions from time to time. Jenson was all business, while Rosekrants and Hague used a more casual approach when asking Andy about everything from where he grew up to his religious beliefs. During the 30-minute grilling, Andy held his own, even injecting a modest amount of humor to be remembered.

"Do you go to church, Andy?" Jenson asked.

"Yes, sir, every Sunday," Andy answered.

Jenson's eyebrows raised as he asked again, "Every Sunday?"

Andy understood the implication because they just asked if he could take a kill shot because the commander gave a green light. They feared that if someone was too devout to their faith, they might not be able to follow that order.

"Which church do you attend?" inquired Rosekrants.

"Second Baptist Church on the Katy Freeway, sir," replied Andy.

"Every Sunday?" Jenson asked again incredulously.

"Yes, sir. Without fail." Then, Andy let them off the hook, "I have an extra job there directing traffic." The room erupted in laughter, and Andy smiled. He hit a home run with that one.

When the interview ended, Andy was dismissed and instructed to schedule an appointment with Dr. Rodie, the HPD Psychologist. All finalists had to complete a mental evaluation as part of the selection process. Andy was familiar with the doc because Rodie conducted presentations at in-service training. He particularly enjoyed Rodie's down-to-earth personality and his seemingly compassionate nature. Andy didn't give psychological evaluations much credence, but he had no problem sitting down for whatever bullshit test Rodie wanted.

Andy had to complete a three-part written evaluation which seemed a bit silly to him, including questions like 'Do you avoid stepping on cracks in the sidewalk?' and 'Do you think people are talking about you when you leave a room?' Andy dutifully answered the questionnaire to the best of his ability, and in the follow-up interview, he was shocked at how much Rodie interpreted from the data. For instance, he detected Andy was dealing with stressful issues and invited him to talk about anything bothering him. Andy didn't care to air his dirty laundry to Rodie or anyone else, especially during the final phase of qualifying for a SWAT position, so he held back. Andy wondered if the doc picked up on his trouble with Hurley or his brother's criminal behavior; either way, he wasn't going there. He had locked those concerns away in his box and was not about to open it now.

After the evaluation, Rodie walked Andy to the exit, extending his hand to shake goodbye, and said, "Andy, if you ever want to come back and talk, after this SWAT competition stuff is over, my door is always open."

Andy shook his hand and thanked him. Rodie had seen right through his façade. Although a little creepy, he was also comforted to know Rodie was willing to help.

The next few weeks were a waiting game. Andy continued to patrol the streets downtown and tried not to think about SWAT. Surprisingly, the time passed quickly while he caught up on how much patrol had changed in three short years. Now, shop cars were equipped with computers that sent messages back and forth to the dispatcher. As a result, officers could quickly and easily check suspects for warrants and access criminal records from their patrol unit. This advancement in technology was a considerable asset in everyday policing.

When the top ten list was finally posted, Andy was ranked number one, so he would transfer to SWAT immediately. Beaming with pride and newfound confidence, Andy couldn't wait to tell Terri and his parents about his new position. Terri was pleased, and it was a proud moment when he called home to tell his Mom and Dad. Now he had to make good on this new opportunity.

Sergeant Jenson called and instructed Andy to report to the SWAT office Monday at 7 am sharp, dressed for a workout. The SWAT schedule allocated time for officers to work out on duty, shower, and change into their blue uniforms. Then, they met with supervisors to receive the day's assignment.

Andy hung up the phone and couldn't ignore the butterflies in his stomach, realizing how unprepared he was. All the SWAT officers he had seen around the station looked like athletes. It was intimidating, and the last thing he wanted was to embarrass himself.

Andy arrived early Monday morning but soon realized everyone in SWAT arrived early. Being with like-minded individuals instantly put him at ease. Everyone was friendly and welcoming, more so than in any place he had worked previously. Sergeant Jenson congratulated him and said, "You'll be assigned to Sergeant Hague's squad, and your Team Leader is Billy Clark." Andy met Sergeant Hague during the interviews but knew nothing of Billy.

He spotted his old classmate, Bobby McGirt, among the guys waiting for PT. He knew Bobby casually from the Academy, but they hadn't hung out together. Bobby brought Andy around, introducing him to the guys. "There's your TL," he said, pointing to Billy Clark. Being the TL or Team Leader was the highest honor an officer could receive on the SWAT team. Supervision selected Team Leaders for their experience, tactical knowledge, and leadership skills. TL was earned by gaining the trust and confidence of the supervisors and team members.

Team Leaders coordinated work assignments and training for their team, and to some extent, discipline was also carried out by the Team Leaders. TLs ran the tactical missions on SWAT with the overwatch and approval of supervision. On the other hand, supervisors are selected by the Captain for their ability to supervise, not necessarily their tactical knowledge. They approved or denied the TLs plans and ensured Standard Operating Procedures (SOP) were followed.

Clark walked over and shook Andy's hand, "Welcome aboard!" Andy instantly knew that he was going to like Billy. He was a large, imposing man with a firm grip and kind eyes with a sense of ease about them. He was steady under pressure, and during a critical incident, he would be the one to jokingly say, "You, you, and you panic! The rest of you come with me." Andy was grateful to be on Billy's team, determined to work hard, and tried to impress Billy every chance he got.

"Roll-call!" Sergeant Jenson yelled. The room fell quiet, and everyone grabbed a seat. Jenson called out the list of names, and everyone present responded, "HERE!" Andy tried to remember as many names as he could, but there were just too many with twenty-four guys. As he looked around the room, Andy assumed most of the team had prior military experience, and some may have even served in special forces. Andy couldn't help but feel inadequate, but he was on a mission to earn his place.

After roll-call, Jenson led them out of the bunker for a short jog down Allen Parkway. Andy stayed with McGirt because he ran with him in the Academy and figured he could keep his pace. However, Andy wasn't sure how far they were going, so his goal was to stay in the middle of the pack.

They ran to a large grassy field along Buffalo Bayou and spread out into formation for push-ups, sit-ups, calisthenics, and stretching. Then, Sergeant Jenson led them down the jogging trail alongside the bayou for a long run. Andy didn't find distance running enjoyable, but he wouldn't dare complain. Next, they jogged to Shepherd Street and back, about five miles. Although it was a lot for Andy, he finished right in the middle.

After a quick shower, Clark instructed Andy to meet him for breakfast at IHOP on Memorial Drive. The rest of Billy's team would be there as well, and they could get acquainted. Every entry team consisted of four members. The point man, who was first through the door, and the cover man was second and next in line to provide protection. The Team Leader was usually third and coordinated the team's movements with a rearguard to watch the back.

Billy's point man was Mark McDonald, ex-military and the strong silent type that exuded confidence. The cover man was John Vargas, a new guy who came over a few months earlier, so he was still trying to navigate his way on the team. That left Andy as rearguard, and for now, he was quite happy with that position.

Over breakfast, Billy lined out his plans to get them operational but explained that for now, the team was not eligible to execute an entry. Supervisors wouldn't send a team on an entry with new guys on it because they lacked experience. So, the road forward for Andy and the rest of the team would be grueling with long hours of training.

After their plates were cleared and their stomachs full, Billy pointed at John and Andy and said, "Right now, I need to get you two prepared for Basic School, which starts in two weeks. My hope is, if you guys survive that week, the rest will come easy."

A little nervous about Billy's statement, Andy hoped he was kidding about surviving Basic School, but he would keep his mouth shut and do as he was told.

Becoming Comfortable With Being Uncomfortable

Over the last few months, several seasoned SWAT team members transferred to other assignments within the department. Some of them were part of the original 1974 team and were ready to move on. Many cited the physical demands of working out every day as part of their decision to leave, which was even more taxing than being on call 24/7. There was also the mental stress of constantly living with a pager, always ready to jump when duty called. All these factors tended to grind on the team.

Most team members remained in the position for about four or five years before having their fill and transferring to another sector within the department. Others chose to promote out, preferring a supervisory career path. Everyone knew that committing to the SWAT detail didn't allow for freedoms like planning vacations or out-of-town trips without first obtaining approval. Team members were required to be ready anytime their pager went off. Even a simple evening out to dinner had to include an exit plan. They parked their SWAT vehicle in the driveway at the end of the day, skipping the garage for a quick escape route when necessary. Pagers were attached like appendages, worn everywhere you went, and they couldn't help occasionally wanting to throw the damn thing out a window.

As a result, eight rookies were added to the SWAT team, and Andy was proud he was one of them. A rigid concrete parking lot served as the inspection area for the new guys standing in formation in the early morning darkness. The parking lot was part of the old Holmes Road Dump, an abandoned waste facility on the southeast side of Houston. It was mothballed by the city years ago, and now the K9 team used it as an office and a place to train police dogs. The maze of brick buildings, rusted pipes, and tanks sprawled the 100-acre fenced property.

SWAT Standard Operating Procedures (SOP) mandated that every Houston SWAT officer complete Basic SWAT School as part of the training curriculum. Their Team Leader had been mentally and physically preparing them for this challenge, and all eight rookies were nervous knowing this week was coming. Andy's heart was pounding, standing at attention, waiting for whatever came next.

The TLs went about their last-minute checks and offered advice to their young subordinates while waiting for the sergeants to start inspection. The air was warm and humid, and Andy was already beginning to sweat, mostly from nerves and their cumbersome equipment. Everyone wore bulky ballistic vests, heavy boots, and a hard, uncomfortable helmet. The supervisors took their sweet time inside the air-conditioned K9 office, preparing for the week of intense instruction.

Andy was thankful to be there, but he was apprehensive about what was to come. Billy Clark was aware Andy lacked prior military experience, so to compensate for the deficiency, he worked with him on what to expect and military mannerisms. Previously, Andy had never worn a ballistic helmet or fired an AR15, so all of this was new. Nevertheless, he stood by, ready to prove he could measure up, knowing it would be one of the most challenging weeks in his young life.

SWAT teams across the state usually conducted their own Basic Schools, and each one was a little different. In Houston, a Basic SWAT School consisted of a week of grueling physical and mental endurance. A military-style training loaded with marching, running, yelling, and PT, LOTS OF PT! A standard 8-hour workday was a thing of the past, and no one dared to think of putting in for overtime. The days began before the sun was up and concluded long after dark—the day ended when the brass said so, not one minute sooner. Lunch breaks were approximately 30 minutes or less and varied from day to day. Students devoured whatever they could stash in their pack in the allotted time. Andy brought either a can of tuna fish or chicken, chips, and an apple because they were nutritious, packed easily, and were less likely to spoil in the hot Texas summer heat.

As the first light of dawn peeked over the horizon, the anticipation was stifling. The unbearable silence added to his anxiety as sweat rolled down Andy's forehead. The TLs finished their last-minute prep and stood back in the darkness, waiting for the show to start.

When the three sergeants finally walked out, Andy was shocked; their entire demeanor changed. The same three friendly and cordial supervisors during his first three weeks transformed into total assholes who looked like they were about to bite someone's head off.

The inspection lasted about 20 minutes; Jenson moved from man to man in the formation, thoroughly checking everything from personal hygiene to issued weapons. If anything was not pristine, a physical or mental punishment followed, sometimes both. Push-ups, additional sprints, standing under the hot sun wearing full gear, including a helmet to eat their lunch, or anything else Jenson could think of. Before the week ended, he was committed to finding something wrong with everyone. If Jenson could see even the tiniest speck of dirt on a weapon, he would remove the gun from the student's holster and throw it in the dirt. Preferably a mud puddle if he could find one. Followed by endless push-ups, and no one paid the price alone; if one student was doing push-ups, everyone was.

When the day ended, every muscle in Andy's body ached, and he had blisters on both feet. Their uniform requirements mandated that they wore leather Cochran combat boots which were hot and heavy, with stiff soles lacking cushioning. But boy, they sounded good while marching on concrete and shined up real pretty. They weren't suitable for running, but Jenson didn't care. As an old-school military man, he couldn't stand a boot that didn't have a spit shine. Andy wasn't aware you should break in leather boots before running in them, so they were stiff and rigid. Within the first hour of PT on Monday, blisters had already formed, and by Tuesday evening, his socks were soaked with blood.

Each night, he soaked his feet in warm salt water, and when he slid on his boots the following day, he held his breath and pushed through the pain. Although the first 20 minutes of exercise were excruciating, his feet became numb to some degree as long as he kept moving. Standing back up was agony if he stopped and sat down for a break. Many years later, Andy learned a phrase from a Navy SEAL that would have served him well that week. To survive the grueling training throughout hell week, "You have to become comfortable with being uncomfortable."

After PT each morning, they hustled into a small classroom and sat down in cramped desks while they cooled down. The curriculum was so engaging that Andy often forgot about the pain coming from his feet. First, the Team Leaders lectured on pertinent topics, including camouflage, cover, and concealment. Next came team concepts such as stealth entries and searching for barricaded suspects. So much more was involved in a successful SWAT operation than Andy had ever imagined.

On Thursday, the topic of chemical agents came up during class instruction and how to properly use a gas mask. Unfortunately, one of the curriculum objectives stated that all students had to be contaminated.

Everyone knew what was coming, and the anticipation only exaggerated the effects. As a final test, they had to search a gassed building wearing their masks. CS was the agent they used, which produced a toxic smoke. The rooms were so full of gas it was challenging to see. Even with his mask on, Andy felt the chemical agent burning the back of his neck and other areas of his body where moisture collected.

The exhausting search took approximately 30 minutes. Then, Sergeant Jenson gathered the students in an interior room. Andy couldn't distinguish anyone specifically between the smoke and the gas masks obstructing his vision. But he heard Jenson's muffled voice demand them to take their masks off and announce their name and payroll number before they were allowed to exit the building. Much to his dismay, Andy was the first student Jenson named, "Wallace! You're first," he yelled.

Andy was hoping to watch one or two others go before him so that he would know what to expect, but no such luck. So instead, he took a deep breath, pulling off his mask and holding his breath. Immediately, he felt a type of immense pain he had never felt before, particularly when the chemicals started burning his eyes. The sensation felt like being jabbed with a million needles, excruciating, stinging bolts of pain pulsating throughout his body. When he finally tried to breathe, it felt like his lungs were being pulled out of his throat. He simultaneously wanted to vomit and gag, but he held back.

After shouting out his name and payroll number, Jenson allowed him to leave the building. Andy stumbled down the hallway, struggling to find his way out. Knocking into walls, coughing, gagging, and when he tried to open his eyes for a quick peek, the pain involuntarily forced them closed. Then, at last, he felt a large hand grasp the back of his vest. Billy Clark guided him the rest of the way out, softly reassuring him, "This way, son!"

Once outside, Andy collapsed to his knees, gasping for fresh air. Clark grabbed the water hose and sprayed his whole body down. Andy fell forward on all fours, gagging, mucus streaming to the ground. Still in full gear, Billy hosed him down from head to toe, and Andy didn't care about the wet gear; all he wanted was relief from the gas.

Within a few minutes, the effects of the CS began to dissipate, and Andy's body started returning to normal. He was slightly embarrassed about his reaction to the gas until he saw his teammates come out of the building. Unfortunately, some of them were far worse off than Andy. One of the students stumbled out of the building, fainted, and fell face-first onto a sidewalk, breaking off his front tooth. He was conscious again after copious amounts of water, and they tossed him back in formation to complete the day. Jenson barked out, "You can fix that tooth next week," and that's precisely what he did.

The last day of instruction included rappelling. Considering he had a fear of heights, rappelling was especially challenging for him. So, he was undoubtedly a bit panicked to learn his first-time rappelling was off a 9-story building at the dump. Nevertheless, when it was his turn to go, Andy carefully listened to Sergeant Rosekrant's instructions and slowly and steadily backed off the roof's edge. He kept staring at the 3/8" nylon rope that held his weight, as it was the only thing between life and/or certain death nine stories below. Andy's heart raced, and even though every instinct told him walking down the side of a 9-story building was crazy, he knew he had to go. The rope looked like a thin piece of dental floss, but he focused on Rosekrants' calming voice and his breathing.

Andy was remarkably calm, taking that first step off the edge and starting down the rope. As he descended the wall, he began to gain confidence, found it a lot less scary, and even a little fun bounding off and dropping down. When Andy reached the ground, he saw Lieutenant John Guinn, quite majestic in his freshly starched SWAT uniform. The brim of his baseball cap was pulled down to his mirrored aviator sunglasses. He was a stoic figure, and this was only the second time Andy had seen him. Guinn observed Andy take his first step off the building, admiring how he dealt with the fear of falling.

Not only was Lieutenant Guinn a SWAT Commander, but he was also a full bird Colonel in the Airforce Reserves, known for his prolific, thought-provoking, and quotable comments. Now that his feet were firmly planted on the ground, relief and pride washed over Andy. He was grateful he made it without any serious mistakes, especially in front of the lieutenant. He hoped Guinn was impressed by his performance as well.

Andy turned to the Lieutenant for his critique. Guinn smiled and said, "Wallace, when faced with danger and your own fears, you reach within yourself and find the courage to overcome and perform."

"Yes, sir," Andy proudly replied and walked away. He hoped to remember the gracious comment, but for now, he was just glad to have survived the 9-story trip.

Even though Basic SWAT school was only a week, it felt much longer. When it was finally over, eight candidates had proven themselves worthy of joining the team. Graduation was short and unremarkable, but the entire team arrived to shake hands and welcome the newest members aboard.

Once dismissed, Andy headed home to enjoy a couple of days of relaxation with Terri. His feet were killing him, and he couldn't wait to remove his boots and give them a good soaking. It took two weeks for his blisters to heal completely, but Andy referred to them as learning portals, 'marks left on one's skin when knowledge enters your body.' He felt physically prepared to go into the week and but now he understood the importance of mental toughness.

The First Callup

Andy's first call-up as a full-fledged SWAT officer came in the wee hours of the morning with a phone call from Billy Clark. A female with a handgun barricaded herself in a home in the southwest part of town, and patrol was requesting SWAT. Although Andy made a couple of call-ups during the three weeks before Basic School, he was only allowed to observe. This time he would be assigned an active position and all the responsibilities that came with it. "I'm on my way," Andy replied and hung up the phone.

Quickly, he dressed into his black Battle Dress Uniform (BDU) and ran out the door. BDU was an old military term that had carried over into law enforcement. SWAT adopted the look as a uniform that would distinguish themselves from the HPD blues patrol officers wore. Andy's SWAT vehicle was an unmarked blue and white equipped with two police radios, one to monitor patrol channels and the other for SWAT. Driving onto the highway, he switched his radio to the southwest channel to monitor the activity as he sped toward the scene. The officers sounded anxious, describing an intoxicated woman staggering around with a gun, taunting them. Andy feared she might take one step too far, and it would be over before he arrived.

He was the first SWAT officer to make the scene. He parked and nervously rushed to gather his gear. Now that he was qualified with his AR15, he grabbed it as his weapon of choice. It made a sobering sound when he released the bolt to slam home on a live round. He hoped this ended well.

In the pre-dawn darkness of the quiet suburban neighborhood, Andy made his way toward the objective. Sergeant Rosekrants was the first SWAT supervisor on the scene, running a makeshift command post (CP) out of his vehicle. When he spotted Andy, he yelled, "Get to the front of the house and take a perimeter position. Send those patrol officers back to me."

Two uniformed patrol officers hid behind a parked car, their pistols drawn. Andy crouched down and hurried toward them, announcing in a low voice, "Coming in." They turned and looked when Andy asked, "What you got?"

One of them pointed across the street and replied, "This crazy bitch keeps coming out of that house and screaming that she's gonna kill us."

"Does she know you guys are over here?"

"No, I don't think so. Sarg is down the street, and he's done all the talking."

"OK, I got this now. They want y'all back at the command post," advised Andy.

"OK," and they eased into the darkness toward Rosekrants.

The SWAT Team was held in high esteem, so they took his directions without question.

He found a cover position over the hood of a car when suddenly the suspect's front door opened, and he spotted the outline of a woman. He struggled to make out her face as she started yelling something. She was highly intoxicated as she staggered out a few steps, so Andy pushed the button on his mic and whispered, "Suspect is at the front door." The Motorola mics had a remote push-button actuator with a small microphone strong enough to pick up the slightest whisper, which was essential in this situation.

Andy had no sooner transmitted the message when he saw Bobby McGirt out of his peripheral. When Bobby spotted the woman, he ducked behind a car in her driveway, but it was too late; she already saw him, agitated, she began yelling, "YOU! BEHIND THE CAR! I SEE YOU MOTHERFUCKER!"

Andy whispered into his mic, "Bobby, get out of there," but he couldn't move without being exposed.

When Bobby didn't move, she was further incensed and started walking toward him, holding the handgun out in front of her as she haphazardly stumbled across the lawn. Andy was becoming increasingly worried as this unfolded. He looked down his rifle sights and tried to aim. But unfortunately, the weapon's iron sights were difficult to line up in the darkness, and he whispered to himself, "Please, please, please, go back inside." With no snipers in position yet, Andy was McGirt's only cover.

As the suspect unsteadily walked closer to Bobby, yelling obscenities with a pistol in hand, Andy feared he might have to take her life. Bobby was in his peripheral nervously shifting positions, using the car for cover. Andy tracked the woman's movement through his sights, switched the safety off, and tried to control his breathing. He needed to stop her before she shot Bobby. Why did this have to happen to him on his first call-up?

Slowly, he began to take the slack out of the trigger and focused his sights on her upper torso, praying that she would stop. A second before he fired, she lowered her pistol and turned away. Quickly, Andy released the pressure on the trigger and let out a sigh, whispering, "Thank God!"

The drunk woman continued yelling, "Get out of my driveway." Then in disgust, she walked back toward the house.

Andy tracked her every step back to the front door, mumbling, "Keep going. Just keep going, bitch." Finally, she walked inside in a fit of anger and slammed the door shut behind her. Andy switched his safety back on. Once he relaxed from the moment's tension, Andy realized he was weak from the adrenaline dump draining his body. But, at least for now, he was grateful it was over.

Bobby used the opportunity to run across the street to Andy's position. He rounded the car and crouched next to Andy as they peered over the hood.

"Wow! That was a close one," said Bobby in a low voice.

"I'll say. I almost shot that bitch!"

"I knew you had my back," Bobby said confidently while they watched the front door. "That's why I just stayed down behind the car. I knew if she kept coming, you would take her."

Andy didn't say anything, but Bobby's confidence made him feel good. The fact that Bobby would put his life in Andy's hands made him realize what part of being a team was all about.

The call-up continued for several hours. Finally, more Team members arrived. Eventually, it became a controlled operation because the negotiators could finally get the woman on the phone and start a dialogue with her. Once she began to sober up, she came outside to surrender.

When the React Team handcuffed her, Andy couldn't help but walk over and make eye contact. With an expression of contempt, she stared defiantly back at him. She would never know how close she was to death. After staring at each other for a few seconds, she lowered her head, and Andy walked away, wondering if all the call-ups were this exciting. He was about to find out.

FOURTEEN

You Can't Fix Crazy

Sunday morning, Andy worked an easy extra job babysitting an empty building under construction. The pay was good, and best of all, he could bring his portable TV to watch the Oilers football game while he sat in his car for 8 hours.

He was sipping his coffee and waiting for the start of the game when his pager started beeping. In far northeast Houston, there was a call-up at a residence near Homestead Road. A family had taken in a Cuban refugee who was part of a recent mass exodus from the Castro regime, the Cuban Boat Lift. Castro utilized the opportunity to open his prisons and mental institutions and flood the United States with as many criminals as he could eradicate.

A loving and generous family decided to help one of those refugees. They had enough room in their home to extend an extra bedroom for the young man, and they welcomed him to stay until he could get on his feet. The family worked hard adjusting to life with their new tenant, but recently they had become concerned about the man's erratic behavior, and for good reason. It turned out their house guest was an escapee from a Cuban asylum for the criminally insane.

The family left the man home alone that Sunday morning while attending church services. While the residents were at church, the man rummaged through their home and found a pistol. When they returned, the woman exited the car and made her way to the front door while her husband helped the children out of their car seats. At the front door, the woman was met by the refugee, who then shot her in the abdomen. Then, the refugee quickly retreated into the house. Wounded and screaming, she staggered into the yard, desperately trying to flee her attacker. Finally, the mortally wounded woman stumbled around the side of the home, collapsing to the ground.

The husband immediately grabbed their kids, rushed them next door to a neighbor's home, and called the police. With the children safe, he returned to the house to check on his wife but found her lying on her side in the grassy yard with her eyes fixed open, terrified. Devastated with grief, he walked back to the neighbor's front steps, trying to get his emotions under control long enough for the police to arrive.

Andy called the supervisor managing his extra job and explained he had to leave, then sped off toward Homestead Road. He was one of the first to arrive on the scene, so he geared up and hurried toward the collection of police cars, where he spotted Sergeant Hague.

Hague instructed Andy to work his way over to a metal shipping container on the west side of the house. "Find a good spot for containment and radio me your location. I will send someone to you as soon as I get more people."

"Roger that," Andy answered and rushed toward the perimeter. After rounding the corner of the storage container, he slowed his pace. Of course, you always had to consider that their information could be incorrect and the suspect outside. Slowly and cautiously, he cleared the side of the container. Then peering around the edge, the dead woman's body was lying just a few feet away. Her body was facing him, eyes fixed open and staring in his direction. Eerily, it felt like she was looking directly at him.

He tried not to focus on her as he scanned the area for anything to potentially report. He radioed Hague his location and advised he had a good view of the objective. Occasionally he noticed something in his peripheral move and snapped his head and eyes back to the body, but she was long past dead. Even though he could have sworn her eyes blinked a few times, he knew that wasn't possible. Over time, her death stare was distressing, but Andy had to hold his position. Worsening an already nightmarish situation, fire ants soon found her body and crawled all over her face, particularly her eyes. Andy thought he was going to be sick.

Suddenly Hague radioed Chuck McDonald was headed his way. Andy quickly responded, "Roger that," and hurried back toward the opposite corner of the shipping container to watch for him. Andy wasn't going back to that corner, he hated to do it, but it was Chuck's turn in the barrel.

Andy waved Chuck over to him and pulled his rifle up to cover his approach. Chuck ran past and stopped a few steps behind the container. He leaned against the metal building, huffing and puffing from the short sprint. "Thanks, Andy. Where do you need me?"

"At the other corner," Andy responded. "I'll cover the garage from here."

"OK. Got it!"

Andy smiled at his good fortune and waited for Chuck's reaction.

It took the negotiators roughly 30 minutes to contact the suspect on the house phone. After attempting to reason with the deranged man, it was clear they weren't going to get anywhere. The unhinged man wanted to speak with the manager of the Houston Astros and demand to play professional baseball, his passion in Cuba. The negotiators played along with his request as they tried to get him to leave his weapon inside and come out. But he wasn't ready; he wanted to see someone from the Astros management first.

As Andy intently watched the garage for any movement, he heard Chuck's voice behind him, "Hey Andy." He turned around, and Chuck was walking his way.

"There's a dead woman over there, and she's looking at me."

"I know. That's why I'm over here."

"You asshole!" Chuck replied; disgusted, he turned and walked back to his post. Laughing at Chuck's misfortune, Andy returned his attention to the garage. A few minutes later, Chuck yelled, "Well, at least come cover me!"

"OK," Andy replied. Then, walking back toward the corner, he wondered what the hell he meant by 'cover me.'

"I can't handle it anymore. I'm going to run out there and cover her face. Can you cover me?"

"Sure, thing."

Chuck pulled a white handkerchief from his pocket and stepped back a few steps to get a running start. "Ready?" Chuck asked.

Andy readied his weapon toward the house, "Yep!"

In a dead sprint, Chuck ran to the woman's body. He slid to a stop just short of the corpse and gently placed the handkerchief on her face. Then he turned around and sprinted back faster than Andy had ever seen him run. Chuck ran right past Andy and around the corner of the container before he slowed down enough to come to a stop. He bent over, hands on his knees, gasping for air, "Whew! I couldn't take it anymore. I didn't care if that son of a bitch shot me. Every once in a while, I swear it looked like she blinked!"

"I know, same here! Better you than me," replied Andy. He smiled and walked back to his corner, and Chuck shot him the finger.

A couple of hours later, the negotiators dressed one of their own in a suit and tie and convinced the suspect he was from Astros management. They advised him his contract was already drafted to become an Astro. Now, all he had to do was leave the gun inside and come outside and sign it. The suspect fell for it hook, line, and sinker and came out only wearing underwear. Yet another confirmation of how crazy this man was. The react team quickly closed in on him, and when the suspect realized the gig was up, a short struggle ensued, but he quickly lost the fight and was hauled off to jail.

Andy couldn't help but give the woman's body one last glance as he picked up his gear to walk back to the CP. Through no fault of her own, she died in her yard. She had lost her life trying to help a man that was beyond help. Andy could only hope that they would put this guy away where he couldn't hurt anyone else.

The next day at the office, Chuck vowed revenge, "I don't know how or when, but I'll get your ass back!"

Andy just laughed and said, "What? I took my turn in the barrel. It was your turn!"

"Maybe," Chuck replied, "But I still owe you!"

They both smiled, but Andy knew Chuck was just waiting for an opportunity to strike and get even.

Pranks were commonplace on SWAT, and they had several ways of getting back at one another, especially in the morning during PT when the lockers were unattended. If someone left their locker unlocked, they might find their socks missing, only to be later discovered in the break room freezer, soaked in water and frozen stiff. Another favorite was for the guys to put Icy Hot balm in the crotch of someone's underwear. You didn't notice when you first put them on, but after a few minutes, the heat kicked in, and you instantly knew what was happening. The only remedy was to strip down and get back into the shower while being laughed at.

A few weeks later, SWAT was requested to respond to a crazy man living in the Spring Branch area of town. Currently, he was living with his mother, and when two Constables tried to arrest him on a mental health warrant, he shot at them. Thankfully, no one was hit, and the Constables backed off and called SWAT. When Andy arrived on the scene, he remembered the house from his patrol days. The mentally ill man's name was Jim Smothers, and Andy had previous run-ins with him. He was crazy then, and his condition hadn't improved.

You couldn't negotiate with him. His demands were all over the place, but the negotiators were at least able to talk him into letting his mother go. She came out of the garage and walked around the corner of the house to the waiting SWAT officers. Negotiations failed after several more phone conversations, so the Captain decided to gas the place.

At dusk, they deployed tear gas smoke grenades inside. Pyrotechnic grenades put out a lot of gas, which was good, but they had to get close enough to throw the canisters into a window or another opening in the house. Agitated, Jim was taking potshots at anyone attempting to get close; thankfully, he hadn't hit anyone yet.

The stand-off lasted throughout the night, and after a while, Andy found it almost amusing. Just like a cat and mouse game with this idiot. SWAT created a diversion to draw him to one side of the house, which usually meant he would fire a few errant gunshots while they delivered canisters of gas to the other side. Then, he ran back and fired off a few rounds in that direction. The back and forth went on for the duration of the night, and when the morning sun made its appearance, it was evident how much damage the house had sustained.

They had put so much gas inside the home that smoke was boiling out of the soffit vents in the roofline. Even though they hadn't thrown any canisters into the attic, it found its way up there from the over-pressure.

After daybreak, Andy was asked to throw a gas canister into a nearby window. With the thick smoke built up in the home, he couldn't see anything through the glass, but they believed Jim was in another part of the house. It turns out they were wrong. When Andy pulled the pin and chucked the grenade through the glass, Jim walked back into the room. As the canister began to release the CS smoke, Andy heard Jim curse, and a gunshot rang out. The bullet whizzed past Andy as he scampered back to safety. Once he rounded a tree, he looked back and saw a bullet hole in the glass where he had just been standing. Luckily, the home's exterior was brick, and the rounds couldn't penetrate the walls. He couldn't help but chuckle at his good fortune.

Smoke was permeating out of every opening and crevice of the home. The gas cloud was so severe that neighbors several blocks away were complaining. Any exposed skin on the perimeter guys was irritated from the prolonged exposure, so they donned poncho-style raincoats for protection.

When their supply of CS gas ran out, the Captain, frustrated, said, "Enough! Let's try something else. Can we trick him into coming outside? Either that, or let's just shoot the asshole, but this nonsense has got to stop!"

They devised a plan and called him on the phone. The negotiators advised Jim they were ready to call a truce, but they needed him to sign a release of liability statement. It made perfect sense in Jim's deranged thinking, and he fell for it.

"OK! Come on in, and I'll sign it," Jim said.

"Oh no," objected the negotiator, "You have been shooting at us. You need to come out and meet us halfway."

"Where?" Jim asked.

"Out the front door," the negotiator replied. "Leave your guns inside and walk out. We'll be waiting."

Jim hung up the phone, and the negotiators looked at each other and crossed their fingers.

The plan was dispersed to the team members surrounding the perimeter, and Sergeant Hauge was elected to wave a piece of paper from across the street. Once safely tucked behind a large oak tree, he would convince Jim to come out in the front yard, unarmed. They just needed him to walk out past the roof's edge for the trap to succeed.

Paul Kandi and Robert Richer were positioned on top of the roof directly above his front door. They were waiting to jump on him as soon as he stepped out far enough. The trap was set, and all they needed was the rat to take the bait.

Andy had a front-row seat to the most incredible show on earth, or it seemed that way to him. He was behind a large oak tree not far from Hauge, waiting for Jim to open the door. All he needed now was some popcorn and a Coke.

When the front door opened, a massive plume of smoke rolled out of the house. After some of the smoke cleared, they had a visual of Jim. The CP radioed Paul and Robert, confirming the door was open and to be ready. Paul and Robert stood on the roof, fully decked out in their green ponchos, gloves, and gas masks, without an inch of skin exposed. From Andy's position, they looked more like aliens from outer space than SWAT officers, standing side by side with their ponchos draping over them.

Jim anticipated a trap, so he cautiously waved for Hauge to come to him.

Hauge stepped out from behind the tree, waving the piece of paper in the air. "I have it right here. You just need to come to sign it."

"Come over here," Jim answered, motioning him over.

"No, sorry. You have to come out in the open, so I can see you are unarmed."

Apprehensively, Jim glanced left and right and saw no one, so he stepped out of the door closing it behind him.

The gas cloud eventually dissipated around him as he nervously looked back and forth. He had tucked a pistol in his waistband and was carrying an extra magazine in each back pocket. Hauge was concerned but knew that Jim didn't stand a chance if Paul and Robert could get a good drop on him.

They continued to coax each other for a few minutes, trying to get the other to step out further. Jim wanted this to end just as badly as the SWAT team did. He was tired from staying up all night, and the gas had been eating at him too. Finally, he decided to take a chance and took a step off the porch, just enough for Paul and Robert to see him directly below. They stepped off the roof in perfect formation and fell onto the unsuspecting crazy man.

Andy watched in amazement as the ponchos parachuted open from the fall; now, they looked more like capes. Paul and Robert resembled superheroes descending from the roof and landing perfectly on their target. The impact drove Jim to the concrete sidewalk with a thud. The added weight knocked the air out of his lungs, and the fight was over. He was abruptly rolled over, cuffed, and the nightmare call-up of Spring Branch ended.

From across the street, the negotiators recorded the entire capture. The next day, while conducting a critique, the team enjoyed repeatedly watching the video. Batman and Robin are flying in to save the day! Every time it played, they high-fived each other for a job well done. They hoped Jim would never be released from the mental facility because he'd never fall for that again.

Evil Woman

Billy knew his inexperienced team needed to sharpen their skills before becoming operational, so the following days were packed with tactical training. Billy focused on approaching barricaded suspects and the skills necessary to slow search a structure. Mark McDonald taught them to use mirrors mounted on poles to peer inside doorways and around corners. The concept was, "Find the ambush before you find yourself in it." Billy would add, "Distance is our friend. If possible, we always work from distance." Andy loved training days and was eager to learn everything he could from his mentors.

One of the equipment devices they were taught to handle during training was ballistic shields. Ideal to use anytime armed resistance was expected and capable of withstanding bullets and other strong projectiles. The shields were large, heavy, and difficult to maneuver, but Billy would say, "If we miss the ambush, these things can make up for a potentially deadly mistake." They taped flashlights to their rifles to use the weapons and lights together. Joe Vargas designed a specialty bracket instead of using tape. Later, flashlight companies picked up the idea, and it became trendy. If he had patented the idea, he would have made a ton of money, but at the time, his focus was learning to become an effective SWAT officer.

Recently, Mark took the detective exam and scored high enough for a promotion. Billy needed to prepare for that inevitability, so he was training Andy and Joe to replace him. At times, Andy would be the point, which was a position Joe occasionally worked. But it really didn't matter because they mixed together like peanut butter and jelly. They were becoming close friends and spending a lot of time palling around off-duty.

Mark was an open book, sharing his talents. Unfortunately, their time with him was short, so they tried to gain as much as possible from his expertise. Soon enough, Andy and Joe would be working with a new rearguard while Mark moved on to a new career.

It was just after midnight when the phone awakened Andy from a dead sleep. It was Billy. An elderly woman had gone off her rocker and held her bedridden husband hostage. Officers tried to take her into protective custody on a mental health warrant, but she pulled a large butcher knife and chased them out of the house. Then, she threatened to kill her husband and herself. Officers on the scene requested SWAT and asked them to bring the new tasers everyone was talking about.

Several stories were broadcast by the news media about SWAT testing the first-generation electronic discharge weapons. Tasers were designed to resemble a flashlight. The device fired two barbed darts connected to the device with tiny, long copper wires capable of transmitting 50,000 volts of electricity. The jolt of electricity would cause temporary incapacitation by disrupting individuals' voluntary control of their muscles.

The team trained with them for a short while, and they appeared to work alright, but they hadn't tested them in the field yet. It was another tool in their arsenal to disarm someone without deadly force. And this might be the perfect opportunity to put them to the test.

When Andy arrived, Billy yelled, "We have the entry!" Andy was surprised command post had chosen them for entry in a hostage situation. Billy reviewed the current intel with the team, "She has her husband in the back bedroom. He's disabled and unable to get out of bed. She's threatening to cut his throat, and she has two large butcher knives. The react team has visual contact with her through the sliding glass door leading into the kitchen, so here's the plan..." Billy pointed at a crude diagram of the house, "We're going to covertly enter the garage through this pedestrian door. Once we're inside, we'll post up at the door leading into the house. Then, if they give us the OK, we will enter the hallway and cut her off to the bedroom where her husband is."

Andy was surprised when Billy handed him the taser. Then, he said, "You guys grab your equipment and meet back here in 5 minutes." Everyone nodded and split in different directions to grab mirrors, breaching equipment, and a shield.

Soon, with their gear ready, everyone was standing outside the CP, and the pressure was mounting. After extensive training, they knew they could do this, but it was the first entry for Andy and Joe, so they hadn't proven themselves to the team. Mark patiently waited; his confidence was undeniable. Considering how many times he had done this kind of thing before, it was just one more time.

Stepping out of the command post, Billy was all business as he said firmly, "Let's go," and marched off into the darkness on a mission. They followed him to the garage, and he motioned for Joe to try the knob. Carefully, Joe slowly turned the doorknob, confirmed it was unlocked, and nodded to signal. The react team reported the woman's current location in the kitchen, so Joe eased open the door.

Inside the garage, it was even darker; everyone momentarily paused, trying to get their bearings. Then, steadily they made entry and quietly moved through the cluttered garage toward the interior door. Within a few minutes, they stood at the ready, using their senses to observe their surroundings. In the distance, they heard the woman's voice yelling at negotiators over the phone. They could almost make out what she was saying, screaming obscenities. It was comforting to know she wasn't close, and hopefully, the negotiators could keep her talking. Once they finally adjusted to the darkness, Billy radioed, "Team is in position."

"Clear. Stand by," Sergeant Jenson replied.

"Relax, guys," Billy whispered. "We may be here a while. Negotiators have the ball now."

There was always an unspoken competition between the SWAT team and the Negotiators. Although they both had the same mission, they had very different approaches to getting there. SWAT utilized a combination of tactics and equipment to gain an advantage and reach a tactical resolution. Negotiators relied upon their verbal skills to convince the suspect to surrender. Both divisions were led by different lieutenants who worked for the same Captain. The Captain listened to both lieutenant's viewpoints and considered his options. Generally, he chose the negotiators option because it was the safest, but if negotiations failed, hopefully, the SWAT option was still available.

Enraged, she slammed the phone down and walked toward the back bedroom, yelling at the top of her lungs, "YOU MOTHERFUCKER! I AIN'T TAKING THIS SHIT NO MORE!" Andy's heart pounded as Billy pointed to the taser Andy was holding, indicating he should be ready. Andy flipped off the taser's safety as Joe grabbed the doorknob so she couldn't unexpectedly open the door. They huddled in the darkness, listening to the hostile voice approaching.

Andy looked down at the light coming from under the door and saw the shadow of her feet walk past, heading toward the back bedroom. It was too late to cut her off now, so the team had to hope she wouldn't kill her husband. Sergeant Jenson's voice came over the radio, "Suspect is off the phone." Andy thought, 'No shit!'

Billy keyed his mic, "Bull to CP, she walked past us to the bedroom."

"Clear," Jenson answered.

They heard the older man yelling, and it sounded like she was slapping him. "YOU SON-OF-A-BITCH," she cried, "YOU DID THIS!"

The assault was difficult to listen to, but it didn't appear life-threatening. Billy keyed the mic and whispered, "She appears to be beating the hostage."

"Clear, standby," CP responded.

Kneeling in the darkness, they wondered what the Captain was waiting for. More than likely, the negotiators were arguing to get her back on the phone. Andy knew it was a tough decision.

When the phone in the kitchen started ringing, the beating came to an abrupt halt. Joe's grip tightened on the doorknob while they watched her footsteps walk past the door toward the ringing telephone. As she passed by, she mumbled in her low and sinister voice. Her voice eerily sounded like a sound bite straight from a horror movie.

She picked up the phone and shouted into the receiver, "WHAT?" Andy continued to wait for the signal to move into the hallway and separate her from her husband, but it never came. As frustrations mounted, they sat there coiled like a spring ready to go. Finally, the CP radioed, "Suspect's on the phone." Andy smiled at the continued communication delay.

Finally, Sergeant Jenson's voice came over the radio, "CP to Bull. Meet Ms. Piggy at the garage entrance."

"That's clear," Billy responded, then whispered to his team, "Hold what you got, guys. I'll be back."

Ms. Piggy was the radio code name for Sergeant Hague, who would deliver a new plan.

Soon, Billy returned and quietly whispered that the older woman was standing next to the glass sliding door in the kitchen. The react team planned to break the glass and shoot her with a taser. "When we hear the glass break, we'll open our door and be ready for her if it doesn't work. Got it?" Everyone nodded in agreement. Billy continued, "Andy, I need you upfront with that taser. Don't miss!"

"Roger that," Andy nervously replied.

For what seemed like hours, they waited in the darkness listening to her ranting in the distance. The smell of men sweating in heavy gear filled the stagnant air.

Andy's frustration was building as he wondered what was taking so long. He knew it wasn't an easy decision, but he was ready to do this. Suddenly Jenson's voice came over the radio, "All officers stand by. React, you are good to go." Andy's heart pounded as he realized this was finally going to happen.

Then, the loud shatter of breaking glass at the far end of the house and the shrill of a woman's scream. When Joe opened the door, the hallway light hurt Andy's eyes, temporarily making it challenging to see. With his shield facing the kitchen, Mark leaned in. Andy raised his taser to the ready. Johnny Williams, a member of the react team, shot her with his taser, but she didn't go down. Instead, with barbs embedded in her back, she screamed bloody murder, running toward Billy's team and Johnny in pursuit with the connected taser wires.

As Andy leaned in to get a better look, he could hear the unmistakable sound of the taser clicking. Holding two colossal butcher knives in the air, she was headed directly at him. Bolts of electricity sparked off the knives, the electricity dancing around her. He aimed his taser and fired both darts into her chest. The electricity intensified, but she kept stumbling past them like an evil witch on fire. Andy stepped out to follow her and keep his wires connected. Suddenly he realized he was side by side with Johnny, chasing her down the corridor.

Past her into the well-lit bedroom, her husband sat up in bed screaming at the sight of his wife running toward him with bolts of electricity dancing off the knives. He laid back on the bed and covered his head to protect himself from what was about to happen. If she killed the hostage, Andy knew his future in SWAT was over.

As she entered the bedroom, she collapsed to the floor. The tasers had finally taken their toll. Andy and Johnny turned off their devices and grabbed her hands. She wrestled to break free, but they had her pinned. Eventually, her incessant screaming got the best of Andy. "SHUT UP BITCH," he yelled at her, but it didn't have any impact as she continued incoherently cursing.

Mark and Joe rushed into the bedroom to check on the older man, still covered with sheets. Joe reached down with both arms and lifted him, carrying the frail man out of the room. He had been bedridden for so long that he was down to a mere 80 lbs. The old man looked back to check on his wife; still concerned for her, he yelled, "Don't hurt her!" No one understood how he still cared for the woman who had tortured him.

Once the old woman was handcuffed, they sat her up, but she kept resisting and yelling. Billy was pleased with the outcome and patted his guys on the back, giving them a congratulatory, "Good job!" It was just another day at the office for Mark as he reassuringly smiled at Andy. It reminded him of the old saying, "I'd rather be lucky than good."

The Donut Caper

Supervision was pleased with how Billy's team handled the elderly woman, saving the hostage. They could now resolve more dangerous situations by utilizing less-lethal tactics and avoiding deadly force. The only issues discussed during the critique identified performance concerns with the tasers, but everyone agreed to continue testing them.

Call-ups were coming in regular succession now, and Andy had gained a lot of experience. At least two or three times a week, they were deployed. However, most of the calls were barricaded mental cases that continued endlessly. Frequently, due to the unstable nature of their illness, a resolution would take hours to negotiate. The SWAT guys referred to this as babysitting because it was generally a waiting game once they had the individual surrounded. Some patrol officers jokingly said SWAT stood for, Sit, Wait And Talk, and there was some truth to it.

Occasionally some excitement ensued when a suspect challenged the perimeter. The team went to great strides to avoid using deadly force, sometimes even at the risk of their own lives. Taking a suspect's life was considered a failure, but sometimes they had no other option. SWAT was deployed to use their specialty skills, talents, and equipment to save lives, including the suspects.

Mark had been promoted to a much-deserved detective's job. He would be trading in his vest for a suit and tie. Everyone was sad to see him go because there was so much more to learn from him. Moving forward, Billy assigned Andy to the point position and kept Joe as cover. Most of the time, it was difficult to know who was point and who was cover anyway, so Joe didn't mind. Mickey Sharp was transferred from another team to be Billy's rearguard. Andy and Joe were already well acquainted with Mickey because they all went through Basic School together, so he fit right in.

After a long day of training, Andy and Terri were about to sit down for dinner when the phone rang. Billy began to describe a hostage situation at a 7-Eleven on Telephone Road. Even though Andy's stomach was growling, there was no time to eat, so he grabbed a breakfast bar on the way out. Terri stood in the kitchen, wondering if dropping everything and running out the door like a superhero would now be a fact of life.

When Andy arrived at the scene, he grabbed his gear and hurried to the command post for an assignment. Unlike barricades, hostage situations were time-sensitive. Once a barricade surrounded the suspect, time was on their side. The suspect eventually went to one of three places, the jail, the hospital, or the morgue; it was their choice. But, during a hostage situation, the life of an innocent person was at risk. And if they had a chance to make a difference, they needed to be within proximity.

When Andy approached, Billy stood outside the CP, "Get a shield and move up near the front door. I'll be there as soon as everyone else arrives."

Andy wasn't sure what was going on yet, but he did as he was told. Jimmy Levine was standing at the corner of the store as Andy moved up behind him. "Hey, Jimmy, what you got?"

"Oh, hey Andy," replied Jimmy. "The crook is a black male about 6 feet tall and slender. I don't know what he is wearing, but supposedly, he has a pistol. That's about all I know."

"What's the hostage look like?" asked Andy.

Jimmy answered, "The store clerk. I think he's a white guy, but not sure. He was last seen wearing a uniform 7-Eleven shirt."

Later on, they learned the suspect attempted to rob the store just as a patrol car pulled up. The officer saw the suspect holding a pistol on the clerk, and the stand-off began. Finally, the suspect moved the clerk into a storage room behind the counter and demanded the police stay back or he would murder the clerk.

Negotiators called the store phone once the perimeter was secure and all the snipers were in place. Because the phone was on the counter, the suspect refused to come out of the storage room to answer it. The team heard the phone continually ringing. Sometimes they heard the suspect yelling, but no one could decipher what he was saying. The predicament went on for hours. Finally, the negotiators resorted to yelling over loudspeakers to communicate with the suspect, "You will not be harmed if you come out and answer the phone," but he wasn't buying it.

Supervision delegated Billy's team to covertly enter the building and deliver a throw phone to the suspect. The delivery distance was limited, but the phone was equipped with a microphone, and two small cameras were hidden on its exterior, allowing the negotiators to spy on the suspect. Billy briefed his team on the assignment, describing how they would enter the store and take positions along the front counter. Once they were set, they would make voice contact to inform the suspect about the phone.

Just before dawn, Billy was given the green light to enter. "All officers, radio silence. Bull's team is making entry." Andy opted to leave his rifle outside and carry in only his pistol and stripped his vest of anything that had the potential to make noise. Quietly, Andy crawled across the floor. Since he hadn't eaten since yesterday, his stomach was growling, but the moment's excitement dominated his thoughts.

Steadily, he slowly pushed the glass door open and disabled the bell at the top. Normally intended to alert the clerk when someone walked into the store, which was exactly what Andy didn't want right now. He eased inside, crawling along the floor toward the counter. Once the rest of the team was inside, they spread out around the counter to create angles.

Bobby McGirt was designated as the eyes for the CP, so he would be the only one reporting movement over the radio. With the exterior glass wall, McGirt had the perfect line of sight into the store. Understanding Clark wouldn't be able to whisper without the suspect hearing him; Bobby was instructed to report their movements.

Andy slithered along the floor until he reached the end of the counter. Joe filed in next to Andy, leaving Billy and Mickey near the cash register. Billy signaled for Andy to move further down to create an 'L' ambush pattern of cover; this training technique provided a devastating advantage. Behind a product display, Andy found a spot where he could lay down and see directly into the storage room. If anyone started walking out of that room, he would see them first.

He was becoming comfortable with being uncomfortable; all his fears had long evaporated from his thoughts. At 6 am, with the sun peaking over the horizon, the fatigue was taking its toll. He had been awake for over 24 hours, and lying motionless on the floor made it worse. The store was completely silent except for the refrigerator compressors running in the background. As Andy looked around to stay alert, he noticed an entire bank of glass door refrigerators lined the far wall of the store.

Billy decided they were ready, so he signaled his team to standby. He yelled out, "YOU IN THE BACK OF THE STORE! THIS IS THE POLICE. ARE YOU OK?"

"HEY! DON'T COME IN HERE! I'LL KILL THIS MOTHER FUCKER!" A voice from the storage room yelled back.

"I'm OK," a second voice then squeamishly replied, presumably the store clerk.

"We're not coming in there," Billy yelled back. "We just want to give you a phone to talk with us. Can I throw a phone in there for you?"

After some mumbling in the background, the suspect said, "OK, but don't come in here motherfucker!"

"We are not coming in. I'm gonna throw the phone to you now!" Billy waited for a response, but there wasn't one. He then moved down the aisle, pulling the phone wire behind him. "I'M GONNA THROW THE PHONE NOW. IT'S GONNA HIT THE FLOOR AND BOUNCE TO YOU, OK?"

Following a long delay, a low voice replied, "OK." Billy waited a few seconds and then stood up and threw the phone with one hand as he peeled off the phone cable with the other. Billy perfectly threw the phone; it landed in the hallway and bounced out of sight.

Within a few minutes, the negotiators were speaking to the suspect. Andy relaxed a little as he listened to his demands. Ultimately, the suspect wanted the police out of the building and a getaway car. Since his demands were out of the question, the conversation went back and forth for about an hour.

Anytime Andy temporarily relaxed, his mind immediately wandered back to his hunger pains. He realized he was lying next to a display case of Little Debbie's donuts. The white powdered sugar donuts Andy loved as a kid looked delicious. While listening to the suspect's voice in the distance, his eyes were deadlocked on those beautiful, delicious donuts. Soon, the urge was more than he could withstand, so he reached over and grabbed a package off the shelf. He carefully watched the storeroom as he slowly opened the package of donuts with one hand and held his pistol with the other. The sound of the clear plastic wrapper crackled as he struggled to open it without making any noise. He finally got a donut and put the entire thing in his mouth. It was dry and hard to swallow, but he didn't care. He loved the taste, and it took him back to his childhood. Reaching for another, he heard Joe snapping his fingers. Andy glanced over and saw Joe with his hand out. Andy stopped chewing and pointed at the display of donuts as if to ask, 'You want one of these?' Joe nodded his head and smiled. Andy reached over and took another package and tossed it to Joe. He then heard another snap coming from Mickey's position. Andy looked over and saw the same expression on Mickey's face. Andy nodded and grabbed another package of donuts, took aim, and threw them across the room.

Amused, Billy watched the donut caper. Due to the seriousness of the situation, he didn't approve, but he also understood these young men hadn't eaten for over 16 hours. As long as it didn't compromise their positions, he was willing to overlook it. Andy made eye contact with Billy as he pointed at the donut display with the same expression 'Do you want some?' Billy shook his head no. Andy shrugged his shoulders and kept eating.

When Andy finished his donuts, his parched mouth needed some milk. Two aisles over, there was a refrigerator holding a variety of beverages, including milk and orange juice, just waiting for Andy to quench his thirst. Granted, he would have to crawl in the open for a few feet, but he'd be back before the suspect knew what happened if he hurried. He looked at Joe and pointed at the glass display of milk. With partially eaten donut crumbs still stuck to his teeth, he grinned and nodded his head. Andy glanced over to Mickey, who was giving an enthusiastic thumbs up. Andy motioned for Joe to cover him while he crawled to the milk, so Joe moved down the counter and brought his rifle up to the low ready.

As he nervously watched the hallway, Andy slithered along the smooth tile surface, pistol in his right hand. He could hear the suspect talking, so he figured that was a good sign. As he reached the refrigerator, he eased it open, and the rush of cool air hit his face. Andy grabbed three pints of milk and gently closed the door. He crawled back with the bounty of milk carefully tucked under his left arm and his pistol in his right hand. After tossing Joe and Mickey their milk, they settled back as the hunger pains receded.

Bobby McGirt saw the entire donut incident through his binoculars. On the first toss, something caught his eye. When he focused on the second toss to Mickey, he wasn't sure what was being thrown. By the time Andy tossed the milk, Bobby realized these guys were in there snacking while everyone outside went without. Although McGirt was pissed, there wasn't anything he could do except watch.

After a couple more hours of negotiations, they convinced the suspect to release the hostage. The clerk came out of the storage room with his hands in the air, and they quickly escorted him to safety and handed him off to the perimeter team.

Still speaking with the negotiator, the suspect began to cry. He knew it was over, and the only three options he had were to commit suicide, surrender, or come out shooting. Suddenly the suspect sat the phone down and yelled, "I'm coming out!"

From the end of the counter, Billy made voice contact, "OK. Leave your weapon in there and slowly show us your hands!" Slowly two hands appeared in the doorway, and Billy called out, "That's it. Keep coming." The suspect exited the storage room, and they took him into custody without further incident.

The entire scene was soon turned over to detectives, and Sergeant Jenson came over to congratulate the team on a job well done. As Jenson shook Andy's hand, he noticed some white powder on his lips and around his mouth. "What is that white stuff?" Jenson asked, pointing.

Andy quickly wiped his mouth with the back of his sleeve, "Nothing, Sarg."

Jenson looked puzzled as he walked away.

During the critique, McGirt spilled the beans about them eating donuts in the store. Some of the guys found it funny, but the supervisors were not happy. Some even spoke of it as theft. Finally, Billy stood up for his guys and said that he allowed it, and if they had a beef, it was with him. Considering how much respect everyone had for Billy, no one wanted to go there, so the issue died.

Andy was embarrassed he had given in to his hunger when everyone outside had the same issue and couldn't do anything about it. He vowed never to let his personal needs take over his decision-making again.

The next day, Mickey stopped at the store on his way home from work to make things right. He picked up three pints of milk and three packages of sugar donuts, carried them to the counter, and paid for them. Then he placed them neatly back on the shelf and walked out of the store with the receipt and the clerk's name. Quizzically, the clerk watched Mickey walk out of the store empty-handed. Mickey smiled all the way home, knowing the wrong had been made right.

With Every Ending, There Is a New Beginning

Early one morning, Andy got the call no one wanted to get. His brother Tommy notified him that the doctors found malignant tumors in his Dad's lungs, and he was dying from cancer. After being a smoker his entire life, it had finally caught up with him. He fought hard, just like he lived, but he lost his battle with the dreadful disease a few short months later. Most of the SWAT team and a few of his former teammates from Narcotics attended the funeral services. Andy and the rest of the family greatly appreciated their presence and support.

There is also a new beginning with every loss in the circle of life. A few weeks later, Andy and Terri were overjoyed to announce they were expecting. In early June, Terri gave birth to a baby boy they named Bryce Alan Wallace. The spitting image of Andy and the apple of his eye.

Despite the good news, Andy and Terri were still coping with the loss, and Poodle was having a much harder time living alone. They visited her as often as possible but getting in the SWAT book for out-of-town travel was difficult. Only four operators could be off at once, so they couldn't see her as much as they wanted. Holding Bryce seemed to ease Poodle's depression when they visited, at least for a while.

Andy's dream of raising a family in the country made the long commute to work worthwhile. To make ends meet, he had to take on a lot of extra jobs. Even though they didn't have a lot of cash at the end of each month, they were paying the bills and getting by. Andy only wished his father could be there to see his family grow.

Facing His Fears

During football season, the Oilers Organization reached out to the Chief of Police and requested for the SWAT team to participate in the opening ceremonies at the next game. For part of the pregame show, they wanted a couple of SWAT officers to rappel from the top of the Astrodome right before the National Anthem. After the Chief approved the request, it was up to the team, and no one liked disappointing the Chief.

The top of the dome spanned 220-feet to the playing field below, which was the equivalent of a 22-story building. The team had never had a reason to rappel from that height, so they didn't know if their ropes were long enough. The only way to know for sure was to climb to the top and find out.

Sergeant Rosekrants served as the Rappel Master for the team; he was in charge of deciding who would participate in the pregame festivities. On Wednesday morning, when a skeleton crew would be present, he was permitted to bring them to the Dome. Andy still remembered seeing the Dome for the first time as a child, attending an Astros game with his parents. So, he was excited at this chance to rappel down onto the 50-yard line in a place that he was in awe of. Never in his wildest dreams did he think he'd become a Houston cop, much less a

SWAT officer. To top it off, he now had the once-in-a-lifetime opportunity to rappel from the 8th wonder of the world.

Early that Wednesday, fifteen guys volunteered to meet Sergeant Rosekrants at the north entrance of the Dome. After signing liability waivers, they rode the elevator to the top floor and then climbed the stairs to the catwalk opening. Once the metal gate was unlocked, they could see the entire path to the gondola above. The catwalk floor was made of an expanded metal grate, with chain link fencing for the sides. As they started up, you could see through the metal grate down to the green football field below. Looking down only intensified Andy's fear of heights, so he kept his head upright and his eyes focused on the gondola.

Some guys who were more comfortable with heights began joking about the sturdiness of the catwalk, which encouraged a couple of outliers to jump up and down, causing the entire walkway to sway back and forth. Then, finally, Rosekrants turned and shouted, "Hey, knock it off! You guys get serious. This shit can get your ass killed if you're not careful!" Although that certainly didn't help Andy's anxiety, he was grateful they weren't jacking around anymore.

The gondola was encircled with oversized lights and speakers pointed down toward the field. The Dome was lit by natural sunlight coming through the roof's skylights. In wonderment, Andy looked around as Rosekrants tied the ropes to the sturdy pipes he found within the structure. A small tour group was below on the ground, and several workers were preparing the field for the upcoming game. At that height, everyone below appeared the size of an ant, just milling around.

Once the ropes were tied, he threw them over the outer railing, and Andy watched their free-fall descent as they whipped down. At least several feet short of the playing field, the rope line ran out, but assuredly Rosekrants said, "Don't worry, guys. They'll stretch the rest of the way by the time you get to the bottom."

Andy looked at him, waiting for a laugh that never came. Then, as the brutal realization was setting in that Rosekrants was dead serious, he pointed to Andy, "Wallace, you're first!" Now Andy was beyond scared; he was petrified! He was at least hoping a few guys would go before him to verify everything was good, but that wasn't to be.

He started tying a Swiss seat with the nylon webbing material he had been issued and then hooked it to his carabiner. Large carabiners were the only descending device they used, so you had to loop the rope through twice to provide enough resistance. Uneasiness spread over Andy, his heart racing, as Rosekrants glanced at his rig and casually instructed, "OK, just climb out over the speakers, and you're good to go." Andy wanted him to double-check his rig, but Rosekrants just slapped him on the back and pointed. Apprehensively, Andy climbed over the metal railing between two huge speakers. Silence fell over the group, overwrought, with every eye transfixed on him. The quiet wasn't particularly reassuring to Andy. Except for Rosekrants, everyone else seemed just as scared as he was.

Once he made it to the edge of the railing, he looked back at Rosekrants, who nodded with approval and a huge grin, bits of tobacco stuck in his teeth. Rosekrants barked, "You got it son! Now go!" Andy thought, 'Oh God, please let it be quick!' He loosened his grip, leaned back, pushed off with his legs, and started his 220-foot descent to the Astroturf below.

Once he was a few feet down and realized the rope and rig would hold his weight, his fears subsided. After about 30 feet into the descent, the twist in the rope working through the carabiner caused him to start spinning. He eased his grip to speed up his descent, but that only caused him to turn more rapidly down the rope. As the Dome spun around him faster and faster, he became disoriented. He forgot all about the height as he tried not to vomit when suddenly his feet landed on the field, and the rope popped out of his carabiner. Rosekrants was right; the rope did stretch enough but not an inch to spare as he stood flat-footed on the playing field. A few more feet would not have been as pretty a landing.

Andy was never so glad to be standing on solid ground as he looked up, barely able to make out the guys in the gondola. "How was it?" one of them yelled down.

Andy forgot who might be listening as his emotions got the better of him, "THAT WAS A SCARY MOTHERFUCKER!" Everyone laughed, and then over his shoulder, he heard several people clapping and snickering. Andy turned around to see the tour group had stopped to watch the rappel, and now they knew more than they bargained for.

After everyone took turns rappelling, they gathered their equipment for the long walk back to their vehicles. Andy took some ribbing about his inappropriate outburst, taglines insinuating the team might not be invited back. Although Andy wasn't chosen to rappel during the actual ceremony, it wasn't because of his vulgar language; he lost out to some men with more seniority. Nevertheless, his time would come, and as Lieutenant Guinn would say, "He faced his fears and performed." That's all that matters anyway.

FIFTEEN

Allen Parkway Inn

The physical demands of SWAT PT were beginning to take their toll on Billy now that he was in his late 40s. The daily grind and monthly physical testing hindered him as he got older. It was time for the rigors of SWAT to become a memory, so he accepted a transfer to the Criminal Intelligence Division, where he would serve as a plainclothes investigator. During their time together, Billy was Andy's mentor and a father figure, so Andy hated to see him go. Even though Andy still had much to learn from him, he understood that everyone had their time, and this was Billy's.

Jose Martinez was selected as Billy's replacement, and as far as Andy was concerned, he was the next best. As a SWAT operator for years, he had the previous experience necessary to lead Andy, Joe, and Mickey. Andy was excelling in his role as an operator, and as a result, he was occasionally asked to test new equipment.

The latest product up for evaluation was a less-lethal impact munition, commonly called a bean bag round. The canvas bags were filled with sand and fired from the same 37mm gun the team used to fire tear gas. The bean bag rounds were designed to deliver enough force to temporarily incapacitate a dangerous suspect giving a long enough window to get them handcuffed. On the positive side, they allowed the team to maintain distance, but they produced a considerable amount of smoke and muzzle blast. SWAT discontinued the use of tasers, but they were issued citywide to patrol supervisors with mixed reviews. Their performance was substandard at best.

Luckily, the perfect opportunity to test these new munitions came along within a couple of weeks. The team responded to a call west of downtown at Allen Parkway Inn. After midnight, a guest approached the front desk night manager demanding keys to the exercise room. Once she explained the fitness room was closed for the night, he became enraged and started threatening her. She was scared and retreated to the office, locked the door, and called 911 while the man pounded on the door.

When officers arrived, they attempted to reason with the angry man, but the confrontation escalated. A struggle ensued, and an officer deployed a taser, to no avail, on the unhinged man. The melee moved from the lobby into the restaurant as officers kept reloading the taser, firing it again with little effect. The suspect started launching salt and pepper shakers at the officers as he backed into the kitchen area, where he found a couple of large butcher knives, changing everything. The officers backed away to containment positions and called SWAT.

When Andy arrived, one of the new SWAT Sergeants, Andy Flores, was on the scene giving directions. He had just finished Basic School, so he was still learning the ropes and running a temporary command post. "Hey, Andy. Go inside and back up Vargas and Levine in the restaurant. Send the patrol officers out here to me. I'll send in more guys as soon as they get here," Flores instructed.

"Roger that," Andy replied and hurried into the hotel.

Joe Vargas tried to talk the suspect down on one side of the room. The man was enraged, swinging knives in the air like he was some sort of a ninja fighter. Several tiny wires hung off his torso from the taser rounds deployed. The man was manic and oblivious to the pain.

Jimmy Levine was positioned on the opposite side of the restaurant, crouched down behind a cash register. Andy navigated to the other side of the diner and eased up behind him. The suspect would lunge at Joe one minute, then run towards Jimmy's location and threaten him the next. Each time, stopping just short of being shot, almost as though he knew how far he could go. Joe and Jimmy kept yelling, "Drop the knives!" but the deranged man cursed them. Occasionally he would stop and aggressively stab them into the countertops.

Sergeant Jim Russell arrived and rushed into the restaurant with a 37mm loaded with the new bean bag rounds. Jim was the other new sergeant on the team and was eager to lend a helping hand. "Hey guys, I have an impact round ready." If there was ever an excellent time to see this new weapon work, it was on this crazy guy from hell. As more SWAT officers arrived, slowly, a perimeter was established surrounding the man. The situation would be resolved right there, one way or another.

A negotiator attempted to talk the man down, but he had none of it. Screaming at the top of his lungs, he paced back and forth like a caged animal. Eventually, Sergeant Flores entered with a second bean bag gun. Once he positioned himself behind Joe, they now had two less-lethal weapons. The tense conflict could not continue much longer. Something had to give.

Suddenly the knife-wielding suspect charged Jimmy one time too many, and Sergeant Russell fired the 37mm. The muzzle blast lit up the dark kitchen smashing him in the abdomen, temporarily stopping the madman in his tracks. He recoiled and retreated behind an oven, checking his wound. Although the impact injured him, surprisingly, it didn't put him down.

He charged toward Joe, knives extended, causing Sergeant Flores to fire his launcher. The round hit him with such force it spun him around, forcing him to retreat again. Even though the impacts were taking their toll, the crazy man refused to go down. Instead, he stumbled around behind the ovens, yelling and cursing the team. The oven concealed the wounded suspect from the waist down, bobbing and weaving behind it.

The team saw this as their opportunity to end the confrontation, so they moved forward to get a better angle on him. Even though it was difficult to see through the smoke, both sergeants aimed and fired again as the negotiator yelled, "PUT THE KNIVES DOWN." The man went down instantly as the sergeants reloaded for another shot. The negotiator kept yelling, "SHOW US YOUR HANDS. WE CAN HELP YOU!"

When he didn't show himself, Russell directed Andy, "Move around and get eyes on him." Andy nodded and slowly crept around the oven with his rifle at the ready. The suspect was flat on his back, gasping for air, "He's down!" Quickly, they closed in, and Joe kicked the knives out of the suspect's reach. His eyes rolled back in his head, and Flores radioed CP, "We need the paramedics here quick!"

Paramedics arrived and loaded the unconscious man on a stretcher and rushed him to an awaiting ambulance. Large bruises and contusions covered his torso from the bean bags. His body endured an unbelievable amount of force before finally giving in.

With peace restored, the team shared personal recollections of the incident, and both Russell and Flores took credit for the shot that finally put him down. "I hit that son-of-a-bitch right in the solar plexus," boasted Flores.

"No, it was my round, Andrew," Jim replied. "I'm the one who had a perfect shot to his chest!"

Flores insisted, "When my bag hit him, he fell to the floor!"

Those two were still arguing about who's round did the job when a patrol supervisor walked in and announced the suspect had stopped breathing and coded. He continued, "They don't know if he's gonna make it." Russell and Flores instantly changed their stories, blaming the other for firing the final round. Andy was amused by how quickly the credit for the shot changed once they learned the suspect might not survive.

It was later determined that one of the rounds hit the suspect in the throat crushing his trachea. By the time paramedics performed a tracheotomy, he had been without oxygen for several minutes. Although they finally got him breathing again, the damage was done. He lay in a coma at Ben Taub hospital for about 3 months before succumbing to his injuries.

Much to their amazement, no drugs or alcohol were detected in his system. With no identification and no fingerprints on file, no one knew his real name. The hotel register was signed under an assumed name, so they could not verify who he was. And no one ever came forward to claim his body. Eventually, he was buried in the County Morgue cemetery under John Doe.

Houston SWAT became infamous for being one of the few teams in the country to have killed someone with a less-lethal impact weapon. A distinction they would have rather forgotten.

House of Horror

For monthly firearm training, the team utilized the Ramsey Prison Range. Located approximately 30 miles south of town, it was a state-of-the-art facility, and they allowed Houston SWAT to train there for free. It was well worth the 45-minute drive to take advantage of the incredible resource. Typically, they ventured into the prison at lunchtime and ate with the guards. The meals were reasonably priced and incredibly good, so they took full advantage of the all-you-can-eat, home-style cooking. The downside was that Andy didn't particularly care for being disarmed at the gate and walking through the convict's mess hall to reach the guard's dining area. Following the Warden past hundreds of inmates who hated their guts was a little unnerving, but Andy obliged.

After lunch, they were notified the Katy Police Department requested their assistance with an armed suspect. Katy was a small suburb on the west side of Houston and one of the many surrounding cities part of a mutual aid pack. Katy PD had responded to a shooting at a residence and believed the shooter was still inside.

Quickly the team loaded their gear, and within minutes, a stream of SWAT vehicles sped toward Katy, TX. The call was a potential hostage situation, so they needed to get there as soon as possible; time was of the essence. About 40 minutes later, the procession of vehicles exited the freeway and entered the quiet neighborhood.

A lovely part of Harris County, the middle-class neighborhood rarely saw anything more than a burglary. SWAT officers and a gauntlet of news trucks poured into their quaint community. Andy quickly parked and grabbed his gear. Then, Jose told him they had been assigned the entry. Jose cautioned Andy to be prepared for the possibility that the suspect may start shooting again. Two hours prior, the neighbors reported sounds of gunfire, and the house had been quiet ever since. Katy PD called out to anyone inside, but there was no response. They feared the shooter was waiting to ambush the police upon entry.

Urgently, SWAT took control of the scene, and negotiators started ringing the phone inside. From intel discovered by the officers, they were informed several generations of a Vietnamese family lived at the residence. Recently, one of their daughters ended a relationship with a young man stalking her. Earlier in the day, the man threatened the woman and her family multiple times and left work a short time later. Typical of Vietnamese refugees at the time, multiple generations lived in one home, struggling to make ends meet. The negotiators suspected there could be as many as eight people inside.

Jose tried to prepare his young team for the carnage they may find inside. "If we get the word to search the house, let's just take it slow. It's a shit sandwich, so let's eat it one bite at a time."

They nodded in agreement as Jose went over the plan.

"It might be gruesome, but don't let it distract you. This asshole might be waiting for you to make a mistake. Let's use our mirrors and shield and work on the problem as we always do, no matter what we find. Got it?" They kept nodding, but Jose was concerned. He didn't want his team taking this one, but it was their turn, so he wouldn't pass it off to another group.

The negotiators continued calling the phone and tried making contact with loudspeakers but still no response. Some perimeter members were asked to approach the windows to look inside, but they were covered with heavy drapes. Command post considered their options and then gave Jose the green light to search the house for anyone who might still be alive.

"OK, Let's do this," Jose said.

"Roger that," Andy replied, and the team equipped themselves.

Jose continued, "The shooter may be an Asian male wearing blue jeans and a white t-shirt. They think he's armed with a pistol."

The CP then broadcasted, "CP to all officers; the team is entering the building. Radio silence."

Practicing standard procedure, they started at the front door utilizing their mirrors to see around angles and held their shields for protection. Andy opened the door and looked through the ballistic viewport into the darkroom. A woman sat on the couch with a massive gunshot wound to her head, blood splattering the wall behind her. Although she appeared to have been killed instantly, Andy stared at the woman's chest to make sure she wasn't breathing. Her stillness confirmed his suspicions.

Doorways were common ambush points, so Andy and Joe moved through quickly, ready for the worst. Once inside, they paused behind their shields, listening for any signs of life. The house was dreadfully silent as they mapped where to begin their search.

Jose moved inside and motioned them down a hallway that led to the bedrooms. Andy carefully stepped over the woman's outstretched legs, the first of several bodies they would find throughout the house of horrors.

Several victims fled to different rooms to escape their attacker, locking the bedroom doors behind them. But the shooter kicked them in. The victims must have been terrified as they were hunted room by room.

An elderly woman was lying in a bed with a tiny infant next to her in the last bedroom. Lying side by side, they were both executed by a single gunshot and died instantly. More than likely, the grandmother shielded the infant when she died. Andy gazed at them for a few seconds, amazed they appeared so peaceful; you would have thought they were sleeping if not for the bullet wounds to their heads.

Andy and Joe advanced toward the kitchen and mudroom. They were the only remaining rooms, and so far, they hadn't found anyone they thought was the killer. Andy peered into the kitchen with his mirror; Joe covered as they spotted a young woman lying on the floor, face down in a pool of blood. As Andy stepped over her to see into the mudroom, he spotted a man's legs extended out, flat on the floor.

Their voice commands remained unanswered, and they eventually moved in and found him dead from a self-inflicted gunshot wound. He was wearing a white t-shirt and blue jeans, same as the description, with a pistol next to his open hand. 'Why would someone do something like this?' Andy couldn't help but wonder.

After a quick secondary search of the house, they turned it over to homicide detectives. Tragically, every room had at least one dead body. Although this was Andy's first time witnessing a mass murder, he wasn't bothered by it. He felt sad for them but didn't feel any emotional attachment. In a few short minutes, he had seen more carnage than most people could imagine in a lifetime. The images didn't bother him, but he never wanted to see them again, so he opened the box in the back of his mind and safely tucked them away.

Man's Best Friend

On a warm summer night, HPD Homicide Detectives attempted to execute a murder warrant for a man indicted by a Harris County Grand Jury. Upon arrival at the residence's front door, there was an exchange of gunfire. Luckily, no one was hit, and the detectives quickly backed off and called for SWAT. Soon, the house was surrounded, beginning another stand-off between police and an armed criminal.

When Andy arrived, he was impressed by the size of the suspect's yard. It was the longest chain-link fence he had ever seen, and it wrapped around over an acre of property. Now that his team was down on the rotation list for entry, Andy assumed he'd be set on a perimeter position somewhere.

Pinky Wilson was the Team Leader assigned control of the perimeter; he typically managed the sniper team. Even though he was an old-timer nearing the end of his SWAT career, Pinky pulled his weight, and Andy admired him.

Wilson requested Andy work his way around to the rear of the house and find a place to contain the suspect should he exit through the back. "Get inside the fence if you can. Just let me know where you end up. This guy has already shot at the detectives, so be careful."

Once he reached the back fence line, he spotted several mature oak trees. He carefully lined himself up behind one of the large trees and climbed the fence. Then, he dashed to the closest tree and tried to catch his breath while familiarizing himself with his surroundings. The yard was completely dark except for a small light at the back door, illuminating the porch.

Andy radioed his position and settled in for a long containment. Then, unexpectedly, the back door opened, and out trotted a large dog, with the door closing behind it. The dog sniffed around for a minute, found a good spot, and lifted his hind leg to pee. Andy thought about reporting the movement to the CP, but even a whisper might alert the dog of his presence, and he feared the dog could be aggressive.

Even though the tree provided cover, he didn't want to put himself in a position where he could get pinned down if the suspect discovered his location. Also, if he ran for the fence line, the dog would surely catch him before he could hurdle it. So, he decided to sit there motionless and hope for the best.

Eventually, the dog made his way in Andy's direction, picking up his scent while sniffing the ground. The dog barked once and then again, unsure of the shadowy figure by the tree. Andy took a chance that the dog was friendly and quietly tried to call it over, "Here, boy," whispered Andy. "Come here, boy." Finally, the dog quit barking and curiously inched toward him. Andy squatted down to appear calm and passive, hoping the dog would get the hint.

Slowly, Andy extended his hand, allowing the dog to approach and smell his scent in greeting. The dog happily started to wag his tail, and Andy breathed a sigh of relief. Within a few moments, the dog acted like they were old friends. It turns out he was just a giant puppy who craved all of Andy's attention. Andy needed to get back to his job, but the dog did not appreciate being ignored. The dog started barking again in a playful attempt to get his attention. Unwilling to risk alerting the suspect of his whereabouts, he squatted back down to pet the puppy again and observed the house for movement.

Annoyed at the dog's constant demand for attention, Andy stood up to focus back on work when suddenly the dog started humping his leg. A definite line had been crossed, and Andy quickly shoved him off. The dog didn't appreciate the rejection, so he started barking again. Andy promptly squatted down and motioned him back, "Shush, come here, boy." The dog quieted and walked around as Andy stroked his head and checked to see if the barking drew the suspect's attention.

The young puppy, with pent-up energy, resumed humping his leg again. Andy pushed him away, and once again, the dog started barking. The back and forth continued for a few more minutes until Andy finally gave in and let the dog hump his leg as much as he wanted. At least the dog wasn't barking anymore, and there was no one around to see it, so Andy let it happen. Eventually, the dog got bored and walked off to inspect the rest of the yard.

After several hours, they gassed the house, but the suspect wouldn't come out. So, the next step was to send Bubba Arnold's team inside to search. During the team's search of the home, they eventually found the suspect hiding in a wooden armoire. When they made voice contact, the suspect pointed a pistol and tried to shoot them. The SWAT team returned fire, hitting the suspect several times. Even though he was severely injured, he survived.

As the ambulance left with the wounded suspect, Andy looked in the backyard for the dog, who almost gave his position away. Once the shooting started, the terrified dog ran under the house and never returned. Andy was relieved that no one was there to see what happened between him and man's best friend because he would have never lived it down. He thought to himself, sometimes you just do what you gotta do.

Ice Water in His Veins

On a quiet Sunday afternoon in northeast Houston, a gunman walked into the Popeye's Fried Chicken on Jensen Drive demanding money and threatening the store manager behind the counter. As the employee nervously fumbled to get cash out of the register, everyone else in the store escaped running out the door, leaving the manager alone to deal with the robber.

Once the register was empty, the gunman shoved the manager into his office and demanded he open the safe. The store employee said he couldn't because he didn't know the combination.

"Well, if you don't find a way to open the safe, I will kill you," the gunman threatened. As the manager struggled with the combination lock, the gunman restlessly paced back and forth, barking demands. Unbeknownst to the gunman, the manager had already triggered a silent holdup alarm, and HPD was on their way.

With every second that ticked by, the armed robber became more agitated. Antsy and impatiently watching for the manager to unlock the combination dial, the gunman glanced out the window and saw an HPD patrol car pull into the parking lot. Immediately, he made a mad dash for the front door, but it was too late; the restaurant was surrounded by three patrol cars. Exasperated, the gunman fired an errant shot at the closest patrol unit, causing the officer to duck and run to another unit. Unfortunately, the officer left his driver-side car door open and the keys in the ignition in his haste.

"Y'all better get the fuck back," warned the gunman, slamming the glass door shut and retreating to the manager's office. He reached the office in time to discover the manager trying to get a pistol out of his briefcase. For years, the manager carried the firearm to the store to be prepared if something like this happened. The robber clocked the manager on the back of the head with his gun, nearly knocking him out. He grabbed the other pistol, holding one in each hand, and pistol-whipped the manager, cursing him for the fix he was in. He screamed,

"Get up Motherfucker," and the manager staggered, trying to get to his feet. "Come on," the robber yelled, shoving him toward the door.

Bleeding badly from his head wound, the manager used one hand to cover his injury and pushed open the door with the other. Hiding behind the manager, the robber again warned the police, "Y'all better get the fuck out of here, or I'll kill this motherfucker!" The officers didn't engage the hostile suspect; they crouched behind their patrol cars, waiting for SWAT.

Andy usually worked a security job at the movie theater on Sunday afternoons. Two hours into his shift, his pager went off. Using the office phone to call dispatch, he learned about a developing hostage situation at Popeye's. He relayed to the dispatcher he would be en route and abruptly left the theatre to make the call-up. Several SWAT officers were on the scene when he arrived, and the CP was rolling up. Quickly, he dressed, grabbed his gear, and listened to the chatter between SWAT officers deployed around the restaurant.

The sun was starting to set as Andy approached the CP for an assignment. Sergeant Rosekrants asked him to stand by, "I'll need you on the react team once I have enough guys." Andy agreed and stood back, waiting for further instruction.

Over the radio, Gary Tilson reported his position on the rooftop directly across the street from the restaurant. Tilson was one of the best snipers on the team, and supervision utilized his skillset for critical positions. He noted a police vehicle parked not far from the front of the restaurant had its driver's door open. The CP followed up with the first responding officers, who admitted that the keys were left in the ignition in the heat of the moment, posing a big problem if the suspect were to use it as a getaway vehicle.

Jenson checked with the captain and radioed their decision, "CP to all officers, the rule has been invoked." The suspect was not to leave the scene, even if deadly force was needed to stop him.

By the time negotiators started calling the store phone, it was dark outside. Finally, after ringing several times, the manager picked up, "Hello?"

"This is the Houston Police Department; who am I speaking with?"

"My name is Earl Johnson. I'm the store manager."

"Are you OK?" asked the negotiator.

"Yes, but he wants you to get out of here, or he's gonna kill me," replied Earl shakily.

"Can I speak with him?"

Earl turned to the gunman, "He wants to speak with you."

"Give me that," the gunman scorned, grabbing the phone. "Get the fuck out of here," he yelled into the receiver.

"I am officer McCoy with the Houston Police Department. Who am I speaking with?" the negotiator asked.

"Fuck you! You and your cop friends better get the fuck out of here, or this motherfucker is dead. YOU HEAR ME?!"

"OK," McCoy answered, "But we can't just leave. So why don't you just let him go, and we'll talk about what we can do for you."

"FUCK YOU!" the robber yelled and slammed the phone down. Furious his demands wouldn't be met, the gunman stomped around the manager's office, pointing the gun at Earl and threatening his life. Occasionally he'd stopped to peer out the windows, but the parking lot was dark except for a few streetlights. He could see a handful of patrol cars parked around the perimeter, but no one was moving. Paranoid that Earl may have another gun hidden; the robber restrained him with some rags he found in a closet and tied his hands behind his back.

Andy was assigned to an ad-hoc react team positioned behind a 6-foot cedar privacy fence next to the restaurant parking lot. Their task was to ensure the suspect did not reach the patrol car.

The gunman was through with negotiations and refused to answer the phone, becoming more flustered with every ring. His last option was the open patrol car, so he decided that was his ticket. Violently, he yanked Earl, put a pistol to his head, and used his other arm to maneuver his torso, walking behind him to the glass door.

Since the react team couldn't see the parking lot, they were surprised when Tilson's radio announced the suspect had opened the front door. They did, however, hear the suspect yelling, "Get back motherfuckers, I'll kill him!" As the situation escalated, everyone tensed and nervously shifted their long weapons close to their bodies.

"Do not come outside," bellowed the loudspeakers. "Go back and pick up the phone. We need to talk to you!"

"I'M THROUGH TALKING!" he screamed in a frenzy. He forced Earl out the glass door, turning his head left and right, looking for cops.

Tilson's rifle scope was equipped with enhanced optics to give him a better view of the suspect. With the scope's precision, he saw the suspect carried a pistol in each hand, and the hostage looked petrified. The gunman forced Earl another step forward. He didn't know that SWAT was on the scene and never thought to look up at the rooftops.

Tilson was lying on top of a hardware store directly across from the restaurant, with a gas station between them. Although he had a good rifle rest position, the station's roof limited his view. If the gunman walked out too far, he would lose sight of them. If he needed to take a shot, he would have to do it before they walked much further.

Andy nervously crouched behind the fence, listening to negotiators plead with the gunman to go back inside. Occasionally he peered between the cedar planks for a glimpse, but it was too dark to see much. Tilson reported the suspect was slowly moving toward the patrol car, and the suspect would soon be out of range; he would lose his shot.

At the command post, Jenson turned to the captain for a decision. They couldn't allow him to get in that car. The best option was to stop him with a sniper shot at this juncture. The Captain leaned back in his chair, staring at the ceiling as he wrestled with how to proceed. Deciding to end a life was never an easy decision to make. Finally, Jenson radioed, "CP to Tilson, let the man die."

"That's clear," Tilson replied matter-of-factly. "I'll be off the radio to set up the best shot."

The radio went silent as everyone quietly waited for what they knew was coming next.

With the gas station rooftop in the way, Tilson stood up to get a better view. He would have to take a free hand shot with nothing to steady his rifle. The gunman anxiously kept turning his head left and right, making it difficult for Tilson to choose an impact point that would cause immediate incapacitation. The pistols were revolvers, and with the hammers back, the slightest squeeze would end Earl's life. Tilson's aim needed to be perfect.

The night air was still. Over the loudspeakers, the constant pleading continued, "STOP!! Go back inside and pick up the phone." Everyone waited for the crack of the 308-caliber rifle, which would signal them to go and make sure the suspect was down. Everyone knew Tilson was an excellent sniper, but this was an incredibly challenging shot, even for him.

Tilson struggled to steady his rifle, focusing on his task. The shot left zero room for error; the bullet would pass an inch from Earl's head before reaching the gunman. The best point of impact was just below the nose. If he could sever the brain stem with the bullet, it would cause the suspect to lose all movement instantly.

Tilson slowed down his breathing, carefully observing the gunman anxiously twist his head left and right, with Earl pulled tightly against him. He needed the gunman looking in his direction for an optimal shot, so he timed his movements. Back and forth, Tilson counted in rhythm and started squeezing the trigger. One, two, three, BANG! The shot broke; its trajectory passed within a few inches of the gas station roofline as it sped at a downward angle toward its target. It had to travel 76-yards and hit a moving target with less than a fraction of an inch for error.

Andy heard the rifle shot crack through the night air and then a blood-curdling scream. He thought, 'Oh my God! He missed,' as the team sprang forward toward the parking lot. They rounded the fence and found the gunman lying flat on his back, arms outstretched, with a large pool of dark blood oozing from his head. Earl was lying beside him, screaming incoherently in terror. The bullet passed within an inch of Earl's head, striking its target, instantly cutting off all communications between the gunman's brain and his muscles. He fell to the pavement like a limp rag doll, and Earl fell with him. But, besides the trauma and loss of control of his bladder, Earl was unharmed.

They helped Earl up off the ground and pulled him around to the other side of the patrol car. When he tried to stand on his own, his knees buckled, so they sat him gently down on the curb. An ambulance arrived to evaluate Earl's condition and pronounce the gunman dead. The gunman's reign of terror was over.

Andy looked up from the parking lot and could make out Tilson's silhouette, standing on the hardware store roof. Tilson had his rifle leaned on his hip, watching the hustle and bustle in the parking lot below. Andy assumed Tilson's heart rate didn't fluctuate much because of the ice water in his veins, and he was just glad he was on their side.

Still Smelling Like a Rose

On a phone call with his mom, Andy discovered Mike had cut a deal with the District Attorney and was charged with possession of a controlled substance, not part of the Ecstasy manufacturing. He was sentenced to three days in the county jail and given credit for time served. Once he paid his fine, the case would be behind him. Andy was amazed that once again, his brother had pulled it off. Just like Teflon, nothing stuck to him. Even though Andy was glad Mike didn't have to serve time in prison, he wondered if the punishment was enough of a deterrent.

That spring, Terri surprised Andy with the news that she was pregnant with their second child. Their hopes were set on a girl, and sure enough, Emma Marie Wallace arrived in January, and their family felt complete. Although life was a little hectic now, the extra bundle of joy was all worth it. Now Bryce was old enough to go fishing and hunting with Andy, and they were best friends. Soon enough, Terri returned to teach her High School Government classes, and the busy schedules of working parents and raising two children kept them running. However, life in the country seemed to keep them centered, and the home they shared was their sanctuary from the rest of the world.

They Call Me the Fireman

At 1 am, Jose's phone call startled Andy awake. Their next call-up was at a convenience store on MLK Boulevard. Patrol responded to a silent holdup alarm and arrived before the robber escaped. When the suspect noticed the police officers out front, he tried to flee out the back, but the door was locked. The store clerk took advantage of the opportunity and ran out the front doors into the waiting arms of the police.

Once the gunman realized there was no way out of the situation, his behavior became erratic. He would have to go back to prison if he was arrested, and the premise sent him over the edge. In front of the gauntlet of patrol cars with officers at the ready, he held the gun to his head and threatened to take his own life.

As SWAT officers arrived, they slowly replaced the patrol officers, and it turned into another babysitting assignment while the negotiators attempted to call the man. Jose's team was assigned to the react position on the side of the building. Since they had zero intention of going inside the store, an entry team was unnecessary.

Fred Locke was the sniper covering the front of the building and reported the suspect was brazenly piling up several items in the middle of the floor near the counter. The man was removing boxes from the shelves and building a mound of trash. Everyone could see where he was going with this when the suspect doused the pile with a can of lighter fluid.

The mood changed inside the CP when Sergeant Jenson turned to the Captain and asked, "If he sets a fire, do we go in then?"

"Well, we will have to do something!" the Captain fumed.

Sergeant Flores left the CP to prepare the react team for entry into a burning building. Jose agreed with the assessment and added, "OK, but I think we need Scott Air Packs if we are going to enter a building on fire."

"Agreed, I'll work on that," replied Flores. "You guys get a plan ready, and I'll have the equipment here as quickly as possible."

Jose instructed his team, "If the fire isn't too large, we'll go in, but we aren't firemen!"

Soon, a firetruck arrived on the scene with four Scott Air Packs. The firefighters gave them a quick tutorial on properly using the equipment. Already wearing bulky ballistics vests, the team had difficulty donning the tanks on top of them. Then, they were forced to discard their helmets for the face masks to fit.

"When you start to hear an alarm bell, you are getting low on air, and you need to exit the building," the fireman instructed. "The tank will give you approximately 30 minutes of oxygen depending on how fast you breathe." Andy nodded; that should be plenty of time. Once they practiced properly wearing the mask and breathing through them a few times, they turned them off to conserve air. Then, with all their equipment squared away, the firefighters wished them well and left.

Andy was concerned about how much weight he was wearing and having difficulty staying calm. He still needed to carry a shield and be able to use his weapon. It was all getting to be a bit much. But he didn't want to risk dying of smoke inhalation, and bullets were even more deadly.

Fred reported the suspect was taunting the perimeter guys by dancing around the mound, holding a lighter over the pile. The negotiators continually called the phone, but the suspect refused to answer. As a last resort for communication, they were broadcasting over their loudspeakers, "Please put down the lighter and pick up the phone," to no avail.

Suddenly, Fred's voice broke the radio airways, "Suspect is lighting the pile." Jose advised his team to mask up. Quickly, they threw on their masks, and the air automatically started flowing with every breath. In the darkness, they tried to overhear Fred describe the suspect's actions over the wheezing sound of air circulating through the masks.

The negotiators were still shouting for the suspect to stop lighting the pile just as a box caught fire. The tiny flame flickered as the suspect provokingly danced around without a care in the world. Jose motioned his team forward, so Andy lifted the shield and walked to the corner. Then, Fred radioed an update that the flame had died, so they retreated and removed their masks to conserve air. They had already been breathing through the tanks for at least 5 minutes, and Andy wondered how much air was left. The team was frustrated, their backs aching from the weight of the extra equipment.

For a few minutes, tensions temporarily calmed when the suspect picked up the phone to speak with negotiators. Then, clearly upset with the conversation, he slammed down the phone and found another can of charcoal lighter fluid. Fred radioed an update describing the man pouring another canister of fluid over the pile and flicking his lighter to set it ablaze.

Once again, Jose announced, "Mask up," and the air started flowing. Andy found the sounds of rushing air heaving in and out incredibly distracting. The suspect picked up the phone again in a few minutes, so Jose directed, "Unmask, save your air." During that block of time, Andy used a lot of oxygen, and he continually worried about how much was left.

The suspect suddenly slammed the phone, immediately followed by Fred urgently reporting over the radio, "Suspect is standing over the pile with a lighter."

"Mask up," Jose yelled. Once again, Andy hoisted the heavy shield, and the sounds of his labored breathing were all he could hear.

"The pile is on fire," Fred reported.

"That's clear," replied CP. "Jose, you are good to go in."

"CP, that's clear," Jose responded. Starting toward the edge of the building, he could see the reflection of the flames dancing on the windshields of the patrol cars parked in the front row. The thick, dark smoke was already pooling at the door, and Andy was glad they didn't have to breathe it. The flames were licking up to the ceiling as Joe reached and opened the glass door. Scanning through the ballistic viewport, Andy tried to see through the smoke. They knew the suspect was armed, but where was he?

Just as he started through the door, Andy's alarm bell sounded. 'Oh SHIT,' he thought but couldn't turn back. Instead, he pushed onward, walking into the room, desperately trying to see and ignoring the sound of his alarm. Immediately, he heard two more air pack alarms going off, and he knew they were all in the same predicament.

Andy and Joe moved past the burning pile, covering the store while Jose and Mickey used fire extinguishers on the mound. It took four large extinguishers to put out the flames entirely. The smoke was thicker now as the pile smoldered.

The team took defensive positions in the store, and Jose removed his mask to yell, "YOU, IN THE BACK! COME OUT WITH YOUR HANDS IN THE AIR, AND YOU WILL NOT BE HARMED!" Andy figured if Jose could survive without his mask, he would take his off as well. Soon all four of them had their masks off as Jose continued yelling for the suspect to surrender.

Finally, the suspect walked out of the storage room with his hands in the air. It turned out he wasn't that crazy after all. He didn't want to die; he merely wanted to raise as much hell as possible before going back to prison. They hauled him off, and the Fire Department ensured the fire was out.

During the critique the next day, the question came up, 'What would happen if one of those air packs took a bullet in a firefight?' They heatedly debated with several different opinions, but Andy wanted an answer, not a hypothesis. So, the next day he spoke to the Firefighters in charge of air packs at HFD. They didn't know either, but they were willing to find out.

Andy facilitated a test at the range, and everyone came excited to witness the result, even the Captain. On a target stand, they placed a fully charged air pack and shot it with a .308 sniper rifle from 100-yards. On impact, a blast of fog obscured the bottle as it took flight. It flew at least 50-yards straight up, like a rocket, and almost back to the firing line where they stood. For a moment, Andy thought they would have to make a run for it, but the air pack hit the ground roughly 10-yards in front of them.

The group stood in amazement, absorbing what had just happened. Andy wanted to shoot another bottle, but this time with a 180 lbs dummy strapped to it. The Captain stepped in and advised there would be no more testing because he would not risk someone getting hurt. Andy didn't get his answer; it would have to wait for another day.

You Got a Quarter?

After completing Advanced SWAT school and several instructor-level classes, Andy became a confident operator who loved his job. He was strategically building his SWAT resume with his ambition set on becoming a Team Leader one day. Other guys were moving to career ladder positions within the department by making rank or accepting less strenuous jobs. Joe and Mickey had taken the Sergeant's Exam and scored high enough for promotions, so they too would be moving on. Andy was sad to see them go, but he understood why they were leaving.

Instead of increasing his salary through promotions, Andy chose to work a few additional jobs to help with the ever-increasing costs of raising a family. At the Marriott hotel on the West Loop, he picked up a night security job working Wednesday night from 6 pm to 2 am. He went with very little sleep for that one night a week, but the pay was good. To avoid the long drive home, he often left his shift and headed directly to the office to grab a few hours of shut-eye on a padded bench in the CP.

One night, driving out of the hotel parking lot at 2 am, Andy was exceedingly exhausted. He was struggling to get to the office without dosing off. As he entered the West Loop ramp, all three lanes ahead of him were nothing but a sea of red brake lights. His heart sank, assuming there was a wreck ahead. He knew he had a duty to check on any potential injuries, but the stop would cost him precious sleep. As he inched closer to the source of the slowdown, a car was swerving from one lane to another. All surrounding vehicles backed off, afraid to pass him. Even though Andy knew he had to stop this idiot, he was relieved to see it wasn't a car accident.

Carefully maneuvering behind the obvious DWI, he flipped on his dashboard's red and blue strobe lights. At first, the driver didn't respond, so Andy hit his siren approaching the Memorial Street overpass. Sluggishly, the car eased over and rolled to a stop just short of the bridge. Making traffic stops on the freeway was never ideal; this was particularly precarious because his unmarked SWAT vehicle wasn't equipped with overhead emergency lights. The location was another obstacle because they ended up next to a steep hill that led to the service road below, adding to the uneasiness. One unbalanced step off the pavement would mean taking an extended tumble down the grass embankment to the access road.

Andy hoped there would be an available DWI unit to take over. Cautiously, he exited his vehicle and glanced back to see if any wayward vehicles were coming. The freeway traffic was light, but that wouldn't last long. All the bars closed at 2 am, increasing the likelihood of more dangerous DWIs. Traffic accidents killed more cops in Houston than bullets, so walking on the freeway always scared him. He nervously approached the car, strobing the windows with his flashlight and spotting a man's face behind the wheel. His bloodshot eyes struggled to focus. This guy was blitzed out of his mind. Andy leaned down and directed his flashlight to the passenger seat, hoping that his companion was in better shape, but not so much. Her eyes were staring back with the same glazed, drunken expression. Andy instantly knew he couldn't allow these two to move another inch; they were an immediate danger to others on the road.

"I need you both to step out of the car," Andy sternly directed.

"Yes, sir," the driver slurred, opened the door, and struggled to stand.

Andy walked between the cars and stepped over to the edge of the pavement. He flashed his light at them and yelled, "Over here!" Holding on to the vehicle to support themselves, they staggered toward Andy. Precariously perched on the barrier's edge, he nervously glanced down the freeway for another intoxicated driver. "Stand right here," he instructed, pointing to a spot on the edge of the pavement as far from the moving traffic lane as possible.

He retrieved the man's driver's license and advised the couple to wait there as they used each other as support to stay upright. Andy returned to his car and asked the dispatcher if a DWI unit was available to check with him, but unfortunately, there wasn't. He dropped his head on the steering wheel and inhaled a deep breath in defeat. He was stuck with this mess. Irritated and sleep-deprived, Andy raised his head and glared at the couple leaning onto each other, cursing the predicament they put him in.

In the distance, he spotted an all-night diner, Toddle House. Brightly lit up about a block away on Memorial Drive as if it were calling his name. From previously dining there, he knew a bank of pay phones lined the front of the restaurant. Suddenly Andy had a brilliant idea because he hadn't mentioned the DWI stop to the dispatcher; there wasn't proof he pulled one over. Feeling empowered, Andy briskly made his way back to the couple.

"You got a quarter?" Andy asked the drunk man. Puzzled, the man struggled to get his hand into his blue jean pocket while Andy nervously watched for approaching traffic.

Suddenly the man came up with a shiny quarter; showing it to Andy, he proudly replied, "Yes, sir."

"You got someone to call that can come to get you?" asked Andy.

"Yes, sir," he replied.

"Who?"

"My brother."

"OK, here's the deal," he said, pointing to the restaurant, "You can go to jail or walk over to that Toddle House and call your brother to come to get you. What's it gonna be?"

"I'll call my brother, officer." The woman nodded her head in agreement, and they both smiled, relieved. "Thank you, officer!"

The two hugged each other, realizing they weren't being arrested, and nearly lost their balance. "WATCH IT," Andy yelled as he reached out and grabbed them just before they fell off the edge. The couple regained their balance, still struggling to stand. "Wait here. I'm gonna lock your car." The two drunks nodded their heads in agreement. Andy walked around the driver's side, removed the keys from the ignition, and dropped them on the floorboard out of sight. He turned on the emergency flashers, locked all four doors, and shut the driver's door. Either they would have to get a spare set of keys or have the car towed. More importantly, they wouldn't be his problem anymore.

When Andy looked up, his heart sank. They were gone. He ran back to the edge of the pavement and flashed his light down the hill. There they were, rolling arm and arm toward the service road. The trip to the bottom felt like forever as Andy watched in incredulity. Finally, they stopped just short of the pavement, lying flat on the grass. Both were gasping for air, and they raised their heads to look for perspective.

"ARE YOU OK?" Andy yelled. They nodded. "DO YOU STILL HAVE THE QUARTER?"

He struggled to his knees and checked his pocket. Then, triumphantly, he thrust the quarter in the air, "YES! HERE IT IS!"

"OK, YOUR KEYS ARE LOCKED IN YOUR CAR. DON'T COME BACK HERE. YOU CAN'T GET IN. GO CALL YOUR BROTHER!" The man nodded his head, and they helped one another to their feet.

Andy got back in his car, cautiously pulled back onto the freeway, and sped away. He anxiously checked his wristwatch to calculate how much sleep he could get if he hurried. The dispatcher called his radio number to verify if he needed anything, but Andy didn't respond. Instead, he drove to the office feeling accomplished. It's possible he just saved a life or two, even if he didn't do it by the book. Pulling into the SWAT parking lot, Andy's mind started running through all of the worst-case what-if scenarios: 'What if someone rear-ended the parked car on the freeway?' 'What if another drunk hit the couple on Memorial Drive while walking to the restaurant?' 'What if they were mugged waiting for his brother?' The endless possibilities raced through his mind when he finally laid his head down in the CP. He stared at the ceiling, trying to sleep, but it wasn't happening.

Before long, he heard people arriving for the day, leaving no hope for sleep. Andy hit the coffee extra hard and hoped to get off early. The lack of sleep made PT a struggle, but he managed to get through it and then grabbed a shower. Still worried about the drunk's car, Andy swung by Loop 610 to check on it on his way to training. Approaching the Memorial Drive overpass, he was as nervous as a whore in church. The anticipation was unbearable until he topped the crest, and sure enough, there it was. Still parked on the shoulder with the flashers blinking. He eased back in his seat, relaxed, and thought, 'Well, at least something went right last night.'

SIXTEEN

Nothing New

Andy's relationship with his brother Mike was virtually nonexistent. Although he hadn't seen him for nearly four years, he kept up with his whereabouts through his Mom's stories. Mike didn't show up to the family events anymore because he was usually traveling on some business deal, so they didn't cross paths. Even though it was probably for the best, he missed the good times shared with his brother. At least he hadn't heard of any more arrests, so hopefully, Mike learned his lesson.

Wrong House

Andy pulled into the SWAT parking lot as the first morning light was creeping between the downtown skyscrapers. He parked, took a deep breath, leaned back, and closed his eyes. Running on fumes from a late-night extra job, he thought a short nap might help. Instead, he was startled when the dispatcher's voice broke his moment of peace, requesting a SWAT unit. Sergeant Flores answered, "901. Go ahead." Patrol was asking for SWAT on the Westside channel; they had a barricaded suspect in a townhome complex. Flores replied that he would change the radio channel and activate the team.

'You have got to be kidding me,' thought Andy, shaking his head in disbelief. He needed that nap in the worst way, but it was not to be. He rubbed his face trying to wake himself up, and radioed the dispatcher he would be en route as he reluctantly drove off toward his next adventure. Upon arrival, Andy realized what was reported as a townhome complex were tiny identical patio homes with individual addresses. Andy drove through the middle of the complex and headed toward the flashing police lights.

Flores was on the scene talking with patrol when he spotted Andy, motioning him up the street toward the objective. Andy nodded and hustled toward a patrol officer standing watch near a garage. The officer informed Andy the homeowner lived alone with his two large dogs. At about 5 am, he awoke to his front door being kicked in. Alarmed, he jumped out of bed, and the dogs headed for the door, attacking the intruder. With a dog attached to each arm, the man was spinning around the living room, banging into walls, screaming, and struggling to get away from the canines. The dogs clamped tight to the intruder, refusing to release their grip.

With the intruder distracted, the owner bolted out the front door toward his neighbor's house, instinctually slamming the door behind him. He pounded on his neighbor's door until he was let in to call the police. As he described the incident to the 911 operator, he could still hear a violent struggle coming from his home. After hanging up, everything next door was now quiet. He worried about the safety of his dogs and what might have happened to them, but he wasn't going back in there. So instead, he waited safely inside his neighbor's home until the police arrived.

Andy asked the officer if anyone had seen movement inside.

"I think the dogs are moving around in there."

"Have you seen any signs of the intruder?" asked Andy.

The officer shook his head no but added, "If he's still in there, he must have gotten away from the dogs, or they killed him."

Andy nodded in understanding and radioed the information to Sergeant Flores.

Within 30 minutes, most of the team was on the scene, and the situation was well underway. After several attempts to reach the suspect by phone, the negotiators set up their speakers. The intruder may have made it to a closet or another room to hide from the dogs, preventing him from answering the phone. After broadcasting over the speakers for about thirty minutes, CP decided to probe inside the home with a camera pole.

The extendable pole held a small camera that projected an image to a small TV screen at the operator's end. It could be directed to look around corners, attics, or windows. Navigating the pole, they moved from window to window and eventually spotted the man lying on a bed in the master bedroom. Both arms were bloodied, and his shirt was partially ripped off. He lay motionless, and they weren't sure if he was alive. This was their best opportunity to get the dogs out of the house.

Andy was covering the front door when Sergeant Flores approached with the homeowner to lure the dogs out and get them safely away. The animals were pacing around the living room, impressively large, weighing at least 150 lbs each. They stood watch, on high alert, saliva drooling from their mouths. When one of the dogs spotted Andy, he immediately lunged at the window, in attack mode. Startled, Andy jumped back and asked the homeowner, "Are you sure you can control those things?"

"Yes, sir. Just give them to me one at a time," the owner replied.

Andy said, "OK, I'll crack the door open, and you reach in and grab hold of one. Then, pull the dog out, and I'll close the door behind him, but do not let that dog loose. I ain't getting bit! Understand?" The owner nodded his head in agreement.

Flores consented to his approval with a slight nod as he reached for the doorknob. The door was badly damaged from being kicked in, so Andy had to use his shoulder to force it open, and the dogs went wild, running around in circles and snapping at each other. The narrow opening was wide enough to allow the owner to reach in. The owner gingerly grabbed one of them by the collar and pulled it out the door. Andy kept his legs arched back far enough for the dog to pass, and the owner proceeded to walk his dog toward the sidewalk. Right behind the first dog, Andy quickly shut the door. The second dog growled and barked. The homeowner took the dog to his neighbor's house and secured him in a bedroom.

Andy radioed the window team, "Is the suspect still on the bed?"

"Yes, no movement yet," they confirmed. The homeowner quickly returned and extracted the second dog, and Andy exhaled a deep breath watching the massive beast walk away with his owner.

Sergeant Flores advised Andy, "I'm gonna put together an arrest team. Stand by." Andy agreed. Now that the dogs were no longer part of the problem, he relaxed. Flores returned with Paul Kandi and Robert Richer.

"Andy, you keep lethal protection, and I'll have the taser. We're gonna ease into the bedroom, and I'll wake him. Then we'll roll him off the bed and cuff him. Got it?"

"Roger that, Sarg," Andy replied. Andy entered the home and moved over to the bedroom door while Paul and Robert searched the rest of the house to ensure it was clear. They quickly returned and lined up at the bedroom door. Andy radioed the window team about the suspect, "No movement. Occasionally, we hear him snore. It's clear. We're about to enter."

Slowly, he eased open the door and spotted the suspect lying on his back with one leg on the bed and one partially off the side. He scanned the room for weapons as he listened to the labored breathing of the intruder. The team quietly eased around both sides of the bed as they prepared to wake him. Once they were in position, Flores reached down and nudged the suspect's leg. He didn't wake up at first, so Flores shook his leg and said, "HEY, POLICE OFFICERS! WAKE UP!"

The suspect awakened to four men in black standing over him, and he screamed in terror. Paul and Robert grabbed each arm, and the fight was on. They quickly overwhelmed him to the floor, and he was cuffed. The suspect flailed and screamed as if aliens were attacking him. When Flores searched his pockets for a weapon, he only found a wallet. Inside, he noticed the address on the driver's license was just a few doors down the same street. Apparently, this guy was high on something, hallucinating all sorts of strange images as he kept screaming wildly.

They dragged the intruder outside and turned the house over to patrol. Once the equipment was picked up, they headed back to the office to finish their workday. Later, the Captain received a call from the detectives explaining what led to the incident at the scene. The man had used PCP and tried to make it home. In his intoxicated state, he accidentally went to the wrong house and tried to use his key. He got frustrated and kicked in the front door when his key wouldn't work. That's when the homeowner's dogs attacked him. He fought back until he got to the bedroom, where he shut the door and escaped the animals. Then, he laid down on the bed and passed out until the team was standing over him. There's no telling what was going through his mind when he saw four guys in helmets and tactical vests staring down at him. It must have been the worst trip of this guy's life, and he was still paying the price. He was sitting in jail with both arms bandaged from canine lacerations and booked on a felony charge of forced entry into a habitation.

Their First Test

The team was transitioning again, which happened about every three to four years, but this was a massive shift. The personnel changes took place over several months but were noticeable, nonetheless. The grind of being on call 24/7 and the physical demands of everyday training eventually took their toll. However, supervisors didn't change as frequently. Keeping someone at the helm with experience created a necessary consistency of operation; however, there was a new Captain and two new sergeants this time. As a result, three Team Leader positions opened up, and several guys put their names in for consideration, including Andy. An opportunity for new leadership, new energy, and fresh ideas was undoubtedly what Andy hoped to bring.

Supervision interviewed the candidates and chose Andy as their first pick. When his name was announced at roll call, it was one of the proudest moments of his career. Making Team Leader was his goal from the first day he met Billy Clark. He hoped to measure up and become the leader others admired. Within a few months, Gilbert Reyna and Paul Kandi were also assigned Team Leader positions, and a new generation of leaders was born. Even though they were young and still learning, they were eager to make a difference.

These young TLs were first tested during a hostage situation in a second-story apartment in southwest Houston. What started as a family disturbance quickly escalated into a man taking a young girl hostage. After the girl's mother ended their relationship, he threatened to kill the girl and himself. Patrol had the apartment surrounded and requested SWAT, and within 45 minutes of arriving, SWAT officers took control.

Andy was designated the perimeter TL, and because suspects had tried to tunnel through sheetrock walls to escape in the past, he placed team members in adjoining apartments on each side of the objective.

Negotiators had the suspect on the phone, trying to coax him out, but he was highly agitated and threatening to take the innocent girl's life. The only phone in the apartment was wall-mounted in the kitchen, and the cord extended about 6-feet. Therefore, if he was on the phone, he had to be in the kitchen.

Paul Kandi hurriedly prepared his team for all possible scenarios as the assigned react TL. Gilbert Reyna was spearheading the entry position, which provided him the luxury of studying the floorplans of adjoining apartments. He realized the neighboring apartments mirrored one another. What if they created an alternate entry point into the suspect's apartment by tunneling through the bedroom closet? Having another way in was advantageous, and the suspect's bedroom was as far away from the kitchen as possible. Gilbert planned to quietly remove the sheetrock from each side of the wall while the negotiators continued talking to the suspect. When he bounced the idea off the command staff, the new Captain was apprehensive the suspect might hear them and harm the hostage. After Gilbert's continued assurances, the Captain relented but instructed him not to tunnel completely through the wall, at least not yet.

Before becoming a police officer, Gilbert worked construction and was experienced hanging sheetrock. If they took their time and with the right tools, he knew that they could dismantle a sheetrock wall with very little noise. They only needed carpet knives, boxcutters, and water tubes to dissolve the chalk in the drywall as they worked. Gilbert gathered the necessary equipment and picked up a ballistic shield as a precaution just in case the suspect heard them and started shooting. He gently leaned the shield against the wall and crouched behind it to begin the arduous process.

Once Andy finished setting the perimeter, he collected the fiber optic scope from CP and headed inside to help Gilbert. The negotiators had the suspect on the phone, so the time was right. Slowly, Gilbert bore a small hole into the sheetrock with a hand-cranked auger. In the distance, they heard the suspect's muffled voice yelling as Gilbert slowly turned the drill bit, occasionally stopping to squirt water in the hole. Within a few minutes, a hole was drilled through both sides of the wall, and they were ready to insert the scope.

Andy fed the fiber optic wand through the hole as Gilbert leaned back to look through the scope. Gilbert turned the scope from side to side, straining to focus the camera lens. Abruptly, he flinched backward. "She's there!" Gilbert whispered.

"Where?"

"Right there on the other side of this wall," Gilbert whispered and empathically pointed.

"What? Are you sure?" Andy whispered.

Gilbert stood up and motioned for Andy to step out of the closet so they could talk without whispering.

"What did you see?" Andy asked.

"She's right there on the other side of the wall," Gilbert replied. "I saw her move. I think she's tied up or something."

"Holy shit! Can we get her out?"

"I don't know, maybe!" Gilbert answered as he keyed his radio to tell the CP what he had seen.

The Captain was nervous about trying something that risky, especially with two untested TLs. Reluctantly, he advised Gilbert to cut a larger hole on their side of the wall, but he didn't want them going through the other side. So, Andy and Gilbert started back in, cutting a space large enough to crawl through. Next, they removed their side of the sheetrock and pulled out the insulation. Now only one piece of sheetrock separated them from the hostage and her freedom.

Negotiations were getting nowhere, and the suspect became increasingly hostile over time. "I'll kill that little bitch, and there ain't nothing you can do about it," the man raged.

In case things went south, Andy kept his rifle at the ready. If necessary, he planned to punch his barrel through the remaining sheetrock wall creating a port to defend the hostage. Although it wasn't a great option, at least he had plan B. Gilbert took an agonizing 20 minutes to prep the sheetrock for removal. He had cut through the chalk of the drywall, but not the paper lining, just in case the suspect walked into the closet. Finally, the Captain, frustrated with negotiations, decided to go with Gilbert's option. Gilbert smugly grinned at Andy when he got the go-ahead because he knew they could do this.

"I'll cut the rest of the way through and ease the sheetrock down. You hold coverage on the door in case he hears us. I'll reach in and pull her out, and then you can move the shield over the hole and hold cover."

Andy nodded and said, "Got it!"

Gilbert walked out to brief Paul on the plan as Andy returned to his cover position. Andy nervously sat in the dark closet, looking at the blank wall, knowing the young girl's life depended on a flawless operation. He wondered, 'What if she freaks and doesn't want to go with us?' 'What if he hears us and a gunfight ensues?' 'What if we can't get her through the opening?' All of it was too much to worry about, so he focused on the job at hand.

Gilbert returned with Paul and tapped Andy on the shoulder as he whispered, "OK, here goes nothing." Then, down on his knees, he used a boxcutter to carefully cut the thin paper lining holding the wall in place. The wall released within a few seconds, and Gilbert slowly eased it down to the carpeted floor. Now, the suspect's voice was loud and clear. Gilbert peered inside, instantly making eye contact with the young hostage. Even though she was bound and gagged, Gilbert lifted his index finger to his lips, signaling her to remain quiet.

Gilbert was halfway through the opening when he reached out and gently took hold of the young girl's arm. Instinctually, she knew they were there to help and didn't resist. He pulled her toward the opening, but with her arms bound behind her, she wouldn't fit. Andy wondered what was taking so long, but he didn't have the luxury of looking down as he focused on covering the doorway.

Gilbert pulled a knife from his vest, cut the bindings around her hands, and gently nudged her through the opening in the wall, handing her off to Paul. Paul rushed her out of the apartment and down the stairs to the awaiting paramedics for a medical evaluation.

Andy laid the ballistic shield sideways, covering the hole, and posted his rifle over the top. He took a deep breath, trying to calm himself, but he wanted to scream for joy. Without the suspect having any clue, they managed to pull off a hostage rescue. She was safe, and the only question now was what the suspect would do when he found out.

The suspect was still dangling his leverage when the time came to break the news to him. The negotiator had been biding time, waiting for the most opportune moment to tell him.

"Listen to me motherfucker! I'll kill that bitch!"

"You ain't killing no one," the negotiator interrupted.

Shocked at that unexpected response, the suspect momentarily paused and then doubled down, "OH YEAH, SO YOU DON'T THINK I'LL DO IT?"

"YOU AIN'T KILLING NO ONE BECAUSE YOU DON'T EVEN HAVE HER ANYMORE; WE DO!"

The phone dropped to the kitchen counter. Hurried footsteps headed in Andy's direction, and the suspect appeared in the doorway. The suspect looked down at the space where his hostage once was and then spotted the hole in the sheetrock wall. In its place stood a black ballistic shield with 'POLICE' written in bold white letters. He spotted the end of Andy's rifle just over the top of the shield and gasped as he jumped back out of view. Andy smiled as he listened to the suspect scurrying back to the kitchen like a scared rabbit.

The man picked up the phone, and his tone completely changed, "OK, I want to give up. I'm coming out. Don't shoot!"

They gave him specific instructions on how to surrender, and Paul's team took him into custody without further incident. The scene was turned over to patrol and homicide detectives as the perimeter team started picking up their equipment.

Andy walked toward his car to stow his gear and spotted Paul and Gilbert, high-fiving, relishing in their accomplishment. A special moment because their hard work and training led to this successful mission. There would be many more to come in their young careers, and unfortunately, some would not end so well.

Billy Jack

For Southeast Texas, the weather was freezing, and Andy wasn't dressed for it. Driving home from a long cold day of training at the range, Andy blasted the car heater to warm up. When the dispatcher radioed, requesting any SWAT unit on the air to respond, his heart sank. His hopes of making it to the house for a hot shower and some chow weren't going to happen.

Sergeant Russell answered the radio call while Andy slowed down, looking for the next exit off the freeway. The dispatcher reported a man was threatening suicide at a sporting goods store on the Gulf Freeway. Patrol evacuated the employees and customers, but the man was still inside, armed with a rifle. "That's clear. We'll be en route," Russell responded. Exhausted and a little disappointed, Andy knew his day wasn't over.

Within 15 minutes, he pulled into the store parking lot alongside Jerry Gieger. Jerry was one of the newer guys on the team. He was tall and lean, and his perfectly groomed head of hair earned him the nickname Ken Doll, after the male figure in the Barbie collection. As one of the newest additions, Jerry was eager to contribute and constantly proposed new ideas. But unfortunately, most were just a little out of the norm to be accepted right away.

As the first Team Leader on the scene, Andy directed Jerry to follow him, and they entered the store. A patrol supervisor caught Andy up on the specifics. The suspect was said to be a suicidal Vietnam veteran who was sitting at the back of the store near the gun counter. Initially, the suspect had asked a retail associate to look at a rifle and ammunition. The associate placed the items on the counter, and the desperate man grabbed the weapon and quickly loaded it. Then, erratically, he pointed the gun at the clerk and ordered everyone out of the store. "I'm going to die today, and unless you want to come with me, you should get the fuck out of here," the veteran screamed to the store patrons, wildly waving the rifle.

Andy was given a solid description of the suspect and headed further into the store to get a fix on his location. At the end of one of the aisles, he spotted two patrol officers, so he and Jerry soundlessly moved toward them. The officers pointed at the suspect's leg; the man was sitting motionlessly. Andy thanked the officers and directed them back toward the front of the building.

Taking a moment to look around the store, the surveillance mirror near the ceiling caught his attention. Andy strained his eyes, trying to focus on the reflection of the suspect. The butt of the weapon was on the floor between his legs, the barrel resting on his chest, with the rifle to his throat. His elbows were leaning on his knees with his hands folded behind his head. Andy radioed he had a visual of the suspect. Russell replied that he was on his way as more teammates entered the store and found positions of containment.

Jerry tugged on Andy's arm and whispered, "We can take this guy." Andy shook his head no, "Just hold what you got until Russell gets here." Jerry whispered again, "I mean, he's not looking around. I'm not even sure he's awake. We can sneak down and get close enough to pop him with a taser."

In principle, Andy agreed, especially now that they had the latest generation of tasers. They were more powerful and incredibly reliable. The more he thought about it, the more he liked the idea. The only stipulation is they would have to get within 21-feet of the suspect to be within range for the darts.

Sergeant Russell carefully walked up behind Andy and asked, "What you got, Andy?" He quickly summarized Jerry's idea, and the concept resonated with Russell too. "Let me go to the CP and explain what you guys have," he whispered. "Then, I'll see if they'll sign off on it." Andy smiled as he watched Russell walk away.

Much to his surprise, Russell radioed approval for the plan, but first, they wanted to give the negotiators a chance to communicate with the suspect. If that failed, the constant noise over the loudspeakers would help mask their movement. "Roger that. Standing by," whispered Andy.

Jerry smiled, "See? We can do this!"

Andy nodded in agreement, although he didn't particularly care for the idea of getting close to a suicidal man with a rifle.

Negotiators tried voice contact over a loudspeaker for the next 20 minutes, but the suspect never budged. He didn't even look up. Was he asleep? Or waiting to lure someone close enough for an ambush? Andy had no way of knowing for sure. Finally, Russell radioed, "Andy, you are clear to move forward."

"Roger that, moving now," Andy quietly responded.

As Jerry grabbed his arm, he stood up, "Let's take off our boots." Andy was puzzled, so Jerry continued, "If we are barefoot, he won't hear our footsteps."

Astonished, Andy watched Jerry take off his boots and then his socks. It was all very reminiscent of the famous movie *Billy Jack*. The star was former military special forces and skilled in martial arts. Before kicking anyone's ass, he always took his boots off first. It was pretty logical if you thought about it. Even though it was another one of Jerry's edgier ideas, it could work, so Andy followed suit and took his boots off.

Barefoot, they quietly moved over one aisle to make their way toward the suspect. Jerry was crouched with his rifle pointed forward as they eased toward the gun display full of pistols. Behind the cabinet was an endless array of rifles on the wall. If he intended to shoot up the place, this guy had access to any weapon he wanted. Andy was convinced the man just wanted to kill himself, and he was trying to get the nerve to do it.

They leaned around the corner at the end of the aisle and spotted the suspect's feet in unison. They bent a little further forward and followed his legs up to his torso. Andy switched on the laser aiming device equipped with the taser, and the suspect spotted it. Slowly, he turned, looked at them, and smiled, anticipating an end to his agony.

Andy squeezed the trigger, and the weapon fired, shooting two darts into the suspect's upper body. You could hear the constant clicking from the electrical impulses generated by the device. The man's legs lurched straight out, jerking violently from the shockwaves pulsating through his body. Jerry and Andy sprang forward, disarmed him, and cuffed him to take advantage of his incapacitation.

The despondent man began to cry and mumbled between sobs, "I just want to die." They pulled him to his feet and started walking him toward the front of the store. His head was downcast in shame. As they turned him over to patrol, Andy couldn't help but feel sad for him.

Sergeant Russell was speaking with the patrol supervisors when he noticed Andy's bare feet. He looked up and asked, "What the hell?"

"Don't ask Sarg," Andy answered as he and Jerry walked back to collect their boots.

On the ride home, Andy felt a sense of satisfaction thinking back on how they handled the troubling situation. They saved the man's life, which felt fantastic, but he was most proud of how they accomplished it. He was looking forward to sharing the story with Terri over dinner and a couple of stiff drinks. Plus, he couldn't wait for the critique the next day.

Sergeant Russell began the critique of the previous day's incident and then tossed the debrief to Andy for an explanation of the arrest. Andy detailed how they found their position and Jerry's plan to taser the suspect. Having some fun, Andy pointed at Jerry and said, "So, then I turned around and saw Billy Jack here, taking off his boots." The entire team burst into laughter, and Jerry just smiled.

Once again, it was an unconventional idea, but a good one, nonetheless. The mission got a stamp of approval, and Andy was building confidence with the supervision as a TL capable of getting the job done.

Release the Hound

With another opening on the team, Andy talked his old buddy, Donnie Parker, into trying out. During the selection process, Donnie was a natural and easy choice. He and another seasoned guy, John Marvin, were assigned to Andy's team, and together they made a great point and cover. Donnie was taller, so it was natural for him to work behind John in the cover position. Once they trained together, they reminded Andy of how well he and Joe Vargas worked together back in the day.

Donnie was an avid scuba diver who often traveled to Cozumel for weekend get-aways. Sergeant Russell also loved to dive and would sometimes tag along. Practically a local, Donnie knew his way around the tropical island and all of the best diving spots. They would even manage to sneak in a night dive during a quick two-day trip. While on their travels, Russell was notorious for eating anything and everything. He was fearless when trying the food, even from sketchy street vendors selling who knows what. And sometimes, there was a price to pay for his adventures. It wasn't unusual for Russell to come back with what they commonly called Montezuma's revenge. The symptoms consisted of a nasty case of diarrhea for a few days, which sometimes required a trip to the doctor. But that didn't stop him, and on this trip, he was just as daring. To Donnie's amazement, Russell still ate and drank everything in sight.

As they landed back in Houston, Russell's stomach was already beginning to cramp and rumble in discomfort. While waiting for their luggage in baggage claim, Russell made a beeline straight to the restroom. Donnie laughed, grabbed their bags off the carousel, and stood near the exit.

Finally, Russell caught up to him and smiled. "Do you think that street taco was a good idea?" asked Donnie.

"Probably not, but damn, it was good!" Russell replied. They laughed and picked up their luggage for the short walk to the parking garage.

The following day Russell arrived at work, still suffering from Montezuma's revenge and all its glory. "Are you gonna make it, Sarg?" Andy asked.

"Yeah, but I think it's gonna require a trip to the doctor. I have an appointment this afternoon," Russell replied.

"Why don't you just take the rest of the day off?" Andy asked.

"I would, but we're shorthanded today, so I better hang around."

The team had just finished a late breakfast after their morning workout when a call came in about a barricaded suspect in a video parlor on Westheimer. The area was known for sex-oriented businesses, and video parlors were constantly robbed. However, the owner activated a silent hold-up alarm this time, and patrol arrived before the suspect left. After an exchange of gunfire, the suspect retreated into the business. Unfortunately, patrol didn't get the rear exit covered quickly enough, and when they finally did, they discovered the back door wide open. The guy may have escaped, but no one knew for sure, so they requested SWAT to come out and search.

Upon arrival, Russell commented, "We're not staying here long. He's probably not even in there. So, get your team together, and let's conduct a quick search so we can turn this over to the detectives. The Homicide boys are already here."

"Roger that, Sarg," Andy replied. Russell clearly wasn't feeling well. "I'd like to take Mondo with us if you guys are OK with that?" Andy asked.

"Sure, let me know when you're ready."

Mondo was the nickname of the K9 handler SWAT had been working with. Django was his canine companion, and the team worked well with the duo. Considering the building was more than likely empty, now was the perfect opportunity for some additional training time.

"Grab your gear and meet me at the front door," Andy instructed John and Donnie. Within a few minutes, Andy radioed the CP they were ready. After an awkward silence, Russell finally responded, "That's clear. Stand by. I'll be right there."

Several minutes went by as everyone wondered what the hold-up was, and then Russell came walking out of a nearby business tightening his belt. Another round of diarrhea forced him to find a public restroom. He was suffering, but he refused to give in; that just wasn't in his nature.

"Hey Andy, I want to follow you guys in and watch the dog work, if that's OK," Russell asked.

Andy didn't have a problem with it; Russell was more like one of the guys than a supervisor. "Sure, thing." Andy turned and motioned his team to proceed. They entered the building and quickly cleared the lobby area while Django worked ahead of them. Mondo commanded Django to search a room and then pulled him back to allow Donnie and John to verify it was clear.

Next, they entered a maze of narrow hallways with rooms on both sides that wound through the rest of the building. Each room was essentially a tiny booth containing a single chair with a video screen built into the wall. Customers paid to sit in a private room and watch pornographic videos, and God knows what else. The place was nasty, and Andy wanted out of there as soon as possible.

After clearing one hallway of booths, Russell signaled Andy to hold up. He looked back, baffled until he realized Russell was having another attack. No restrooms were located in that part of the building, but Russell had to go NOW! It was going to happen somewhere, and Russell sure as hell wouldn't let it happen in his pants.

He backed into one of the booths and yanked down his pants without a second to spare. A God-awful sound like the bowels of a sick animal echoed through that part of the building. Andy and his team looked at each other, snickering. Of course, everyone knew what he was doing, and it was hilarious until the stench hit them. The noxious odor permeated the hall, and Russell walked out of the booth, buckling his belt. Andy shook his head in disgust and disbelief, and Russell just shrugged his shoulders.

Andy motioned to resume the search. He wanted to immediately get the hell out of that part of the building. They continued working one hallway after another, searching every booth. Some of the doors to the stalls were open, some closed, but Django didn't care. He sniffed each one, entering each open door as he searched.

Andy figured the building was empty by the last hallway when they sent Django down for one last run. He quickly returned without alerting, so Andy nodded for John to check again.

The last door was closed, so John reached out and turned the latch for the door to swing open. As John leaned around behind a shield, he flinched when he spotted something. Then, abruptly, he stepped back and signaled that he could see the suspect. Andy motioned for them to return as he glanced at Mondo. "What the fuck?" Andy whispered in an accusing tone.

"I don't know?" Mondo answered in a puzzled voice. They glanced down at Django like they couldn't believe he missed the guy. Django sat there looking back at them, eager to please.

Once John and Donnie were back, Andy asked, "What did you see?"

John answered, "I saw his feet; he's in that last booth."

"OK, I'll make voice contact." Andy said as he yelled out, "YOU IN THE BOOTH! WE SEE YOU! SHOW US YOUR HANDS NOW! SLOWLY PUT YOUR EMPTY HANDS OUT WHERE WE CAN SEE THEM!" There was no reply. They waited for a few seconds, and then Andy yelled, "SHOW US YOUR EMPTY HANDS NOW OR I'LL SEND THE DOG!" There was no reply. Andy whispered, "Do you think he's alive?" John shrugged his shoulders.

Andy looked back at Mondo and whispered, "I'd like to send Django down there again now that the door is open. Are you OK with that?"

"Sure," Mondo replied.

Andy laid his hand back on Mondo's shoulder, emphasizing, "If he still has a gun, he might shoot your dog. Are you sure?"

Mondo looked down at Django's eager eyes and then at Andy, saying, "He knew the job was dangerous when he took it!"

Andy chuckled and said, "OK!" He looked back at Russell, who gave his thumbs up of approval, so he patted Mondo on the shoulder and whispered, "Release the hound."

Django started back down the narrow hallway, methodically sniffing at each door. He seemed relaxed because he had already searched these booths, but he was startled with surprise as he reached the last one. Then, without hesitation, he leaped into the booth and out of view. From the hallway, they could only see Django's tail. From inside the booth came the growling and snarling sounds of the dog mauling someone.

Not a single scream was heard as they listened to Django chewing someone's ass. Every time Andy witnessed a K9 bite a suspect in the past, there was always a lot of screaming involved. The pain of a dog's locked jaw and ripping flesh is excruciating, so he wondered if the man was dead.

Django started to drag the man out of the booth, so Andy yelled, "SHOW US YOUR HANDS, AND WE'LL CALL OFF THE DOG!" But there was no reply. Instead, they spotted a boot and then part of the leg that Django had his teeth clamped into as he lurched backward. Both hands slowly came into view as Django continued tugging. Finally, the suspect's hands were open, and he turned toward the team in surrender. Even as his terrified face appeared, he didn't seem worried about the dog.

Andy tapped John to move forward and take him into custody. They didn't waste any time cuffing the suspect, and Mondo removed Django. The man's leg was mauled to the bone, and he never once screamed. He must have understood that he could survive a dog bite but not multiple rifle rounds.

As they walked the suspect out of the building and turned him over to patrol, the detectives met Russell at the front door. "Can we start our investigation now?" one of the detectives inquired, tired of waiting.

"Sure! It's all yours. We're just grabbing our gear," Russell replied.

The detective walked into the lobby and took a whiff, "What the fuck is that smell?"

"I think the asshole took a shit somewhere," Russell casually replied.

"Oh my God!" the detective replied. "How did you guys work in here with that stench?"

"Well, it's better than tear gas," Russell joked with a smile.

The detective walked down to one of the booths and opened the door to discover a massive pile of diarrhea and exclaimed, "OH MY GOD! THAT SICK MOTHERFUCKER!" Russell grinned, walking out, listening to the detectives curse the suspect.

SEVENTEEN

Brass Protects Brass

While Andy was pouring his first cup of coffee, Sergeant Russell's voice announced over the PA, "Andy, report to the Sergeant's office." He thought it was rather unusual to be needed this early in the morning as he stirred his cup and headed toward Russell's office.

"Morning Sarg," Andy greeted, walking in.

"Hey Andy, morning," replied Russell.

"What's up?"

"Well," Russell took a deep breath and paused, thinking about how to phrase this lightly, "You know the new guy, Scott?" Andy nodded and sipped his coffee. "Well, he hasn't been working out that well on Reyna's team, and we're hoping that a change of pace might be what he needs. Are you up to taking him under your wing?"

"Sure, Sarg, whatever you need. What's his major malfunction?"

"We're not sure. That's what we want you to find out. He's sharp and has the physical skills, but he can't seem to put it all together."

"Got it. I'll see what I can do," Andy replied helpfully.

"Thanks, Andy. I'll let Scott know to report to your team today."

Andy's rearguard was recently promoted and moved onto another opportunity, so he had an opening. Scott was a nice enough guy, so hopefully, he could get him up to speed.

Later that morning, as Andy was finishing his training report, Scott walked in, "Looks like you drew the black bean with me, Andy."

"Not at all, Scott. Welcome aboard." Andy replied, stood up, and shook hands to welcome him officially. They sat down and had a productive conversation as Andy laid out how he ran the team and his expectations. The meeting went smoothly and confirmed to Andy that Scott merely needed more time to come into his own.

Andy was in for another surprise that day when he heard Hurley's name spread around the building. Rumor had it; that he was selected as the new lieutenant over the Negotiators. The position had been open for a month, and several applicants had been interviewed. The last time Andy heard about Hurley, he was working in the Records Division. Andy considered sharing his insights on Hurley with the Captain, but he presumed it wouldn't matter. Not to mention, the Captain may not appreciate a complaint from an officer on a fellow supervisor. So, he kept his mouth shut and hoped for the best.

Sure enough, his worst fear was actualized when Hurley's name was posted on the bulletin board as the new Lieutenant of the Hostage Negotiation Team. Andy was livid, although there wasn't anything he could do about it now. To lay out the training schedule for the next month, Andy called a team meeting in his office. John and Donnie warmly welcomed Scott, and by the end of the meeting, they appeared to have the foundation of a good foursome.

As a closing note, Andy earnestly added, "Just one more thing, guys. This Hurley guy...the new Lieutenant, don't trust him."

"What's the deal with him?" Donnie asked.

"Let's just say we have a history," replied Andy. After an uncomfortably awkward silence, Andy stood up and looked at his watch, "Hey, it's 4 o'clock! Let's go have a beer to welcome Scott to the team!" Everyone agreed and headed to the icehouse bar down the street from the office, where on occasion, they held their after-work team meetings.

A couple of beers deep, the guys tried to get Andy to loosen up and elaborate on Hurley, but he stuck to his script, "We just have a history that goes back to my Academy days, and I have never liked him." With places to go, everyone finished their beers, said their goodbyes, and left the bar. Driving down Dallas Street, Andy spotted a liquor store and pulled in to buy a bottle of Jack Daniels for the drive home. The long commute took 45 minutes, and he needed something more substantial to calm his nerves and get his mind off Hurley. Then he bought a fountain drink, drove around to the back of the convenience store, and poured a stiff one. With his first sip, his tensions eased. Then he pulled onto Louisiana Street for the long drive home.

Terri wasn't home yet when Andy pulled into the driveway. He poured himself another drink and waited on the front porch. Andy never sat on the front porch unless he wanted to talk, so she knew something was bothering him the moment she pulled in. Terri unpacked her school stuff and sat beside him to hear all about it. The venting helped, and Terri was an excellent listener, but the issue wouldn't miraculously disappear. It was something that Andy would have to deal with, and only time would tell how it would turn out.

Even though he didn't sleep much that night, that didn't stop him from being punctual the next morning. To beat the traffic, he preferred to arrive at work early. Then with the jumpstart to his day, he could knock out his paperwork over a cup of coffee. Having the time to focus on the day ahead was good, and he wanted to do right by Scott. Andy was experienced in training new guys and was prepared to give it his all.

Walking down the hall to grab his second cup of coffee, Andy ran into Hurley. The moment he had been dreading, and sure enough, Hurley still had the same shit-eating grin. Hurley held his hand out to shake, and instinctually, Andy extended his but didn't smile back. Andy was repulsed by having Hurley's hand in his, but it happened so fast that he was shaking hands before he knew it.

Emotionless, Andy looked at Hurley. Then Hurley broke the silence, "Hey Andy, look, I know we've had issues in the past, but I want to start fresh. Let bygones be bygones. What do you say?"

Andy nodded and matter-of-factly replied, "Sure," then pulled his hand back and walked past Hurley without another word. Just then, he thought of Hurley's old saying, 'What goes around, comes around,' and sure enough, it was coming around again.

As Hurley watched Andy walk away, he knew that he wouldn't let it go. Even though Hurley didn't have authority over him, he did have rank, he was a lieutenant, and Andy wasn't. If things came to a head, he would have the upper hand with the Captain because 'Brass Protects Brass.' The saying originated from the brass-colored badges supervisors wore and how they protectively banded together. Confidently, Hurley smiled and walked away.

The week was flying by, and Scott's training was going exceedingly well. As anticipated, he completed everything expected of him. As a bonus, he got along with John and Donnie. The team was coming together as a cohesive unit, and Andy hoped supervision recognized it. To avoid running into Hurley, Andy tried to stay out of the office as much as possible, so he called Sergeant Russell and told him Scott was good to go. Russell thanked him for his efforts and agreed to put his team into the rotation for the next call-up.

The next afternoon, Andy was cleaning his equipment in the office parking lot after a long training day. Usually, he pulled into the covered garage area of the building but knowing he might see Hurley there, he stayed outside instead.

His equipment was scattered on the pavement surrounding his trunk when his pager went off. 'Well, SHIT!' Andy thought to himself. There was a hostage situation in the Allen Parkway Tower office building. His response time would be quick with the location right down the street, but he needed at least 10 minutes to put his gear back together.

Soon he was pulling out of the parking lot and headed toward Allen Parkway, listening to the radio chatter from the units on the scene. The jilted lover of a female employee on the 24th floor had taken her hostage with a pistol. He held her inside a small conference room and threatened to kill her and anyone who tried to rescue her.

John Marvin was on vacation, so Andy would move Donnie up to the point position, and Scott would be his cover. The move slightly troubled him because Scott was untested, but there was no reason not to, and hopefully, he was ready.

As he stepped off the elevator of the 24th floor, Sergeant Russell yelled, "Andy, take over the React position." Andy would be responsible for an emergency assault. He considered passing it on to another team because of Scott, but he didn't. Instead, he found an office to stage his team directly across the narrow hallway from the hostage. They didn't know if the suspect had barricaded the door at this juncture, so he radioed Donnie to bring some breaching equipment with him on his way up. When Scott arrived on the scene, Andy asked him if he was good with being Donnie's cover today.

"Sure, I got it!" Scott replied without hesitation.

"Good, let's set up here and wait for Donnie."

Andy spotted Steve Noble walking out of the elevator and motioned for him to join them. Once in the room, Andy asked Steve if he had been given an assignment.

"No, I just got here."

"Good," replied Andy. "You'll be my rearguard following behind Donnie and Scott." Andy handed Steve a flash-bang, "Here, you'll need this. If we breach the door, I want you to deploy this banger as soon as the door comes open. Then follow us in. Got it?"

"Roger that," confirmed Steve.

Before coming to SWAT, Steve had been involved in multiple shootings, indicating he could remain steady under pressure, boosting Andy's confidence in his plan.

By the time Donnie arrived with the ram, Andy had obtained a floorplan of the room across the hall. He laid out the drawing for his team, thoroughly planning their entry and handing out detailed assignments. Finally, Andy pointed at Donnie, "OK, I need you to go straight across the room and be our San Diego Chicken!" The nickname was coined for the individual assigned to move across a room to draw the shooter's attention, which created an advantage for everyone to move in and engage.

"The corner fed room contains a long conference table to the right. I'm not sure where the shooter and hostage are. Scott, you hook to the right along this wall," Andy said, pointing at the floorplan. "I'll step in behind you, which should give us a triangle on him. One of us will have a shot, no matter where they are. As soon as you have a clear shot, take it. Don't hesitate. If he has the gun, he dies. Got it?" Donnie and Scott nodded their heads in agreement.

"OK, let's stack up in order and be ready. We could be deployed any second. I'm going to check with the Lieutenant and get the rules of engagement. If anything occurs in my absence, Steve, you step in and take my spot. I'll run back as quickly as I can to help but don't wait on me. Donnie and Scott's routes stay the same. Got it?" Everyone agreed.

Andy quietly stepped out of the small office, leaving the door open to ensure the guys had nothing obstructing their way if they needed to go. Peering at the door across the hall, he knew that the young woman's life depended on how well they did their job. Andy spotted Lieutenant Chesney and motioned for his attention. Chesney was the new SWAT lieutenant who recently transferred from the Internal Affairs Division (IAD). He was friendly enough, but many guys were suspicious of him coming from IAD as a by-the-book type of guy. Based on his previous experience, Chesney wasn't a tactical guy, at least not yet. His concerns aligned more with policy and SOPs than tactics.

"Hey Lieutenant, we are set and ready," Andy said and briefed Chesney on the plan. Chesney was in agreeance and requested Andy explain it again to the Captain. The Captain was on board with it, but he wanted first to get the negotiators' thoughts. 'Why does the Captain care what the negotiators think regarding a tactical plan? Especially now that Hurley was over them,' Andy thought.

"Hurley," the Captain called, motioning Hurley over, "Andy, run the plan down to Lieutenant Hurley."

Andy was in complete disbelief he had to tell Hurley anything, but he didn't have a choice. Hurley looked to Andy, "What you got, Andy?" Reluctantly, Andy reviewed the plan again while the Captain and Lieutenant Chesney stood listening. When he finished, Hurley looked at the Captain and said, "OK, but we have the guy on the phone. The conversation is going well. We shouldn't do anything unless he starts shooting."

Unable to contain himself any longer, Andy blurted out in frustration, "If we hear gunshots, she's dead! He can't miss from that range."

Angerly, Hurley turned back, glaring at Andy, and elevating his voice, "You don't know that!"

The conversation quickly escalated when the Captain was forced to step in, "OK, let's see if we can get some eyes into that room. Can we get some fiber optics in there?"

"I'll check into it," complied Chesney.

"Until then, Andy, we wait for gunshots or my command. Got it?" the Captain sternly ordered.

"Yes, sir," Andy replied, gave Hurley the go-to-hell stare, turned, and walked away. Hurley arrogantly smirked, gloating about winning the argument.

Through a small gap found in the acoustic ceiling tile, Paul Kandi was able to sneak a fiber-optic wand into the room. Now, he had a fisheye view of the oval conference table with the eight surrounding office chairs. He spotted the top of the woman's head, but the suspect was talking on the phone under the table. Andy relayed the Captain's decision to his team when Paul radioed. "Andy, do you want to get a look into the room? I have a fairly good view on my screen."

"Sure thing," Andy replied and hustled back to Paul's position.

"She's right there," Paul said, pointing to the screen. "I think he's under the table from the phone cord trailing underneath it," he theorized.

"Roger that!" Andy replied. "It doesn't look like the door is barricaded."

"Nope. And the maintenance guy told me the doorknob doesn't have a lock."

"Right. Thanks," Andy replied and hurried back to his team. After reviewing the floorplan again, Andy pointed, "She's right about here, and he's under the table. Donnie, you should have a good view of him as you sweep across the room but stay low to see beneath the table. Do you want to go with a rifle or your pistol?"

"I think I'll go with my pistol. At that range, it shouldn't matter, and I'm more flexible with my handgun."

"Cool! That's your call." Andy turned to Scott, "How about you?"

Apprehensively, Scott chose, "I'll go with a pistol too."

"Good, are you OK?" Andy conferred with Scott. Scott gave a reassuring nod and a thumbs-up. Andy continued, "If we hear gunshots, we bang before entering, right?"

"Right," Steve responded.

"If we hear shots, she's probably already dead, so we might as well give ourselves an advantage," Andy said, disgruntled. "OK, let's get in order and try to relax. We may be here a while."

The negotiations dragged on, and occasionally, Andy heard the hostile man's voice through the thin walls. A few times, the woman desperately pleaded with her captor. The voices were getting louder and more frequent; this wasn't positive. Andy knew a surprise entry was her best hope, but Hurley had the Captain's ear. The Captain trusted negotiating with a man who came there to die and take her with him. To Andy, it was unfathomable. Experience dictated this could easily result in a murder and then a suicide.

Again, voices in the room elevated, and the woman started screaming, terrified, "No, NO!" A gunshot rang out, and Andy's worst fear came to fruition. Instantly, the team sprang forward and moved across the hall. Donnie didn't even glance back, reaching for the doorknob. Steve moved to the other side of the door and pulled the pin on the flash-bang. Donnie turned the knob and pushed the door open, and Steve proceeded to toss the bang in the room. Even though it was all happening in the blink of an eye, everything was going precisely as planned. After the flash-bang exploded, Donnie launched into the room at breakneck speed. Behind him, Scott stepped through the threshold and hesitated. Andy pushed him and yelled, "GO!"

Scott shouted back, "I CAN'T SEE!" There was smoke from the flash-bang, but nothing more than they practiced with during training. Then, hearing gunfire, Andy knew Donnie was in a gunfight and needed backup. Peering over Scott's shoulder, he saw Donnie moving across the room with his pistol extended, but Scott was frozen in place. With Scott of no use, he shoved him out of the way and took his route into the room. Andy turned right along the wall and saw the woman's legs stretched out under the table. The gunfire ceased.

"He's under the table!" yelled Donnie. "I think I got him!"

Andy dropped to his knees to ensure the shooter was down, but he was obviously dead or dying. Donnie yelled, "I got him! Take her!" Andy reached down with one hand and grabbed the woman's legs to pull her out from under the table.

He looked at the woman's face to assess her injuries. Her eyes were open and fixed as she made a gurgling sound, attempting to breathe. Pink frothy blood boiled from her throat; it was coming from her lungs. He assumed she wouldn't survive with severe injuries, but they had to try. "SUSPECTS' DOWN! WE NEED PARAMEDICS!" Andy radioed and jumped to his feet. He grabbed her legs, dragging her lifeless body behind him, heading toward the door and out the threshold.

The paramedics were just down the hallway. They rushed a gurney forward and quickly took over her care. Andy let go and stepped back, attempting to regain his composure. He knew she was dead, and the sight of such a pretty young woman killed when she still had her entire life in front of her made him sick. But, until that gunshot rang out, she had a chance. Unfortunately, her fate was sealed after that.

Andy forced himself back into operational mode, returning to the room. Scott was silently standing to one side. At that point, he was nothing more than a spectator, and when their eyes met, Andy's eyes shot daggers.

On the other side of the table, Donnie watched the suspect for any signs of life. He suffered a gunshot to the head, and blood oozed from his wound. "Did you shoot him in the head?" Andy asked Donnie.

"I'm not sure. I know I fired at least once, but I can't tell you where my round hit. I heard him fire, too; it's possible he shot himself. I'm not sure." Donnie was perplexed, attempting to recall the gritty details.

"No worries," Andy said reassuringly. "Just as long as you are OK."

"I'm good," Donnie answered.

Homicide detectives arrived and requested a brief description of what happened. Andy and Donnie walked them through the scene. Steve and Scott stood by, answering an occasional question directed their way. The autopsy later showed Donnie's round hit the suspect's upper torso and severed his aorta. He was bleeding out when he put the gun in his mouth and pulled the trigger, causing his massive head wound. The coroner ruled the death self-inflicted, although he indicated that Donnie's round would have also been lethal.

The team collected their equipment and headed down the elevator to stow their gear. Donnie gave a blow-by-blow of his recollection during the long elevator ride to the lobby. Andy didn't pay much attention; he was focused on Scott's actions or lack thereof. Specifically, his refusal to enter the room. Andy was confident Scott would stick to the story that he could not see through the smoke, but they both knew it was bullshit. Andy was stewing, and the more he thought about it, the more enraged he became. Scott knew it too and didn't say a word but occasionally glanced over at Andy on the ride down. Andy wouldn't look at him, furious; he just kept his jaws clenched shut. Sometimes it is best not to speak, and he was just as upset with Scott as he was with Hurley.

Andy made his way to the car and dumped his gear in the trunk when Sergeant Russell walked up and asked him if he was alright. Andy paused, then turned and spilled his guts, "No, I'm not OK, Sarg! I want Scott off my team! He's a fuck up!"

"What are you talking about?" Russell asked, surprised at Andy's admission. Andy explained. "OK, I see your point," Russell replied. "But this is not gonna happen now. You guys need to go to Homicide, write your statements, and we'll talk in the morning."

When Russell started to walk away, Andy blurted out, "She never had a chance Sarg."

Russell stopped, pausing for a moment, "I know. He was going to kill her from the start."

Andy interrupted, "No, once Hurley convinced the Captain to wait for a gunshot, her fate was sealed. We could have taken that guy Sarg; at least would have had a fighting chance!"

Russell thought about what Andy said, dropped his head, and, in a low-pitched voice, said, "Yeah, that's not right," then he turned and walked away. Russell was a good man, but he wouldn't win a fight against the Captain or Hurley. He was in the same predicament as Andy.

As soon as Andy could, he called Terri, knowing that she was home from school by now. If she saw the news before he called, she would worry. "Hi, Babe. I just wanted to let you know I'm OK." Terri had heard him say that many times before when shootings were involved. Occasionally the news media ran the story before Andy could call, but he always tried to get there first.

"What's going on?" she asked.

"Watch the news. You'll see, but I wanted you to know that we're all OK. I'll see you as soon as I can."

"OK, drive safe," she replied, hung up the phone, and hurried to turn on the TV.

After writing their statements and speaking with detectives, they discovered the crime scene officer found a bullet embedded in the doorway's threshold. The shooter fired at Donnie upon entry, and Donnie returned fire as he tracked the suspect across the room. Once Donnie's bullet hit the shooter, he decided to finish himself off.

The puzzle pieces fit together, but Andy's mind was elsewhere. First, he needed to have Scott removed from his team before someone lost their life because of his cowardice, and then he planned to find a way to get back at Hurley.

Once they finished, Andy pulled out of the parking lot and headed toward his favorite convenience store. Due to his frequent stops on the way home, the store clerk knew him. When Andy set his fountain drink on the counter, the clerk smiled and said, "No charge." The TV was on, and the clerk was watching the local news. Andy glanced up, and on the screen, he saw himself walking across the parking lot. He appreciated the clerk's token of gratitude.

Andy thanked him and pulled around the back of the store to fix his favorite elixir for the long drive home. On his drive down highway 288, he replayed the events from the scene. Vividly, he saw Donnie move across the room in a fight for his life over Scott's shoulder. He could hear Scott's false cries that he couldn't see, just a lie safeguarding his deficiency. Andy was now well aware of what Scott's problem was. When it counted, and everything was on the line, he was incapable of doing his job.

Andy's thoughts drifted over to Hurley and the battle ahead as he took a few more sips. He had anticipated it as only a matter of time before Hurley became a problem, but it happened much quicker than he expected. Hurley cost a young woman her life or at least a chance at survival. He was pissed Hurley had that kind of influence on the Captain. He wanted to press the argument, but it was a battle he couldn't win, and besides, the Captain would never admit his mistake. Brass Protects Brass.

Innocence Lost

An internal investigation was underway regarding Scott's performance during the Allen Parkway incident. Supervision held private interviews with everyone on Andy's team, trying to get to the bottom of what happened. Scott defended his actions by stating the smoke from the flash-bang temporarily blinded him. Donnie informed the supervisors that he was unaware of what occurred behind him because he was in the middle of exchanging gunfire. Steve witnessed Scott stop in the doorway, but he couldn't see into the room from his position; therefore, he couldn't confirm or deny how thick the smoke was.

Andy acknowledged Scott did well during training but added that he shut down and didn't do his job when it mattered most. Then they proceeded to ask several follow-up questions regarding Scott's development and how to correct the problem, but Andy didn't have an answer.

Following the interviews, the staff considered everyone's statements and called Andy back into the office. The Captain began the conversation, "We think Scott has potential, and maybe we rushed him. We want you to work with him some more. Do you think you can do that?"

"I guess so," replied Andy. "I have no problem working with Scott. I just don't want to make an entry with him. Maybe at some point, but not right now. I'm not ready to trust him."

"Fair enough," the Captain added. "Dismissed." Andy left the room knowing that wasn't exactly what the Captain wanted to hear, but it was a compromise.

The next few days around the office were incredibly uncomfortable. Scott knew Andy didn't believe his story about temporary blindness, and he didn't appreciate being called out to the superiors. Nevertheless, the two tolerated each other and tried to work around their differences. Andy orchestrated multiple training events designed to exploit Scott's weaknesses, but each time Scott performed well. Frustrated, Andy began questioning his judgment. Maybe he had been too tough on him. After all, it wasn't as though he was without fault. He had screwed up operations before; no one's perfect.

Andy drove home, sipping on his signature Jack and Coke. The smooth elixir was becoming a necessity to calm his nerves on every ride home. Somehow, it helped him make sense of the day, and after a few more sips, he felt better. If nothing else, it made the 45-minute trip fly by as he tried to leave his problems at work.

The pager went off about midnight, and Andy jumped up to get ready. Before going to bed each night, he always prepared the coffee pot, so the first thing he did was punch the brew button and then get dressed. By the time he was ready to walk out, there was enough coffee to pour a tall one for the road. The entire routine pissed off Terri because after a couple of hours, the coffee pot turned off, and by the time she got up, the coffee was cold and stale.

While he listened to the police radio, he sped toward Southwest Houston. A Vietnamese gang masterminded a home invasion on a Vietnamese family. After the Vietnam war, a large population of Vietnamese refugees settled on the city's southwest side. Due to experiences in their homeland, they didn't trust the police, and they also didn't trust the banking system after losing everything. This resulted in large sums of cash being hidden inside the homes of many Vietnamese families. If a robbery occurred, they never reported it to law enforcement. The families accepted the loss, moved on, and the gangs exploited these customs.

The victims included an elderly Vietnamese couple residing with three generations of family. It wasn't uncommon for fifteen people to live in a three-bedroom home to reduce expenses. An armed gang forced entry into the house and threatened to kill anyone who resisted. They began restraining each person in the home with tape, and when the roll ran out, they reverted to using phone and extension cords found throughout the house.

Once everyone was secured in the living room, three gang members searched the residence for money and valuables while the gang leader took his time threatening the family. Infuriated by their silence, he started pistol-whipping the family members, one at a time. Even the elderly matriarch, or 'Momason,' wasn't spared the abuse; he violently struck her several times. Soon fellow gang members carried out the collected money and jewelry, laying everything down on the living room floor. Infuriated that he was lied to about the amount of expected valuables, the gang leader beat the victims with greater force. The 12-year-old granddaughter was the only family member spared from the beatings because he had a likeness for her. Once he was satisfied he had taken everything he could, he told the other members to watch the family. Then, he grabbed the small girl by the arm and violently dragged her down the hallway as she screamed and cried. Momason pleaded with the man to leave her alone, but her pleas were ignored. He pulled the girl into the first bedroom and slammed the door.

He stripped the young girl naked and tied both of her hands to the headboard. She thrashed, trying to resist her assailant, but that only angered him further, slapping her. He raped her, and when he was finished, he left her lying there as she quietly sobbed.

The gang was waiting in the living room with their captors when the leader strolled back into the room. As he finished buckling his belt, he made eye contact with the Momason and smiled. She was well aware he had violated her granddaughter, and she could only hope she was still alive. He yelled, "Don't look at me bitch!" in Vietnamese, then walked over and grabbed the old woman by her hair. She screamed in pain as he torqued her head to face him and asked, "Who lives next door, you old whore?" When she replied that she didn't know, he assumed she was lying and demanded, "Tie all these motherfuckers together and let's go next door. If anyone gets up, kill them!" He yanked the older woman by her hair to her feet as she screamed in pain. Then he violently pulled her, stumbling toward the front door. The three remaining gang members busily tied everyone into two groups and threatened to kill them if they attempted to get loose.

The gang leader held his pistol to the older women's head and told her to do precisely as he instructed or he'd shoot her. Terrified, she nodded in understanding, then he shoved her off the porch into the darkness toward the house next door. To gain a glimpse inside his next potential target's home, he nudged the older woman over to a window. The old woman quietly whimpered in pain as he whispered, scolding, "Shut up bitch." Inside the home, the neighbors sat in their living room watching TV. He confirmed his suspicions; they were Vietnamese as well. "You're going to knock on the door and get them to open it, you hear me?" She nodded, and he forced her onto the neighbor's porch, waving behind him for his cohorts to follow.

Reluctantly, the older woman knocked on the door and called out to one of the women living there. After being friends for a long time, she hated the chaos she brought to their doorstep. "OK, coming." Slowly, she cracked the door open, surprised to see her neighbor.

"Hello," she said cheerfully, attempting to mask the panic and pain in her voice. Just then, the gang leader pushed the older woman inside and barged in behind her.

The four gang members quickly dominated the home with the same brutal tactics, tying everyone up and searching for anything of value. The leader relished his power over the newfound captors and how well his plan worked. He continued his brutal threats and demanded compliance, or he would kill everyone.

A family friend arrived to watch a movie, but he immediately heard screaming inside the home when he stepped onto the porch. Sneaking over to the closest window, he peeked in and was stunned to see everyone on the floor with their hands tied behind their backs and a crazed man waving a gun. He quickly and quietly backed away from the house and ran to his car. Since he didn't know anyone in the subdivision he trusted, he decided to drive to the convenience store at the entrance of the subdivision to call the police.

When he turned into the convenience store parking lot, a police vehicle was parked out front. From outside the surrounding glass windows of the store, the family friend spotted a uniformed officer playing a video game inside. He threw his car in park and ran inside for help. Hysterical, the panic-stricken man spilled his guts to the officer about what he witnessed just a few blocks away. "Come with me," demanded the officer, hurrying to his patrol car. The officer radioed the dispatcher he had a potential home invasion in progress and sped into the subdivision with the frightened witness.

As they turned onto the victim's street, the witness pointed and exclaimed, "Right over there, just past that tree!" The officer turned off his headlights and parked his patrol car in the shadows. Then, he firmly advised the man to stay inside the vehicle for his safety, pulled his pistol, and hurried across the lawn. When the officer eased up to the window and peered around the edge, he saw precisely what the witness had described. He snapped back and hurried to his patrol car, confirming the home invasion and radioing all responding units to approach quietly. Last, he requested the dispatcher get SWAT rolling because this could quickly turn into a hostage situation.

Within a few minutes, patrol surrounded the house, but they were still unaware of the victims of the first home invasion. So instead, all efforts were focused on the second home as more officers arrived and quickly took cover positions.

With the influx of officers on the scene, it was only a matter of time before one of the gang members spotted them. One of the gang members saw an officer running along a hedgerow; he screamed out, "COPS!" and panic spread amongst the gang. Leaving their victims tied up, the four of them rushed toward the back of the house to find an escape route. First, they tried to open the back door, but the family had nailed it shut to prevent a burglary. Next, they scurried like rats to a back bedroom and attempted to open a window, but it was also nailed closed. Finally, in a panic, one of the men threw a chair through the window, and the shattering sound of breaking glass echoed throughout the backyard.

Three officers were positioned in the back for containment. However, the yard was completely dark, so all three officers kept their flashlights off for fear of being spotted. Suddenly, one of the suspects jumped headfirst through the window and sprang to his feet. In the darkness, it appeared he had a gun, and all three officers opened fire. The suspect crumbled in a heap to the ground. When the remaining gang members saw their cohort shot by police, they decided not to follow him.

When the hostages heard gunfire, they used that as their opportunity to escape. The officers immediately recognized the victims on the well-lit front porch with their hands still bound behind their backs, stumbling out the door. One of the gang members disguised himself as a victim and ran out with the group. The officers yelled for the escaping family to come to safety as the two remaining gang members scurried around inside, attempting to formulate a new plan.

As the officers gathered the family and attended to their needs, the victims quickly noticed the outsider. "HE'S WITH THEM," one victim yelled, nodding toward the gang member. To deny the allegation, he shook his head, but officers noticed his hands weren't bound, so they grabbed him. He was quickly handcuffed and searched as the family members cursed him for what he did. He dropped his head in shame once he realized the gig was up.

Andy was speeding inbound on Hwy 59 with his emergency lights flashing when an officer yelled over the radio, "Shots fired!" 'This might be over before I even get there,' thought Andy, but he continued driving. A few minutes later, he parked on a side street near the police vehicles and grabbed his gear. As he hurried to the command post, Sergeant Flores called out, "Hey Andy, hang around for a minute. The Captain's here, and he said he might want to use gas. He's gonna want to talk to you."

The Captain had just finished speaking with the patrol supervisors when Andy saw him walking back to the CP. "Morning, Captain," Andy greeted.

"Hey Andy," he replied and got straight to business, "Patrol thinks they have everyone accounted for except maybe two or three hijackers. An older woman among the rescued victims indicated this situation started at her house next door. No one's been in there yet, so I need you to put a team together and verify. We don't think there are any bad guys left but be careful."

"Roger that, Captain," Andy replied. As Donnie and John walked toward the CP, Andy intercepted them, "Hey guys, this way! We're going to check this house next door." Scott was approaching, but Andy looked the other way and walked toward the neighbor's house.

As they paused near the neighbor's front porch, Andy spotted Tony Garcia and waved him over. Even though Tony was assigned to Gilbert's Team, he knew Gilbert wouldn't mind if he borrowed him. Although Tony was one of the smaller guys on the team, it certainly didn't impede him because he was pretty sharp and a good operator.

"What'cha need, Andy?" Tony asked.

"Can you be my rearguard while we check this house?"

"Sure thing," Tony replied, and they stacked up for entry.

The team entered and immediately discovered three people bound and gagged on the floor. They moved past the victims, continuing to search the house. When Andy entered the second doorway, a young girl was lying naked on the bed with her arms tied to the headboard. He couldn't leave her like that, so he slung his rifle and started untying the phone cord. As Andy worked to release her restraints, she sobbed in pain and embarrassment. Calmly and kindly, Andy motioned for her to be quiet and stay put, and she nodded her head in understanding.

The moment they finished clearing the house, they immediately broke formation and moved to the living room to free the victims. Assuming it would be best for the woman in the room to console the young girl, Andy helped her to her feet and guided her to the bedroom. The instant she spotted the girl, she ran to her side. As they sat on the bed crying and comforting one another, Andy left the room to give them some privacy. Then, they turned the house over to waiting Homicide Detectives and headed back to the CP.

The negotiators brought in a translator to announce commands over the loudspeaker in English and Vietnamese. The suspects were repeatedly advised to come out of the house with their hands in the air, but there was no reply. The Captain waved Andy over while he and Hurley discussed their next move. Hurley put his hands on his hips, disgusted the Captain cared what Andy thought.

"Andy, if the commands don't work, we need to clear the house. To my knowledge, I think a couple of suspects remain inside, and they're probably just hiding. What do you think?"

Andy replied, "This has been going for a while now. These guys aren't crazy; they just don't want to go to jail. The safer option would be to use some gas."

"I hate to gas their home," the Captain replied. "They've been through so much already."

Andy nodded, "I agree, but I don't think it will take much. One grenade in the front room should do it."

The Captain considered his options when Hurley intervened, "Captain, give me another hour. I think we can get them out without fucking up the house."

After a few seconds of consideration, the Captain said, "You have 30 minutes." Then, he turned to Andy, "Get a gas team ready and stand by."

"Yes, sir," Andy replied. He walked away thinking how Hurley didn't give a shit about that house or the family. He just didn't want to relinquish control and lose an argument.

Soon, the Captain became restless, and the more he thought about it, the more he wanted this situation over. To Hurley's dismay, he advised Andy to proceed with the gas option. In confirmation, Andy nodded and headed toward the front door with a gas grenade. He could hear the A/C compressor running; therefore, the system would help circulate the gas throughout the house, making his job more manageable.

John cracked the front door open, and Donnie tossed the grenade inside. After bouncing on the floor, the grenade rolled into the living room; then, they heard the familiar pop of the device deploying. John closed the door, and they backed away to watch and wait. Typically, it took several minutes, but to their surprise, the front door flew open within a few seconds, and both suspects stumbled out, coughing and sneezing.

The team moved in and cuffed them face down. The two gang members were incredibly small in stature; they couldn't have been more than 5'6" and maybe 120 lbs soaking wet. 'These are the guys that created all this havoc?' Andy thought to himself. Seeing they were nothing more than little punks infuriated Andy. They jerked the suspects up and walked through the front yard toward the CP. Andy's memory of the young girl on the bed was still hauntingly vivid, and these were the guys. One or all of them defiled a child, and even though he was glad they were caught, it wasn't enough. They deserved street justice for what they did.

Walking through the darkness, Andy spotted some large tree roots extended from a giant oak tree. He couldn't stop seething over the crime these assholes committed. As they stepped over the root, Andy used his leg to whip the feet out from under the suspect he was leading and shoved him to the ground. The suspect slammed his chest first on a large root, and a loud groan erupted from him on impact. Watching this punk trying to catch his breath, Andy felt content. He violently yanked him back to his feet by the handcuffs, "Oh, I'm sorry. Did you trip?" Andy smiled.

They handed the suspects over to awaiting patrol officers, and the Captain walked up behind them, "Good job, guys!"

"Thanks, Captain," replied Andy. From a distance, Hurley stood glaring. Andy smiled at him and walked off toward his vehicle to dump his gear.

Paul Kandi's Team cleared the house to ensure no one else was inside and opened the doors to ventilate. Paul yelled to Andy, "You're not gonna believe why they came out so quick?"

"Yeah, that must have been some good stuff," Andy replied.

"Better than that." Paul said, "Guess where they were hiding."

"Where?" Andy asked.

Paul pointed down the hallway to the A/C return air grill lying on the floor. They both had a good laugh. While those punks hid in the return air chase, the A/C pulled the gas directly to them. They kicked the grill open after inhaling a full blast to escape the fumes. At least they found something to smile about out of a senseless tragedy. Andy didn't have his customary drink on the long ride home that night. Instead, he focused on the pain those bastards felt trying to get out of the door. He tried not to think about the girl. He regretted pushing the asshole to the ground because he never condoned brutalizing a prisoner. Andy had allowed a moment of anger for the innocent girl and what she lost that night to get the best of him, but that didn't make it right.

EIGHTEEN

FUBAR

A Special Operations Detachment from Fort Bragg, North Carolina, sought realistic training locations in Houston. Houston had many old buildings set for demolition, precisely what these guys needed to conduct training in a real-world environment. Utilizing sites the operators had never seen, they wanted to test their tactics and equipment. Hands-on simulations were the best way to prepare them for deployment anywhere.

The Army relied on local law enforcement to show them around the city and point out potential training sites. Sergeant Flores appointed Andy as their liaison because he had knowledge of several buildings being gutted for remodeling and some scheduled to be leveled. Anytime the Army used a facility for training exercises, it endured a significant amount of damage, but if it was going to be torn down, it didn't matter. The most crucial issue was the potential liability; so frequently, the Army would sign hold harmless agreements and pay damages. Some property owners felt a patriotic duty to help these warriors prepare to defend America worldwide, but others just cared about the money.

Andy had been previously assigned as a liaison and enjoyed working with the Army guys, so he eagerly looked forward to helping them. Although the specialty-trained military forces took things to another level, both used similar tactics. The D-Boys used helicopters to get in and out quickly, working primarily at night with equipment Houston law enforcement didn't have access to. The heightened training was beneficial for SWAT to learn to train under pressure. Although some of the techniques and scenarios were unrealistic for their jobs, the training was cutting edge and beyond their comfort zone.

Andy showed them around town for the next three days while his team trained with Gilbert's team. Andy knew of several locations that would be of interest to the Army, especially the Texas State Hotel. The 12-story building, situated in the heart of downtown, was already set for demolition. However, the Army could negotiate permission to do whatever they wanted with the facility if they agreed to board it up when they were finished. Compared to the other contenders, it was a crown jewel because its helicopters could deploy to the roof and use the surrounding high-rises for sniper positions during their complex exercises.

The scenario the Army concocted was quite impressive. The mission was to capture a valued package from enemy forces somewhere on the 8th floor. The package was a briefcase containing top-secret documents stolen from a US Embassy. Helicopters would deploy operators onto the roof in the cover of darkness while snipers took shots on targets positioned near windows. The targets were representative of sentries posted to guard the perimeter.

Operators would fast-rope onto the roof and then rappel down all four sides of the building to the 8th floor. Using explosive devices, they would breach the exterior windows and gain entry. Once inside, they would search for the package and take out enemy targets along the way. They were only allotted 20 minutes to complete their mission and make it back to the roof to evacuate on the helicopter.

Andy listened intently as they went over every detail of the operation. Everything had to go perfectly for it to work, but Andy knew that most things this complex never went perfectly. One of the guys asked, "Do you want to go with us?"

"What do you mean?" Andy asked.

"Well, you guys can do rep training with us during the day and then go on one of the hits that night. We'll probably do several scenarios anyway," the operator replied.

"Oh my God! That would be awesome!" Andy said enthusiastically.

"Cool! We'll make that happen," the operator replied and returned to planning.

Andy could hardly contain his excitement; he couldn't wait to tell his team about this fantastic opportunity to train alongside some of the best warriors in the world. If they pulled off a scenario like this, they could do anything.

One of the guys turned to Andy and asked, "Can you do something for us?"

"Sure, anything," Andy eagerly replied.

"Well, one of our guys is leaving the unit. He's moving on to another assignment in DoD, and we have a tradition when someone leaves," he paused, and the group smiled as they looked at each other.

"OK, what's that?"

"Well, his name is Josh Schmidt, but we call him Smitty. You know, he is a real tough guy, a male chauvinist, martial artist kinda guy." Andy nodded in understanding. "We want to have him arrested, but it must be by a female officer. Oh, and we'd like to capture it on video. You know, from one of the dashcam videos in patrol cars?"

Puzzled, Andy asked, "OK, but what's he getting arrested for?"

"We'll set him up with a sixpack of beer and make sure he drinks one before leaving the training site if you could have the female officer waiting down the road to pull him over. Then she can pretend she smells beer on his breath and arrest him for a DWI, but we need to get it all on video. That would be awesome to show the guys," he said, grinning at the thought.

Nervously, Andy smiled back, unsure how he would ever pull this off. "OK, what happens then? We don't really take him to jail, right?"

"No, just turn him over to us, and we'll take it from there." Sheepishly, Andy agreed because he didn't know how to tell them no.

That afternoon he called his old buddy Joe Vargas. When Joe left the team, he was promoted to Sergeant, and he was now working in the Criminal Intelligence Division. Joe knew absolutely everybody and had a knack for being able to coordinate events and pull favors from around the Department. However, this particular favor would require all of his talents. After Andy explained the prank the D-Boys wanted to pull on Smitty, Joe couldn't wait to help, and he got a kick out of being involved with his old team again. He immediately started calling in favors and trying to find a female officer willing to play the role. Andy left everything to him, understanding that if anyone could pull it off, it was Joe.

With the training scheduled for three months down the road, Andy was grateful to have some lead time. But before he knew it, two months passed by, and the D-boys were calling to check on logistics. More importantly, they wanted to know if Andy had the kidnapping set, so he called Joe regarding the capture plan. "Are you good to go?"

"You're talking to the kid," Joe answered. "The kid is always good to go."

"Cool, any problems with doing it in three weeks?"

"You just be there motherfucker, and the kid will be there. In fact, go look now! I'm already there. If it has to be, it's up to me!"

Andy laughed; Joe was always a jokester and notorious for talking in riddles. At times though, Andy just wished he would give him a straight answer, but it wasn't his style.

When the big day finally arrived, the D-Boys landed at Ellington Airforce Base on a massive Galaxy cargo plane. Everyone from SWAT supervision was waiting to welcome the squadron to Houston. After deboarding and collecting their gear, they drove to an abandoned apartment complex in Pasadena, which would be their home base for the week. From that location, they would conduct daily rep training and then every night fly out to various target locations throughout the city.

Safety protocols were slim, considering they were constantly pushing the boundaries. Due to the inherent dangers, it wasn't uncommon for someone to get injured during their training. SWAT observed from the sidelines, and the D-boys let them jump in whenever they were allowed. The Captain never particularly warmed up to the idea because of the possible liability. He felt the risk wasn't worth the reward, but he allowed it just the same.

Thursday rolled around, and they had saved the Texas State Hotel for the last full day of training. They worked on the techniques they would need to pull it off all day. Rappelling was a significant part of the operation. They used Petzel Stop devices to stop the descent when the operator released the grip automatically. If the devices weren't attached correctly to the rope, it would malfunction.

The entire day Andy's team worked with one of the Army teams on anchor points and properly securing ropes. Next, they practiced attaching their Petzels and descending the three-story building. Mastering that skill set was imperative because the 12-story tower would not forgive a mistake. The final training exercise was fast-roping out of a helicopter, an exhilarating new experience for Andy's team. The descent from the helicopter to the ground took mere seconds.

With the evening fast approaching, they grew increasingly confident in their skills. Andy paid particularly close attention to Scott's performance. Surprisingly, he did just as well as everyone else during the reps. The actual test would be later that night when the pressure was on. After attending a scenario briefing, the Sergeant Major conducted a safety meeting on the rules of engagement. Then, before allowing the team to descend the building, two safety monitors on the roof checked for any potential safety concerns. It was as safe as you could make a dangerous job.

Most downtown dwellers returned home by midnight, so they decided to begin the operation then. Only cops, drunks, and drug dealers were still roaming around that time of night. The Houston Police Department was briefed on the exercises that would take place, and some patrol cars were positioned to prevent anyone from gathering around the hotel.

The Blackhawk helicopters took off with operators onboard, and the operators returned on a compact French-made helicopter. The smaller bird was just large enough to carry the necessary passengers and small enough to land on the edge of the hotel's roof. Andy's team was scheduled as the last run of the evening. With four D-boys, they would board the aircraft and fly to the hotel, where they would fast-rope to the roof. The D-boys were responsible for rappelling down to the target window and breaching it. Their Team Leader advised Andy, "Once we're in the window and offline, use our ropes. When the ropes go slack, put your Petzel on and go. The rope will be in the window, so you can't miss."

Easy enough, Andy nodded and replied, "Roger that." Donnie, John, and Scott were listening, so Andy turned to them and confirmed, "You guys got that?" They nodded in agreement, and Andy paused specifically on Scott to ensure he was up for the task. However, he noticed the same unsteady look in Scott's eyes he observed during the Allen Parkway Tower incident. So, Andy asked again, "Scott, are you alright?" Scott nodded, but Andy wasn't assured.

At 2 am, Andy heard the Blackhawk approaching, so he conducted a last-minute equipment check with his guys. Sergeant Flores knew Andy's team was next, so he walked over and hollered over the sounds of the approaching helicopter, "Andy! Keep an eye on Scott. Don't let him get hurt." Andy nodded in agreement. However, he found it a bit irritating that Scott needed to be watched. Everyone was nervous, Andy was no exception, and they were operating at a level far beyond anything they had previously encountered.

The Blackhawk landed, and they jumped in for the short 10-minute ride downtown. The big bird lifted off and ascended into the night, and as Andy looked out, he realized they were flying without any lights. The D-boys obtain special permission from the FAA to fly at low altitudes and in conditions usually not permitted. Even the police helicopters and Life Flight knew of the Army helicopters and their flight paths to avoid them.

Night Observation Devices (NODs) were fixed to the pilot's helmets and shielded their eyes, enabling the pilots to see in low light environments. Andy was amazed at how low in altitude they were traveling, especially so quickly. The pilots were from Fort Campbell, Kentucky, and the Black Wing Squadron was the best in the Army. The D-boys always preferred their pilots because they would fly anywhere and try anything.

With the side doors of the aircraft open, it felt like they were only inches above the streetlights and houses as they streamed past in a blur. Andy was nervous and impressed simultaneously as he watched the pilots acting like this was a walk in the park. Considering these pilots were trained to fly at this advanced skill set internationally to avoid radar detection, this mission would be no different. They were perfectly relaxed flying, discussing, and pointing at landmarks and buildings in Houston, enjoying the city as sightseers. Andy wanted to scream at the top of his lungs, 'HEY! WATCH THE ROAD,' but he didn't want to sound like a pussy, so he kept quiet.

As they began their approach into the skyline of downtown Houston, they increased their altitude on the Blackhawk, weaving between skyscrapers toward the Texas State Hotel. Curiously, Andy noticed cars traveling on the streets below and wondered what they thought about a mysterious black helicopter flying between buildings. The pilot hovered over the hotel, and the D-boys deployed fast-ropes off both sides. Everyone efficiently exited, with two operators following directly after Andy's team. Everyone was on the roof in a few seconds, and the crew chief released the ropes to the roof below. And just like that, the pilot pulled pitch, disappearing into the darkness of night.

The only sound remaining was the subtle noise of the D-boys stretching out rappel ropes. Andy momentarily paused and observed, trying to take in their technique as the D-boys hustled over the edge of the hotel. The Team Leader tapped his first two operators, and down they went. Andy leaned over the brick ledge bordering the roofline to sneak a peek. The ledge extended approximately 3-feet, so the operators climbed over it to descend. Seeing straight down a 12-story building at night was frightening, so he decided it wouldn't be in his best interest to do that again. Instead, he focused on his equipment and the task at hand. The D-boys descended to the target window when rifle shots sounded from all directions. The gunshots signaled the assault as snipers engaged the targets predetermined in the hotel. The rifle reports eerily echoed off the surrounding buildings.

A massive explosion rocked the 8th floor, sending glass fragments falling to the street below. Although the same simulation was practiced during training several times throughout the day, the sound was deafening in the calm of the night. In a flash, the D-boys flew through the window opening, like bats returning home after a night of foraging. Andy's team held onto the ropes, and when they went slack, they knew the D-boys were no longer attached. Donnie and John hooked up their equipment first and eased over the ledge while Andy anxiously waited to follow. He glanced at Scott, who was again standing like a spectator. "Scott! Grab your rope!" Andy yelled. Scott snapped out of it, grabbed the last rope, and began winding it through his Petzel.

Andy swung his leg over the brick ledge to start down when he recalled Sergeant Flores' warning. Looking over at Scott, he yelled, "WAIT!" Scott stopped, nervously looked at Andy, and crawled back from the edge. When Andy checked Scott's Petzel, sure enough, the rope was wound backward. Scott was about to rappel off a 12-story building with the device hooked up incorrectly. Infuriated with Scott's stupidity, Andy scolded, "You stupid shit! You hooked it up backward!" Scott looked down, confused, and Andy correctly rewound the rope. "THIS IS ELEMENTARY SHIT, SCOTT! NOW GET YOUR ASS DOWN THE ROPE!"

Scott fixed his eyes on the rope, never looking up or down, and started over the brick ledge again with Andy directly behind. The darkness and height were fueling Scott's anxiety, causing his descent to take much longer than it did during training. Since only one operator could enter at a time, Andy was stuck waiting at the window. Andy screamed, "GO SCOTT," agitated, knowing they were already behind schedule. Finally, through the window, with their feet firmly on the floor, they unhooked their Petzels. Gunshots rang out several floors above them, which meant Donnie, John, and the D-boys were shooting the bullet traps on their way to the roof. Andy was fuming. To make matters worse, you could hear the approaching helicopter, which was their ride home. "Forget the fucking targets, just get to the roof as fast as possible," Andy yelled, running out of the room.

As Andy entered a long straight hallway running to the left and right, the building was pitch black. The floor was laid out in a standard hotel floorplan with doors on both sides for as far as the eye could see. Smoke from the explosion and previous gunshots hung in the air as Andy pointed his light directing, "You go that way, and I'll go this way. If you find the stairs, yell out!" Scott nodded, and they ran off, searching for their way out. Frantic, Andy looked in all directions until he reached the end of the hallway; the stairway must be on Scott's end. He ran back, yelling, "Did you find them?"

"NO," Scott replied in the distance.

The stairwell had to be in his direction, it didn't add up, so Andy picked up the pace and headed toward Scott. Halfway down Scott's assigned section, the hallway veered to the right. He flashed his light, and sure enough, there was the stairway. "SCOTT! YOU DUMBASS! It's right HERE!" Scott didn't say a word as he ran back to Andy, appearing astonished.

The helicopter sounded like it was hovering over the building; Andy took off running up the stairs. He didn't care if Scott made it or not, but he wasn't going to miss that flight out. Scott was at his heels, running up the four flights of stairs as fast as their legs could carry them. After only a few seconds, Andy was through the rooftop door and spotted the safety guys. They pointed toward the waiting helicopter hovering on the side of the building. The bird was precariously perched, one skid on the brick ledge while the remainder of the aircraft hovered in space.

Andy leaped in the open side door and squeezed in amongst the operators already packed in like sardines. The French-made helicopter was significantly smaller than the Blackhawk. Scott jumped in behind him and wormed his way toward the back. The pilot nervously looked around to determine how many people were on board when the two safety's jumped in as well. Everyone was well aware this was the last flight out, and if they missed this one, they would have to ride back with the cleanup crew and equipment trucks several hours later.

Just as the pilot pulled pitch to leave, the helicopter strained with the extra weight. As the engine revved and the bird fell from the roof, there was a moment of weightlessness. Andy clutched onto a handle and wondered what kind of joy ride they were about to experience. Soon, the helicopter began shaking and violently vibrating, attempting to ascend. As the aircraft leveled, they were barely clearing the streetlights, then they rounded the side of another building and flew toward the training base.

Upon landing, they gathered to conduct a hot wash. It was optimal to complete any operation's down and dirty critique directly after a mission while the events were fresh in everyone's memories. Before the analysis, Andy was in complete awe of these guys' fearlessness and flawlessness; then, he discovered several mistakes had occurred.

The Team Leader sternly questioned, "What the fuck happened with the charge?" The faulty window breaching charge sent glass fragments into the operator's legs suspended on the ropes. They sustained minor slices on their pant legs, and some of the cuts drew blood.

"I think it went off before I had it set against the window, Sarg," the breacher answered.

"That's a FUBAR!" the TL shouted. A term meaning 'Fucked Up Beyond Recognition,' or a bad mistake was made. "I want to know how that happened?" insisted the Team Leader.

"Well," the breacher answered, "I guess I was just a little bit jacked up from the height and the darkness, Sarg."

The Team Leader seemed to accept that answer. Andy was relieved he was not the only one who was scared to death. Apparently, they got scared too; but they didn't show it. Just then, a safety officer walked over and asked the TL why everyone didn't have their own rope. The TL explained they were trying to cut down on logistics. "Well, we just heard from the equipment guys." The safety officer explained, "One of the ropes had a deep cut from the jagged window glass."

"Oh shit," the TL exclaimed.

"Next time, everyone gets their own rope," the safety officer scorned.

"Roger that," the TL acknowledged. That meant that someone from Andy's team possibly came down on a rope that was badly cut. It could have been a deadly mistake.

Still livid with Scott, Andy held his tongue, knowing he might say something he regretted later. Donnie asked Andy if they should conduct their own critique, "No, you guys go home and get some rest. We don't have to be at the office until noon." Driving away, Andy knew precisely where he was headed. He bought a Coke at the nearest convenience store and fixed himself a drink. He was now carrying a bottle in his trunk for situations like this. Tonight, he needed it more than ever. It was becoming a habit, and Andy knew it wasn't good, but he couldn't make the long drive home without it.

When he pulled into his driveway, he sat in his car for a moment and finished the last few sips of his calming medicine. He quietly walked in and undressed in the bathroom to prevent the light from waking Terri. He was exhausted as he eased into bed for a few hours of rest. He could tell she was fast asleep by his wife's breathing as he lay there, staring at the ceiling. He couldn't stop dwelling on Scott's mistake and how things could have ended much differently. What would Terri do if he had come down on the damaged rope and didn't make it home? Finally, he let the Jack Daniels calm his mind, and he drifted off.

The following day he drove to work with a particular goal. Again, he would confront the supervisors about Scott, and this time there was no room for compromise. If Scott weren't immediately removed from his team, he would resign from his TL position and move to another team. He poured his first cup of coffee and sat down at his desk, contemplating how to argue his case. He was still fuming, repeatedly reliving last night's events. Not only could Scott have killed himself, but Andy would have been held responsible.

Just then, there was a knock on his office door. "You got a minute?" Scott asked, sticking his head in.

"Sure."

Scott stepped in, "Well, I just wanted to tell you that I am sorry about last night and thank you for catching my fuck up. That could have been bad for me."

"Yes, it could have."

Scott went on to say, "Look, I know I have a problem. I'm working on it, but I will go to the supervisors and request to be moved off your team. Maybe there is something else I can do because I don't want to leave SWAT. I think I need more time to adjust."

Andy recognized his sincerity. By coming to Andy himself and admitting what they both knew, he had no choice but to accept it. He offered Scott his blessing and decided to wait to see what happened. If his superiors asked for his side of the story, he would tell the truth, but he didn't wish Scott any further grief.

Later, Andy heard his name announced over the PA system and to report to the Sergeant's office. 'Well, that didn't take long,' he thought. He was surprised to see Lieutenant Chesney with all three sergeants when he walked in. Conspicuously, the Captain wasn't present, but everyone else sat in a semi-circle waiting for Andy's version of last night's events. In full detail, he described Scott's missteps. Some follow-up questions ensued about Scott's future, but he didn't offer an opinion.

The leadership staff ended up creating a new position for Scott. He would be a full-time equipment guy responsible for inventory and maintenance moving forward. They desperately needed someone to ensure everything was accounted for and functioning correctly, and it was a good fit for Scott.

With his usual cup of Jack and Coke, Andy made the long drive home that afternoon, but today's drink celebrated how everything worked out. He couldn't wait to tell Terri the excellent news and hoped it was a turning of a page for his team.

Andy's excellent mood was instantly crushed when he walked into the house, and Terri told him to call his Mom. She had already called twice, and it seemed important. 'What now?' Andy wondered as he dialed her number. Mike was arrested again. This time by the Texas Department of Public Safety while driving to Houston late last night on US Hwy 59 in a rental car. When he was pulled over, he was found in possession of a large amount of anabolic steroids. Steroids could be purchased over the counter in Mexico, so his regular travels now made sense. Moreover, the State Legislature had recently reclassified steroids as a Class 1 narcotic, the same class as cocaine and heroin.

Andy's Mom was highly distraught, worried sick about what would happen to Mike. He attempted to comfort her by reminding her how many times Mike had gotten out of trouble before, and it was possible this time would be no different.

These Guys Are Crazy

As he drove to work, Andy couldn't help but worry about the mess Mike had made for himself. Also, he could see how taxing this was on his mother, and at her age, she didn't need this kind of stress. So, Andy did what Andy does best; locked the thoughts and worries away and focused on the task at hand, capturing Smitty.

Now that training week was complete; the much-awaited capture was set for later this evening. The plan was unfolding perfectly, and after confirming with Joe, all details had been coordinated with the female officer. As an assigned officer to the accident division, she was permitted to go anywhere inside the city without question.

The night sky closed in on downtown as Andy and Joe anxiously waited in the front seat of the Bomb Squad van. Just down the street from the Texas State Hotel, the D-boy's van was backed into an alley, where they were loading their equipment for the trip home. The roads were almost empty; most of the downtown workers had already gone home for the day. Andy was assured Smitty would be driving the last van out that evening. They planned to have him drink a couple of beers and then take the remainder of a six-pack to the hotel. Then, when they were about to leave, they would page Andy.

On a backchannel, Joe radioed the officer, verifying her position. "Standing by on Smith Street," she responded.

"OK, I'll let you know when he pulls out," Joe said.

"Clear," she radioed back.

Joe turned to Andy, "You don't think this guy would do anything stupid if it looks like he's going to jail, do you?"

"God, I hope not," Andy answered, sitting in the dark, stressing about everything that could go wrong.

His pager went off, and '0000' was displayed on the screen. It was time. "That's IT!" Andy exclaimed, "That's the signal!" They were nervously shifting in their seats as Joe started the engine. Just ahead, they spotted Smitty leaving the hotel carrying a brown paper sack, and entering the van.

When Smitty pulled out northbound on Smith Street, Joe radioed the officer, "He's headed your way. Be sure your dashcam's on when you pull him over."

"Clear," she responded.

After following Smitty for a couple of blocks on Smith Street, they noticed the patrol car up ahead. "That's the white van approaching you now," Joe radioed. She pulled in behind the van and turned on the emergency lights.

Smitty pulled over, and Joe parked a few car lengths back for a good view. The officer asked Smitty to step out of the van and stay at the back of the vehicle. With her flashlight, she shined inside the van, peering around the interior, then she located the brown bag containing the remainder of the beer and pulled it out. Smitty's head dropped, realizing this situation had just drastically deteriorated.

Joe and Andy chuckled as they watched the officer walk back to Smitty and conduct a field sobriety test. In full view of the video camera, she dragged him through a litany of tests. Then came the moment of truth when she asked Smitty to place his hands behind his back.

Andy had been worrying himself sick that he might lash out, run, or do something worse to the officer, and this little prank could turn into a nightmare. But instead, he breathed a sigh of relief as Smitty turned around and submitted to the officer's request. She cuffed and placed him in the back seat of her car as Andy said, "Let's roll!"

Joe put the van in drive and pulled alongside the patrol car. Then, after yanking ski masks down over their faces, they jumped out toward the police car.

The officer had her dome light on, in park, with Smitty pleading his case from the backseat. "I'm with the DoD, and I am in town training with your SWAT guys. Call any of them, and they will tell you." Smitty was so busy attempting to convince the officer of his innocence that he didn't notice Andy and Joe until the door flew open. Smitty looked up to see two masked men reaching in to grab him. "Oh, Shit," Smitty exclaimed, instantly realizing what this was about. And although he was relieved he wasn't going to jail, he worried, not knowing what he was about to be in for. "Look, guys, we don't have to do this!" Smitty begged while Joe and Andy pulled him out of the vehicle and forced his face down on the pavement. Then, Joe handcuffed his ankles, and with a dog leash, Andy tied his ankles to his handcuffed hands.

The officer watched the entire series of events unfold from the driver's seat, not once getting out of her patrol car. Anxiously, she looked around, hoping no one could see what was occurring right outside her vehicle. Andy pulled a ski mask backward over Smitty's face so he couldn't see anything, and Joe taped the mask in place. In seconds, they lifted Smitty and tossed him into the back of the Bomb Squad van. Joe gave the officer a thumbs-up, and she smiled. Andy slammed the van doors and peered around to see if anyone had just witnessed the abduction. A wino stood on the sidewalk with his mouth ajar. Andy realized the derelict saw the whole thing. So, he just politely nodded and smiled. In shock, the drunk continued watching until they sped away.

Smitty was sprawled out on his stomach, hog-tied, in the back of the empty cargo van as they entered the freeway on the drive out of downtown. He pleaded through the ski mask; voice muffled, "Come on, guys! We don't have to do this."

"Shut up!" Joe yelled back and continued southbound on Highway 288 toward the dump.

A few minutes later, they entered the Holmes Road Dump, and several of the D-boys were standing near a row of chain-link dog cages typically used by the K9 units. Andy rolled the window down, and Joe pulled up the van, stopping beside them, "He's in the back!" The D-boys opened the back doors, yanked Smitty out, and dropped him on the pavement. He landed with a hard thud. Then, without hesitation, they pulled knives out of their pockets and sliced his clothes to shreds.

"Come on, guys. Enough! Stop! You don't have to do this," Smitty continued pleading with the guys, but it didn't matter; he was naked in a flash.

Andy and Joe stepped out to watch the show, wondering where in the hell they were going with this.

They removed the dog leash, exchanged the handcuffs with their own, and shoved Smitty into a cage. He screamed at his captors as they closed the door, cursing obscenities. Then, completely unfazed, they just told Smitty to shut the fuck up. Lying on his side with the hood still pulled down over his face and hands cuffed behind him, he vowed revenge. Andy thought that was the end, but it turns out they were just getting started.

Next, they rolled out a heavy-duty 2-inch firehose customarily used by the K9 crew to pressure wash the cages and opened it full blast on Smitty. The force of the water violently shoved him, pinning him to one side of the cage, and he continued cursing at the top of his lungs.

"We got it from here, guys. Thanks for everything," one of the guys said, tossing back their cuffs to Andy.

"What are you gonna do with him now?" Andy asked.

He smiled and said, "We'll leave him here for the night. We're staying in the K9 office, so we'll come out every hour and hose him down again. Did you get the video of the traffic stop?"

"I'll get it from the officer tomorrow when I take her cuffs back," replied Joe.

"OK, see you then."

As Andy and Joe drove away, the water torture was still in full force. When they pulled onto the freeway toward the office, Andy finally said solemnly, "Do you believe that shit?"

For a moment, Joe didn't say anything and then mumbled, "Holy shit." Parking the van, they both felt rather guilty about their involvement in Smitty's torture, but it was too late now. As they headed their separate ways, they could only hope he never found out who captured him.

The following day came much too early for Andy as he drove back to the office, sipping a cup of coffee. Passing the Holmes Road exit, he wondered how much torture the poor bastard must have endured last night.

Upon arrival at the office, he immediately started a pot of coffee in the dayroom; he would need it today. Right as he walked into his office, his desk phone was already ringing, "Hello?"

It was Joe. "Did you hear?"

"Hear what?"

"He escaped!" Joe said.

Of course, he had to be talking about Smitty, "How?"

The D-boys were drinking, living their best lives, and about every hour, they went outside to hose him down again. Finally, around 2 am, they came out to discover the cage open, and Smitty was gone.

"What the FUCK?" Andy asked.

"Well, apparently, they used cheap aluminum cuffs," Joe continued. "He must have rubbed the chain on the concrete long enough to grind the chain links down and break them. Even though he still had cuffs on, his hands were free, so he opened the cage and ran away, naked as a J-bird."

"OH MY GOD!" Andy interrupted.

"Wait. It gets better. He ran toward Scott Street and ducked into a subdivision. After stealing a pair of pants and a shirt hanging on a clothesline, he went to find a phone and call some buddies. On a street corner, flagging traffic was a prostitute, so he asked if he could borrow a quarter to use the payphone. When she handed him the quarter, she saw the handcuffs on his wrist and assumed he was an escaped prisoner. She wanted the crime stopper's money, so she walked across the street to phone the police."

Andy interrupted again, "SHIT! Don't tell me that he got arrested!"

"Well, not really. While waiting for his buddies, standing under the streetlight, three police units arrived first. They threw him down on the ground and cuffed him."

"OH, MY GOD!" Andy blurted out, panicked. "I knew Murphy was gonna jump on our backs!"

"Hold on," Joe interrupted. "It turned out OK. He started telling them who he was and what happened, and one of the officers was on the dive team and was aware the D-boys were in town. So when Smitty's buddies showed up and identified themselves, the story checked out."

"HOLY SHIT!"

"They finally released him to his buddies."

"Where is he now?" asked Andy.

"Sleeping it off at the hotel," Joe replied.

They agreed to meet up later before going to the 'piss up.' That's what the D-boys called a party they threw on their last night in town. It was a traditional going-away party where they handed out gifts to the hosting Agency and told the funniest stories from their training visit. Andy and Joe were tense about running into Smitty at the event. But they were expected to attend, so they agreed to go together and leave early.

The party was in a nice bar in the private patio area west of downtown. An extensive buffet was set up, and they even had an open bar. Everyone was in great spirits, swapping stories about the week. The training operation was a big success, and they were leaving for Fort Bragg in the morning. After talking to some D-boys, Andy found out Smitty was cool about everything last night. Also, he didn't have a clue who captured him. Which was a relief, and when he spotted him across the room, he was drinking a beer and laughing with some of his buddies.

The helicopter pilot who gave them the ride of their life off the Texas State Hotel the other night was leaning against the bar. Of course, Andy had to ask if that was all for show or what, so he strolled over and introduced himself. "Hey, I'm Andy from the Houston Team, and I was on your flight the other night leaving the hotel." The pilot nodded and smiled. "Man, that was quite a ride you gave us."

Curiously, the pilot eyed Andy, grinned, and then asked, "Oh, were you on the last run?"

"Yeah, when we flew off the hotel, it was a rollercoaster of a ride."

"Well, I tried to pull pitch and get some lift, but we were too heavy." He paused to take a sip of beer and continued, as if this kind of thing happens all the time, "I found out later that a couple of the safety guys jumped on board, and we had already maxed out the weight limit, so the bird just couldn't climb."

"Wait, so we were falling?" Andy asked, puzzled.

"Yeah," the pilot replied with a laugh. "I figured if we fell off the roof, I could get some airspeed on the way down, and then we'd get enough lift to climb out."

The response hit Andy like a ton of bricks, "So, what would have happened if you couldn't get enough lift?"

The pilot smiled, stuck his beer out, tapped Andy's glass, and said, "Well, we wouldn't be here right now, would we?" Then, he busted out laughing, not caring either way.

Andy nervously laughed as they drank to their toast. Finally, he thanked him and walked away thinking, 'These guys are crazy.'

Andy left the party early for his long drive home, and he couldn't stop thinking about the pilot's cavalier attitude. He was amazed at what these guys did and the risks they took. He couldn't understand how anyone could just go for it and see what happens when life and death were at stake. It must be the type of mindset necessary to do that job. 'Thank god they're on our side,' he thought to himself, driving off into the night.

The next day, Poodle called and said Mike wasn't offered bond due to his previous arrests. He had hired an attorney, but he was awaiting his preliminary hearing in county jail. The family was helping with his attorney fees. However, no one expected Andy to chip in, considering the bad blood between them. After talking it over with Terri, they decided to chip in the same amount as his brothers, but he didn't want Mike to know. It was $5,000 apiece, and that was $5,000 Andy really didn't have to spare, but they scraped it out of savings. Although they were living comfortably, they were still paycheck to paycheck, and that large of a sum would hurt. Andy appreciated Terri's understanding when she said, "We have to help Andy; it's your brother." It made him love her even more.

Their home life was focused on raising Emma and Bryce. Andy took his young son hunting and fishing as often as possible, and Terri enjoyed her girl time with Emma. Life in the country was as simple as they could make it with their busy schedules, and every minute they spent together was precious.

Django Strikes Again

On a Friday afternoon, a hijacker walked into a downtown bank and robbed the teller with a handgun. As he ran out the door, he caught the attention of two officers walking their beat, and they gave chase. The robber jumped into his closely awaiting parked car and took off toward the freeway. A patrol car fell behind him and chased him out I-45 toward Galveston until he broke down in a parking lot on Monroe Street. Cornered, he put his pistol to his head, threatening suicide, so they slowly backed off and called SWAT.

Andy's team was on react assignment, and they called in Mondo and his dog Django to assist, the same K9 team they had last worked with at the video parlor. "If the suspect gets out of the car and starts running, you send Django. So we ain't chasing him. Got it?"

"Sure, no problem," Mondo replied.

Andy was armed with a single shot 40mm that fired an impact projectile designed to deliver enough force to incapacitate. Donnie was given a 12 gauge pump shotgun with the same impact rounds. Although the shotgun was not as accurate as the 40mm, it could shoot several rounds in a few seconds. "If he starts walking away, I'll shoot first," Andy instructed Donnie. "If it doesn't put him down, you start hitting him with the shotgun rounds until I reload."

Donnie replied, "Roger that!"

With a bullhorn, Hurley attempted to persuade the suspect to get out of the car and leave his pistol inside. Sure enough, he finally exited the vehicle but still had the gun in his hand. Uneasily the man paced back and forth at the vehicle's rear, pointing the gun to his head. It looked like he was trying to get the nerve to run or shoot himself from the outside perspective. Nevertheless, Hurley continued his commands over the loudspeaker.

Suddenly the guy started briskly walking away, and it became painfully apparent he wasn't stopping. Hurley shouted for him to return to his car, to no avail. And Andy aimed and squeezed a shot. The projectile hit him right in the ass; he jumped from the impact and started hobbling away. Andy yelled to Mondo, "SEND THE DOG!" Mondo released Django, and he took off like a hair missile with teeth. Donnie pelted the man's backside with 12 gauge projectiles as Django closed the distance. When the suspect glanced back and saw Django coming, he decided he wouldn't hang around for that. He put the pistol to his head and blew his brains out in the parking lot. His body collapsed to the ground with a thump.

Django, already on his orders, didn't care if the man was dead or alive. When he reached the body, he mauled the man's leg. The team closed the distance, and Mondo pulled Django off. The man was dead.

Several guys stood around gawking at the gore, but Andy turned and walked away. There was a time when it didn't bother him to see dead bodies, but now it was becoming increasingly complex, and he started avoiding it as much as possible. The images in his mind were beginning to pile up, and his box was overflowing, making it challenging to keep them tucked away. If they weren't secured, they would haunt him later, usually in a dream, so he tried to avoid adding another image.

Hurley was miffed that he was unable to talk the guy into surrendering. Andy passed him in the parking lot. "Bet you loved the trigger time," Hurley sarcastically commented. Andy wanted to come back with something but thought better of it and kept walking. It was another call where everyone lost and another image for Andy to deal with.

NINETEEN

No More Egg McMuffins

Rob Striker was assigned to Andy's team as Scott's replacement for the rearguard, appearing to have the qualities he needed in a team member. Rob got along with everyone and was eager to pull his weight. In Andy's view, he would fit right in, although he thought the same thing about Scott, so he decided to hold his final judgment until Rob proved himself. Finally, after several weeks of training, Andy was satisfied with his performance and ready to use Rob on their next entry.

A three-person home invasion team was working in the southwest part of town. They established a pattern of breaking into the homes of wealthy disabled people who lived alone. Detectives were baffled at how they found their victims. They had yet to discover one of the robbers was a driver for an oxygen delivery service. Throughout the area, he was responsible for delivering oxygen tanks to patients. Inside the home, he scoped out the premise, and if the place looked profitable enough and the patient appeared helpless, he notified the gang leader about the potential target.

The leader, Gary, was a hardcore ex-con. A ruthless individual with a never-ending rap sheet who vowed never to return to prison. Even the other gang members feared him. It didn't help that he always carried a sizeable shiny pistol that he loved to intimidate people with. Besides running the home invasion team, he also dabbled in burglaries and car thefts on the side. He was a walking crime spree, willing to kill anyone in his path.

The delivery driver was particularly excited about a house he visited in Belaire. When he called Gary, he went on and on about the expensive furnishings and how the owner had to be worth a significant amount of money. The man was bedridden, and even though caretakers were present throughout the day, he was alone at night. After liking what he heard, Gary gathered the team for a hit later that evening.

Around 3 am, they approached the house from the backyard in the dead of night. They kicked in a pedestrian door on the attached garage and stormed the house with guns and flashlights. The bedridden man was awakened and realized what was happening, so he reached under the bed and set off a silent hold-up alarm. The alarm company immediately started monitoring the residence using the installed microphones in the home.

The burglars had most of the obvious valuables gathered within a few minutes, but Gary wasn't satisfied; he wanted more. To get the homeowner's attention, he forcefully slapped him across the face. The man recoiled from the strike, looking at Gary in horror. Then, Gary put his lips to the victim's ear and whispered, "Where's the fucking money, asshole?"

"I don't have any here," the man pleaded. "It's all in the bank!"

Not convinced, Gary firmly pressed the pistol to the man's temple and demanded, "I'll put your worthless ass out of its misery if you don't tell me where the cash is NOW!"

The rest of the gang was too busy searching for valuables to notice the police cars pulling in front of the house. With guns drawn, officers quickly surrounded the home. Once they found the back door kicked in, they assumed the suspects were still inside.

As additional units arrived, the officers created a perimeter before making voice contact. One of the suspects spotted a patrolman and started yelling, "FUCK! IT'S THE COPS! Cops are here!" Gary calmly walked to the window and gradually peeled back the curtains to find numerous police vehicles surrounding them. His partners were panic-stricken, running around the house, looking for any way to escape. In every window they looked out, police shined flashlights. They were trapped, and the gig was up.

Even though Gary knew this day would eventually come, he wasn't about to give up. "Look, I'll walk out the front door and start shooting," he told the other two. "You make a run for it out the back."

"No way, man, they'll just kill us too if you start shooting."

"Well fuck you then, you cowards! Go ahead and give up! I'm going to the attic to hide. If they find me, I'll just shoot it out with them, but I ain't going back to prison!" Angrily, Gary stomped off to find the attic entry.

The other two momentarily looked at each other and dropped their guns on the floor. Then in surrender, they opened the front door and loudly announced, "WE GIVE UP! DON'T SHOOT!"

"Come out with your hands in the air," instructed one of the officers. "Leave your weapons inside and walk toward my voice!"

The two dejected burglars conceded and were taken into custody without incident.

Gary climbed into the attic, pulled the door closed behind him, and smiled. He was well aware this might be his final stand, so now he just needed to find the perfect place to hide and try to take some cops with him, given a chance.

The bedridden man had been lying there watching them panic. He was terrified of the possibility that Gary might take him hostage. Once the place was quiet, he crawled out of bed and slowly dragged himself to the front door. Right away, the officers spotted him and ran forward to pull him to safety. Due to the cuts and bruises the victim endured from the beating, an ambulance transported him to a hospital for evaluation.

When officers questioned the two suspects, they informed the officers Gary was still inside and unhinged. The officers called out to him over their PA system, but there was no response. After about 30 minutes, the on-scene supervisor requested the dispatcher get the SWAT Team rolling their way.

At 5 am, Andy's pager went off. Already up and dressed for the day, he hurried out the door, speeding toward Southwest Houston. The Captain was already on the scene when Andy arrived, and negotiators were busy readying speakers for communication. The Captain told Andy, "This one is yours if we decide to go in, or would you rather gas?"

"Let me talk to the prisoners and get a better look at the house," replied Andy.

The Captain nodded, "OK, take your time. We're going to try to communicate with him first."

'No shit,' thought Andy as long as Hurley was there; good luck getting him to relinquish control. Andy walked over to the patrol car holding the two suspects and opened the back door. Both men were stunned; neither expected to see a SWAT guy in full tactical gear with an M16 slung across his chest. Andy stared at the two derelict-looking crooks and said, "Tell me about this guy." Immediately they started talking over each other. "Stop," Andy interrupted sternly and pointed to the man nearest him. "YOU! Tell me about this guy." The other one dropped his head, disappointed he wasn't chosen.

"His name is Gary, and he's a crazy motherfucker," the suspect blurted out. I don't know how much time he's done in prison, but he said he ain't going back."

Andy interrupted again, "Are you sure he's still in there?"

"Yes...well, I think so. Last we saw him, he told us to surrender, but he said he would rather shoot it out with you guys. He was going to hide in the attic and hope you don't find him."

"What kind of gun does he have?"

The other suspect jumped into the conversation and said, "It's a pistol! A big shiny one!" Quite proud he managed to get a few words in.

"Any other weapons?" confirmed Andy.

"Nope, that's it," he replied. Andy had everything he needed; he shut the door and walked away.

At Hurley's instruction, the negotiators broadcasted demands for Gary to pick up the phone. The phone rang for at least 30 minutes with no response, agitating Hurley. Without a resolution soon, he was worried this might require a tactical solution, and he despised the idea of losing control. Whenever he could not negotiate a successful surrender, he considered it a personal failure.

Before long, the Captain became tired of waiting, so he radioed Andy to ask if gas was the best option. Unfortunately, the wooden shingles on the house wouldn't be able to hold gas, "And besides," Andy added, "This poor man has been through enough. I hate to fumigate his house with tear gas. Gary may have committed suicide, and we could be gassing a dead body for all we know." The Captain agreed. Andy's plan entailed entering the home through the same door the suspects kicked in. They would methodically clear the house, and if he found Gary, they would try voice commands. Based on the information Andy obtained, Gary might be in the attic, "If we don't find him in the living area, we'll call in negotiators and let them try to coax him down from the attic if he's alive." It was a solid plan, and the Captain gave Andy the green light to go when ready.

Andy gathered his team and reviewed the plan. They would work behind shields and use their poles to open doors ahead of them as a precaution. Additionally, he spoke with Paul Kandi and Gilbert Reyna about using their people to fill in behind them and maintain a watch over the rooms once cleared. By the time they approached the garage door, it was just after daybreak. From the exterior, they could clear most of the garage with a camera pole and then enter for a quick search. They moved to a small mudroom that led inside the house, and evidently, the homeowner was a hoarder because junk was stashed everywhere. The clutter made searching difficult, creating hiding places in every nook and cranny.

Paul and Gilbert were brought in to keep the garage and mudroom secure as Andy's team pushed forward with the search. Next, they cleared a small library that led to the largest kitchen Andy had ever seen. Huge custom kitchen cabinets lined the walls, and each one needed to be searched. Although it was tedious and time-consuming, their safety depended on it.

Still working their way through the kitchen, they maneuvered a long pole to open the broom closet door. Inside must have been at least fifty maroon cone-shaped hats stacked on top of each other. Staring at the columns of Shriner's caps, they wondered what would possess a guy to have so many, but they had work to do, so Andy nudged his guys to move on.

Next, they cleared a small breakfast nook leading to a formal dining room. The search was becoming exhausting. Carrying around that amount of extra equipment was cumbersome, but it was necessary because each room presented another potential ambush. Paul and Gilbert's guys occupied the rooms once they were searched, giving Andy's team a sense of security, knowing they had their backs. Paul snapped his fingers to get Andy's attention while working another threshold. Andy glanced back, and everyone behind him had taken off their helmets and was wearing the Shriner's caps. Peering down the walkway, he could see into several rooms, and at least six guys were lined up, grinning and pointing at their hats. Andy couldn't help but chuckle and decided this was an excellent place to take a break. John and Donnie posted on the door, setting their shields down for protection and relaxed behind them for a breather. Gilbert passed out Shriner caps, and they took turns trying them on as they quietly pointed and snickered at each other. It was a minute to decompress from the tension and a lighthearted moment they needed.

Within a few minutes, everyone was back on their feet, buckling their helmets, and ready to resume the search. With each empty room, the tension increased. If Gary was down here, he had to be in one of the remaining rooms, and when they finally met, it was not going to end well. Andy breathed a sigh of relief when the last room was cleared, and Gary was nowhere to be found.

Andy's stomach was growling, and his guys were hungry too. The call-up started long before anyone could eat breakfast, and now it was 9 am. He radioed the CP and asked if they could order something to eat while they took a break and let negotiators do their part. The Captain was on board and ordered Egg McMuffins from a McDonald's down the street.

Walking in like he owned the place with a bullhorn in hand, Hurley pointed to one of the attic openings and yelled for Andy. Even though he hated to answer the call, he had no choice.

"What'cha need?" Andy asked.

"Can you open this attic hatch so we can talk to him?"

Quizzically, Andy asked, "You don't think he can hear you with that bullhorn?"

Condescending, Hurley replied, "I want to be able to hear him. Now can you get it open or not?"

Andy replied without inflection, "Yeah, sure." He asked John and Donnie to grab some shields and lights. "Let's get this hatch open for the negotiators." After a few minutes, they gained entry and cleared the area. Then, they posted shields for security, and Andy told Hurley he was good to go. Andy sat down in another room and tried to rest a few minutes as he waited for his Egg McMuffin. He took off his helmet and asked Paul, "You still got one of those Shriner's caps?" Paul smiled, handed him one, and Andy put it on. He took a deep breath, let it out slowly, and giggled while the negotiators blared their message into the attic.

Finally, the McMuffins arrived, and everyone chowed down. Andy was starved, and even though they were cold and soggy, they tasted fantastic! He quickly finished his meal and discussed a strategy with Paul and Gilbert, still donning their Shriner's caps.

"What do you guys think?" Andy asked as he pointed to the hat.

Paul smiled and said, "I like it!"

"Do you think he's up there?" asked Andy.

"Yeah, but I think he's dead," Gilbert said and took another bite of his breakfast sandwich. "I think he crawled up there in a corner somewhere and offed himself with his pistol." A scenario they had each witnessed play out many times before.

Andy scanned the ceiling using a thermal imager, a new device they had borrowed from the fire department. If Gary had been lying in one place for a while, his body heat could have permeated through the sheetrock. Unfortunately, the imager didn't locate his position, but it was worth a try. Now it was time to call his team and discuss the next move. "I want to open the other ceiling hatch so we can see more of the attic." Andy ran his plan past the CP, and much to Hurley's chagrin, the Captain agreed. He asked Gilbert and Paul to work the other hatch with box lights. Soon they could see most of the attic, but no Gary.

With all other options exhausted, the only thing left was to go up and search. "Are you guys good with this?" Andy asked, checking with John and Donnie. Considering they would be first up the ladder, Andy wanted to make sure they were comfortable with the idea. John and Donnie were good to go, so Andy radioed the CP that they were ready to enter.

"Clear," Sergeant Russell responded. "All officers maintain radio silence."

Behind small shields, John and Donnie slowly eased up the stairs as Andy watched from below. They scanned in opposite directions back-to-back as they softly ascended into the dark opening. Andy feared that all hell was going to break loose at any second. His heart was hammering in his chest as his guys cautiously climbed the stairs one rung at a time. Within a few seconds, they were positioned at opposite sides of the opening. With a million places for Gary to hide, they shined their weapon lights past the 2 x 4 bracing and air-conditioning ducts meandering throughout the attic.

After them, Andy climbed the ladder and realized they had each spotted something, seeing them both staring intently at different spots. Neither one dared to shift their eyes off what they were watching as they waited for Andy. He eased up to John first and whispered, "What'cha got?" John was focused on a large mound of blown insulation near an eave of the roofline. It was large enough for Gary to be lying under, and at one end, there were two exposed boot tips. "Yeah, I see it," Andy whispered. "Hold what you've got. I'll check with Donnie." John nodded, keeping vigil on the mound.

Andy crawled to Donnie and whispered, "What'cha got?" Donnie pointed to a large mound of insulation similar to John's, except this one lacked boot tips. "John's mound looks better than your mound. I'll call Rob up to watch this one, and we'll check John's first." Donnie nodded in agreement. Rob came upstairs and changed positions with Donnie. Then, Andy signaled them to spread out and move through the maze of ductwork toward the suspicious mound. They were precariously forced to walk on ceiling joists to avoid falling. Although it wasn't a good situation, they had no choice.

Getting only as close as they dared, they spread out, surrounding the mound of insulation. Andy glanced at his team and signaled that he was about to start voice commands. Donnie and John braced for a reaction. "GARY," Andy firmly shouted, "We see you. Show us your hands." No response. "Come on, Gary. No one's hurt. Just show us your hands." Still only silence. Andy was becoming increasingly convinced Gary was dead. After growing tired of it all, he probably crawled under the insulation and ended his life. The insulation would have most likely muffled the sound of the shot.

At the other hatch, Paul and Gilbert, still wearing their Shriner's caps, leveraged their camera pole to peer around the opposite side of the attic. Their rifles were left on the kitchen table. Even though they could hear Andy's voice commands, they had no idea what he was seeing. Box lights pointed in all directions, trying to light up the space as much as possible. Andy kept giving commands without response. His eye peered through the rifle's red-dot optic, and he watched for the slightest sign of Gary's breathing, but the mound remained motionless.

Andy repeated, "Gary, we see..." and mid-sentence, Gary sprang up from the pile of insulation, wearing a ski mask, and his arm fully extended with a pistol pointed directly at them. Instantly, gunfire erupted, causing Andy to lose sight of Gary in the blinding flash of the muzzle blast. During the barrage of gunfire, Andy couldn't help but think about the pistol and how it was just as Gary's buddies described. The gun was big, alright! At least a 40 caliber, possibly even a 45. And it was shiny too. 'It must be a nickel or stainless-steel finish,' thought Andy as he watched the red-dot optic and squeezed the trigger. It all happened so quickly, Andy figured he had fired three or four rounds in a heartbeat, but it was six. Even though he could still see part of Gary's body through the insulation, his arm was down, and the pistol was out of view. Intuitively, he stopped shooting, released the trigger, and looked over the top of his weapon to reevaluate the threat.

When all hell broke loose, Gilbert was stretching a firepole into the attic to adjust the direction of light. Startled, he turned and ran toward his helmet and rifle but forgot the pole. After falling sideways into the kitchen cabinets, the pole knocked Gilbert backward onto the floor. Paul knocked off his Shriner cap and mistakenly grabbed Gilbert's helmet. Realizing his error, Paul tossed the helmet to Gilbert and rushed to his feet to gather his rifle. Surrounding the attic opening, they backed into defensive positions, wondering what the hell happened up there. The fun and games were over. Once the shooting stopped, Gilbert and Paul anxiously worried that Andy and his team had walked into an ambush. Feeling helpless, they could only wait.

John and Donnie opened fire when Andy did, shooting several rounds. Miraculously, all three stopped shooting at the same time, and the attic fell silent again. Gary's body leaned against a rafter, preventing him from collapsing entirely. He was shot to shit, his hands down by his side.

"You guys OK?" yelled Andy.

"Yeah, I'm good," replied Donnie.

"Me too," confirmed John.

Andy broke the radio silence, "Shots fired. All officers are OK. The suspect is down. We're gonna need paramedics up here."

"CP clear," replied Sergeant Russell. "They're on their way."

Andy said, "I'm gonna move up and see if I can find the gun. You guys cover me."

"Got it," Donnie replied.

Andy cautiously stepped from one joist to another, easing over to Gary. The loose insulation was at least 12-inches deep, so he didn't see the gun. He swept a few layers away, but still, no pistol, so he left well enough alone because he didn't want to disturb the crime scene. Moving back toward his team, John and Donnie were exchanging their recollections of what happened when Sergeant Russell came over the radio, "CP to Andy, Sergeant Flores is bringing the paramedics forward." Andy keyed his mic just as John asked Donnie how many times he fired. Everyone on the scene was listening, including the media outside the perimeter. Then, in the background, they heard Donnie's voice, "I don't know, but I was a shooting motherfucker!" By the time Andy realized what he had done, it was too late to let go of the mic. Everyone heard the transmission.

Sergeant Russell radioed, "CP to Andy, have Donnie hold it down."

Andy replied, "That's clear." Some might have been appalled at his comment, but to the SWAT guys, it was Donnie merely trying to describe what he remembered, and it was a phrase they commonly used, especially when they were excited.

Paul and Gilbert weren't sure what happened up there, but when they heard Donnie's voice, they laughed, relieved they were OK. 'Shooting Motherfucker' became Donnie's new nickname, but he took it in stride.

The paramedics crawled up into the attic and pronounced Gary dead. The scene was soon turned over to Homicide, and Andy and his team drove downtown to write their statements. Andy stopped at a payphone and called Terri at work, but she was in class, so he left a message that they were alright. Another one of those calls she was getting too frequently.

Andy's observation of the suspect's pistol was spot on. The investigation determined it was a stolen, stainless steel, 10mm, semi-automatic. When they autopsied Gary's body, he was wearing women's underwear. The embroidered initials on the panties matched an unsolved rape case. Another crime had been solved, and the perpetrator was administered the death sentence. He was a sick piece of shit, and his reign of terror was over. In Andy's opinion, the world was a better place without him.

During the next day's critique, the Captain vowed never to buy Egg McMuffins again at a call-up. "We'll just stick to burgers or pizza from now on." He was superstitious about things like that, but the most important thing was that his guys were alright and got the job done.

As part of HPD policy, Andy and his team were assigned to visit Dr. Rodie, a requirement of any officer involved in a shooting. The meeting went well, but Andy felt like Rodie could see right through him once again. He sensed that Andy was fine with the shooting, but there was something else. Rodie then asked about his family and if he planned to tell his kids about the shooting.

Andy answered, "No, of course not. My daughter is a toddler, and my son is only 6."

Rodie replied, "Well, OK, but your son goes to school, right? So, I'll bet he plays with friends in the neighborhood, right?"

"Yeah, so?"

"Well, I'm sure you have neighbors who know about the shooting. What if their kids hear them talking and say something to Bryce? Would you rather he hears it from you?" Andy looked down and thought for a few seconds. Then Rodie said, "Well, just think it over. I know you'll make the right decision."

He stood up, shaking Andy's hand, and walked him to the door. "Oh, and Andy..." Rodie added, "If you ever want to talk, my door is always open." Andy nodded and walked away because he couldn't go there, not yet anyway.

A few days later, while Andy and Bryce were fishing, he thought about what Rodie said. The time seemed right, and before he knew it, he blurted out, "Bryce, you know I'm a cop, and I get the bad guys, right?" Bryce nodded his head, looking straight ahead. "You know that sometimes I might have to shoot a bad guy to protect myself, right?" Bryce remained silent but nodded in understanding. "Well, a few days ago, I had to shoot a bad guy. Are you OK with that?"

Bryce turned to his dad, "Is he dead?"

Andy swallowed hard and answered, "Yes."

Bryce looked down, thinking it over, and then asked, "Dad? Did he have a son?"

Andy was blown away. He didn't see that coming. Teary-eyed, he answered, "I don't know, son. I don't know."

Bryce stared out over the water, accepting his answer, but it was all Andy could do to fight back the tears. Not another word was said, and Andy hoped he never had to have that conversation again.

Captain Dynamite

Like the seasons, Andy's team changed from time to time, and it was transitioning again. Donnie had witnessed enough dead bodies and all the blood and gore that comes with it to last a lifetime. It was time to move on to something less intense and away from Hurley. Even though Andy tried to talk him out of transferring, Donnie's time had come just like Andy's would someday. John had matured into Team Leader material, and supervision asked him to take a vacant TL position, so he would be leaving as well.

An innate bond comes from trusting someone with your life, and Andy couldn't help but think back on the great times they shared. Donnie was always the jokester, and Andy would miss that. One time in particular, when they were training at Camp Swift, just East of Austin, Donnie wanted to lighten things up after a long day. So, when they got to their Quonset hut to clean up for dinner, he stripped down to his underwear and combat boots and evolved into the character he called Captain Dynamite. He wore his helmet and goggles and then added green flight gloves and tied a towel around his neck as a cape to complete the ensemble. Then he proceeded to walk into a courtyard area between several huts and began performing a series of bodybuilder poses. At least fifty SWAT officers from around the state attended the same training. One of them spotted Donnie, and word quickly spread as they poured outside to cheer him on. Instantly, he became a celebrity amongst the group, and his nickname was forever changed from Shooting Motherfucker to Captain Dynamite.

And then there was John, who was such a big fan of the Batman movie series that he purchased an authentic full-length suit, including a mask and cape. When he dressed up, he looked precisely like Batman from the films. Occasionally, John would walk into the office unannounced, strutting around in his suit, imitating Batman for some laughs.

One summer morning, during their quarterly PT qualification run, John decided to surprise the guys. Everyone was lined up in their shorts and tennis shoes to complete the quarter-mile track at Memorial Park. Summer in Houston is scorching, and that day was no exception. The park was full of joggers on the adjacent 3-mile trail. Just as Sergeant Flores started the countdown, "Ready, Set...."

John jumped out of his car in his Batman suit and ran to the track, yelling, "WAIT!"

Flores stopped the count, and the whole group cracked up laughing. John hustled to line up with everyone, and Flores yelled, "Ready, Set, GO," and off they went with Batman alongside. People started pointing and laughing, and steam began pouring out of his mask. The suit was hot and didn't ventilate, so John was on the verge of passing out when he entered the 8th lap. Even though he was hurting, John refused to quit and finished the run well under the 16-minute limit.

From time to time, Andy enjoyed pulling pranks as a coping mechanism to escape from the seriousness of the job for a short while. The laughter lightened the mood from the reality of their daily risks.

Andy didn't like running alone, so he would announce his intentions in his best John Belushi impersonation from his famous role in *Animal House*. He motivated his fraternity brothers to join in by yelling, "WHO'S WITH ME?" No one went on Andy's first attempt, so he would walk back in and start pleading again, "Come on, guys! Let's GO!" Next, he would yell a war cry, "WHO'S WITH ME?" and thrust his arms in the air, running out of the gym. It usually took three or four tries before he had guys willing to run, and everyone else was grateful he was gone.

He enjoyed intimidating the new guy by introducing himself and then nonchalantly mentioning they all showered together. With a straight face, Andy leaned in and whispered, "I'll save space for you in the shower," winked, and walked off. It was all he could do to keep from cracking up when he saw the look on the new guy's face. Then, to add to the prank, he waltzed around naked in the locker room with a bar of soap stuck in the crack of his ass, yelling, "Has anyone seen my soap?"

By the end of the day, fatigue usually set in, and the funny stuff didn't seem as entertaining anymore. The stress of the job, Hurley, and what lay ahead for Mike weighed heavy on his mind on the long ride home. Alcohol had become another coping mechanism, making the ride more manageable, but his worries were always just below the surface.

Mike's preliminary hearing went well, resulting in an affordable bond, so he was out of jail for the time being. The District Attorney had a reputation for being an aggressive prosecutor who was highly successful in obtaining convictions. Additionally, a conservative jury had no problem sending people to prison. In Andy's opinion, sending someone to prison for steroids was extreme, but it was the law. He was deeply worried about what it would do to his mother if Mike ended up in prison.

Boiling Point

Andy was reviewing training records in his office, awaiting news on his newest team member. During one of the training classes he conducted for patrol officers, Andy met Gary Barkley and convinced him to try out for SWAT. Because of his natural talent and abilities, Andy thought he would be the perfect addition to the team, and sure enough, he was just selected by supervision.

Gary was quiet and unassuming, nothing like Andy, but the team didn't need another peacock. More importantly, Andy recognized Gary's potential. Recently, his team picked up Larry Molten from Gilbert's group, which he was happy about. Larry or Mo, as everyone fondly called him, was an exceptionally good operator. After spending a few years on Gilbert's team, he was already trained in the position. Andy was confident these two would make a great point and cover, and they'd be operational in no time.

Rob Striker was progressing well as the rearguard and good enough to move up, but Andy asked him to stay on just a bit longer. Ideally, it's never preferable to train up an entirely new team. He needed someone watching his back that he could trust. Rob saw the big picture and agreed to stay on.

To further complicate matters, changes were underway in supervision. Sergeant Russell recently transferred to the Narcotics Division because he had his fill of Hurley. Andy saw his leaving as one more nail in his SWAT coffin. Hurley was slowly ostracizing anyone who opposed him. It was only a matter of time before he set his sights on Andy, and he couldn't understand why the Captain didn't see it.

Sergeant Flores walked into Andy's office with good news for a change that morning. Gary was joining his team, and now his job was to get them up to speed. A task Andy had done many times before, but this would most likely be his last. He felt his days in SWAT were limited, but he would make the most of his time left.

Over the next few weeks, Andy rigorously worked with his new team, and just as he suspected, Gary was picking up the skill sets quickly. He performed well enough to work the point position with Mo over his shoulder at the cover. They were a perfect fit and eerily reminiscent of how John and Donnie had worked together. Andy was proud to have been the one who recognized Gary's talent and recruited him to apply. This team would be his legacy. His responsibility was to train the leaders of tomorrow's SWAT operators, and long after he was gone, they would pass those skills on to the next generation.

Andy's pager went off while working on covert searching techniques at an abandoned house in Southeast Houston. Portable telephones or cell phones recently flooded the market as the latest technological advancements now made returning calls to the office instantaneous. In the Heights area of town, there was a hostage situation in progress, so they quickly broke down their training gear and left in a hurry.

The suspect was holding his young son hostage in a back bathroom. Since SWAT supervisors had yet to arrive on the scene, Hurley held the highest rank and took control. In direct violation of the Standard Operating Procedures, Hurley brought negotiators inside the house. Established protocol stipulated that only SWAT Officers are allowed inside the inner perimeter unless the individual is being escorted by SWAT personnel. Although none of that seemed to matter to Hurley because he was in charge.

Andy was the first Team Leader to arrive, and Hurley met him in the front yard, "I've already set some guys inside to replace patrol."

"WHAT?" Andy asked incredulously. Another clear-cut violation of SOP standards. Only a Team Leader or SWAT Supervisor was authorized to set inner perimeter positions.

"You can check them, but I needed to get those patrol officers replaced."

"Whatever," replied Andy, rolling his eyes.

Hurley spun around and threateningly grabbed Andy's arm. "Look, we are not killing this guy! Understood?" he growled.

Andy yanked his arm out of his clutches and said, "Like I said, whatever." Insulted by the comment, he intentionally didn't reply. He would never kill anyone unless he had to, and he knew his guys wouldn't either. Hurley's insinuation infuriated him.

When he walked inside, two negotiators were setting up a throw phone, and two patrol officers were standing in the living room observing. Tony Garcia was posted up outside the master bedroom door. The suspect yelled demands from inside the room. Andy eased next to Tony and whispered, "Whatcha got?"

Then, without taking his eyes off the room, Tony leaned back and pointed, "He's got his son in that bathroom."

"Is there any way out of there?" Andy asked.

"It doesn't appear so," Tony replied.

Later on, the team discovered the suspect retreated to the bathroom to avoid an arrest for child abuse. He held his 2-year-old son captive in his arms with a 12-inch butcher knife to the toddler's throat. The suspect said, "You don't think I'll kill him? I will! I promise you; I will!"

"Who is the suspect talking to?"

Tony leaned back, "OJ."

OJ was another member of Gilbert's team, and he was positioned in the closet with a clear shot of the father. He remained quiet and didn't engage the suspect except to occasionally demand, "Put the knife down!"

Now Andy understood why Hurley was afraid they would kill this guy. According to State Law, lethal force was already authorized because the man could slit the child's throat at any moment. Andy worriedly thought about the similarities to the Allen Parkway Tower incident, and he remembered how that turned out.

Mo arrived, popped his head over Andy's shoulder, and asked, "You need anything?"

"Yeah," Andy replied. "I need to replace OJ. He's been in there a while and must be getting tired of keeping his pistol at the ready."

Mo nodded his head, "Pistol?"

"Yeah." Andy replied, "The distance is only a few feet across the room."

"OK, just let me know when," Mo said. Then he took off his rifle and leaned it against the wall in preparation.

Andy keyed his mic and whispered, "Andy to OJ, are you ready for a break?"

"OK, if you have someone."

"Mo is coming your way." Andy turned to Mo and said, "Back down this wall slowly. I don't want to startle this guy. Lieutenant Hurley said that we aren't gonna shoot this son-of-a-bitch, but you do what you have to. Got it?"

Mo nodded his head and eased past Tony. Slowly, he backed down the wall to OJ. The movement agitated the suspect, adding stress to the existing dynamic. While OJ slowly walked out of the room, the suspect continued yelling threats. Eventually, he slightly calmed down, but things remained at a stalemate.

Anxiously, Hurley pushed the throw phone to Andy. Hurley thought, that if they could speak without yelling at one another, it might diffuse the situation. To prevent potentially startling the suspect, Andy loudly announced he was tossing a throw phone into the bathroom. The phone landed with a thud directly inside the door, beside the suspect.

The man knelt and picked up the throw phone, holding the child with his other hand. Immediately, he started speaking with the negotiator while he cradled the boy on his knee. Finally, things seemed to settle down a bit. Andy hated to admit it, but the throw phone was a good idea.

After several minutes, Mo was tensing in his stance and needed to be replaced. Holding a pistol steady on a target was exhausting over time, especially with a young life hanging in the balance every second. Andy decided it was easier for him to take Mo's place since he was already at the doorway, so he backed down the wall with his pistol at the ready. "I got it, Mo," Andy whispered as Mo lowered his gun and eased behind Andy, walking out.

Andy's worst fear was directly in front of him. The suspect's butcher knife was pressed to the boy's throat. Thoroughly disgusted, Andy thought, 'This guy needs killing!' Glaring with contempt at the man's face, his pistol sights perfectly aligned. Without hesitation, he would put a round in this guy's head if they were in any other situation. Hurley put them in this dangerous predicament of gambling with a boy's life, betting the father wouldn't kill his son. In the end, it was quite simple; Hurley was the Lieutenant, and Andy was merely an officer. Besides, at least two other SWAT officers witnessed the same thing and hadn't pulled the trigger. Andy thought about the woman lying on the 24th floor of the Allen Parkway Tower. He couldn't fathom seeing a toddler sliced across the throat by his own father; it was too much to bear. The only way to guarantee this child's survival was to take the shot, but he didn't.

Over Andy's pistol barrel, he and the suspect stared at one another as he continued speaking to negotiators. Although he was unable to hear the conversation, he could tell the man was not buying it. Infuriated at the look Andy was giving him, he laid the phone down and screamed, "You want to kill me? Go ahead! I'll slit his throat before I die!"

'Not if I put this round right there,' Andy thought, looking through his sights. The intensity heightened, "You don't think I'll do it? I'LL KILL HIM RIGHT NOW! I'LL DO IT MOTHERFUCKER!"

Andy had enough. Assured with his decision, he clicked the safety off his Colt 1911 and began squeezing the slack out of the trigger. Lastly, he made the final adjustments to his sight alignment, and the shot was about to break. This nightmare was about to be over, and he figured another one was about to start. Andy was well aware this would ultimately cause a confrontation with Hurley but that he could live with as long as this little boy lived.

"ANDY! Hold what you got!" ordered Hurley. Andy snapped out of it and slowly released the pressure on the trigger, inhaling a deep breath. Somehow, Hurley knew what was about to happen. Precariously, Andy stood there, somewhere between life and death, as he waited for the pendulum to swing one way or the other. "Pick up the phone, and let's talk!" Hurley demanded. Finally, the man looked down, picked up the phone, and started speaking to the negotiators again.

Andy took another deep breath and lowered his pistol a few inches. He straightened his finger along with the slide and clicked the safety back on. He wondered if the man knew how close to death he was. One more pound of pressure on the trigger, and it would have gone another direction. Andy despised this asshole and Hurley for putting him in this unstable situation. This needed to end. It needed to become another memory squeezed into a box that was already full.

After another hour of negotiations, the man finally let the child go and surrendered. Andy took pleasure in placing the cuffs extra tight on his wrists and yanking his arms up behind him, shoving the suspect forward. He complained aloud about inhumane treatment, but Andy didn't care. Truthfully, he was starting to enjoy mistreating these assholes, and he hated who he was becoming.

Patrol hauled the suspect away as Andy was storing his gear. Hurley walked past Andy and arrogantly commented, "See? I told you we weren't killing this guy." Andy pretended not to hear him, but inside he was seething in anger. Even though he wanted to turn and belt Hurley in the mouth, he knew better. That type of action would end his SWAT career, and he wasn't ready for that. Although he wasn't sure how much more he could take.

At 5 pm, he pulled into a convenience store and loaded up on a huge fountain drink, and mixed a strong one. An all too familiar habit. The long drive home was filled with emotion as he sipped his drink and replayed the day's events. He was torn between what happened today and the Allen Parkway incident. Was Hurley right, or did he just get lucky? Either way, Andy was an emotional wreck with tears streaming down his cheeks. Sipping a concoction to numb his senses, he hoped he could get ahold of himself by the time he got home.

TWENTY

The Grand Jury

Andy was subpoenaed by the Grand Jury investigating the attic shooting. Donnie and John had received one as well and assumed it was a formality. Seeing Donnie again on the day of the hearing was like a reunion. While they waited, they talked and laughed for the next hour as the DA presented the case to the Grand Jury.

Eventually, the DA walked in and broke up the fun. The Grand Jury didn't have a problem with the shooting. Everyone was no-billed, but some members of the jury requested to hear more about what happened in the attic. The DA asked if one of them would be willing to fill in a few details. John and Donnie simultaneously pointed at Andy as he sighed and said, "OK." As the TL, he should be the one to go.

"It's not official testimony or anything like that. Again, strictly off the record, but they wanted to hear more if you don't mind."

"No problem," replied Andy. He turned and hugged Donnie goodbye and told John that he would see him back at the office later.

Walking into the room, Andy noticed that the Grand Jury was predominantly comprised of elderly women and one older man. Everyone smiled, stood to greet Andy, and shook his hand, making him feel instantly comfortable. They were simply interested in a good story and wanted to learn what it was like to search a dark attic for a man ready to kill you.

He sat down and began telling the story from the beginning, detailing the home invasion, their strategies throughout the search, and how they ended up in the attic. Several of the women were fully engrossed in the story the further he got into it. Finally, Andy decided to pour it on thick and use some of his storytelling talents. When he started to tell them about what they saw in the insulation, Andy went to great lengths to describe the dark, eerie surroundings.

Several women leaned forward in their chairs, hanging on to every word as Andy tried his best to illustrate the entire scenario. Then, he decided to add a little excitement to the story, so when he reached the point where Gary rose from the mound, pointing the gun, Andy elevated his voice in suspense, "AND HE JUMPED UP!" The jurors jumped back in their chairs, and two of the ladies let out a scream. He tried not to smile, but that was the reaction he was hoping for. They wanted to know what it was like in that attic, and Andy put them right where they wanted to be.

After his storytelling session, Andy stood up to leave, and the jurors complimented his bravery and the job of the SWAT team. Humbly, Andy shook their hands, then he excused himself and walked out of the room.

The DA followed him to the elevator, patted Andy on the back, and said, "Good story," chuckling. "I thought a couple of those ladies were about to have a heart attack."

Andy smiled and said, "They wanted to know." At that moment, the elevator opened, and Andy stepped inside.

The DA laughed and said, "You're right. Don't ask if you don't want to know." He waved and walked away as the elevator door closed.

Danger Is No Stranger

Call-ups were consistently coming in, one after the other, and Andy immersed himself in work. Instead of dwelling on the inherent dangers of the job, he relished the difficulty the situations brought. The more challenging and intense the assignment, the more he thrived. The threats were more amusing than frightening, and the team often laughed about nearly being shot.

Tonight, they faced a woman in a car threatening to kill her baby. The car was parked in an open lot on the Katy Freeway, where patrol had first confronted her. She was obviously mentally deranged because one moment, she would be tending to the baby like a doting mother, and the next minute she had a knife to its throat, threatening to kill her. The call-up began in the afternoon, and now it was past 10 pm. Due to her irrational behavior, negotiations were inconsistent and got nowhere.

As the Team Leader assigned to the perimeter, Andy's main challenge was how to stop the woman's car if she decided to drive away. Typically, an armored vehicle was used to block the car's path, but Hurley would have none of it, arguing it might set her off. For once, Andy didn't disagree with him. Gilbert and Paul shared the react and entry responsibilities because one team wasn't sufficient to assault the vehicle if it came to that.

The woman and infant were situated in a late model Cadillac, and negotiators called her husband to the scene to help coax her out. First, they recorded the father's desperate pleas to let the baby go and played them over a loudspeaker, but the woman didn't respond. Also, he brought the spare key to the car. If they could manage to do it without her noticing, the team could use the key to unlock the doors.

The team found an identical car at a nearby Cadillac dealership and practiced stealthily approaching it from the rear, using the blind spots. Moving in double columns, one was assigned to the driver's side and the other to the passenger. Paul and Gilbert mapped out, crawling to her door and using the key to quietly unlock it. They practiced with several teammates inside the vehicle listening for noises and watching the rear-view mirrors.

After several practice runs, they felt confident they could get to the car unseen and unlock the door without her knowledge. Additionally, they were prepared with breaching equipment to bust the windows to create a distraction. Plus, it guaranteed another entry point if the key failed.

The Captain approved the plan. Reluctantly, Hurley agreed to assist. He would cautiously move to the front of her car and conduct face-to-face negotiations. If Hurley could keep her looking straight ahead and talking, the team would have a better chance of saving the infant. Andy couldn't wait to watch the entire plan executed. His only regret was that he wasn't part of it.

Around midnight they were given the green light to start. The infant needed to be changed and fed, but the mother ran out of formula, and now the child constantly cried. The more the baby wailed, the more agitated and irrational the woman became. Slowly, Hurley walked to the front bumper and offered a bag containing baby formula and some diapers. The desperate woman began erratically brandishing the knife and yelling for him to get back. They leveraged the opportunity with her attention focused on Hurley.

The team scurried from the darkness to their respective places to begin the crawl to the car. They quickly traversed the 10 yards to the back bumper and then split to approach each side. Paul and Gilbert rounded the driver's side with the woman still screaming at Hurley. Hurley placed the sack of formula on the hood as a focal point. Then Paul slithered up to her door with Gilbert directly behind him. They stayed under the car as much as possible, and Paul rolled onto his back for a better view putting the key into the lock. Inserting the key without making a sound took him several seconds, and then he slowly rotated the key until he felt the linkage move. Finally, they had the door unlocked. And thankfully, she hadn't heard anything, still threatening Hurley.

The team was set, and Gilbert signaled Andy, who stood watch from several yards away. Andy radioed the CP that the team was in place and standing by. The Captain gave the decision one last consideration and then gave the thumbs up. "CP to Gilbert, RESCUE, RESCUE, RESCUE!" They sprang to their feet in unison and tossed the flash-bang onto the hood. At the signal, Hurley stepped back and covered his ears. The device exploded with a large booming sound and a brilliant flash of light. The woman was terrified, screaming and covering her face. All four windows exploded from the breaching tools, and the shattering noise completely overwhelmed her.

Paul lunged through the broken window behind her and grabbed her arm with the knife. He pulled her arm back against the seat. She screamed and struggled, trying to free herself from his grip. Simultaneously, the remaining three doors flew open. She let go of the baby to fight for the knife with both hands, and

Gilbert saw his chance. He grabbed the infant, pulled her from the woman's lap, and handed the child to Hurley. Then, frantically, he carried the screaming baby to the awaiting ambulance for a medical evaluation. At the same time, Paul struggled to get the knife from the mother. She tried to bite and kick the officers, but she slowly lost the battle. Finally, Gilbert grabbed her legs and pulled her out of the car, feet first onto the pavement.

They handcuffed her as she finally fell limp, too exhausted to continue the fight. She seemed to accept that it was over as patrol hauled her off for a mental evaluation while the guys stood around high-fiving each other for a job well done.

The news media captured the entire incident on video and broadcasted it on every channel the following day. The camera solely focused on Hurley running with the baby. When he was interviewed on camera, he took credit for almost everything. Andy was a little miffed, but other than his disdain for Hurley, he didn't care who took credit. He was grateful to be part of a team that could pull something like that off without a hitch.

The news cycle hadn't even finished running its course when the next challenging call dropped. In the Galleria area, a deranged pedophile had taken three small girls captive in his upstairs apartment. Following a tip called in by neighbors, patrol stumbled onto his crimes. After a confrontation at his front door, the suspect slammed the door shut and threatened to kill the girls if police attempted entry. The scene quickly escalated into a stand-off, and SWAT was called.

Andy was again assigned the perimeter. So, he strategically stationed guys in the surrounding apartments to prevent the suspect from tunneling through the sheetrock walls to escape. When he located attic hatch openings, he placed men there as well. Most apartment buildings had common attics, enabling the suspect to traverse unimpeded into other apartments.

Gilbert was on the entry assignment and staged his team in one of the neighboring apartments. They situated fiber-optic scopes to track the movements of the suspect and listening devices to determine if the girls were alive. The team located the girls in the bathroom, and the suspect was anxiously pacing the apartment like a caged animal as he spoke with negotiators.

The suspect threatened to "set this place on fire" on more than one occasion throughout their phone conversation. Proactively, Gilbert requested the CP call a Fire Department cascade truck. They might need the Scott Air Packs to enter if he followed through on those threats.

A few doors down from the objective, they found a fire hose access panel and stretched the hose out as a precaution. Once the fire truck arrived, CP sent four Air Packs to Gilbert, and within a few minutes, they were adjusted over their vests and standing by. The situation was eerily similar to the call-up at the convenience store a few years ago, and they could only hope the oxygen lasted longer this time.

The situation momentarily lightened while the negotiators tried to talk the man into surrendering. Eventually, he hung up the phone, refusing further communication.

Minutes later, Gilbert smelled smoke. He quickly directed his guys to focus their scopes on the objective and confirm if there was a fire. Flames were flickering in the kitchen, and Gilbert sounded the alarm over the radio, "Gilbert to CP, we have flames in the objective. Are we clear to enter?"

There was a short pause while the supervisors discussed their options, then came the reply, "CP to Gilbert, you are a go for rescue!" The team hurried to assemble at the front door.

The suspect started the fire as a distraction, hoping he could enter the attic and sneak out of the apartment unnoticed. Rob Striker was holding security on one side of the attic when he spotted the hatch door open. Andy stood below Rob, peering up into the dark hatch opening, watching Rob's reaction. He wished he could climb up and help, but it was too late.

Rob noticed light shining up through the open hatch, so he raised his rifle to the low ready and waited. The suspect's head popped up through the opening with smoke billowing around him. "POLICE! FREEZE!" Rob yelled as he shined his rifle-mounted flashlight in the man's face. He ignored Rob, proceeded to pull himself up into the attic, and started crawling in the opposite direction. Rob radioed Mo, posted at the next attic entry, "He's coming your way, Mo."

"Clear, I'm coming up," responded Mo. Then, quickly, he climbed the ladder into the attic to stop the suspect from escaping. Soon he was trapped and forced to surrender, but the apartment fire below was still raging.

Gilbert overheard the radio traffic exchanged between Rob and Mo. With the suspect in the attic, they immediately breached the doorway. Flames were shooting up the back wall of the apartment as they pulled the fire hose in to fight the fire. Gilbert rushed to the bathroom, where he found the girls tied together in the bathtub. "IN HERE," Gilbert announced as he slung his rifle behind his back and bent over to cut them free. He must have been a frightful sight in full tactical gear with an air tank strapped to his back. But, somehow, the young hostages knew he was there to help, so they didn't resist his efforts to release their bindings. One by one, the girls were carried out through the smoke while the rest of his Team finished extinguishing the fire. Gilbert radioed that all three hostages were safe, and cheers erupted from the command post.

The pedophile was handcuffed and hauled down from the attic. Firefighters ensured the fire was extinguished. All three girls were turned over to Children Protective Services to be reunited with their families. The guys quietly congratulated each other for a job well done.

Andy fixed a good one for the ride home. He knew the team accomplished something special today, and everyone played a part. There was no denying they were a very skilled team, and they knew it.

Silver Bullet

Summer was coming to an end, and the tropical storm season was in full force. The weather during September along the Gulf of Mexico created the perfect combination of warm water and atmospheric conditions necessary to produce severe storms. Houston was notorious for attracting them, and a large storm was headed directly for Galveston. However, this tropical storm wasn't strong enough to cause panic or mass evacuations because people had become immune to anything that wasn't at least a category three hurricane.

Andy was up late preparing for the storm's landfall, securing the patio umbrellas and lawn furniture. He was utterly exhausted and slept through his pager going off. In far west Houston, a call-up was in progress. A man wanted for aggravated assault was holed up in a second-story apartment. The call wasn't unusual or unique, so they treated it as another babysitting event waiting for negotiators to talk him out.

After an hour on the scene, the CP noticed Andy wasn't present. Sergeant Flores called his home phone. Still half asleep, Andy groggily answered, "Hello?"

"Hey Andy, you want to come out and play in the storm with us?" Flores asked.

"Sure, Sarg," Andy replied. "Whatcha got?"

"Oh, just your everyday, run-of-the-mill, barricaded gunman," Flores answered. "Nothing to get all upset about, but if you want some overtime, come on out. The storm is on its way, so wear your galoshes."

"OK, headed that way," Andy replied and hung up the phone.

It was 3 am by the time Andy rolled into the K-mart parking lot on Dairy Ashford Street. The command post was parked between the store and an apartment complex. After parking near the CP, Andy popped his trunk to get his gear on while heavy clouds swirled in the night sky above him. The city lights illuminated the clouds, appearing like waves rolling in from the surf. The wind from the storm was gaining momentum and already starting to howl, but it wasn't raining yet, as he slung his M16 rifle over his shoulder.

In the distance, he heard the negotiators broadcasting over their speakers, "MARK JOHNSON! WE NEED YOU TO PICK UP THE PHONE AND TALK WITH US!" Communications weren't established, so Andy thought they might be there a while. He grabbed a poncho for the rain and his double stacked 30-round magazines and gazed overhead at the night sky as he finished loading them.

Just as he pushed the last round into a magazine, it flipped out and fell to the pavement. When he looked down to see where it landed, there was an explosion and a flash of light. Small particles hit him in the face. Right away, he realized the bullet had exploded. The sound caused an instant reaction. A voice over the radio announced, "Shots fired!"

Andy keyed his mic to advise them of the false alarm, "Andy to CP, that was me. I dropped a round on the pavement, and it must have exploded." There was an awkward silence, and he knew it was a difficult story for them to swallow. The assumption would be he was covering for an accidental discharge of his weapon.

Sergeant Flores replied, "CP to Andy, where are you?"

"Right behind the CP."

"Clear, I'll be right there."

Flores hurried out while Andy was still putting his kit on. "What the fuck, Andy?" demanded Flores.

"As I said, I dropped a round, and it went off," replied Andy.

"Where is it?" Flores asked.

"Fuck if I know!" Andy said, exasperated. He turned the light on his M16 to search the pavement and spotted the casing a few feet away. "There," Andy exclaimed. Flores walked over and picked up the .223 brass. The casing mushroomed open like a flower with petals extending out in all directions.

"Holy shit!" said Flores, amazed. Although Flores didn't initially believe him, he was a believer now. "Where's the bullet?"

"Hell, if I know!"

They shined around the area for a few minutes to no avail, and then Flores said, "Just go on over to the perimeter. We'll look for it when it's light out."

"OK," Andy replied and walked off into the darkness.

All the required positions around the perimeter were assigned. So, Andy stopped at Paul Kandi's react position and listened to the negotiator's broadcast demands. He and Paul exchanged small talk about the stupefying exploding bullet. And then mildly joked about taking bets on whether or not the suspect inside was alive.

Using gas had been kicked around, but they didn't want to risk contaminating the neighboring apartments. "I hate to pump the place full of gas and then have to go in and find his dead body," Paul said.

"Yeah, how many times have we gassed a dead body?" Andy sarcastically asked.

Hurley walked by to check on the negotiators and jumped back when passing Andy, "Watch it!" Hurley yelled, holding up his hands, poking fun at Andy for an accidental discharge that didn't happen. Andy just glared back as Hurley laughed and walked off.

Paul leaned over and commented, "What a dick!" Andy didn't give a shit what Hurley thought, so there was no point in dignifying it with a response.

Eventually, the conversation turned to the many situations just like this one that ended in suicide or when the suspects forced a shootout with SWAT. Somehow, they jokingly tied the man's problems to a woman and claimed, "The vagina got him!" Paul added, "A vagina was the most dangerous thing in the world and has caused the death of countless men." The jokes were crude, and most people would think they had a sick sense of humor, but for them, it was a way of coping with the death and gore they witnessed all too often.

Soon, the first bands of rain from the approaching storm arrived. As they finished getting into their ponchos, a sniper radioed, "Front door is open!" Andy leaned out to obtain a good view of the upstairs landing and spotted the suspect step out and slam his front door.

"Well, I'll be God-damned," Paul said. "The son of a bitch is alive. Go figure!"

Andy laughed, "I would have lost my lunch money on that one!" Then, the rain steadily picked up.

The team stepped into position, and Paul commanded, "GET YOUR HANDS IN THE AIR!" The suspect instantly complied. "WALK TOWARD MY VOICE!" The man casually walked down the stairs and was taken into custody. Paul asked Andy if he would walk him back to the CP so they could quickly search the apartment.

"Sure," Andy responded and took the suspect by the arm. "Let's go," and Andy led him down the sidewalk.

Curious, he had to ask, "What made you come out?"

"Well, I knew it was starting to rain, and you guys were probably getting wet, so...." the suspect responded matter-of-factly.

Andy smiled, "Well, thank you!" They walked to the CP, and the suspect was turned over to patrol.

Andy stopped at his car to drop off his gear.

Gilbert walked by and said, "The vagina didn't get that one."

Andy chuckled and added, "Maybe he's gay?" They laughed.

"Lucky for him," Gilbert said as he walked away.

Andy had to wait around for Homicide to make the scene because when a bullet is fired for any reason, Homicide is required to conduct the investigation. No matter how Sergeant Flores tried to explain the exploding bullet over the phone, the Homicide Lieutenant didn't buy it and insisted detectives make the scene. Andy and Flores were the only officers left at the K-mart parking lot as the storm moved off to the west. The wind was still howling, but the sun peaked over the horizon.

Andy had often wondered, so as they leaned against his car, he asked, "Hey Sarg, what do ya think about Hurley?"

Flores didn't answer immediately. Instead, he carefully chose his words, "He's an asshole, but I never said that."

Andy smiled, thankful someone saw through his bullshit. "Yeah, I hear ya," he replied, letting it go.

An unmarked police vehicle pulled into the parking lot, and Flores said, "That must be them!" The detectives introduced themselves, and then Flores explained what happened. They seemed satisfied with the explanation, especially after Flores handed them the split open casing.

One of the detectives asked, "Where do you think the bullet went?"

"We don't know," Flores replied as he pointed at the parking lot. "We searched the area...." midsentence, something shiny caught his eye. The bullet was glistening in the morning sun. "What the....?" Flores stopped talking and headed toward the shiny object. He walked approximately 30 yards and reached down to pick up a .223 bullet. It was in perfect condition with no groves, proving it did not go down a barrel. Flores walked back and said, "You are not going to believe this," and handed it to the detectives.

"Come on, guys," one of the detectives commented. "That was a little too convenient, wasn't it?"

"I shit you not," exclaimed Flores. "That's God's truth!" The two detectives looked at each other and shrugged their shoulders as if to say, 'Oh well, who cares.'

They recorded the necessary information for their report and said their goodbyes. The next day, Andy was still required to go to Homicide and write a letter explaining what had occurred. Although he never saw the mushroomed casing again, he did get to keep the bullet. He thought back on where he was standing when the bullet launched and where the bullet landed. The trajectory sent that bullet within inches of his head. Once again, Andy dodged serious injury or death, proving the theory, 'I would rather be lucky than good.'

Baby, It's Cold Outside

As winter set in along the coastal bend, the temperature was unusually cold. During that time of year, the team typically focused on training that could be conducted indoors to prevent weather interference. And a great training opportunity became available at the old Southwestern Bell building on Main Street. It was 20 stories tall and offered unlimited possibilities.

The TLs orchestrated a scenario that took advantage of the building's attributes. One unique feature was that each floor had a balcony stretching around the building. They concocted an elaborate scheme to insert two teams of operators onto the roof by helicopter and then rappel down to the 15th floor. They'd attempt to rescue hostages held by a crazed domestic terrorist who compromised the elevators and booby-trapped the stairways.

The training would start promptly at 7 pm. It would be dark by then, and most people working downtown would be gone for the day. Gilbert was assigned to take a team down the outside of the building and enter from the balcony. At the same time, Andy's team would rappel down an elevator shaft beginning at the mechanical room on the roof. Once on the 15th floor, they'd open the elevator doors to gain entry.

The big day was here, and the only hitch was a blue norther due to arrive that evening. So, sixteen operators gathered at the landing zone along Buffalo Bayou with their eyes focused on the dark clouds approaching from the north. Since it was only a 4-minute trip to the training site, with any luck, they'd be inside the building before the weather hit.

They used two helicopters to make the insertions, with two operators standing on each side of the little birds. When the helicopters arrived, the operators stepped onto the skids and attached their rappel harnesses as the engine revved and they lifted into the night sky.

Murphy's Law was in full effect; the norther hit just as the helicopters started their runs. Although rain wasn't expected with the weather front, the temperature rapidly dropped 20 degrees as the howling winds blew in from the northwest. They had already invested too much time and effort into this training exercise to stop now. As long as the helicopters could still fly, they would keep going.

The pilot carefully placed the tips of the skids on the edge of the building since the antennas wouldn't allow for a rooftop landing. The bird hovered precariously as the operators unhooked and shuffled forward, stepping onto the roof. The last few steps were particularly precarious, with the operator's harness unfastened and a small amount of space to clear before reaching the roof. The night sky's darkness added distraction as the rotor wash whipped them around.

Andy was glad that his team was descending the elevator instead of dealing with the outside weather. The great thing about an elevator shaft was the environment never varied. It was always still, dark, and quiet. Stealthily descending the shaft, they entered the 15th floor without the role players noticing. Unfortunately, Gilbert's team wasn't so lucky. The wind tossed the men around like rag dolls, swinging back and forth from one balcony ledge to the next, dangling above Main Street. They fought to remain upright as the added weight of their equipment tried to invert them. Finally, they made it to the 15th floor.

Andy located a storage room near the elevators, and the team hid there until Gilbert's team was in place. Once Gilbert was ready, the two teams launched a rescue that proceeded as planned. When the bad guy put up a fight, he was lit up with multiple simunition rounds for his efforts.

The next morning, from the warm comforts of the SWAT office, they sipped their coffee and shared stories about the night before. With the weather outside still nasty, they dedicated the day to critiquing the scenario and getting gear cleaned and stowed away. No one enjoyed working in bad weather, especially hanging from a rope 200-feet above the city.

Rappel training couldn't have been timelier because they were called to a jumper in the Montrose area the next night. A suicidal man climbed a cellular tower in sub-freezing temperatures but shortly afterward reconsidered.

From what the negotiators gathered, his name was Frank, and he yelled that he wanted to come down, but he couldn't move. Unfortunately, they weren't sure if he was sincere or if he wanted to take someone on the plunge with him. The Fire Department didn't want to take the risk, so SWAT was asked to climb up and evaluate Frank. They could hook him into a rescue harness and lower him down if he wasn't armed.

Andy and John Marvin were rappel masters, so they were chosen to go up and attempt the rescue. To have a better perspective on Frank, they climbed the opposite side of the tower. They planned to climb above him, lower the harness, and lower him to the ground.

Once they started climbing, they quickly noticed ice had formed on the metal superstructure of the tower. Even with gloves on, gripping was difficult, and Andy had to perfectly place his steps to avoid slipping. Reassuringly, they called out to Frank, advising him they were there to help and everything would be alright. After hanging on for several hours, Frank grew weak, his hands stiff from the cold.

When they approached him, he was glad to see them. John started tying off their ropes while Andy cautiously kept his eyes on Frank. Shaking uncontrollably, he was in no shape to fight anyone at this point and just wanted to survive. Once John had the ropes adequately arranged, he lowered the rescue harness, but Frank struggled to get it on. Freezing cold and unable to stand it anymore, Andy climbed down to help Frank secure the harness. Finally, a lucky and grateful Frank was lowered to the ground and arrested.

Chilled to the bone, Andy couldn't wait to get off the tower. Once he finally got to his car, it took several minutes of running the heater full blast for him to stop shaking. He could only hope the next jumper would wait for warmer weather before pulling a stupid stunt like that.

After midnight, Andy pulled into a convenience store and purchased a Diet Coke. Once he mixed a stiff drink, he settled in for the long drive home, alone with his thoughts. He remembered the look on Frank's face and how frightened he was. Andy was scared too, and a simple mistake could have changed everything. Before, he didn't dwell on those details. In fact, he used to love the adrenaline rush and welcomed the risk, but now he had a family to think about. Driving through the night, sipping his elixir, it worried him to think about what would happen to Terri and the kids if he didn't make it home. He hoped to grow old with her and watch the kids grow up, but he now realized that a mistake in his line of work was for keeps.

The following week brought the long-anticipated trial date for Mike. Driving to work, Andy wondered how his defense attorney could get him out of this one. The training schedule was light that week, so Andy could call his mom and get updates on the trial. The trial lasted three days, and the jury returned with a conviction, sentencing Mike to 30 years in prison. Andy was stunned. Even though he knew there were conservative juries in South Texas, the punishment seemed excessive. Poodle was crushed and feared for her son being in prison with violent and hardened criminals. The lawyers mentioned hope for an appeal, but Andy assumed it would fall on deaf ears. More than likely, Mike was doomed to spend several years in the Texas Department of Corrections.

Andy sat on his front porch, sipping a Jack and Coke, contemplating his big brother's fall from grace. He was waiting for Terri to get home to break the news to her as he looked out on the wooded acreage around him. He realized how lucky he was to have her, a beautiful family, and this wonderful home. He was no longer 10 feet tall and bulletproof. Now he worried about a mistake that could take all of this away.

TWENTY-ONE

Picture That

The Narcotics Division requested SWAT's assistance in executing a search warrant on a crack house in the southeast part of town. The fortified home was like dozens of others they had worked before, and their plan to hit the home was standard. Paul Kandi took the lead and briefed the team later that afternoon. And Andy phoned Terri at work to let her know he wouldn't be home for dinner.

Around 5 pm, Paul delegated assignments and assembled everyone for a quick walk-through before loading into the armored vehicle (AV) for a short drive to the staging location. The AV would breach the fortified front door and create a quick entry point. It weighed 28,000 lbs, and the ram weighed an additional 2,000 lbs. Upon impact, the AV didn't just open the door; it knocked it off its hinges. Sometimes, it not only breached the door but took out some of the surrounding walls with it. The ram created an inordinate experience that most suspects never imagined possible and would remain unforgettable.

On one occasion, when they hit a trailer house with the AV ram, instead of opening the door, the impact rolled the trailer off its blocks, landing on its side. A steady stream of water spewed from the broken water connection while the team was forced to climb on top of the trailer, pull the front door open, and drop inside. The back wall of the trailer had become the floor as the entry team climbed over furniture, shouting and searching for the suspect. The suspect and his wife could be heard calling for help from the back bedroom. Pinned under their bed, they offered zero resistance and patiently waited to be rescued. Unlike most warrants, these suspects were glad to see the police, even though they ended up in jail.

Now eight SWAT officers climbed onto the rear platform of the AV while the rest of the team followed in the raid van. The procession pulled out, weaving its way through a busy neighborhood. They drove past houses with children playing in the front yards and people walking their dogs. Everyone stopped and gawked at the sight of an armored vehicle rolling down the street, carrying several heavily armed SWAT guys riding on the back like firefighters.

The AV turned on the target street, reducing its speed while lowering the breaching ram in preparation for the hit. The AV mowed down everything as it plowed through the front yard, even decimating a small tree. The siren sounded as the ram struck the door with tremendous force. The PA blasted, "POLICE! THIS IS A SEARCH WARRANT!" The entire house shook as the door, and several supporting 2 x 4s on either side fell inside the home. The team launched off the back of the AV and quickly moved through the vast opening that used to be the front door.

The warrant execution ended successfully, with several suspects in custody within a few minutes. The ram entry left significant damage to the house, so the team began to secure the breached door. Lieutenant Chesney was overseeing the repairs when he received a call from the Homicide Division about a possible kidnapping in the Heights area. He wrote down the information and called to Andy, "Hey Andy, take your team and head over to North Main and 18th Street. US Marshalls are requesting our help with a hostage situation." He added, "I don't know much about what they need. Just get things started, and the rest of us will be en route as soon as we are finished here."

Andy's team and a few guys Paul could spare sped off toward the Heights in the raid van. Chesney called the Captain at home and filled him in on the new situation. The Captain confirmed he would be en route and asked Chesney to notify Lieutenant Hurley so they could be prepared if it turned into a stand-off.

To obtain firsthand information on the situation, Andy met several US Marshalls on the scene who had been watching the home. The traffickers were involved in an illegal immigrant smuggling ring. Most of the people inside were held captive against their will, and it was typical for traffickers to demand a ransom in exchange for their release. However, everything changed when an informant told the Marshalls the traffickers had two men tied up in the backroom who they planned to kill.

Andy gathered as much intel as possible and formulated a plan to move closer to the house. He sent Ernie Scott and Mark Flake from the sniper team across the street to provide overwatch if they needed an emergency rescue. When Gilbert arrived, Andy asked him to be ready to follow any vehicle leaving the site. "We'll stand by here if we need to enter the house."

"Roger that," Gilbert replied and hurried off to gather his team.

Chesney and Sergeant Flores arrived, so Andy briefed them and relinquished control. Hurley walked up and wanted a briefing as well, but Andy ignored him and walked away. He had more pressing things to deal with, and he loved the idea of Hurley being in the dark. Ernie radioed they were set in a vacant lot across the street, and from their position, they could see two suspects loading something in the back of a Suburban. Gilbert was informed to stand by, and soon the vehicle drove away, with the raid van not far behind, heading for 610 Loop.

Once on the freeway, Gilbert requested two marked police cars pull the suspects over. The Suburban didn't stop right away, and the officers noticed movement inside the vehicle while it was exiting the freeway, rolling to a stop. The traffickers freed the hostage and demanded he leave the vehicle as though nothing had happened. They threatened to kill his entire family if he dared to mention the kidnapping. The hostage opened the car door, walking to the officers with his hands in the air. Red marks and pieces of duct tape were visible on his face and wrists from days of restraints. At first, he tried sticking to the suspect's story, but he admitted he had been held captive under questioning. One at a time, the kidnappers surrendered and were taken into custody. The arresting officers found two pistols hidden under the floormat of the Suburban and a used roll of duct tape tucked under the seat.

Gilbert radioed Sergeant Flores that the two kidnappers were in custody and the hostage was singing like a bird. At least four armed suspects were in the house, and another bound victim they intended to kill. Andy worried the crooks in the Suburban called the house, so he asked the Captain to move forward and prepare for an emergency assault. The Captain was reluctant, especially with Hurley arguing to begin negotiations.

"You don't know how committed these guys are, Captain," pleaded Andy. "If they think they can get away with it, they may do something drastic."

The Captain had to consider both sides of the argument because Hurley argued the exact opposite. "OK. Move your guys closer but stay hidden, don't do anything unless I give the OK. Got it?" the Captain sternly directed.

"Yes, sir," Andy replied. He gathered his team and orchestrated a move along the ditch to the driveway and staged by some parked cars. Gary would lead the way, but Andy warned, "If we're seen, this all goes to shit!"

Andy spotted Erik Mullen and waved him over because he needed a fifth man, and Erik was perfect for the job. Although Erik was new on the team and didn't have much experience, he was sharp and always willing to help. He loved to dabble in photography as a hobby and always carried a camera with him for those spur-of-the-moment shots. Erik hurried to fall in line, and Andy whispered, "Just key off what we do." He nodded, dropped into the stack, and they carefully moved down the ditch.

Gary found a staging spot behind a car at the end of the driveway. It was an excellent place to launch, so Andy keyed his mic and whispered, "Andy to Ernie, do you see us?"

"That's clear. We have the front of the house covered."

"Clear, any movement?"

"Nothing, but several lights are on inside," Ernie responded.

Andy then radioed Flores they were in position and standing by.

Several minutes passed as they awkwardly huddled in the ditch to stay concealed. Occasionally a vehicle would drive by, and they'd hunker down even further to avoid the headlights.

Suddenly Ernie radioed, "Front door is open! Several suspects are heading to the driveway."

The worst-case scenario was coming true. A man and woman were having a conversation in Spanish as they approached the car. The discussion was casual, and Andy's team laid motionless in the ditch, hoping they wouldn't be spotted. The group remained unnoticed as they rounded the front bumper. When she opened the door, the vehicle's dome light shone down on them, and she began screaming. Andy yelled, "COMPROMISE! COMPROMISE!"

"React has been compromised," Ernie radioed as they bolted from the ditch.

The team swarmed both sides of the car, taking the suspects down without incident. The traffickers were caught entirely off guard by the commandos appearing from the darkness. As soon as all four were on the ground and cuffed, Andy realized the hostage must still be in the house, and the element of surprise was gone.

Andy yelled at Erik, "Cover them! We're gonna take the house."

"Clear got it!"

Andy pointed at the door, "Go," they shuffled in behind Gary toward the front door, and whatever waited for them there. The door was partially open with a light on indoors, and Rob pushed it open the rest of the way. Mo tossed in a flash-bang, and BOOM! There was a brilliant flash and thunderous explosion just inside the doorway, then Gary launched through with Mo on his heels.

A male suspect was lying on the floor with his hands raised after suffering the direct effects of the flash-bang, and that was enough for him. A gun sat on the kitchen counter, and the phone was off the hook. He had been calling someone when the room erupted. Rob remained with the suspect while Gary, Mo, and Andy cleared the premise. When they entered another room, they found a Hispanic male lying on the floor in the fetal position, bound and gagged with his ankles taped together. He must have been there for days because his pants were soiled, covered in dried urine.

Andy stayed with the captive while Gary and Mo searched the rest of the house, but no one else was found. Andy notified the CP the house was secure and the hostage was OK. "Clear. The Captain is coming forward." The Captain was likely pissed they entered the house without approval.

Erik made his way inside, asking Andy if he could help. "Sure, let's get this guy up." They began pulling duct tape off the hostage's mouth and eyes. They sat him up, and when they tried to communicate with him, he didn't speak English.

"We should have got a picture of him taped up," mentioned Erik.

"Awe shit," exclaimed Andy. "Yeah, that would have been cool. Too late now."

"Well, maybe not." With his minimal knowledge of Spanish, Erik communicated with the hostage. Finally, the victim understood when Erik pointed at his camera, so he laid back down in the fetal position. Erik taped him up the way he was found and started taking photos. After Erik finished taking his snapshots, he removed the tape again.

"ANDY," rang out the Captain's voice from the front of the house.

"In here, Captain," Andy replied, preparing for the inevitable.

"What smells like shit?" he asked when he walked into the small room with Hurley behind him.

"He does," Erik replied, pointing to the hostage.

The Captain looked at the hostage and then to Andy, "I thought I said don't do anything without my OK!"

"I know, Captain, but I had no choice," pleaded Andy. "We were compromised when they walked out on us, and the hostage wasn't with them."

"How did you know that?" interrupted the Captain.

"No one was bound or gagged. They were all walking separately. When she started screaming, I knew anyone inside the house must have heard her."

"You couldn't know that," Hurley interjected.

"Sure, like you didn't know that father wasn't gonna slit his son's throat," accused Andy.

Hurley's eyes widened in outrage, "That was different!"

"HOLD ON," the Captain interrupted, raising his arms to calm them down, "This isn't the time or the place." Andy and Hurley angrily glared at each other, and the Captain continued, "We'll discuss this later. Is he the only hostage?"

"Yes, sir," Andy replied. "He was laying here, bound and gagged, and the guy in the front room
was on the phone when we entered."

The Captain looked around as if he was starting to understand Andy's predicament. Finally, he turned and pushed Hurley to leave along with him as he said, "We'll talk later."

"I thought the Captain was going to eat your ass," said Erik shockingly.

"Yeah," Andy replied. "He still might. It ain't over." Then, he walked toward the front of the house to check on Rob and the prisoner.

Soon, they turned the scene over to the Marshalls and Homicide detectives, but Andy worried about what tomorrow would bring. The van dropped off everyone at the office, and Andy headed straight for the nearest convenience store. He drove home repeatedly, analyzing the entire call-up, knowing he did the right thing as he sipped his drink. Now the question was how he would explain it to the Captain. Obviously, Hurley would be arguing the other side.

The following day was anticlimactic. The Captain never challenged Andy. Later, Flores told him that during the supervisor meeting, they concluded the right call was made. Of course, Andy was relieved, but he had been looking forward to a chance to confront Hurley. There would be more opportunities. Andy was sure of it.

Dog Days of Summer

The Houston summer roared in full force on that hot and humid morning. While the group cooled down in the air-conditioned office before their workout, Andy filled his team in on the alligators continually showing up in his pond. When he caught one, he would relocate it to a lake in the back of his subdivision. Sergeant Wills was over listening and interjected, "Hey Andy, do you really catch those things?"

Andy nodded, "Yeah, but only the small ones. I don't mess with anything over two or three feet."

"Man, I have some beavers destroying my lake, and I could use a gator to run their asses out of there. Do you think the next time you catch one, you could bring it to me?"

"Sure, Sarg. I'll keep an eye out for one." Once Andy finished his story, they reluctantly braved the outdoors for their grueling workout in the sweltering heat.

After cooling off with a quick shower, Andy was paged to Sergeant Bird's office. When the fugitive detail requested help with the warrant backlog, the Captain agreed. Now there were several blue warrants the Sergeant needed to assign. Anytime a convict's parole needed to be revoked, a blue warrant was issued, returning them to prison. Each warrant contained the convict's last known address, but it would require an early morning execution to apprehend the ex-con. Andy selected a warrant for his team and agreed to track the individual.

The warrant execution plan entailed utilizing the raid van to drive by the location and conduct reconnaissance on the house and surrounding neighborhood. After running their initial checks on the spot, the team agreed to meet at the Shell gas station near the subdivision at 5 am. Since it was possible they may need to first walk by the location, Andy directed everyone to wear street clothes. Then, they'd use raid jackets for identification when it came time to knock on the door.

Andy arrived at the gas station at 4:45 am, sipping on his coffee in the parking lot. Within a few minutes, the rest of the team arrived and reviewed the plan. Rob and Mo would be situated around the back of the house, just outside the fence. The backyard contained a few small dog sheds and no grass from the satellite photos, indicating the yard was the dog's domain. So Gary and Andy would knock on the front door, and hopefully, someone would let them in.

To limit the procession of vehicles moving toward the house, Andy hopped into Gary's car, and Mo jumped into Rob's. They cut their headlights and quietly rolled to a stop a couple of houses away, then quickly moved to their assigned positions outside the residence. Andy banged on the front door, "POLICE DEPARTMENT! OPEN THE DOOR!"

"A light just came on in the back," Mo radioed.

"Clear," Andy replied as he cautiously stepped back to the door and knocked again. "POLICE OFFICERS! OPEN THE DOOR!"

Finally, a woman responded, "What do you want?"

"Police officers, ma'am," Andy responded. "We have an arrest warrant for Thomas Williams."

"He's not here," she replied.

"This address is on the warrant, so you need to open the door," demanded Andy.

An elderly woman peered out of the slightly open door dressed in a housecoat. Andy stepped under the porch light so she could see his police raid jacket. "Good morning, Ma'am. I'm officer Wallace, and this is officer Barkley." He held up the blue warrant and said, "We have a warrant for Thomas with this address, so you need to let us in."

Reluctantly, she opened the door. "Thomas ain't here. You are wasting your time," the old woman mumbled. Andy radioed Rob to join them as the woman sauntered off toward the kitchen.

Rob and Gary started a slow search of the small two-bedroom home while Andy held an over-watch, remaining with the old woman. The tiny house was quickly cleared. Then they stepped into the attached garage to search there as well. A car was parked in one of the stalls, Rob walked over to check the hood, and it was still warm. It couldn't have been there for more than an hour or two.

Next, they searched the vehicle's interior and the rest of the garage. Finally, Gary called out, "Hey Andy, come check this out." Directly below an attic access door, pieces of insulation were on the hood of the car. Andy smiled at Gary and called out to the old woman, "Ms. Williams! Is Thomas in the attic?"

"I don't know."

"You need to tell us now. We aren't going away."

"I don't know," she pleaded and turned to sit back down.

Andy radioed Mo they were entering the attic. Mo replied, "Clear. Standing by."

Andy heard several dogs barking in the backyard, "Are those dogs loose?"

"No," Mo responded. "They're chained to their dog houses."

Andy asked Rob to stay with Ms. Thomas while he assisted Gary with searching the attic. Gary stepped onto the vehicle's hood, slowly pushed open the hatch door of the attic, and moved it off to one side. "Thomas, this is the police department. You need to come down and give yourself up. We don't want to hurt you, but we are not going away," Gary shouted, waiting for a reply that never came.

Gary slowly entered the attic with Andy following closely behind, shining their flashlights in every direction. Immediately Andy couldn't help but think of the last time he searched an attic, but he would have to put this feeling of déjà vu aside and focus on the task. Gary carefully climbed over ceiling rafters and searched behind the scattered boxes as Andy stayed near the hatch to oversee. Then, as Gary was panning his light through the dark attic, he spotted him. "Hey, you," he hollered. "Behind the boxes, we see you!" Andy turned his flashlight toward the boxes, and Thomas raised his head to see where the voice commands were coming from. Then, he ducked back down and kicked the sheetrock below him, breaking a large chunk loose.

"STOP!" Gary screamed as Thomas dropped through the hole he made and fell to the garage floor.

"ROB! HE'S IN THE GARAGE!" Andy yelled.

Rob had followed the old woman to the living room, so he turned and ran back toward the attic hatch. Andy peeked through the opening to see Thomas running through a door to the backyard. "There he goes!" Andy shouted as Rob entered the garage and gave chase.

Thomas sprinted into the dimly lit backyard toward a 6-foot wooden fence, with dogs barking all around him. He slowed down to grab a wooden plank just as Rob grabbed him and pulled him back. They tumbled onto the ground, and Rob struggled to get the man under control. With a pistol in his right hand, Rob only had his left to fight with as he tried to hang on until help arrived. Andy joined the melee as the three rolled around on the muddy ground in the darkness. They didn't dare try to holster them for fear their holsters wouldn't retain their weapons during the commotion. Suddenly Andy realized it wasn't mud after all. The area must contain a lot of large dogs because the entire ground surface was covered in piles of shit, and they were rolling around in it.

Even though Thomas was a big man, he was surprised at his strength as he easily stood up with Andy hanging onto his back. Rob had pinned his legs, but Thomas quickly kicked him loose. Andy had one arm around Thomas' neck, and the other held his pistol as he tried his best to squeeze Thomas unconscious. Instead, Thomas quickly bent forward and flipped Andy over him, forcing him to fall face-first into the feces-covered yard. The impact of the fall on the hard ground nearly knocked him out, and his pistol dislodged from his hand, bouncing away.

Dazed, struggling to see and not to gag from the dog shit in his mouth and covering his eyes and nose, Andy slowly tried to regain his faculties. Finally, his vision focused, and Rob and Thomas were standing above him, fighting over Rob's pistol against the city's night sky. For a second, Andy panicked, not knowing where his pistol was. But right now wasn't the time to look for it, so he jumped to his feet and joined the fight for Rob's gun.

Soon, Thomas realized he wouldn't win the fight, so he let go and took off running, leaving Andy and Rob behind, still struggling over the pistol. As he ran toward the back fence, Gary appeared from the garage and grabbed him before he could clear it. They slid, falling back into the yard, and Andy and Rob caught up and rejoined the struggle. After Mo finally arrived, Thomas was eventually overpowered, pinned, and handcuffed.

Thomas started yelling, "DOGS! WATCH OUT FOR THE DOGS!" Andy ignored his effort to distract them or the barking pit bulls. If they were vicious and going to join the fight, they would have done it by now. At this point, he was completely covered in dog shit and didn't care.

When they walked Thomas inside the home, his mother wailed, "Let my boy go! Don't you hurt him!" Under the garage lights, Andy looked down at his clothing covered in feces and remembered his pistol. He ran back into the yard, and sure enough, it was lying in a massive pile of dog shit. He picked it up, slung off some dung, wiped it on his pants, and holstered it in revulsion.

Mo was the only one not covered in feces, grimacing at the sight and smell of his teammates. But he didn't dare to say anything. Andy was developing a massive shiner on his right eye from the hit to the ground, and Mo was relieved to have missed the backyard wrestling match. Andy radioed for a patrol car to transport Thomas. Gary laid out a couple of towels from his gym bag to sit on as they drove back to the Shell station. Forced to roll the windows down to keep from gagging, Gary couldn't help but slightly chuckle. Andy, however, failed to see the humor as his eye continued swelling.

They stopped at the gas station, and Andy stripped down to his underwear and put on his gym clothes for the ride to the office. From the water faucet on the side of the building, he attempted to wash his hands and face, but there was no way to get his hair clean, so he didn't even try. Rob and Gary tried their best to clean up as well; everyone was cursing and gagging the entire time.

They showered in scalding hot water for at least 20 minutes at the office, trying to remove the stench. When Andy finally finished and looked in the mirror, he had a black eye. But, he was grateful it was his only injury because he knew it could have been much worse if Thomas had gotten ahold of Rob's pistol.

All of the guys around the office got a hoot out of the dog shit story, and Andy took quite a bit of ribbing afterward. Until the story got old, sounds of dogs barking over the PA and finding dog treats mysteriously on his desk became commonplace. He took the banter well from everyone except Hurley, but he didn't take anything well from Hurley.

When the weekend arrived, Andy took the family fishing on the San Bernard River, but heavy summer rain ended their trip early. As they pulled into the driveway, there was a small gator in the pond, the perfect size to transport to the office. He grabbed his cast net, tossed it over the gator, and just like that; he had the reptile captured. Andy grabbed an ice chest to hold the creature for delivery. He couldn't wait to see the look on Sergeant Wills' face!

Monday morning, Andy carried the ice chest down the hall, past the Sergeant's office, to their bathroom. Luckily no one was there yet, so he opened the glass shower door, turned the ice chest on its side, and waited. The small alligator snuck its head out and crawled into the shower a few seconds later. Andy closed the door and carried the ice chest back to the car to stow it, laughing in anticipation of Wills' reaction.

Patiently, Andy sipped his coffee in the dayroom until Wills finally walked in to pour a cup. "Morning Sarg!"

"Morning, Andy."

"Hey, do you still want a gator?" Andy asked.

"Sure do," replied Wills. "You got one?"

"Yep!"

"Great! Where's he at?"

"In your shower," Andy answered and burst into laughter.

Wills laughed too and took a sip of his coffee. There was an awkward silence as Wills walked away, and then after he turned the corner, he looked back at Andy, who just smiled and nodded his head. "No, really, where's it at?"

Andy took another sip and grinned, "In your shower."

Wills stood there with a blank look for a few seconds, then put his coffee down and hurried off toward his office. Within a few seconds, he ran back into the dayroom, yelling, "There's a fucking alligator in my shower!"

"I know. You wanted one, right?"

Wills exclaimed, "Yeah, but not in my shower! How the fuck do I get him out of there?"

Andy shrugged his shoulders, grinned, and said, "I only deliver Sarg!"

Irritated, Wills glared at Andy and stomped off.

Firearms training was scheduled for the day, so his team headed to the Academy range as soon as Andy finished his workout. The following morning, Andy ran into Wills at the coffee machine. "How's the gator business Sarg?"

"Good," Wills replied.

"How'd you get him out of the shower?" Andy asked.

Wills threw his gym towel over the gator and wrestled him into another ice chest. Later that day, he carried the chest to his lake and released him. "Man, when those beavers spotted that gator crawling in one side, they scampered out the other side."

They laughed as Andy added, "Yeah, the party is over, boys!"

Wills said the alligator had ravaged his towel and chewed a massive hole through the middle. "You owe me a new towel."

"Let's call it even, and I won't charge you a delivery fee!"

"Fair enough," Wills chuckled and walked away with coffee in hand.

Live at 5

There was no pattern to the frequency of call-ups. Sometimes they wouldn't get a call for two weeks, and then the floodgates would open with two or three on the same day, sometimes simultaneously. Maybe the hot summer days had something to do with it or a full moon, but the work kept coming.

Most of the situations were run-of-the-mill surround and call out. Of course, Hurley would take credit for talking the individual out. Often the person just needed to sober up or take their meds to start thinking rationally. Others were simply scared and wanted to ensure they wouldn't be shot when they surrendered.

One suspect was so convinced that SWAT would kill him that it took the negotiators nearly two hours to convince him that he would not be harmed. He continually insisted the SWAT guys would kill him if he left the safety of his home. Then the negotiator responded, "No, they will not kill you!"

"Yes, they will," the suspect promptly refuted, and on and on, the dialogue went, getting nowhere.

Finally, the negotiator asked, "Why are you so convinced the SWAT guys will kill you?"

After a short silence, the man said, "Well, before you guys got here, the cops were trying to talk me out too."

"Yeah, so?"

"Well, they told me, 'OK, asshole, now you've done it! SWAT is on their way, and when they get here, they're gonna kill you!'" It took almost another hour to convince the suspect that the patrol officers weren't serious.

On another call, Andy made the 'Live at Five!' news feed, but not in a good way. Patrol interrupted a robbery at a Jack in the Box restaurant in the Heights part of town. Following a short stand-off, the employees escaped out the front door, and the robber crawled up into the attic to hide. A typical response when there was no place else to go.

After several unsuccessful attempts to contact the suspect, Gilbert's team was tasked with searching the restaurant. Hurley argued for more time, but considering the restaurant was positioned at a major intersection, the Captain was unwilling to keep it shut down for long.

Once Gilbert was ready to enter the attic, Andy moved several perimeter positions in the southeast parking lot. If a gunfight erupted in the attic, the trajectory of Gilbert's team's bullets could exit the building's thin sheet metal in their direction.

It was 5 pm, and most Houston TV stations were broadcasting live. The media had set their cameras a block away but zoomed in on the activity, hoping to capture some action.

The suspect was found behind ductwork in the southeast corner, and Gilbert demanded his surrender. Unexpectedly, he began forcibly kicking the metal which enclosed the awning around the edge of the building. Eventually, the thin metal panel gave way, and the robber dropped out of the attic onto the parking lot outside the building. Surprised, he stood up and looked around as the news cameras zoomed in on him.

The long shadows of the setting sun stretched across the parking lot as the crook ran from the building. "I ain't got a gun! You can't shoot me! I ain't got a gun!" he shouted with his hands in the air, sprinting across several lanes of the empty intersection. The live news cameras followed closely behind him.

Jimmy Chin was the closest perimeter guy and took off running after him. Andy also gave chase as the suspect ran across the deserted intersection with the news cameras rolling. At first, the reporters tried to give a play-by-play of the action, but they couldn't keep up with everything unfolding so quickly.

A shut-down gas station was on the other side of the intersection, with abandoned vehicles scattered about. They maneuvered past the gas pumps, and as they approached the corner of the building, Jimmy closed in on the crook.

Once they rounded the corner, Andy lost sight of the chase, but as he rounded the turn, 'BOOM!' a gunshot rang out. Temporarily stunned by the large muzzle flash, Andy tried to focus on who shot who. A female uniformed officer stood next to the building with her pistol pointed at the robber laid out on the pavement. She was petrified, standing completely still, unable to believe what had just happened. Andy's expression was much the same as Jimmy checked himself for a bullet wound.

The man clutched his stomach, rocking back and forth in immense pain. "I didn't have a gun! Why did she shoot me?"

"I thought he had a gun," she exclaimed.

Andy and Jimmy knelt beside the suspect and searched him, but he was unarmed. "I grabbed his arm as we rounded the building, and he spun on me," Jimmy explained. "That's when the gunshot rang out. I thought he shot me. I didn't even see her. I swear my whole life flashed before my eyes!"

Andy nodded in understanding and walked over to console the officer. "You can holster your pistol." She snapped out of the shock and abruptly holstered her weapon. Andy comfortingly patted her on the back and assured her, "It's gonna be OK. Just tell what happened, and you'll be fine."

Not pleased with her reflexive response, she dropped her head and said, "I could have sworn I saw a gun!"

Andy nodded in agreement and told her, "It's OK!"

The EMTs loaded the robber on a gurney and transported him to the hospital, where he was treated and eventually recovered from his wounds. Later, in a live interview, the Captain had to explain how the suspect escaped the building only to be shot by a patrol officer on the outer perimeter.

The entire event made for excellent television, but it was an embarrassing moment for Andy and the SWAT team. Although, it was a valuable lesson learned about metal awnings surrounding fast-food restaurants. Hurley made the most out of the misstep, using the incident to poke at Andy every chance he got. Andy tried his best to ignore him.

They hadn't had the opportunity to critique the last two call-ups when a barricaded gunman in the Clear Lake area dropped. Andy was assigned the entry team, so he went about learning all he could about the suspect.

Nearly everyone despised the suspect; even his children disowned him and moved away. Months ago, he kicked his wife out of the house, and she had become destitute, living in homeless shelters and relying on the kindness of friends to get by. The man constantly harassed his neighbors, and they knew the day would come when he went completely off his rocker.

That day came quicker than anyone expected. He shot at patrol officers responding to a domestic argument between him and his next-door neighbor. After firing at the officers, he retreated into his house and threatened to kill anyone in his yard.

Paul Kandi's team moved around to the backside of the detached garage. They would provide a barrier if the suspect attempted to reach his vehicle. The paranoid suspect had motion sensors surrounding the garage that sounded an alarm inside the house. Once alerted, the suspect picked up his rifle and walked out his back door, looking toward the garage with his rifle pointed in Paul's direction.

A SWAT sniper was positioned at the rear of the house, approximately 50 yards away. He and an observer were watching the man approach the garage. "Suspect's out the back door. He has a rifle. He's walking toward Paul's location," the observer reported.

"Clear," the command post responded. "You have a green light. Do not let him get to the garage!"

Everyone silently waited for the sound of a .308 rifle report. The sniper carefully watched, hoping the man would turn around, but he didn't. Instead, the gunshot cracked through the quiet neighborhood, the bullet found its mark, and the man instantly crumpled to the ground.

After paramedics pronounced him dead, the team picked up their equipment and waited in front of the house for Homicide and the Medical Examiner's office to arrive and begin their investigation. Andy stood out front with several other SWAT officers mulling over what just happened. He glanced over his shoulder and noticed a small crowd of neighbors gathering. As they chatted amongst themselves, they slowly inched toward the scene.

Reluctantly, one of them stepped forward as the spokesman for the group. He patiently waited to get someone's attention, but Andy avoided eye contact. SWAT never liked talking with emotionally involved family and friends, and it wasn't their job. Moreover, they had no idea if this guy had been a friend or family member, so it was best not to engage.

Finally, the man got the nerve to call out, "Excuse me, officers?"

Andy was the only Team Leader in the group, so everyone looked to him. He didn't want to be rude and ignore the man, so he turned around and asked, "Can I help you?"

"Yes, sir," the man nervously responded. "I was wondering, or rather we were wondering," the man said as he glanced back at the neighbors, "Is he dead? I mean, is Mr. Johnson, OK?" he asked solemnly.

Andy paused, trying to think of how best to answer without invoking an emotional response from someone who cared about the man. "Well, unfortunately..." As he struggled for the right words, Andy said, "Mr. Johnson is deceased."

The man's expression suddenly changed to glee as he turned to the group, thrust his arms in the air, and yelled, "HE'S DEAD!" The group spontaneously burst into cheers, with some even high-fiving one another. It was like the Wicked Witch had been expelled from their neighborhood, and now they could finally live in peace. The group walked away, grateful the neighborhood could return to normal.

Once they cleared the scene, Andy headed to a convenience store to fix an elixir for the long ride home. He thought about Mike and what life must be like for him now. He was transferred to Ramsey prison, the same prison where the team used to train. Even though it wasn't far from his house, and he wanted to visit, the time wasn't right yet. So, Andy took another sip and realized how fortunate he was to live in the country, where life was simpler and his neighbors were acres away. The problems of the congested city didn't make it that far, and his long drive home was worth it.

TWENTY-TWO

Nightmare in Katy

After Arnold Price lost his job working at a steel mill in Detroit, Michigan, his life quickly spiraled into depression and alcoholism. His loving wife of 12 years, Angie, had become scared of his controlling and abusive behavior. Together, they had five young children, so she desperately tried to save their marriage.

One night, after his abuse became more than she could endure, she called the police for help. A stand-off ensued between Arnold and patrol officers, and as the situation escalated, a SWAT team responded. Once they had the house surrounded, they tried to reason with him, but he was having none of it. Eventually, they tricked him into walking out his back door for more cigarettes and booze and ambushed him. SWAT hit Price with impact munitions, they wrestled him to the ground, and police took him into custody.

He pled guilty to the battery of his wife and resisting arrest and was sentenced to 30 days in the county jail. The entire experience was enough to sober him up, and he swore to turn his life around. Once out of jail, Angie and Arnold patched things up and decided to move to Katy, Texas, for a new job opportunity and a fresh start.

Arnold worked a factory job west of town, and the family rented a modest 3-bedroom home in Katy. Unfortunately, it didn't take long for him to start drinking again, and soon he was caught with booze at work and was summarily fired.

Once again, Arnold's vicious cycle of spiraling down into a drunken depression occurred. All his children were terrified of him, especially when he was drunk, so they tried to stay out of his way. When Angie realized there was no path forward, she threatened to leave and take the children with her. "You ain't going anywhere. You so much as even try, and I'll kill you and the kids before I lose you," Arnold angrily promised.

Angie feared going to bed that night and anxiously worried about what she should do. Finally, after lying for hours listening to him snore, she garnered the courage to make a move. Quietly, she dressed, slipped out the door, and walked down the street to the Katy Police Department.

Petrified and shaking, Angie spilled her guts to the night shift Sergeant about her abusive husband. He reassuringly calmed her and told her not to worry; they had handled many similar situations. All he needed to do was talk some sense into Arnold. Even though she argued that it was not a good idea, she eventually relented and gave him their phone number.

When Arnold answered the phone, the sergeant introduced himself and told him that his wife was in his office. Then, with authority, he lectured how they don't put up with this sort of behavior in Katy, and he better straighten up his act, or he would end up in a Texas jail. Arnold didn't take constructive criticism well and calmly asked to talk to Angie. The Sergeant explained that he could come to the station to speak with her, but he wasn't falling for that again. "Listen, you tell that bitch that she better get back here now, or I'll kill these kids, and there ain't nothing you or anyone else can do about it," Arnold shouted, slamming down the phone.

Stunned, the Sergeant turned to Angie, "Well, that didn't go well."

The situation escalated beyond the Sergeant's paygrade, so he called the night shift commander and explained the situation. As a smaller town, the Katy Police Department didn't have its own SWAT team or negotiators. Instead, they had a mutual aid agreement with the City of Houston. So, when the Katy Police Chief was called at home, he agreed to make a formal request to the Houston SWAT team and their negotiators for help.

Just after midnight, Andy's pager woke him from a dead sleep. Katy was a 40-minute drive, so he stumbled into the kitchen and turned on the coffee maker like he had so many times before. He had no way of knowing how different this "typical" call would turn out.

The staging area was a block down the street from the suspect's house because they didn't want Arnold to know that the SWAT team had been called. As more operators arrived, they quietly deployed toward the objective in the cover of darkness and took containment positions around the house. Andy was assigned the react position, so he gathered his guys and moved forward to find a staging location. Due to the size of the home, Andy needed additional operators, especially with the number of children they needed to rescue. He asked Mark Levey and Dan Mayfair to join his team, making six. A solid number until more men were available.

The team quietly crept through the bushes toward Arnold's house, using the garage as a staging area. They knew nothing of Arnold's capabilities or what kind of weapons he had, but his wife mentioned he owned a handgun. This part of Katy was so quaint and peaceful. It was difficult to believe someone living here threatened to kill their entire family. Sergeant Bird arrived and gave Andy a quick debrief. "OK, what are the rules of engagement?" inquired Andy.

"I don't know that yet but hold what you've got for now unless you know he's killing those kids," replied Bird.

"Roger that."

In the command post, supervisors analyzed the situation and tried to develop a game plan. After Hurley spoke in length to Angie about their history, he had a strategy. Confidently, he walked straight into the CP and started bending the Captain's ear about how this guy needed a dose of reality. "We need to tell Arnold what kind of mess he's in. Right now, he thinks he's dealing with a small-town PD. He needs to know that the entire Houston SWAT Team is just outside his door. He isn't crazy. He's a drunk. He needs to know that he's surrounded and has no option but to surrender."

Although the Captain was skeptical about such a rigid approach, Hurley was convincing as always. Skilled in the art of debate, after a few minutes, the Captain conceded.

Sergeant Flores radioed to the men standing perimeter that the negotiators would attempt phone contact. However, to be prepared if the call drew a bad reaction, Andy requested an explosive charge be set on the utility door first. Hurley didn't want to wait, but the Captain agreed. Charlie Shirk, a member of the Bomb Squad who facilitated explosive breaching for the team, was assigned to place the charge.

Quietly, Gary Barkley led the Team to the utility side of the house where Charlie placed the charge; all he had to do now was hit the initiator, and the explosion would breach the door. Precious seconds at the threshold could save lives, maybe their own. Andy radioed they were standing by. Flores broadcasted, "All Officers, negotiators are ringing the phone."

Always worried of the first phone contact in a hostage situation, Andy eased forward and whispered, "Be ready, guys."

Flores radioed, "Suspect is on the phone."

When Arnold answered the phone, Hurley didn't hold back as he authoritatively explained who he was and that the house was surrounded. Then, Hurley demanded he leave his gun inside and walk out with his hands in the air. After an awkward pause, Arnold sneered in a low, ice-cold tone, "I told you what would happen if she didn't come back," and hung up.

Shocked at his response, Hurley slowly lowered the phone and looked at his negotiators with a blank stare, unsure of his decision. Nervously, he worried about what Arnold meant. Had he miscalculated Arnold's intentions? Surely, he wasn't serious about killing the kids. He advised the captain that Arnold was thinking it over.

Flores broke the air, "All officers, the suspect hung up the phone." Everyone anxiously awaited an update on the suspect's reaction. Usually, CP relayed what was said, but nothing so far. So, they stood beside the house in the darkness of the warm summer night, wondering what was happening inside.

Suddenly pounding sounds vibrated through the exterior wall. The sound was muffled, but there was a steady, loud noise, at least five or six times and then silence again. It only lasted a few seconds, and Andy anxiously whispered, "What was that?"

"I don't know," Rob Striker whispered back as he strained to hear more.

Mo chimed in, "I think he's hammering. Maybe he's barricading an inside door."

Although Andy wasn't sure what it was, he hoped Mo was right. But he had to report it, so he keyed his mic and whispered, "Andy to CP, we just heard sounds inside the objective. We think he may be barricading an interior door."

"That's clear," replied Flores.

Feeling sick, Andy looked at his guys for reassurance. Maybe he knew better and just didn't want to go there. He hoped for the best as he tried to convince himself that the noise was hammering, and he was sticking to that.

Hurley explained to the Captain that the suspect was in a defensive state of mind and was barricading himself. "He's trying to keep us out, so he must be worried about us coming in." Hurley preferred the idea of Arnold being a little intimidated. He decided to call Arnold back and double down, but the phone just rang. Unsure, he hung up the phone, wondering why Arnold didn't answer. 'Surely, he wouldn't...', Hurley thought, picked up the phone, and dialed again.

After ten unanswered attempts, Hurley asked the Captain to check with the perimeter guys to determine if anyone could hear the ringing. "Maybe he yanked the phone out of the wall, and it's not ringing on his end."

Flores radioed, "CP to all perimeter officers. Can anyone hear the phone ringing?"

After a short silence, Andy keyed his mic, "Andy to CP, we are right next to what appears to be a bedroom wall, and we don't hear the phone."

"Clear," Flores replied.

"That's it!" Hurley exclaimed. "He's pulled the damn phone out of the wall because he doesn't want to talk." The Captain wanted to believe him, but he wasn't convinced.

Hurley directed his guys to position their stadium speakers around all four sides of the house and start blasting messages to Arnold. "Give us some sign that you're OK?" No response.

Paul Kandi broke the air, "Kandi to CP, do you want to deploy devices?" Typically, the next course of action would be to deploy listening devices and motion sensors.

"That's clear," replied a supervisor.

When Paul hurried back to the CP to collect equipment, the supervisor on duty appeared worried. Unaware of any new information or Hurley's hard-core tactics, he dismissed his somber eyes and gathered what he needed. Within a few minutes, they had several devices planted around the house. They began monitoring for the slightest sounds, but nothing was coming from inside after listening for more than an hour.

Hurley continued with the stance that Arnold was scared and barricaded somewhere, so they weren't detecting movement. "We need to make some noise and get him moving around." The Captain was desperate for good news, so Flores requested the perimeter team make some noise. The group threw rocks and any other small objects they could find onto the roof and against the side of the house, making as much noise as possible. But still no movement.

Hurley doubled down and argued, "We need to break some windows. That will surely draw a reaction!" Reluctantly, the Captain agreed with Hurley's strategy; he wasn't going to change course now. So, one at a time, Gilbert's team broke the bedroom windows and listened for a response.

At almost 6 am, daylight was starting to peek over the horizon, and Andy's team attempted to relax a little. They had grown weary and incredibly frustrated after standing at the ready for hours. Andy was in the middle of chewing on a breakfast bar when Flores requested he report to the CP.

"What the fuck?" Rob asked.

"Who knows." Andy replied, "Look if something happens while I'm gone and you think you need to go, don't hesitate. Trust your instincts." Andy looked at Charlie, "If they call for a breach, you hit that damn thing and make the door go away." Charlie nodded. Andy gave his guys a wink walking away, and mumbled, "Let's see what words of wisdom they have now."

When he rounded the garage corner, he spotted the Captain, Chesney, and Hurley standing by the CP. 'Uh-oh! What the fuck did I do now?' he wondered. As he got within speaking distance, he said, "Hey guys. Fancy meeting you here." Andy's humor was not appreciated; everyone looked concerned. "What's up?"

Chesney handed Andy a key to the house, "We got this key from the wife. It should open any exterior door. We want you to search the house covertly. Do not engage if you find the suspect. Just back up to a place that you can hold, and we'll bring in a negotiator to start talking."

"OK, but what if he starts shooting?" Andy asked, concerned for their safety.

Chesney nodded, "Of course, defend yourselves, but hopefully, he won't know you're there."

Hurley stepped forward defensively, "Look, we don't want to provoke this guy. Just find him, and we'll take it from there."

Intentionally, Andy didn't look at Hurley and directly replied to Chesney, "Roger that. We'll see if we can find him."

The Captain appeared distressed. 'We've been in many situations like this before, so why is this one giving the Captain so much grief?' Andy wondered, observing his high-strung demeanor. Most of the team was utterly unaware Hurley had decided to go tough guy on Arnold, with approval from the Captain. But, of course, now that he and Hurley were in this together, the Captain was second-guessing that decision.

Andy explained the plan to his team along with the rules of engagement. The utility door was the best entry point, so Charlie removed the explosives. Andy asked his team, "You ready for this?" Everyone nodded, but they weren't sure what he was asking. He wanted everyone to be mentally prepared for what they might find.

Now that the sun was up, there was plenty of light to work with. Gary tried the key in the deadbolt lock, but it wouldn't fit. With his flashlight, he peered into the keyway and spotted the problem. A key was broken off inside the lock, and it was hopelessly damaged. If Arnold had fixed one lock, he most likely fixed them all. "Andy to CP, the lock has been sabotaged. The key will not work. Permission to manually breach the door?"

The Captain dropped his head as the realization set in that Arnold was more cunning than they expected. After contemplating the fix they were in for a minute, he reluctantly nodded his approval to Flores. "CP to Andy, clear to breach."

Mo was in position with the ram, Andy gave the signal, and the door burst open with a mighty swing. Mo dropped the ram and hurried back while they waited for a reaction. For a few seconds, they carefully watched the empty doorway; then, Andy tapped Gary to clear the threshold behind a ballistic shield. Next, they quietly entered the utility room and then the kitchen, where they paused to listen for signs of Arnold or the children, but there was only silence. They methodically cleared the dining room and living room, noticing almost every room had pictures of the kids. Everyone looked so happy and innocent. Andy pleaded to himself, 'Please let them be OK,' fearful the worst might be waiting for them.

They only had the bedrooms left and paused to take a breather while Kandi's team used a camera pole to clear the back bedrooms from the outside. Soon everything but the master bedroom had been searched. Andy was convinced that Arnold was waiting for them there.

Listening devices and fiber optics were set on the bedroom wall to find out as much as possible. Gary used a stethoscope and heard something. He snapped his fingers to get Mo's attention, and Mo listened to a similar sound. They motioned Andy over and whispered, "We think we heard a baby cry. It was only for a second, and it sounded muffled, but we heard something." Andy figured Arnold was covering the baby's mouth to keep it quiet. It only confirmed what a sick bastard he was.

Fiber optics under the door provided a view of the bedroom, but they couldn't see into the bathroom and the closed closet door. Andy got permission to breach the exterior window of the master bedroom to get a better cover position on the closet. George Gregor breached the glass within a few minutes and slowly cleared the room. He had eyes on everything and a perfect angle on the closet door.

Andy was ready to end this thing one way or the other. He radioed the CP, "Are we clear to enter the master bedroom?"

There was a long silence, and the CP responded, "Stand by for the Captain to come to your location."

"Roger that," Andy replied as he wondered what the fuck? The Captain never came forward. Maybe he just wanted to see for himself?

Andy told his guys to hold as he walked back through the house toward the mudroom. He met Chesney, the Captain, and Hurley standing in the kitchen. He immediately knew something was up by the look on Chesney's face. Hurley pushed forward to do the talking. "Andy, you can make entry into the bedroom, but we think he's in that closet." Andy stared at Hurley but didn't respond. He couldn't believe Hurley was giving the instructions. Hurley continued, "Once you open the closet door, just get back. We don't want to shoot this guy even if he has a gun. So back out of there and let us talk to him." Andy couldn't believe what he was hearing. It was just like the Allen Parkway Tower incident. Hurley was rolling the dice with innocent life once again.

Andy looked at the Captain, but he wouldn't make eye contact. Then, in an intimidating manner, Hurley moved closer to Andy and demanded, "Can you do that, or do we need to get someone else?"

That struck a chord with Andy because he was never one to shirk responsibility, so he took it as a challenge. He could tell the Captain and Chesney were just as uncomfortable with this idea, but they said nothing.

Andy replied without looking at Hurley, "I got it."

Hurley smiled and said, "OK then." He turned around and smirked at the Captain as if to say, 'I knew he'd do it.' Andy walked directly to George, who was still posted in the window, and whispered, "If we open that closet door, will you have a shot?"

George calmly whispered back, "Yep," without even taking his eyes off the room.

Andy said, "Good! Here's the deal. Hurley said we are not to shoot this asshole, but I'm telling you that if you have a shot, take it. If you see the bastard with a gun, you smoke that motherfucker. Got it?"

"I got it!" George replied without hesitation.

Andy knew he would do it too as he smiled and slapped George on the back. Andy motioned his guys away from the bedroom so that he could speak without whispering, "OK, we're gonna take the bedroom. The doorknob is locked, so Mo will breach it. We'll scan it, and then Dan and Mark will move across and clear the bathroom while we cover the closet."

Andy pointed at Mark and Dan, "Once the bathroom is clear, open the closet door and get back. George has a shot from across the room. If the shot isn't there, he'll give us the go, and we'll take the room."

"Roger that," Mark answered.

Andy decided not to tell anyone about his conversation with Hurley. He wished he hadn't mentioned it to George because it may have put doubt in his mind. Besides, he knew his guys would do what was right. Fuck Hurley!

Once everyone was in place, Mo breached the bedroom door, and just as they figured the room was clear, Andy sent Mark and Dan to the bathroom. They moved in quickly, then Dan turned around and waited for the signal. Andy nodded, and Dan yanked the door open. George glared over his rifle as he shined his light into the dark closet. "HE'S DOWN! GO!" George yelled, and Rob sprang forward toward the closet with Andy right behind him.

The closet was a mess, with clothes and pillows scattered around the floor. Blood was splattered everywhere, and several bodies were sprawled among the pillows. Andy's worst nightmare had come true. Those sounds weren't hammering. They were muffled gunshots, and now he was looking at the results. He spotted Arnold, still on his knees, and leaned back against a wall. The top of his head was gone, and blood and brain matter were everywhere. The kids were splayed around him in a semi-circle with gunshot wounds to their heads. Some were shot in the face and some in the side of the head as if they had turned away from their executioner.

One of the pillows had burn marks, indicating Arnold had used it as a makeshift silencer. Andy felt weak in his knees, but the stronger emotion of anger was pouring out of him as he wanted to drag Arnold out of the closet and shoot him again.

Rob was scanning the horrific scene, trying to make sense of what happened, when suddenly he noticed the face of an infant girl looking up at him. He yelled, "We've got a live one here!" Andy glanced over just as Rob scooped the baby up and took off, noticing one of her arms was barely dangling by some flesh and tendons. Andy quickly scanned back to the carnage, double-checking the other kids, but their wounds were not survivable. Finally, he became overwhelmed with emotion and couldn't take anymore. The lid on the box in Andy's mind had flown open like never before, and the memories of all the tragic scenes and dead bodies were racing through his brain. He struggled to keep his composure as he mentally chased the images, trying to get them tucked back in the box.

Andy walked out of the closet without saying a word to anyone. He had lost all sense of tactical command as he stumbled out of the bedroom toward the front door and into the yard. He purposely faced away from everyone as tears began to stream down his face. He tried his best to fight back the emotions, but they kept coming in waves.

Looking off into the distance, his sense of purpose started to gain control. In the depths of his mind, he mustered the strength to close the box. Wiping away the tears, he took a few deep breaths knowing he still had work to do.

Sergeant Flores' voice came over the radio, "CP to Andy, give us a status!"

"Andy to CP, Rob has the baby; the rest are DOA. We'll need EMTs forward to pronounce them." Rob ran outside with the baby and handed her over to waiting EMTs. She was rushed to the hospital with a severe gunshot wound to the arm. An injury she eventually recovered from.

Everyone stood in silence, occasionally consoling one another as they waited for the detectives to make the scene. The banging sounds repeatedly played in Andy's mind. He couldn't help but wonder, 'What if....' but then he had to let it go.

When the detectives arrived, Andy recognized one of them from several of their previous scenes. A likable guy who was always professional and never failed to impress. He asked Andy and the team to go downtown and write formal statements as soon as possible.

When they were leaving to ride back to their cars, the same detective ran after them, yelling, "Andy, where's the gun?"

Surprised by the odd question, he replied, "I don't know. I assume somewhere in the closet. I didn't want to disturb the crime scene by rummaging around for it."

Puzzled, the detective replied, "Well, there better be a gun in there!"

'What the hell did he mean by that?' thought Andy, taken aback.

Detectives eventually located the gun in a tangled mess of clothing in the closet, but the comment bothered Andy for days. The same detective committed suicide the following year while sitting at his work desk. Andy realized he wasn't the only one dealing with death and its unintended consequences.

Except for Andy and his team, everyone was released to go home for some much-needed rest. It was almost noon when they finished their statements, and Andy was exhausted. He desperately needed some sleep, but he was afraid of what his dreams would bring. Although he fully acknowledged that he shouldn't, he drove to his favorite convenience store and fixed a drink for the long ride home. Then, taking a long sip of the mind-calming elixir, he tried to clear his thoughts, pulling out of the parking lot. Andy just wanted to get home as quickly as possible to hug Terri and the kids.

When he arrived, he realized the house was empty because everyone was still at school. He walked into the silent house and glanced at his family pictures hanging on the wall, and the memory of Arnold's home came flooding back. Sadly, he averted his eyes and took a big swig of his drink as he walked toward the bedroom, trying to clear his mind of the haunting scene. He sat down on the side of the bed and lost it again as tears poured down his face. Finally, eyes closed and sobbing, he laid back, trying to relax, and slowly drifted off into a deep sleep.

The smell of dinner cooking woke him, and he realized Terri and the kids were home. After getting much-needed hugs, he engaged in small talk with the kids. Terri sensed that he didn't want to talk about the call-up, so she didn't bring it up. Instead, they enjoyed a nice meal and precious family time that Andy needed more than anything.

The following day, while he was storing equipment in his car, Lieutenant Chesney called out to him. It was rather unusual to see Chesney in the back of the parking lot, so this was probably no chance encounter. Chesney got straight to the point, "Hey Andy, I want to apologize for yesterday."

Quizzically, Andy asked, "What's that, Lieutenant?"

Chesney continued, wanting to get through this as fast as possible, "Yesterday, in the house, when we asked you not to shoot that guy, even if he had a gun. That was wrong, and we shouldn't have put you in that situation. I didn't say anything then, but next time I will."

Andy was not sure what to say. "I understand. I appreciate it." Chesney nodded his head, absolving his conscience, and walked away.

Andy wanted to tell him what he thought of Hurley, but the overwhelming feeling that brass protects brass held him back. Chesney never criticized Hurley or the Captain. He merely admitted his responsibility. Just the same, Andy appreciated the gesture.

Later that afternoon, they conducted a formal critique of the Katy call-up, and the Captain was present. He never attended critiques, but they had never lost four hostages before. Andy took up a significant portion of the debrief, explaining the sounds of gunfire and how they mistook them for hammering. He also detailed the clearing process and how they eventually made it to the master bedroom.

The Captain and Chesney stood in the back of the room, hanging on to every word. The Captain was particularly concerned about Andy's debriefing, as they occasionally made eye contact with each other. Andy never mentioned their meeting, instead went directly to describing how they entered the closet. He concluded by saying he had come to terms with losing the hostages. "I've played those sounds over and over in my mind. I've wondered what might have happened if we recognized them as gunshots. But, by the time we blew the door, entered the threshold, and worked our way to the bedroom, we couldn't have stopped anything. Arnold was right! He was going to kill those kids and himself, and there was nothing we could do about it." Andy finished by making eye contact with the captain, who nodded in agreement and walked out. Now that the Captain was satisfied with Andy's account, he could put this behind him, or at least he hoped so.

That afternoon, Andy made the long drive home, sipping his drink and somewhat relieved that the critique was behind him. However, this time his mind drifted to thoughts of his big brother. Mike had been in prison for a couple of years, and Andy couldn't help but worry about him. He now realized the importance of family and longed for the relationship he and his brother once shared. In hopes of healing old wounds, Andy decided to write Mike a letter. He would hope for the best and prepare for the worst.

Monster in Bear Creek

David Ruiz had been living a lie for the last year, and now it was crumbling around him. He lied to his girlfriend about their relationship and lied to his wife about the time he was spending at work. Eventually, David's girlfriend discovered he was married and living with his wife, mother-in-law, and three children in the Bear Creek area of Houston. In addition, his wife found out about his girlfriend, so she planned to divorce him. As of late, David had become mentally unstable, and in a heated argument, he shot and killed his wife in the living room. Since his mother-in-law witnessed the murder, he killed her as well.

As he stood there, coming to grips with what he had done, he knew his life was over. His wife of 10 years was dead, and he couldn't go on with his children or girlfriend knowing what he had done, so he decided to kill them all. When the two male kindergarteners arrived home, they dropped their backpacks by the back door. David persuaded his sons to come into the kitchen with a promise of an after-school treat and shot them. Their daughter was in the third grade and the last one home. After David lured her upstairs to the master bedroom, she received the same fate.

The only person remaining was his girlfriend, so David called her and excitedly explained his family had moved out and invited her to come over and see where they would spend their lives together. Unbeknownst to her, it would be a very short life because he killed her in the kitchen. David left a trail of bodies scattered throughout the house. Afterward, he wallowed in self-pity and insanity. Initially, he intended to commit suicide, but somewhere along the way, he changed his mind and decided he could clean everything up and go on with a new life. To slow the decomposition of the bodies, he turned the A/C down to its coldest setting. Then, he drove to Walmart to purchase several bleach bottles, air fresheners, and boxes of mothballs.

After three days passed, David still lived with the decomposing victims in his house. The stench of rotting flesh had drastically worsened. First, he tried to dispose of the kid's bodies by dissecting them into small pieces. Then he tried to burn them in his fireplace but was unsuccessful. So, he moved on to plan B, placing body parts inside a large plastic trashcan and covering the corpses in bleach. He closed the lid and stumbled around the house in a psychotic daze.

The family of David's girlfriend began to worry about her, so they filed a missing person's report with HPD. Two Homicide detectives were assigned to follow up on the investigation. When they met with the family, they learned David Ruiz was her boyfriend. Accordingly, they visited David's home and spotted the missing woman's vehicle when they pulled into the driveway.

After several unanswered knocks on the front door and ringing the doorbell, they decided to walk around the house to investigate further. One of the detectives peered through a window and spotted four bottles of Clorox sitting on the living room floor. From previous experience, he knew that bleach was commonly used to clean up a crime scene, so he needed to find out more. He found an unlocked window, and as soon as he opened it, the pungent odor of decomposing flesh filled his nostrils. While he was crawling inside to check for victims, David stepped around the edge of the fireplace and shot the detective in the abdomen. The detective fell back outside the window, reeling in pain on the ground. Unable to move, his partner grabbed him and pulled him to cover.

With the detective rapidly losing blood, they decided to get out of there. While running to their car, more shots rang out from an upstairs window. Thankfully, the shots didn't hit anything, and the detectives hightailed it down the street to safety. They urgently radioed for help, and soon, an army of law enforcement was headed their way. An ambulance arrived and hauled the wounded detective to the hospital, where he underwent emergency surgery and started the long road to recovery.

It was Valentine's Day, so Andy and Terri were getting ready for a night out. They had plans for dinner at their favorite restaurant and then a concert. They were looking forward to a night without the kids and spending some quality time together, but it was not to be. Andy's pager displayed, 'Barricaded suspect, possible hostages, one officer shot.' Terri's heart sank. All Andy could do was look at her and shrug his shoulders. The disappointment was nothing new, and their best plans had been spoiled so many times before; still, she somehow learned to deal with it.

Rob Striker had just flipped the switch on a blender of margaritas when he heard his pager. Dropping his head in disappointment, he closed his eyes and absorbed the reality that his night of rest and relaxation would not happen. As Rob glanced over to his wife, she intuitively knew their plans had just changed. After an apologetic look, he hustled off to get dressed. Sitting on a lawn chair in their beautifully landscaped backyard, she sipped on a margarita and watched him drive away.

Deputies from the Harris County Sheriff's Office surrounded the house. No activity had occurred since David fired at the detectives. Gilbert was assigned the entry team responsibility, and Glenn Silva had the react position. As the SWAT team arrived, they quickly replaced the deputies around the perimeter. Negotiators continually called the phone to no avail. Finally, they set up speakers to broadcast commands to the suspect. Intelligence flooded into the CP, and now they were able to determine David Ruiz was indeed the man who lived at the residence and shot the detective.

Darkness was settling over Houston. Long ago, Andy wrote off any chance of making his dinner date with Terri. After three hours passed with no sign of

David, the captain began to think he had committed suicide. Much to the chagrin of Hurley, the Captain sent Gilbert's team inside to conduct a slow search to find David. Hurley argued that David could have retreated to his safe space and still had hostages, but the Captain quickly dismissed his argument and approved Gilbert as a go for entry.

Due to the expansive two-story house, Gilbert asked Andy if he would share the entry responsibilities with them. The two teams merged into one stack at the back door as Dan Mayfair used the ram to breach. The stench of rotting flesh wafted out the open door, and the smell was unbearable. It took them a minute to adjust to the putrid smell, and everyone knew this would be horrendous. Nevertheless, they had been in these situations before, so they persisted. The team could see past the kitchen and into the living room where a female body was propped up at the kitchen table, partially covered in a white sheet, and the kid's backpacks were stacked neatly by the door where they had left them. They quietly eased into the kitchen, past the dead woman's body, who was later identified as David's mother-in-law.

Andy spotted a large green plastic trashcan in the middle of the kitchen, which seemed out of place. Curiously, he lifted the lid and shined his light down inside. The toxic fumes of bleach filled the air. Inside were several pieces of flesh, but he wasn't immediately sure if they were human. It wasn't until he spotted a small ear on what appeared to be a child's head that he realized what he was looking at. Disgusted and shocked, he instantly dropped the lid and turned away, but it was too late. The horrific image would be forever seared in his brain. Andy was struggling to remain composed. The constant stench and the sight of a child's body parts had Andy on the verge of vomiting, but he stifled the urge and focused. There was still more work to do.

They spotted burnt flesh and body parts in the fireplace in the living room where David had tried to dispose of his son's bodies. What kind of monster could do this? And where was he hiding?

Before going upstairs, a negotiator was brought in to call out to David, but there was no response. Gilbert pushed his team onward, up the stairs, and into the master bedroom. The team discovered two more dead bodies lying on the bed. One was a middle-aged woman who was more than likely David's wife based on the pictures around the house. And a young girl who must have been their daughter. They appeared to have been killed somewhere else and then laid out on the bed. A handwritten note was left on a pillow by the girl's head. Andy leaned over and read it, 'I hate what I have done to her. She was my favorite.' A rush of hatred flushed through Andy, and he could only hope to inflict justice when they finally found David.

As they continued clearing the upstairs bedrooms, they eventually found David's lifeless body under a bed in the kid's bedroom. A self-inflicted gunshot wound to the right temple, and the pistol was still in his hand. After shooting at detectives from the bedroom window, he must have crawled under the bed to hide. At some point, he grew tired of waiting for the police to enter his ambush, so he ended it all. David's girlfriend lay on the bed with another note in the last bedroom. He was somehow trying to explain the unexplainable.

Andy couldn't get out of that house of death fast enough. From early in his SWAT career, he recalled the mass shooting of a Vietnamese family. A strikingly similar situation, with dead bodies in every room. Although it didn't bother him then, now everything was different; he was different. The box in his brain was overflowing, and he was sick of death. He couldn't handle another senseless mass murder. Maybe it was time to drop his gear and walk away.

It wasn't until after midnight when they were finally released to get some rest. Homicide allowed the team to report and write their letters for the investigation in the morning. Andy's clothes reeked of decaying flesh, so he stripped down and put on the spare pair of BDUs he carried in his trunk. Even with the windows rolled down, he couldn't escape the smell. He didn't even stop for a drink on the ride home. All he wanted was a hot shower and to try to put this awful night behind him. It had started with the promise of a date night but ended in death and gore, the same way far too many of them were ending these days.

TWENTY-THREE

Tragedy in Conroe

Close Quarter Battle (CQB) training was the day's objective at the FBI Firearms Training Facility in Conroe, Texas. Conroe was a 45-minute drive north of downtown, so they scheduled a whole day to make the trip worthwhile when the team trained there. That part of Texas had the best facility, but they always crossed their fingers that they didn't get a callup because they wouldn't be able to respond quickly.

The facility was co-owned and operated by the local FBI Office and the Conroe Police Department. The team reserved the live-fire shoot-house for the entire day and one of the ranges. Shoot-houses were the best way to train dynamic entry because the rooms and furniture were laid out similarly to the real thing. Although this house was only rated for handgun ammunition, the walls were ballistic, preventing bullets from passing through. Shooting real bullets during training was acceptable if the safety limits were followed and the targets were adequately placed. A catwalk platform was suspended above the rooms where observers could stand and watch the team work below.

Targets were constructed from large sheets of paper portraying life-size images of various individuals. Some images depicted criminals with guns, while the others deceptively had people holding cell phones or similarly sized objects. The differing images forced the team to evaluate the threat as they progressed through their scenarios. The targets were stapled to a free-standing platform, which could be situated around the room. Placement of the targets was crucial, so the supervising Team Leader would strategically set the targets and oversee the training initiative.

Hurley had been making a major power play to dominate control of the SWAT scenes, but the Captain often overruled him for failure to understand SWAT tactics. Hurley argued attending SWAT training would correct the deficiency, and the captain finally relented. Andy just figured the Captain just wanted Hurley out of the office.

Although it was Andy's turn in the rotation to position the shoot-house targets, Hurley convinced Lieutenant Chesney that it would be more helpful if he set up the house for all the teams, allowing everyone to participate in the training. The idea made sense, so Chesney agreed.

The day began in the classroom with a short debrief and a review of the safety protocols. Andy wasn't expecting to see Hurley there with Chesney and the sergeants. He arrogantly smirked as though he was in charge and the center of attention. Chesney announced Hurley would be running the shoot-house, allowing all four teams to participate in the training rotations. Everyone in the room was apprehensive as the realization set in that a non-SWAT-trained person was granted the authority to set targets in a live-fire shoot house. Awkwardly, the guys glanced at each other, hoping someone would speak up and object, but no one did.

To make matters worse, they had invited four finalists from the SWAT selection process to come along for the day and train with them. Lieutenant Chesney thought it would be an excellent opportunity to evaluate their skills and observe their work in a high-stress environment. One candidate was assigned to each team, and they were instructed to stay at the rear of the stack. Most likely, the new guy wouldn't even see a target in Chesney's mind, which made the safety concerns reasonable.

After the debrief, the teams were dismissed for collecting their gear and reporting to the range for some warm-up drills. Paul Kandi walked alongside Andy, "Can you believe that shit?"

Andy immediately understood what he meant, "Not my decision. Not my world. I just live in it!" Paul shook his head and walked away. Paul knew Andy was just as concerned as he was, but what could they do about it? A written policy didn't exist. There wasn't a list of required credentials necessary to set up a shoot-house. But there was always an implied consensus that an experienced operator should do it, or bad things could happen.

Once everyone lined up on the range, they started their warm-up drills, and Hurley began arranging targets inside the shoot-house. In addition, he brought a couple of his negotiators as reinforcements to assist with moving the target stands around and stapling paper targets. Even though he had never operated a shoot-house, Hurley directed precisely how he wanted every target set.

While arranging the targets to his specifications, Hurley came across a pneumatically operated mannequin target, which he thought would be a powerful addition to the training obstacles. The target was constructed from a dense foam material shaped into a man's torso. The specific design was invented to react to the impact of a bullet and collapse once the bullet passed through, mimicking the movement of a person if they were shot. If placed correctly, the bullet would harmlessly pass through the target and stop in the wall.

To gauge a reaction from the teams, Hurley decided to place the mannequin in the center of the first room. Suspects could realistically be in the middle of the room, so why not? Furthermore, if it malfunctioned, the target came with a remote control that could be used from the catwalk and force the mechanism to collapse. Typically, a TL would never consider placing a target in the center of a room because if an operator ended up on the other side, it would create a crossfire. Instead, Hurley relied on his ability to control the target and make it fall on command.

Once the house was ready, Chesney conducted a preliminary scenario review. When he inquired about the potential crossfire hazard created by the positioning of the pneumatic target, Hurley assured him it was perfectly safe because of his ability to control the device. Hurley was quite convincing, but he failed to consider Murphy's law.

Once the warm-up drills concluded, everyone was advised to stay on the range and continue training until their rotation through the house. Gilbert's team was first up, so they walked over, grounded their rifles, and selected handguns due to the ballistic limitations of the house.

Hurley walked out with a swagger, acting like he knew more than everyone else. Gilbert listened carefully while Hurley described a hostage scenario and how his team was instructed to breach the front door and deliver a flashbang. Then, the team would conduct a dynamic sweep through the house until all the rooms were clear. Finally, Gilbert turned to his SWAT candidate and firmly commanded him to stay in the back of the stack. "Keep your muzzle down, and remember you don't have to take a shot unless you're sure." Once the new guy nodded in confirmation, Gilbert told Hurley, "We're ready!"

Hurley climbed up to the catwalk with the target remote control firmly in his grasp. He glanced over at Chesney and signaled a thumbs up. The first run was always a bit nerve-wracking, and they wanted to see how the team would react to the pneumatic mannequin. Hurley was beaming with pride at his simulation and arrogantly yelled down to Gilbert, "The house is clear. It's on you!"

Gilbert signaled his breacher, who gave a mighty swing as the ram slammed against the door and flew open. A flashbang was deployed, detonating in the entry. The day's first run was underway as they swiftly moved through the doorway.

Tony Garcia was Gilbert's point man and the first to see the pneumatic target. Since it had a gun positioned in its hand, Tony shot it twice in the chest. Instantly, it fell forward and was out of play. The rest of the team flowed into the room and efficiently cleared the house. Hurley glanced at Chesney with a cocky look, saying, 'I told you so!'

Gilbert's team performed well. They did not miss any of the shoot targets or engage any no-shoot targets. However, during the short debrief after their run, Gilbert questioned the target in the middle of the room. Hurley was pissed that Gilbert mentioned it. Then, sarcastically, he pointed to the remote control that allowed him to collapse the device if the team missed. Gilbert replied, "Well, all I know is we were taught never to put a target in the middle of a room." Hurley dropped his head in disgust, then looked at Lieutenant Chesney, unable to understand how anyone could question his expertise.

Next in the rotation was Glenn Silva's team, and they also performed well. But once again, Glenn mentioned the safety issues with having a target placed in the middle of a room. Chesney and the sergeants were increasingly uneasy now that two Team Leaders had complained, but Hurley used his power of persuasion to overcome any doubts. After all, he was a Lieutenant, and they were merely officers. Police ranks dictated he knew best.

Kandi's team was up next in the rotation and completed another clean run in the house. Immediately afterward, Paul turned to Hurley and questioned why there was a mannequin in the middle of the room. Paul could not accept an unproven explanation, so he argued the basic SWAT guidelines, setting Hurley off.

Following a verbal altercation, Hurley summarily dismissed Paul and called for the last team to report. 'Why does everyone want to hold up progress?' Hurley irritatingly wondered. Plus, Paul was being quite argumentative with his comments.

The number of complaints by TLs was quickly stacking up. Chesney was concerned, so he asked Hurley, "Why don't we just move that target back against a wall so we don't have this same argument every time?"

A lieutenant losing an argument to an officer was utterly unacceptable, especially after he had been so adamant that he was right. In a halfhearted attempt at appeasement, Hurley offered a small compromise, "OK, let's run this last team, and then I'll move the target to make these guys happy. Jeez!" Chesney didn't care for the compromise, but he agreed, considering there were no issues thus far.

Andy's team was waiting outside the entrance, oblivious to the concerns and discussions regarding the target in the middle. He was uneasy about leading his team into a shoot-house set up by Hurley, and to make matters worse; he had a new SWAT candidate attached to his team.

The candidate's name was Chris, and he seemed likable enough. Throughout the weapon skills work on the range, Andy carefully observed him, and he appeared proficient. Chris was eager to impress the guys and fit in. Since he was competing against three other candidates, he needed to excel at every level.

Andy turned to Chris with a serious stare and said, "Look, you don't have to shoot anything in there. No one will judge you if you are not comfortable taking a shot. Just operate within your skillset and trust your instincts. If it doesn't feel right, it probably isn't." Chris nodded in understanding, but Andy found his vacant expression unsettling. Desperate to be on the team, Chris tried to blend into the group.

Hurley walked out of the shoot-house to meet Andy's team and begin the briefing on the training scenario. Andy refused to make eye contact and just looked down and listened. Then, Hurley hurried to the catwalk to take his position with the remote control and yelled, "The house is clear. It's on you!" Andy nodded to Mo, and he picked up the ram and gave it a mighty swing. The door flew open, and Rob delivered the flashbang through the doorway. A massive explosion rang out, and the team launched forward into the room.

When Gary spotted the pneumatic target positioned straight ahead, he fired two shots directly into the torso, but it didn't go down. Confident of his shot placement, he assumed it was not a reactionary target and turned to check the corner to his right. Mo stepped in and engaged the same pneumatic target with two rounds, but it did not respond. Like Gary, he presumed the target wasn't designed to collapse, or it had malfunctioned, so he checked the left corner, and both men moved along the wall and proceeded to the next doorway.

Andy was next through the doorway and was dumbfounded to see a target directly in front of him. He knew that Gary and Mo had already engaged the target, so he moved on, seeing no value in reshooting it. Instead, he turned to the right and followed Gary toward the next threshold. Rob followed Andy's lead and continued to move to the left. He knew Gary and Mo were too far into the room, and it wouldn't be safe to take the shot.

The target had been shot four times, and it hadn't fallen. Hurley frantically pressed the button on the remote control to override the pneumatic device and force it down, but nothing happened. Chesney, concerned the target did not fall as expected, worriedly looked to Hurley. Hurley repeatedly pressed the remote button at a loss for another course of action.

Chris stepped through the doorway and quickly spotted the 3D foam target directly ahead. Because he was last on the stack, he didn't realize Gary and Mo had already shot the target. Chris assumed the target was still up for a reason, and due to his lack of experience, he didn't consider how the team had already moved past the mark. So, he raised his pistol and engaged.

Chesney's greatest fears materialized before his eyes. In warning, he screamed out, "CEASEFIRE!" but it was too late. Chris moved to his left, which put him and Andy in the direct line of fire with only the target between them. He put two more rounds in the mannequin to ensure he hit the mark since it failed to move. Entirely consumed by his target, he lost all situational awareness. As he realigned his aim, he didn't pause to consider where his teammates were located. Blocking out all noise distractions, Chris didn't hear Chesney's commands, and he pulled the trigger one more time. The last bullet passed through the foam target and traveled across the room into Andy's back, hitting just below his ballistic vest.

Andy let out a groan, spun around from the force, slammed against a wall, and then slid down to his butt. Pain radiated across to his right side. He felt something warm running down his leg and feared he had pissed himself from the pain. In that instant, he was more worried about the embarrassment of soiling himself than the potential danger. He reached down, touched the warm liquid, and saw blood covering his hand. Then he realized he was shot, although he wasn't sure how it happened.

In shock, Andy peered around the room and saw Chris shakingly lower his pistol. Seeing his terrified facial expression, he knew. Rob witnessed the entire ordeal and sprinted to Andy's aid, wildly waving his hands in the air and screaming, "CEASEFIRE! CEASEFIRE!" Gary and Mo were oblivious to what happened behind them, so they continued to clear the remaining rooms and engaged targets as they came across them.

Chesney and the sergeants snapped out of their stunned, momentary pause and hurried down the catwalk toward the stairs leading into the shoot-house. Still holding the remote control, Hurley stood there, horrified. 'How the hell am I going to explain this?' He was completely unconcerned about Andy's life or the trauma caused by his arrogance. More importantly, he needed to spin the story to spread the blame around; Lord knows he didn't want to be the only one left holding the bag.

While Gary and Mo were clearing the last room, they heard Rob's screams. They ran back to help. Andy tried to roll over to get some relief from the excruciating pain. Rob pushed him back and said, "Stay still, brother," and then pulled off Andy's vest. As the blood collected and pooled onto the concrete floor around Andy's waist, Rob realized the severity of the wound.

Chesney radioed dispatch they had an officer down and needed an ambulance immediately. Sergeant Bird darted to the office to grab the trauma kit mounted on the wall just inside the front door. Within minutes, the shoot-house was packed with SWAT operators and first responders offering assistance, but it was becoming too crowded. Finally, everyone was ordered out except for the EMTs. When Chesney glanced up at the catwalk, Hurley was still in the same spot, holding the damn remote control, standing uselessly on the sidelines. Chesney became livid and screamed, "GET YOUR ASS DOWN HERE, HURLEY!" He had listened to Hurley one time too many, and now there would be a price to pay, possibly Andy's life.

Hurley was astounded a fellow lieutenant would speak to him that way. What happened to brass protecting brass? They should be circling the wagons, not at each other's throats. Slowly, he headed down the stairs, prepared to explain his pre-rehearsed version, but Chesney would have none of it as he began to speak. "Just tell the truth, Hurley! What you saw, what you said, and what you did!" Unsure that was a good idea, Hurley walked outside to consider his options.

The EMTs called for a life flight helicopter to transport Andy to Herman Hospital in Houston. His wound was life-threatening, and he had already lost a significant amount of blood. The gunshot wound to his back landed to the right of the spine. The bullet traveled across his lower torso and exited his right side. The EMTs packed the wound with gauze to slow the bleeding, but he needed a trauma room.

Andy fought to stay awake, slipping in and out of consciousness. He could hear the EMTs screaming for him to stay with them. Even though he understood how vital it was, occasionally, he blacked out without warning. Then, he was abruptly awakened by a piercing pain when they lifted him on a stretcher to carry him to the awaiting helicopter. When the helicopter lifted off, Andy thought of John Frost and how his life flight ride must have been much like this.

After losing consciousness for a while, he came to as they were wheeling him into emergency surgery. A doctor reassuringly leaned over him and calmingly said he would recover but that they needed to take his kidney. Then the anesthesiologist inserted a hypodermic needle into his IV, pushed in the anesthesia, and everything went black.

The remainder of the team waited for Homicide and IAD to make the scene back at the range in Conroe. Hurley called the Police Union office and requested a lawyer before answering any questions. With his entire police career on the line, he knew he needed help to save it.

Regardless of how it would turn out, Chesney and the sergeants told their sides of the story precisely as they remembered. Gilbert, Paul, and Glenn dropped the hammer on Hurley and told the investigators what an arrogant asshole he was, which was why Andy was now fighting for his life.

The three of them spoke at length about how they warned Hurley about the target, which only enraged everyone more. Finally, Murphy reared his ugly head, smacking Hurley directly in the face, but he had it coming.

Terri was teaching her third-period class when the school resource officer knocked on the door and asked to speak with her in the hallway. Immediately she worried something had happened to one of the kids. Once she stepped outside, he explained Andy was shot during a training accident. Shocked and scared, Terri gasped and immediately covered her face with her hands when the officer informed her Andy was in emergency surgery at Herman Hospital. Consolingly, he offered to drive her to the hospital, but she wanted to gather the kids and go as a family. He understood and offered any help she may need. Terri thanked him and quickly ran to the principal's office to alert him of the emergency and find instructor coverage for the rest of her classes. After checking the kids out of school, she sped toward Houston, trying to remain strong and calm. But unfortunately, she was headed directly toward the situation she hoped and prayed would never come.

The Way Back

Andy woke up in the Intensive Care Unit, surprised he was still alive. The last thing he remembered was wishing he could see Terri and the kids one last time. The nurse came around and welcomed him back among the living. When Andy inquired about his injuries, she sidestepped the question and said the doctor would be in soon to talk about it.

Terri and the kids were only allowed to see Andy for a few minutes. They exchanged several brief "I love you's" before the nurse asked them to leave so he could get some rest. The next time Andy awoke, the surgeon stood by his bedside,

"Hello, Andy. All things considered, you are a lucky man. Another inch to the left, and that bullet would have clipped your spinal cord, and you never would have walked again." Andy nodded. "I'm sorry, but I had to take your right kidney. It took a direct hit from that bullet, and I couldn't save it."

"That's OK, Doc," replied Andy. "That's why we're born with two, right?"

The doctor paused a minute and then replied, "Well, that's the other side of the story. We did a CT scan of your abdomen and found a large growth on your left kidney. I had an Oncologist take an initial assessment, and he's pretty sure it's cancer. So, we may have to take that kidney as well. Do you understand what I'm saying?"

Andy stared at the doctor, trying to process what this meant for his health. A few days ago, he was a strapping SWAT Team Leader in peak physical condition, and now he was reduced to having his organs removed to stay alive. The doctor attempted to put a positive spin on the situation, "Well, in a way, the gunshot exposed something that might have killed you. You weren't having symptoms, were you?"

"No," replied Andy.

The doctor leaned in and said, "See, you might not have known about that tumor until the cancer was ravaging your entire body, and then it might have been too late."

Andy rolled his eyes and jokingly said, "Oh wow! Lucky me."

He stood to leave, patted him on the leg, and said reassuringly, "We'll bring in a specialist to deal with that kidney as soon as we get you in better shape." Andy nodded, closed his eyes, took a deep breath, and tried to relax.

The doctor met with Terri and filled her in on Andy's dilemma. He added family support was essential, and she needed to be strong for Andy and the kids. "If we take the other kidney, he'll need a donor as soon as possible. We'll get him on the registry and try to find one, but you can always check with relatives. We can test and determine if any of them are a match. Until then, he'll need dialysis regularly."

With Andy rapidly healing, they soon transferred him into a private room. Terri took a leave of absence from work to stay in Andy's room and sleep on a roll-away bed. A friend of hers from school took care of the kids and brought them to the hospital several times the following week during Andy's recovery.

The entire SWAT team visited Andy at the hospital, including many of his old buddies from patrol and narcotics. Andy was touched, so many coworkers thought enough of him to visit, and his room was filled with flowers and get-well cards. John Frost shared stories about his life flight lift, and they compared scars. Unfortunately, the visitation was becoming a problem for the hospital, and soon they had to schedule visitors in advance to cut down on the crowd.

After almost two weeks had passed, they prepped Andy for another surgery. He wasn't nervous; he was just ready to be rid of cancer. He joked with the surgeon about which kidney would be removed, saying, "OK, you're taking the left kidney, right?" The doctor was unamused. "Don't worry, Doc. If you don't find a kidney, check the other side when you go in. You can't screw this up." The surgeon was strictly business and smiled but didn't reply. Andy kissed Terri and the kids as they wheeled him down the hall toward the operating room.

The surgery went as planned, and now, they could focus on searching for a kidney donor. While Andy was recovering in his room, he wondered about going home and how many times he would go through dialysis before finding a suitable donor. At least the surrounding lymph nodes tested clear of cancer, so he wouldn't have to endure chemo.

A week later, Andy was sitting on his front porch, enjoying the view of the woods surrounding his home. He never felt more alive than after his brush with death. He had a greater appreciation for life and considered every day a gift. Although the recovery was slow, he was making steady progress. After receiving four rounds of dialysis, he received the call that a donor was found. The following day, the doctor had him scheduled for surgery. When Andy asked about the donor, he was advised the person wished to remain anonymous.

The transplant surgery went well, and the new kidney started functioning immediately. Although he would have to take antirejection medication to prevent his body from rejecting the organ, that was a small price. He wouldn't have to live with the restrictions of dialysis, and that's all he cared about. Frequently after the surgery, Andy sat, relaxing on his front porch, wondering about the donor. Who was this person? Were they tragically killed like in so many scenes during his career? He would love to thank the family for his new lease on life. After a long and arduous career, Andy planned to retire and move on, but he still had a few loose ends to tie up first.

Paul Kandi and Gilbert Reyna drove out to Andy's house for a visit and to fill him in on the changes at SWAT. IAD concluded Hurley displayed gross negligence and disregarded several safety standards. The investigation noted several Team Leaders repeatedly warned him, but he failed to heed those warnings, which led to Andy's shooting. Since he was too arrogant to retire, he was dishonorably discharged. Through Civil Service, Hurley was appealing the decision, which could potentially result in a trial before an Administrative Law Judge. If that happened, Andy would most likely be called to testify.

The Captain and Lieutenant Chesney survived the investigation. Andy accepted that, realizing they were caught up in Hurley's bullshit like everyone else. Andy had a rare insight into Hurley's behavior patterns because of what happened to Herman at the Academy. Andy wanted to make a full recovery and return to the team. He didn't want to go away quietly. He wanted to retire with dignity, on his feet as an operator and a Team Leader. For now, that was his focus as he started his physical therapy and the long way back.

Burying the Hatchet

Andy suddenly snapped out of his daydream and glanced at the cold prison walls, realizing the correctional officer had been calling his name. He rubbed his face, wondering how long he had been lost in his thoughts and memories of his past. Then, the guard again yelled out, "ANDY WALLACE?"

Andy raised his hand and yelled back, "HERE! COMING!" He struggled to get on his crutches and awkwardly hobbled down the mirror-finished hallway. The corridor led to a row of picture windows with telephones hung on the wall. As instructed, he sat down at window number 6 and waited.

A week ago, he wrote to Mike and asked if it would be alright if he visited. He was overjoyed when Mike wrote back and said that he would have his name put on the visitor list for this weekend. Nervously he sat at the window, waiting to see his brother as he looked around at the cold hard prison surfaces that were his life now.

Andy's brush with death opened his eyes, and he had a newfound outlook on life. He wanted to start fresh, and the first part of that process was finally seeing Mike and burying the hatchet. A loud metallic latching sound indicated the door on the other side of the booth was being unlocked. Mike walked through with a smile on his face, and instantly Andy was relieved and happy to see him. He had hoped their reunion wouldn't be adversarial, and seeing that smile, he knew it would go well. After so much time had passed, his first impression was that he couldn't believe how much weight Mike had lost. He had always been a muscular, athletic-looking guy, but now he had lost at least 20 lbs. He walked with a bit of shuffle, like an older man, as he stepped forward to the glass partition and sat down. Considering that his brother had always been the image of strength and confidence, his frailty was concerning. Unfortunately, prison had reduced him to someone much older and weaker.

"Hey, little brother," Mike said eagerly as he picked up the phone.

Andy smiled and tried to fight back the tears as he answered, "Hey, big brother!" They chuckled a bit and started chatting about family and catching up on what was happening in the free world.

Concerned, Mike asked about Andy's injury and added, "I always thought if you got shot, it would be a bad guy, not another cop!"

Andy smiled and decided to change the subject, "Let's talk about you and what I can do for you here."

"Nothing really, unless you can get me a cake with a hacksaw blade hidden in it," said Mike laughing. They enjoyed one another's company and shared laughs until the guard gave Andy a five-minute warning.

He turned back to Mike and said, "Well, big brother, I guess I will say goodbye for now. Can I come to see you again sometime?"

Mike smiled and replied, "Sure!"

Andy nodded, struggling to stifle his emotions. They said their goodbyes, hung up the phone, and Andy pushed his chair back, reaching for his crutches. Then he noticed Mike grimacing as he helped himself up with both hands. He looked pained, and as he turned away, Andy spotted a bandage. It was a sizeable surgical bandage just under his shirt on his left side. At that moment, Andy realized Mike was his donor. He dropped his crutches to the floor and started beating the glass, screaming, "HEY! MIKE! IT WAS YOU! YOU GAVE ME THE KIDNEY!"

Mike stopped and glanced back as he gave one of his patented winks and slowly mouthed, "Of course. I'm your brother. Have a nice life," as he walked away.

Andy could only watch in silence as the door slowly shut behind him. He sat there stunned for a minute, staring at the door and thinking back on everything. Then, finally, the guard said, "Time to go." Andy snapped out of his thoughts and grabbed his crutches. He got to his feet and started down the long corridor to the parking lot.

The entire drive home, he cried. It wasn't until he drove down his driveway leading to his beautiful home in the woods that the tears finally stopped. Terri came out to greet him and find out how the visit went. The moment Andy got out of the pickup and their eyes met, he lost it again. Terri rushed into his arms as he dropped his crutches, and they embraced in a long hug. Finally, he slowly regained his composure, and they turned to walk into the house. He told her all about the visit and the surprise that would last a lifetime as Terri fought back her tears.

What Goes Around Comes Around

Andy pulled into the parking lot of the Texas Administrative Law building and got out of his car just in time to see several of his old SWAT teammates. It was the beginning of Hurley's Civil Service trial, but it felt like a homecoming for Andy as the group hugged and grab-assed in the parking lot. Just like Andy, most of the team was subpoenaed to testify in the case. But, according to the Judge, none of the witnesses could sit in on the testimony. So instead, a secretary ushered them into a waiting room at the opposite end of the building. Then, when their time came to testify about their recollections on that fateful day, a court clerk would come into the room and request the witness by name.

It was Andy's first-time seeing Chris, the young SWAT candidate that shot him in the back. After the accident, Chris pulled his name from consideration in the selection process. Andy understood why Chris would be reluctant to approach him, so he walked over and shook his hand, "Hey, Chris! How are you?" Chris was unbelievably relieved Andy was friendly with him. As he finally let go of the guilt, he lost control of his emotions, hugged Andy, and repeatedly apologized. It felt good to put Chris at ease, "You're gonna be just fine, and I think you should try out for SWAT again. You never should have been in that shoot-house. It wasn't your fault." Those words were all Chris needed to hear. He didn't reply but nodded his head, wiped his tears, and walked away to collect himself.

One by one, the witnesses testified over the next two days, and finally, it was Andy's turn. As he walked into the courtroom, he immediately spotted the back of Hurley's head at the defendant's table. After that, Andy was laser-focused on Hurley as he walked to the front of the courtroom to take the oath. Hurley looked down the entire time, doodling on a piece of paper.

Once the Judge swore Andy in, he asked him to take a seat in the witness chair. Andy briefly glanced around the room and then returned his focus to Hurley. He desperately wanted to lock eyes with the man who used to intimidate him, but now he reveled in Hurley avoiding eye contact. He could sense his uneasiness, and he wanted to pile it on.

Andy's testimony went as planned, reliving that day's events. If anything, Hurley's lawyer took it easy on him to avoid the appearance of badgering the victim. He simply clarified a few procedural points and then passed the witness. The Judge dismissed Andy and said that he was free to leave. Andy thanked the Judge and stepped down. He stopped at the attorney's desk, handed Hurley's lawyer an envelope, and walked away.

With Hurley's name written across the front, he passed it over to his client and curiously watched to see what was in the envelope. Hurley glanced down at the envelope and then toward the back of the room, but Andy was gone. Then, slowly, he opened the envelope and looked inside. It contained a photo of Herman Munich in his cadet uniform, with a handwritten note at the bottom, 'What goes around, comes around!' The lawyer leaned over and whispered, "What's that all about?" But Hurley waved him off, silently raging inside. He glanced around the room, nervously twitching and shuffling in his seat, and turned Herman's photo face down on the table.

Andy walked to his pickup with a smile as he thought of how small and inconsequential Hurley was in that courtroom and how he wished Herman could be here to see it. Weeks later, he learned the Judge ruled in favor of the City and upheld the dishonorable discharge, so Hurley's law enforcement days were over. With a dishonorable discharge looming over his resume, he couldn't get a job as a dog catcher. Hurley would fade into nothing more than a distant memory, tightly sealed inside Andy's box. Now, he could finally close the lid for good and get on with the rest of his life. A sense of satisfaction washed over him, and that's all Andy needed this time as he pulled out of the parking lot to take the long road home.

This book is based on real events, certain parts have been fictionalized solely for dramatic purposes and are not intended to reflect on any actual person or entity.

Made in the USA
Las Vegas, NV
03 June 2022